Governors State University
Library Hours:
Monday thru Thursday 8:00 to 10:30
Friday 8:00 to 5:00
Saturday 8:30 to 5:00
Sunday 1:00 to 5:00 (Fall
and Winter Trimester Only)

A HISTORY

OF THE

ADULT EDUCATION MOVEMENT

IN THE

UNITED STATES

(Includes Adult Education Institutions through 1976)

MALCOLM S. KNOWLES

Professor of Adult and Community College Education
North Carolina State University

KRIEGER PUBLISHING COMPANY
MALABAR, FLORIDA

Original Edition 1962
Revised Edition 1977
Reissue 1994 with new preface & bibliography

Printed and Published by
KRIEGER PUBLISHING COMPANY
KRIEGER DRIVE
MALABAR, FL 32950

Printed in the United States of America

Library of Congress Cataloging in Publication Data

Knowles, Malcolm Shepherd, 1913-
    The adult education movement in the United States.

    Reprint of the edition published by Holt, Rinehart and
Winston, New York.
    Bibliography: p.
    Includes index.
    1. Adult education–United States–History.   I. Title.
[LC5251.K55   1976]   374.9′73   75-31824
ISBN 0-89464-872-1

10   9   8   7   6   5   4   3

PREFACE TO
THE 1994 REISSUE

The trends during the period 1961–1976 cited in Chapter IX
continued for the most part during the period 1977–1994

SOCIAL SETTING

The population continued to increase, with the most rapid
growth being in the older and immigrant—particularly the Latino
and Oriental—segments. The ferment in the larger cities continued to boil and to produce several major riots. The problems of
poverty, illiteracy, crime, unemployment, health care, and environmental decline continued to command national concern and
attention—balanced somewhat by improvement in race relations
and the status of women. The reduction of the national debt and
growing deficit became a major issue of public policy, greatly in-
hibiting efforts to deal with social problems. The technological
revolution accelerated, with dramatic developments especially in
the electronic media—making distance education more and more
viable.

ADULT EDUCATION

The institutional developments described in Chapter IX continued unabated, with educational services to adults expanding
rapidly in business and industry, colleges and universities, community colleges and technical institutes, the Cooperative Extension
Service and other government agencies, foundations, museums and
art institutes, proprietary schools, public schools, religious institutions, and voluntary agencies.

The term "continuing education" was increasingly added as a partner to "adult education," perhaps reflecting the broadening scope of the field. For example, the Adult Education Association of the U.S.A. became the American Association for Adult and Continuing Education; most university extension programs became "Continuing Education Programs; and many new publications had "continuing education" in their titles.

The volume of publications in the field increased markedly. Whereas the bibliography for the period 1961–1976 contained 135 listings—an average of 9 per year during the 15-year period—the bibliography for the period 1977–1994 contained 251 listings—an average of almost 15 per year during that 17-year period. The titles of these publications reflect a growing interest in such aspects of the field as professional education, community education and development, adult learning theory and practice, workforce education, adult developmental processes, education of the elderly, program evaluation, self-directed learning, lifelong learning, literacy education, experiential education, distance education, nontraditional education and external degrees, religious education, health education, qualitative research methods, competency-based education, transformative education, human resources development, intercultural education, and the future of adult and continuing education.

It became clear during this period that adult education had moved from the periphery to the center of our national educational enterprise.

PREFACE TO
REVISED EDITION

The *Adult Education Movement in the United States*, which was published in 1962, was out of print ten years later. Since there was no other work available to provide a sense of historical perspective to adult educators and others interested in the field, the invitation from Krieger Publishing Company to revise and update it was accepted enthusiastically.

It has been an exhilarating and in some ways startling experience to bring information about developments across the spectrum of institutional settings of our broad field together and concentrate them into the physical space of a chapter in a book. Although I have been an active observer of the field, and have taught many courses on "The History, Philosophy, and Contemporary Nature of Adult Education" to graduate students, it came as a shock to me when I brought the events of the past fifteen years into the focus of a few pages to discover what a feverish period of activity it was.

Since I was removed by more than fifteen years from my role as Executive Director of the Adult Education Association of the U.S.A., and the sense of identification with and responsibility for the field that I experienced in that role, I believe I was able to look at the development of the last fifteen years a little more objectively than perhaps I had the previous ten. But, as I point out in the introduction to Chapter IX, I encountered other difficulties regarding which I need the reader's help.

M. S. K.

North Carolina State University
January, 1977

PREFACE

What is an adult education movement?

In most countries in which adult education has appeared in recognizable form, national programs for the education of adults have tended to take on a rather easily definable character. In England and Sweden, for example, adult education evolved essentially as national movements for the education of workers. In Denmark a network of folk schools was created for the express purpose of refashioning a national culture. In most underdeveloped countries adult education has been used primarily as a means for eliminating illiteracy. In the Soviet Union adult education has served as an instrument of state policy directed at producing loyalty to the state and developing technical competencies required by national plans. In the sense that adult educational activities in these countries have tended to be fairly unified in their aims and institutional forms, they can be identified as national movements.

In the United States, on the other hand, the national adult educational program has proliferated almost haphazardly in response to myriad individual needs and interests, institutional goals, and social pressures. In one sense the absence of domination and control by a single agency, clientele, or doctrine has been a strength. Because of this very freedom and diversification, according to Lyman Bryson, adult education "has penetrated to more phases of life in America than in any other country . . . [and has] expressed the complexity and vitality of American life." *

But in another sense the apparent formlessness of the adult edu-

* Lyman Bryson, *Adult Education*, pp. 13–14. New York: American Book Company, 1936.

cational enterprise in this country has been its major weakness. Confusion about what the adult education movement in this country encompasses and how it should be structured has impeded persistent efforts toward better communication across lines of specialization, toward agreement on common social goals, and toward the achievement of some degree of coordination of activities within the field. This confusion has resulted in disagreements as to what the relevant components of the movement are, how the roles of different agencies should be delineated, which goals the various units should seek in common and which they should pursue separately, and what kind of organizational machinery would be appropriate for relating the parts to some sort of whole. Indeed, there has been a continuing lack of agreement as to whether or not there is such a thing as an adult education movement, the counter hypothesis being that adult education in this country is—and should properly be—a patternless mosaic of unrelated activities.

Perhaps some of the confusion is semantic. The term "adult education" is used to convey three meanings. In its broadest meaning it describes the *process* by which men and women continue learning after their formal schooling is completed. In this sense it includes all forms of experience—reading, listening, traveling, and conversing—that are engaged in by mature people for the purpose of learning. In its more technical meaning, "adult education" describes a set of *organized activities* for mature men and women carried on by a wide variety of institutions for the accomplishment of specific educational objectives. In this sense it encompasses organized classes, study groups, lecture series, workshops, conferences, planned reading programs, guided discussions, workshops, and correspondence courses. In this book the phrase "the program of adult education" will be used to convey this meaning. A third meaning combines all the processes and activities of adult education into the idea of a *movement* or *field*. In this sense "adult education" brings together into a definable social system all the individuals, institutions, and associations concerned with the education of adults and portrays them as working toward such common goals as the improvement of the methods and materials of adult learning, the extension of opportunities for adults to learn, and the advancement of the general level of our culture.

In this book the phrases "adult education movement" and "the field of adult education" will be used to convey this meaning.

The problem is, however, more than semantic. More American citizens have devoted more energy than has probably been expended in all other countries combined to try to shape a coordinated adult education movement in this country. These efforts have resulted in a succession of local, state, regional, and national adult education councils and associations that have met with only small successes and large frustrations in their attempts to create a unified field of adult education.

Why was this book written?

As a participant in some of these efforts at the local and state levels in Illinois, Massachusetts, and Michigan, and as the Executive Director of the Adult Education Association of the U.S.A. during its formative years (1951–1959), this writer shared intimately both the hopes and frustrations of those who were seeking to bring some sort of order out of the adult educational chaos. During this experience I became increasingly concerned that so many policies regarding the organization of the field were being based largely on static conceptions of the needs, interests, and perceptions of adult educational workers and organizational leaders as of given moments in time. Little information existed about the historical origins and developmental trends of the various adult educational institutions, so that it was difficult to see the field as a total system of institutional components and to place the field in the perspective of a sequential process of development. As a result of this deficiency, the field itself and the coordinating agencies seeking to serve it lacked a sense of direction.

In an effort to discover such a sense of direction I undertook to find answers to the following questions:

1. What is the nature of the field of adult education as it has emerged to date? What are its dimensions, its component parts, its general characteristics? How did it evolve, and what genetic principles seem to be guiding its development?

2. What are the dynamics of the field of adult education? What are its needs for coordination? What forces seem to be favoring and opposing coordination?

3. Where does the field of adult education seem to be going?

Because so many others are also concerned about the strengthening of the adult education movement in this country, I feel a responsibility to make my private inquiry public.

How is the inquiry conducted? How is it reported?

The approach used in this inquiry is genetic, in that an understanding of the present state of the field of adult education is sought through understanding its origins and patterns of growth. The inquiry progresses through three sequential steps.

Part One traces the emergence of institutions for the education of adults. The purpose of this step is to discover how the component parts of the field began and how they developed. In order that these developments can be seen in the context of the social environment in which they occurred, they are divided into four broad eras of American history: 1600–1779 (Chapter 1), 1780–1865 (Chapter 2), 1866–1920 (Chapter 3), and 1921–1961 (Chapter 4). The assumption is made that these eras roughly correspond to periods of major change in the social forces affecting the development of adult education, and an attempt is made to summarize these forces for each era.

It becomes clear as the story unfolds that the source material on the origins of adult educational institutions is highly uneven. A few institutions, such as the Cooperative Extension Service and certain social agencies, have been treated by full historical studies. Other institutions, such as public schools, university extension, evening colleges, and libraries, have been favorite subjects for doctoral dissertations. Chapters in yearbooks and other books that are not primarily historical in nature, as well as articles in periodicals, proved fruitful sources of data about some institutions. But there were almost no data about the development of adult education in a number of types of institutions—including business and industry, government agencies, mass media, and voluntary associations. Much of the information about these institutions had to be collected by questionnaire and correspondence. It has been possible, therefore, to obtain a much more complete picture of institutional developments in some categories than in others. Indeed, it will not be possible to compile a comprehensive history of the adult education movement until better documentation of the development of its segments has been accomplished.

Part Two depicts the shaping of adult education as a coordinated field. The purpose of this step is to examine the various approaches that have been made toward interrelating the different components of the field. Chapter 5 analyzes the development of organizations that have been created to perform coordinative functions within particular segments of the field: (1) institutional groupings, (2) groupings around subject-matter interests, and (3) geographical groupings. Chapter 6 describes attempts that have been made to develop national coordinating organizations for the purpose of bringing the component parts of the field into an integrated social system.

Part Three summarizes the findings of the inquiry as to the nature, genetic development, and trends of the adult education movement. In addition to generating working hypotheses about the character of the field from an analysis of the data presented in the preceding sections, in this section I shift from the role of historian to the role of prophet and venture some predictions about adult education's future.

What can you hope to get from this book?

Certainly you should expect to acquire some knowledge from this book, for it contains some factual information about the adult education movement that has not appeared in print before. And the book is purposely rather liberally seasoned with footnotes and bibliographical references so that you can verify or elaborate on the facts about any particular facet of the movement.

Hopefully, you should emerge from a reading of this book with a deeper appreciation of the role of adult education in helping to shape our national culture and a better understanding of its dynamics.

Not to be overlooked is the hope that the book might also provide you with some entertainment, for it presents the drama of an embryonic social force of great potential seeking to overcome the numerous obstacles that lie in its path toward self-fulfillment.

Primarily, it is my hope that by putting adult education in the perspective of developmental growth this book will inspire the thousands of volunteer and professional leaders and concerned citizens who control the destiny of the movement to create their own visions of its unrealized potential and to redouble their efforts to realize that potential. And, incidentally, I hope that a few more scholars might also be inspired to help fill the gaps in our knowledge about the field of adult education.

This book could not have been written if the writer had not had available to him the archives of the Adult Education Association and many rich hours of reminiscent conversation with such architects of our field as Kenneth Benne, Leland Bradford, Eleanor Coit, Paul Essert, Cyril Houle, Andrew Hendrickson, Herbert Hunsaker, Abbot Kaplan, Robert Luke, Howard Mc-Clusky, Harry and Bonaro Overstreet, Paul Sheats, Robertson Sillars, and Thomas Van Sant. To them and many other colleagues in the drama of the last three decades the writer expresses his gratitude, respect, and affection. Credit for whatever scholarly quality this book possesses belongs above all to Professor Cyril O. Houle who, as chairman of the writer's doctoral committee at the University of Chicago, guided much of the research on which this book is based. The shortcomings that can be found occurred while the professor's back was turned.

My wife Hulda, son Eric, and daughter Barbara deserve special words of appreciation for their moral support and helpful comments during the ten years this book was in preparation.

M. S. K.

Boston University
May 1962

CONTENTS

PART IV: SEQUEL (Cont'd.)

PART ONE

THE EMERGENCE OF
INSTITUTIONS FOR
THE EDUCATION OF ADULTS

CHAPTER I

COLONIAL FOUNDATIONS AND

ANTECEDENTS (1600–1779)

THE SOCIAL SETTING

Provincial America was so beset with problems of survival that it would have been reasonable to expect the colonists to find little time or have little inclination to attend to education. But this was not the case. One of the first concerns of the colonists after they established themselves in the wilderness was the provision of some kind of education for their children.[1]

Several forces contrived to produce an educational consciousness in America that early started setting it apart from the education-for-the-elite-only pattern of most of its European mother countries. Perhaps the most basic force arose out of the character of the immigrants themselves and their motivation for coming to the New World. Many of them were members of political and religious minority groups who perceived America as a land of opportunity that would offer them the possibilities and freedoms denied them in the Old World. This kind of initiative tended to create a readiness for learning.

A second strong force was the predominantly Protestant character of the American colonization. In Grattan's words, ". . . the original impulse for the spreading of literacy was, in America, as in Britain of the same decades and later, religious in character; the end sought was the ability to read the Bible as a guide to salvation." [2]

A third force was what Wright calls "the gospel of work," which became a cardinal point in the social doctrine of the Puritans. "One reason for the Puritans' insistence upon education,"

3

Wright points out, "was the fear that ignorance would beget idleness, and idleness, which was the waste of God's precious time—a recurring phrase in Puritan writing—was one of the worst of sins." [3]

Additional forces gained strength as the Colonial period progressed. For example, as political thought moved toward rebellion against colonial status and toward the establishment of independence, an awareness began to emerge that self-government would require an educated citizenry. The expansion of commerce and industry began to make new demands on education for the production of more skilled workers and artisans. A mounting wave of secular knowledge and thought brought on a struggle to disestablish the church as the partner, and in many ways the senior partner, of the state and to break up its monopoly on education. And the opening up of the back country away from the settled regions of the coast gradually produced a frontier section that developed more radical notions about equality and popular government. By the beginning of the American Revolution the stage had been set for dropping the European traditions and creating a new pattern of education that would more adequately meet the needs of a new and unique society.

EARLY BEGINNINGS OF EDUCATION

While adult education during the entire Colonial period was essentially unorganized and primarily vocational, the seeds of certain institutional forms were planted at this time. And certainly the notion that every person can get ahead if he is willing and works hard—which has so greatly influenced the growth of adult education in this country—began to develop during this period.

Apprenticeship

Since survival depended upon the ability to produce the essentials of life, it is natural that the first educational priority of the colonists should have been vocational training. "The earliest form of vocational education in colonial America," Seybolt points out, "was provided by the apprenticeship system. The colonists brought it with them, and it remained, for some time, the only institution which prepared for vocational life." [4]

Apprenticeship was designed primarily for the education of the poor. Many colonial legislatures passed laws requiring that children of the poor be indentured as apprentices so that they would learn a trade and would not be dependent upon public support. Frequently the laws included the teaching of reading and writing as a part of the responsibility of the masters of apprenticed children.

Universities

The first permanent institutional form of education to be created was the university. Sixteen years after the Puritans landed in Massachusetts, in 1636, they founded Harvard College. Harvard certainly had nothing to do with adult education at that time, being primarily a school for training ministers at what would now be considered the secondary school level. But it was the beginning of an institutional form that has grown to an important position in adult education. Other colonies followed Massachusetts in providing institutions of higher learning with the founding of William and Mary College in Williamsburg, Virginia, in 1696; Yale in New Haven, Connecticut, in 1701; the College of New Jersey in Princeton in 1746; King's College (the forerunner of Columbia) in New York City in 1754; and the University of Pennsylvania in Philadelphia in 1755.

Common Schools

The foundations of our public school system were also laid soon after the colonies were established. Originally the responsibility for teaching the young to read and write resided in the home and church. But it early became evident that these voluntary efforts would not be sufficient to insure that general education which was required by the Puritan religious theory. As a result, the famous Massachusetts Law of 1642 was enacted, directing the local town governments to hold parents and masters to their responsibilities and to impose fines on those who refused. This was the first time in the English-speaking world that a legislative body ordered that all children should be taught to read. This law was followed by one in 1647 which provided:

1. That every town having fifty householders should at once appoint a teacher of reading and writing, and provide for his wages in such manner as the town might determine; and

2. That every town having one hundred householders must provide a grammar school to fit youths for the university, under a penalty of 5 pounds for failure to do so.[5]

While the passing of legislation did not automatically result.in schools being established, these two laws set the precedents for state initiative in education on which our public school system is based. The example of Massachusetts was followed by other colonies, and by the time of the Revolution town schools were a common phenomenon. It was not until well into the next century, however, that the principle of public support by taxation became established. And it was not until even later that programs of education for adults were grafted onto this basic educational institution.

The practice of using school buildings for general community activities did develop during this period, however—especially in New England. Often there was no place as suitable as the schoolhouse for the citizens to gather. While these activities were not wholly educational, they set a precedent for the use of school facilities for general community purposes as well as for the education of the young.[6]

Private Vocational Schools

A third institutional form is described by Seybolt as follows:

Town schools made no attempt to meet the needs of the time. The vocational courses were offered only in private-venture establishments. These schools had no definite, or exclusive name; they were called "School," "Academy," "Grammar School," "English Grammar School," "Mercantile and Mathematical School." Their various curricula, identical in essential respects, were designed to prepare young men for vocational life. They were the most popular of all schools of secondary grade throughout the eighteenth century.[7]

These private schools were widely advertised in the newspapers of the day and were largely conducted in the residences of the "masters." They were the chief source of vocational education for adults and were the predecessors of the numerous commercial trade schools and business colleges that provide vocational training for adults today.

Secondary Schools

The earliest attempts to provide something approaching a secondary education were the Latin grammar schools established by masters for private profit or by town authority in the middle of the seventeenth century. This original type of secondary education was modeled after the classical schools of Europe and was designed for the upper classes who could afford tuition and for a few poor boys who were given a free education, chiefly to prepare for the ministry. With the growth of trade and commerce during the eighteenth century a new type of secondary education began to appear with a curriculum devoted to mathematics, science, and modern languages. This new education was provided by "English grammar schools," or simply, "English schools." In the latter half of the eighteenth century the private English schools gradually gave way to a new form, the private academy, which was an effort to combine the values and content of the Latin schools and the English schools into one institution. The academies became the dominant secondary school in America for the next century.

Libraries

Books were highly valued by the very earliest colonists. Wright points out that while a considerable proportion of the books collected in the seventeenth century were "sheer utilitarian works," having to do with medicine, law, government, agriculture, commerce, and military discipline, many volumes were accounted for by the "zeal to perpetuate learning, to keep alive the desire for knowledge, and to provide the instruments of self-instruction." [8] The colonist's library was likely to include a number of Greek and Latin classics, English histories, scientific works, sermons and theological treatises, books on manners, a few books of fiction and poetry, and encyclopedias. In fact, one encyclopedia, Pierre de La Primaudaye's *The French Academy,* was so important in the informal education of seventeenth-century readers that according to Wright "home study, or 'adult education,' in America should regard this book as one of its foundation stones." [9]

The notion of establishing collections of books available to citizens-at-large developed from small philanthropic beginnings. In 1653 Robert Keayne presented the citizens of Boston with a small collection of books that was later supplemented by other donations, all of which were brought together in a library housed in Boston's Town House and opened to the public in 1673. A number of parish libraries were established by the efforts of Reverend Thomas Bray starting in Maryland in 1696. Designed primarily for the clergy, these parish libraries were made available for limited use by the public.[10]

The facility through which books were made available to the largest number of people in Colonial times, however, was the subscription library (also referred to as social library and company library). The subscription library was a voluntary association of individuals contributing to a general fund for the purchase of books. The books were owned in common, and every member had the right to use them. The first of this new type of library was founded, as were so many other adult educational prototypes, by Benjamin Franklin in 1731, as the Library Association of Philadelphia. It is estimated that between then and 1780 over fifty such libraries were established in New England alone.[11]

Although the idea of a free public library supported by local taxes had not yet emerged, the soil was prepared in Colonial times for the germination of one of the most important adult education institutions of our society.

Churches

The single most universal instrument for intellectual activity in these times was the church. Grattan makes this fact clear:

. . . the early New England clergymen made no intellectual concessions to their audiences; they were not exactly popularizers when it came to dealing with the knottiest of theological conundrums; but they **did** use certain pedagogical devices to assist understanding, such as developing the argument under easily noticed heads and subheads, eschewing Latin quotations, and sticking to a simple style to avoid distracting attention from matter to manner.[12]

Although the subjects of the colonial sermons were overwhelmingly theological and their mission was to bring sinners to salvation, Butts and Cremin point out that ". . . John Winthrop as governor of Massachusetts was apprehensive that the Puritan clergy made too much of the classical authors rather than sticking to the Bible, but he was quickly reassured by the ministers themselves that humanistic learning was as necessary for development of human reason as revelation and grace were necessary for faith and salvation." [13] The church was also the scene of midweek lectures on a wide variety of subjects by both clergy and laymen.

The broad program of activities designed expressly for the education of adults that has come to characterize many religious institutions was only dimly foreseen in the Colonial period. Nevertheless, the church was probably the most influential institutional force for the education of adults in the first two centuries of our national life.

Town Meeting

The New England town meeting is frequently characterized as an important adult educational instrument, and perhaps it was, to the extent that it served as a training ground in the art of self-government for the colonists. Possibly it also provided a general formula on which later adult educational programs were based, such as public forums. But the town meeting was essentially a problem-solving, decision-making instrument, not an educational institution, and it left no permanent deposit in the main stream of adult education's institutional development.

Agricultural Societies

In spite of the predominantly agrarian character of the colonial culture, it was not until the middle of the eighteenth century that agricultural societies began to appear. True reports, for example, that in South Carolina a group of planters interested in the cultivation of indigo began about 1740 to hold meetings "which were largely convivial but at which they talked about the indigo industry and means for improving it." [14]

Agricultural fairs were held as early as 1644, but they were primarily for the purpose of selling agricultural products and had little educational significance. In Franklin's proposals for an academy in Philadelphia in 1749 he suggested that "a little gardening, planting, grafting, and inoculating be taught and practiced, and now and then excursions made to the neighboring plantations of the best farmers." [15] This was one of the few recognitions in the literature of the time that agriculture was something that could be taught.

Nevertheless, local agricultural societies had proved so useful that John Adams requested the Continental Congress—although without success—to encourage the establishment of an agricultural society in every state. Such state societies were organized without this encouragement in South Carolina in 1785, New York in 1791, and Massachusetts in 1792.

Benjamin Franklin and the Junto

The only uniquely adult educational institution founded in this period that has survived (at least in name) into modern times was the Junto, a discussion club started by Franklin and eleven cronies in 1727 to explore such intellectual problems as morals, politics, and natural philosophy. According to James Truslow Adams, ". . . we may count the American Philosophical Society, the Franklin Institute, the University of Pennsylvania, the first American public library, and the first Philadelphia mutual fire insurance company as offshoots of the talks at this club." [16] Over the years the Junto evolved from a men's club into a civic organization sponsored by larger agencies, and in 1941 it was revived as an independent adult education institution, with "Fun in Learning" as its motto.[17]

Through all his writings and by the example of his life, Franklin ingrained deeply into the American stream of thought a compulsion toward self-improvement that has exerted a dominant influence on the American attitude toward continuing education. "Franklin, beyond all other early American heroes," according to Grattan, "has claim to being a patron saint of adult education." [18]

Prototypes of Other Institutions

Early forms of three other cultural institutions appeared during this era. The birth of the idea of the museum can be seen in the founding of the Pennsylvania Academy of Fine Arts in 1791 in Philadelphia and the Massachusetts Historical Society in 1790. The first theater was built in Williamsburg, Virginia, in 1716, and New York had a "play house" by 1733. The first newspaper, the *Boston News Letter,* started publication in 1704.[19]

SUMMARY

The general trend of educational development during the Colonial period was away from domination by theological orthodoxies and European traditions of class structure toward more liberal, more secular, more utilitarian, and more democratic conceptions. Although the movement in this direction had not been great by the time of the founding of the Republic, the course for the future was set. And while the institutions that were established for the education of adults were crude indeed, they were the seeds of which we are now enjoying the fruits.

CHAPTER II

⚙

THE GROWTH OF A NATION AND
ITS QUEST FOR THE DIFFUSION
OF KNOWLEDGE (1780–1865)

THE SOCIAL SETTING

Between the American Revolution and the Civil War the United States emerged as an independent, self-governing nation and American society took on a character which set it apart from its European antecedents. During this period the notion that only the rich and propertied should participate in government gave way to the idea of universal suffrage. It was an era of great westward expansion that operated as a leveler of social classes and a breeder of rugged individualism. It marked the beginning of the industrial revolution, with its concomitants of competitiveness among free men, upward mobility, urbanization, immigration of cheap labor, and the emergence of labor unions. The principle of separation of church and state became fixed, and freedom of worship became a constitutional guarantee.

These forces, coupled with the influence of the European Enlightenment, which brought an upsurge of secular thought and interest in natural science, produced almost a compulsion for knowledge. Perhaps the central issue during this entire period, however—and one not fully resolved until after the Civil War—was what form of government we were to have. Indeed, no undertaking of any society ever staked more on the ability of adults to learn than did the founding of the Republic.

12

THE EDUCATION
OF DEMOCRATIC CITIZENS

The first adult educational task of the new nation was to transform an entire people from subjects to citizens—from a people used to being governed by an aristocracy to a people able to govern themselves in a democracy. This process began, of course, well before the Revolution, but the excitement of the Revolution and the elections that followed it, on the local, state, and federal levels, extended the process from a few to the many.

The instruments by which this undertaking was accomplished were informal, disorganized, and in a sense unconscious. Perhaps foremost were events and experiences themselves. As the Beards point out, during the Colonial period "Americans by the hundreds learned to practice and think about the arts of government. They acquired training in drawing up bills and resolutions. . . . They could stand upon the floors of assemblies, defend the projects they favored, argue with their opponents, and carry on business in accordance with the rules of parliamentary law." [1]

More easily identified instruments for the education of adults were the rising flood of letters of correspondence, pamphlets, editorials, books, speeches, poems, and plays which explored the issues and ideas of democracy. Sam Adams, through his letters of correspondence, speeches, and other political activities, organized popular sentiment and communicated to Americans a desire for independence. Thomas Paine's tract, *Common Sense,* which assailed the King and raised a clarion call to revolution, went through printing after printing totaling over 100,000 copies. The writings and speeches of such other Revolutionary leaders as John Adams, Madison, Jefferson, Franklin, James Otis, and Washington were widely known and discussed in humble homes. *The Federalist,* published by Jay, Hamilton, and Madison in 1788, was a primary textbook for the education of the American people in republican ways of government. Paintings by Trumbull, Gilbert Stuart, and Wilson Peale depicted the events—the Battle of Bunker Hill, for example—and heroes of the new nation. Poets joined in the same theme, as illustrated by John Barlow's "The Vision of Columbus"; playwrights, too, as shown by Tyler's comedy, *The Contrast*. Novelists Charles Brockden Brown and James Fenimore Cooper dealt with stories of the struggle for liberty.

Newspapers multiplied rapidly in the Republican era and became a significant instrument for the distribution of knowledge. It was estimated that in 1810 there were 366 newspapers scattered all the way from New Hampshire to the Louisiana Territory.[2] The first daily newspaper was started in Philadelphia in 1784, but by 1809 there were twenty-seven dailies. Several magazines were also founded in this period, the only one of which to survive into the twentieth century was the *North American Review*, launched in 1815.

THE GROWTH AND DIFFUSION
OF KNOWLEDGE

At the same time that the common man was mastering his new role as citizen-ruler, the world of knowledge was being illuminated by the dawn of the age of science. The natural sciences took root on the American scene at about the time of the Revolution. The American Academy of Arts and Sciences was founded in 1780 to promote interest and knowledge in natural history, medicine, mathematics, astronomy, geography, agriculture, commerce, the arts, and all other forms of useful knowledge. Most of the early scientific work was by amateurs and was an avocational interest. Perhaps the most productive of these was Benjamin Franklin, whose experiments in electricity were almost as well known as his writings and acts of statesmanship.

Concrete evidence of this interest in science is given by the experience of Professor Benjamin Silliman (1779–1864) of Yale College. Anticipating the idea of university extension by three quarters of a century, in 1830 Professor Silliman gave a course of popular lectures in natural science for the benefit of a class of ladies and gentlemen in New Haven. It proved so popular that in 1834 he began to lecture outside of New Haven, in Hartford, Lowell, and Salem. In 1835 he gave afternoon and evening courses in Boston in geology under the auspices of the Society for Promoting Useful Knowledge, which Adams reports were "thronged and yielded subscriptions totaling $2,000." [3] By 1859 his lectures had been extended south and west to Pittsburgh, Baltimore, New Orleans, Mobile, Natchez, and St. Louis.

Mechanics and Mercantile Libraries and Institutes

Interest in the spread of useful knowledge was expressed also in the founding of numerous libraries and institutes for mechanics and merchants' clerks. The Mechanics' Apprentices Library of Boston and the New York Mercantile Library, both opened in 1820, stimulated the development of similar institutions in most of the larger cities of the country. Fees in these libraries were lower than for the more scholarly subscription libraries, and the book collections tended toward the more technical needs of young artisans and mercantile workers.

A more continuous and deeper level of educational opportunity for these same population groups was afforded by the mechanics' institutes. Originated in England to meet the need of artisans for technical education at low cost, in leisure hours, and with minimum preparation requirements, the mechanics' institute was transplanted to this country with the founding of the Franklin Institute in Philadelphia in 1824. Its purpose was "the advancement of science and the mechanic arts, the increase of useful knowledge, the encouragement of invention and discovery, and the education of the public in the achievements of science and industry." Its program consisted of several elements: (1) annual awards, (2) a *Journal* to transmit scientific information, (3) a library, (4) lectures by distinguished scientists, (5) research, (6) a museum, and (7) traveling exhibits. Similar institutes were established in Boston in 1826 and later in New Haven, Rochester, New York, and other cities.

Lowell Institute and Cooper Union

In the same spirit, but with broader purposes and programs, were two institutes that have exerted great influence on their respective communities and on the adult education movement as a whole. The Lowell Institute was founded in Boston in 1836 for "the maintenance and support of public lectures, to be delivered in Boston, upon philosophy, natural history, the arts and sciences"; and Cooper Union was established in New York in 1859 "to provide free courses of instruction in the application of Science and Art to the practical business of life." Both institutions have contributed many pioneering developments in the methods and substance of adult education and are still thriving institutions today. Indeed, the Lowell Institute has recently given pioneering leadership in the development of educational television.

The Lyceum Movement

Perhaps the most spectacular offspring of the hunger for knowledge that characterized this period was the lyceum. Henry Barnard evaluated it in the context of its time as follows:

The first quarter of the present [nineteenth] century was marked by a constantly increasing energy in the working of the leaven of educational improvement. Toward the end of that period and during the succeeding decade the ferment wrought so actively as to generate a numerous, heterogeneous brood of systems, plans, and institutions—many crude and rudely organized; many that never reached an organization; many that did their work quickly and well; few that have survived to the present time. Of all these, whether under the names of school systems (infant, free, monitorial, manual labor, agricultural, etc.), or of mechanics' institutions, lyceums, societies for the diffusion of useful knowledge, mercantile associations, teachers' seminaries, school agents' societies, library associations, book clubs, reading associations, educational journals, etc., none created so immediate and general interest, or excited for a time an influence so great or beneficent, as the American Lyceum.[4]

The idea of a national network of local study groups, or lyceums, emerged out of the experience of Josiah Holbrook of Derby, Connecticut, as a lecturer before numerous groups in New England. In October 1826, Holbrook described in the *American Journal of Education* a full-scale plan for the organization of an educational society that would reach every part of the nation. He proceeded to demonstrate that his plan would work by personally organizing the first town lyceum in Millbury, Massachusetts, that same year, and ten more lyceums in neighboring towns during the next year. By 1828 there were around one hundred lyceums in local towns and several county lyceums. The movement continued to spread, and by 1835, according to Mr. Holbrook's estimate, there were about 3,000 town lyceums, over 100 county lyceums, and 15 or 16 state lyceums.

Barnard gives this eye-witness account of the lyceums in action:

Lyceums are associations formed for the mutual improvement of their members and the common benefit of society. Their members meet on frank, cordial, and equal grounds. All declare, by joining a lyceum, that they wish to extend their knowledge; and from the manner in which they associate each may become, by turns, a learner and a teacher. All unnecessary formalities, as well as expenses, are to be avoided, that the way of learning may be rendered as free as possible. . . . These associations may be formed in almost any village or neighborhood by a few friends of knowledge; and by meeting with an audience once a week through the winter, delivering lectures in a familiar manner, exhibiting and conversing of minerals, plants, etc., inviting inquiries, requesting aid in collecting and arranging them, furnishing communications on similar subjects to editors of newspapers, contributing books for a library, arranging for their delivery, etc., and a visible improvement will be made in the aspect of society before the next spring.[5]

Hayes points out that to this purpose of self-improvement was added the higher purpose of advancing the cause of the public schools: "The espousal of the common-school cause gave each lyceum membership something definite to work for, besides their own intellectual improvement. The people who controlled the fate of the common public schools thus convinced themselves of the need of improvement and extension of their schools." [6]

In May 1831, a meeting was held in New York City for the organization of the National American Lyceum, with delegates present representing 1,000 town lyceums. The new organization adopted as its purpose "the advancement of education, especially in the common schools, and the general diffusion of knowledge." An organizational pattern was formulated consisting of a hierarchy of local, county, and state lyceums, each with representation in the national lyceum. Hayes reports that the annual meetings of the national lyceum were poorly attended and that ways were never found to get the county and state organizations functioning properly. The national system therefore gradually withered, and by 1840 it had disintegrated into scattered local lecture series.[7]

Although the national lyceum ceased to exist, many town and county lyceums continued to operate, especially in New England, until about the time of the Civil War. Around 1869 the function of providing popular lecturers for literary societies, women's clubs, and other groups, began to be taken over by commercial speakers' bureaus—often known as "lyceum bureaus." According to a later critic, the educational quality of the lyceum tradition became violated because "bureau managers, being business men, studied lyceum audiences not from the viewpoint of what was the best these audiences might be made to receive, but what could be sold to them with the greatest profit." [8]

The lyceum movement was significant in many respects. Above all, it served the needs of its time. It was one of the most powerful instruments of its time for the mobilization of public opinion in favor of tax-supported public schools. In fact, its very success in this mission presaged its own decline. Moreover, it produced a general intellectual stimulation throughout the country by providing a mechanism for local citizens to study together and by exposing them to the ideas and personalities of such notable giants of American thought as Wendell Phillips, Ralph Waldo Emerson, William Lloyd Garrison, Henry David Thoreau, Henry Ward Beecher, Charles Sumner, Oliver Wendell Holmes, and Susan B. Anthony.

But the lyceum movement also left several permanent deposits in the main streams of American culture and, particularly, of adult education. It spawned the idea of an integrated national system of local groups organized primarily for adult educational purposes. Its experience in this regard without doubt influenced the development of such later organizations as the women's clubs, the service clubs, the parent-teacher associations, and even the modern-day Great Books Program. It developed an educational technique, the lecture-forum, that was later to be adopted and extended by such successors as the Chautauqua, university extension, and public forum movements. Its publication of scientific tracts for home study foreshadowed the correspondence course. Perhaps it even suggested the idea of a national popular movement for the advancement of adult education.

Popular Reading and Public Libraries

The hunger for knowledge that characterized this period was, fortunately, accompanied by a general rise of the ability of citizens to read, by technological advances that made reading materials more readily available, and by the emergence of a significant number of native scholars, authors, poets, dramatists, and artists, who interpreted with contagious pride the evolving national culture. American journalism entered a golden age with the establishment of the one-cent daily paper (the *New York Sun*) in 1833, the invention of the telegraph in 1844, the introduction of the cylinder rotary press in 1846, and the appearance of such journalistic leaders as Horace Greeley, James Gordon Bennett, Thomas Ritchie, and Henry J. Raymond. Literally hundreds of weekly and monthly magazines came into being, of which *Harper's Magazine* (1850) and *The Atlantic Monthly* (1857) have survived to the modern era.

Simultaneously a native literary movement was developing. Whereas in 1820 less than one third of the publications issued in the United States came from American writers, by the Civil War more than four fifths were of domestic origin.[9] Such names as Stowe, Cooper, Hawthorne, Thoreau, Emerson, Prescott, Holmes, Irving, Whitman, Alcott, Longfellow, Lowell, Melville, and Poe came into prominence in this period.

If this was a period of expansion for reading materials, so was it for the facilities of mass circulation—the public libraries. Although private libraries multiplied in connection with lyceums, young men's associations, civic groups, and subscription clubs, the idea of free public libraries began to take hold. A free town library was established in Peterborough, New Hampshire, in 1833, supported by a municipal tax. By 1849 the idea had gained such strength that a state law was passed in New Hampshire enabling towns to establish and maintain libraries by taxation. Massachusetts followed suit in 1851, Maine in 1854, Vermont in 1855, and Ohio in 1867.

However, it was with the opening of the Boston Public Library in 1852 that the free public library as we know it came into existence. With special permission from the state government to tax in support of a library, with a gift of $5,000 from Mayor Quincy for books, and under the leadership of such solid men of Boston as George Ticknor and Edward Everett, a free public library was started to serve the wants of those who could in no other way supply the reading for further education. Boston's example was followed shortly by New York—as the result of an Astor gift of half a million dollars—and by other urban centers of the country. It was characteristic of the early public libraries that they were largely urban and were founded under the stimulus of philanthropy. By the beginning of the Civil War the free public library had become established as an integral part of the American cultural and educational system.

Museums

In this period the museum also had its beginning as an instrument for popular learning in science, history, and art. Borrowed from Europe, where it had developed primarily as a center of scholarship and research, the museum when transplanted to young America took on the coloration of its new environment and became concerned primarily with the diffusion of knowledge.

The great interest in natural science that characterized the early nineteenth century intellectual revolution stimulated the assembling of scientific equipment and objects into classified collections. The universities were the first to organize such collections, but popular collections became institutionalized with the founding of the New York Academy of Sciences in 1815, the Academy of Natural Sciences in Philadelphia in 1812, the Franklin Institutes, and local scientific societies.

The same period witnessed the growth of a substantial number of historical societies as repositories of local history and folklore: in Massachusetts in 1790, in New York in 1804, and in most states of the Union by the Civil War. Adam observes, "The appearance of these forerunners of a museum movement was no accident of chance. They represented the necessary foundation that had to be laid for the creation of a working ideal of American unity." [10]

Art museums barely made an appearance during this period. The Pennsylvania Academy of Fine Arts, established in Philadelphia in 1805, along with a few art collections assembled by universities and by the Smithsonian Institution (founded in Washington in 1846), account for the major collections available to the public at the start of the Civil War.

Voluntary Associations and Agencies

One of the most uniquely American aspects of our culture, and one of the most significant in the future development of adult education—the voluntary association—had already become so visible by 1831 as to draw these often-quoted remarks from a French observer:

Americans of all ages, all conditions, and all dispositions constantly form associations . . . to give entertainments, to found seminaries, to build inns, to construct churches, to diffuse books, to send missionaries to the antipodes; in this manner they found hospitals, prisons, and schools. If it is proposed to inculcate some truth or to foster some feeling by the encouragement of a great example, they form a society. Wherever at the head of some new undertaking you see the government in France, or a man of rank in England, in the United States you will be sure to find an association.[11]

Tocqueville himself connected the principle of association with that of equality, observing that "among democratic nations . . . all citizens are independent and feeble; they can do hardly anything by themselves, and none of them can oblige his fellow men to lend him their assistance. They all, therefore, become powerless if they do not learn voluntarily to help one another." [12] And he went on to generalize that "if men are to remain civilized or to become so, the art of associating together must grow and improve in the same ratio in which the equality of conditions is increased." [13] Tocqueville is here laying down both a goal and a rationale for the informal adult education movement that developed in this country.

While the growth of voluntary associations may have been related to the spread of equality, as Tocqeville hypothesized, it was no doubt influenced by other forces. One was the changing religious climate. With the relaxation of the stiff Calvinistic core of New England theology, the multiplication of sects, greater participation by laymen in the leadership of the churches, and the ground swell of secularism in American thought, the spirit of the churches became more conducive to voluntary citizen participation. Indeed, the churches themselves increasingly took on the characteristics of voluntary associations and stimulated the development of other voluntary associations, such as interdenominational organizations, charity agencies, and hospitals.

The growth of voluntary associations was aided also by increased urbanization, improved communications, and the emergence of such causes as abolitionism, temperance, and the women's movement. The most powerful force of all was, no doubt, the general quest for knowledge and self-improvement that produced such pioneering voluntary associations as the subscription libraries, lyceums, discussion clubs, institutes, and scholarly societies previously described.

Many of these voluntary associations had an action goal to propagandize for, but many of them carried on adult educational programs as their chief activity. Although most of them were narrowly local in their scope and influence, the way was being paved for the formation of the strong national organizations that came to dominate the picture in the second half of the century. The organization of the Young Men's Christian Associations starting in 1851, the United States Agricultural Society in 1852, the Young Women's Christian Associations in 1855, the first industry-wide trade association in the same year, and the National Education Association in 1857 gave an indication of the future direction of voluntary association development in this country.

Churches

While the Protestant churches were experiencing an increasing voluntarism, this fact does not mean that they were yet conscious of any substantial role in the secular education of adults. The Sunday School movement began to be transplanted from England in 1785, and in 1824 the American Sunday School Union was founded. The mission of this movement was completely doctrinal and its clientele was exclusively children. Grattan attributes considerable influence to the American Bible Society (1816) and the American Tract Society (1824) which, "though chiefly concerned with religious work, were definitely concerned also with the promotion of literacy and with satisfying the reading needs of the moderately literate." [14]

Perhaps the most important development in adult education in Jewish religious institutions during this period was the emergence of Reformed Judaism. Of this movement Meland observes:

Having abandoned the racial taboos and practices of the traditional faith which had tended to set the Jew apart from his contemporaries, the Reformed Jew has taken up the task of adapting himself to the environment of modern culture with a zeal not to be exceeded, if, in fact, matched, by other religious adherents. . . . This movement in Judaism has been an energetic influence in behalf of enlightened and socialized living in this country for more than a century.[15]

The earliest form of discrete adult educational activity operated by Catholics was the reading circles that were often founded in connection with parish libraries. An example was the New York City Catholic Library Association established in 1854 "with the object of disseminating Catholic truth and useful knowledge and promoting the moral and intellectual culture of its members." [16] By 1860 this association had a historical section, a debating club, a mechanics' society, and a library of over 1,000 volumes. Catholic young men's societies, which had their genesis in this period, also afforded adult educational opportunities. For example, the Xavier Alumni Sodality, begun in New York in 1863, brought the alumni of all Catholic colleges together "to promote the study of good books and to foster a taste for the sciences and arts." [17]

Agricultural Education

The local and regional agricultural societies, which began appearing after the American Revolution to promote agricultural production through printed materials, contests, and fairs, joined together in 1852 to form the United States Agricultural Society. In 1860 this society reported that there were 941 agricultural organizations in existence in the country, and True reports that during this period these organizations "became more democratic and brought a considerable body of the most intelligent and progressive farmers into active relations with a nation-wide movement for the advancement of agriculture." [18] They were also becoming more aware of the possibilities of enlisting government aid and were actively attempting to promote the formation of state boards of agriculture (the first of which had been established in New York and New Hampshire in 1820), a national Department of Agriculture, and the teaching of agriculture in the colleges. The societies reached their peak in 1861 and began to wane in favor of farmers' institutes, which had spread from Massachusetts starting in 1839 under the auspices of the state boards of agriculture. Because they provided direct instruction in technological improvements in farming, the institutes proved more effective than the societies in meeting the practical needs of the farmers.

The year 1862 represents a landmark in this steady forward march of agricultural education with the occurrence of two events of enormous consequence. One was the establishment of a federal Department of Agriculture having broad responsibility for promoting the welfare of the rural population. The other was the passage of the Land Grant Act—often referred to as the Morrill Act in honor of the Vermont senator who sponsored it for many years—providing federal support for colleges to teach the agricultural and mechanical arts.

THE SHAPING OF A NATIONAL EDUCATIONAL SYSTEM

During the period between the American Revolution and the Civil War the basic pattern of our national system of state-supported elementary and secondary schools, state universities, and normal schools took shape. But this achievement was not accomplished by an easy, automatic process.

Except in certain regions of New England where the free-school idea had become established, the prevailing notion about education at the time of the founding of the Republic was that it was at the most a private responsibility (primarily that of the parents and the church) and at the least a luxury to be indulged in by the elite. Several forces combined to change this attitude to one favorable to public responsibility for education.

Perhaps the strongest of these forces was the growing realization that the success of a free self-governing society depended on the existence of an intelligent citizenry. New requirements for more widespread education were also imposed by the great growth in manufacturing and urbanization. Technological progress cre-ated a demand for more skilled workers and stimulated the organization of workingmen into labor unions, which early supported public education as a means for increasing equality of opportunity and eliminating social ills. The rapid growth of cities produced concentrations of both needs and resources to a degree that caused the cities to champion public education consistently, often in opposition to the views of the rural population.

The new spirit of the West, the political influence of which was symbolized in the election of Andrew Jackson as President in 1828, also greatly affected educational developments. It was on the frontier that egalitarianism reached its highest peak and that rebellion against a caste system based on both education and property was strongest. In the new states there were no traditions and few entrenched interests to overcome. The idea of public education received a further boost by the Ordinance of 1787 for the government of the Northwest Territory, which provided that sections of land were to be set aside for the support of schools in each township. Consequently, the constitutions of most western states, as they were admitted to the Union, made provision for state systems of public instruction.

While there was little opposition to the idea of universal education, it being widely accepted in principle that everyone in a republic ought to be educated, there was strong opposition to the idea of universal public education supported by taxation. This opposition came from private school supporters, many church groups, and some foreign-language groups—all of which saw public education as a threat to their own educational programs. It also came from some members of the aristocratic classes and conservative taxpayers, and was especially strong in rural districts.

A battle ensued that lasted a generation, from 1825 to 1850, and the issue engendered much feeling and bitter antagonism. The process by which the battle was won was strongly flavored with propaganda and social action, but included many elements that can be properly labeled adult education. Public interest was aroused and citizens were stimulated to study and discuss the issues through the activities of hundreds of school societies, lyceums, and educational associations. Many conventions were held in which resolutions advocating state schools were adopted; state legislatures were deluged for years with resolutions, memorials, and petitions. Running debates were carried on in the newspapers and magazines. Public-spirited citizens, as well as professional schoolmen like Horace Mann, traveled over the country making addresses to the people and spreading the vision of a national pattern of universal public education. The result of these efforts was that, as Cubberley phrases it, "In 1825 [common] schools were still the distant hope of statesmen and reformers; in 1850 they had become an actuality in almost every Northern State." [19]

The earliest institution of secondary education in this country, the Latin grammar school, with its rigid classical, college-preparatory curriculum, gradually died out in the second half of the eighteenth century in favor of the semiprivate tuition academy, with its broader and more practical curriculum. But the same forces that brought about the establishment of free public elementary schools began working for the extension of the principle of tax support to secondary schools. In Cubberley's words, "As the colonial Latin grammar school had represented the educational needs of a society based on classes, and the academies had represented a transition period and marked the growth of a middle class, so the rising democracy of the second quarter of the nineteenth century now demanded and obtained the democratic high school, supported by the public and equally open to all, to meet the educational needs of a new society built on the basis of a new and aggressive democracy." [20]

And as in the case of the common schools, the development of free public high schools came about gradually, over much opposition from vested interests and conservative taxpayers, and only after the solution of providing grants to private academies so they could expand facilities and reduce rates had been tried and found inadequate. The first high school was established in Boston in 1821, with Portland and Worcester following its example immediately and New York City following within five years. The basic pattern of high school legislation was laid down in a Massachusetts law of 1827 that required a high school in every town having five hundred families or over. This law was amended in 1835 to permit any smaller town to establish a high school. From these beginnings the idea spread gradually westward and southward, at first only in the larger cities.

By 1860 there was little doubt that the high school, although still subordinate to the academy, would become accepted as a part of the public school system. It represents the first truly American contribution to a national educational system, rejecting entirely the English parallel-class-education idea on which the Latin grammar school and academy are based.

EVENING SCHOOLS

The literature of the field is not in agreement about when the first evening school was opened in this country. Cubberley asserts that "Providence is said to have established an evening school as early as 1810," [21] but the Rhode Island State Department of Education dates the operation of public evening schools in Providence from 1850 on the basis that the earlier evening schools were conducted under private auspices.[22] New York City is usually credited with opening the first evening elementary schools in 1833, but these were discontinued in 1838 because no financing was provided for them and they were not reopened until 1847.[23]

In Table 1 are shown the starting dates of evening schools in both elementary schools and high schools in pioneering cities, as given by three students of this historical development. The reliability of this information was tested by requesting the directors of adult education in the public schools of the cities listed to determine the true starting dates from the reports of the boards of education in their cities. The dates provided by those who responded are given in the fourth column of the table.

No doubt the principal difficulty in firmly fixing the founding dates of the first evening schools is the fact that these new undertakings were highly unstable and often rather informal in their early stages of development.

An examination of the annual reports of some of the pioneering school systems indicates that many of the evening schools were begun in a spirit of great tentativeness and often without much conviction about their rational foundation. For example, three evening schools were opened in 1840 in Cincinnati in re-

TABLE 1

Founding Dates of Evening Schools

	Cubberley[a]	Mann[b]	Greenberger[c]	Knowles[d]
ELEMENTARY SCHOOLS				
New York City	1833	1847	1833 (43)	
Louisville	1834	1834	1834 (247)	
Boston			1836 (250)	1856
Baltimore	1840			1839
Cincinnati	1840		1840 (260)	1840
New Orleans			1845 (325)	
Providence	1810		1849 (373)	1850
Cleveland			1850 (300)	1850
Pittsburgh		1856	1855 (286)	
St. Louis		1859	1857 (340)	1859
Washington, D.C.			1858 (394)	
Chicago		1862		
HIGH SCHOOLS				
Cincinnati	1856			
New York City	1866		1866 (47)	
Chicago	1868			
St. Louis	1868			
Philadelphia	1869	1869		
Boston	1870			

[a] Ellwood P. Cubberley, *Public Education in the United States,* rev. ed., pp. 428 and 587. Boston: Houghton Mifflin Company, 1947.

[b] George C. Mann, "The Development of Public School Adult Education," National Association of Public School Adult Educators, *Public School Adult Education,* p. 2. Washington, D.C.: National Association of Public School Adult Educators, 1956.

[c] Lawrence C. Greenberger, "Adult Education Through Evening High Schools," pages as indicated in parentheses. Unpublished doctoral dissertation, University of Pittsburgh, 1936.

[d] From letters to the author from the directors of adult education in the designated cities quoting from the minutes of their respective boards of education.

sponse to a law requiring "the Trustees to provide a suitable number of evening schools for the benefit of young men over twelve years of age, who are, by the nature of their occupations, prevented from attending day schools." Because attendance became increasingly irregular, the annual report for 1841 concluded: "We are of the opinion that the continuance of these schools for three months is as long as their usefulness can be rendered adequate to the expense incurred for their support." However, the annual report for 1842 indicated that attendance had improved; and with the opening of a night high school in 1856, the annual report of 1857 was able to state enthusiastically,

This School has succeeded much beyond our expectations, not merely in the proficiency of the pupils in their studies, and their steady adherence to the school, the attendance being much more regular than had prevailed in the most successful of the District Night Schools, but especially in the increased numbers attracted to these latter mentioned schools, and the evident zeal for improvement excited among our youth by the opening of a higher course of education . . .[24]

The 1850 report of the Board of Managers of the Cleveland Public Schools announced the opening of the first evening school during the winter term with an enrollment of 135 students whose average age was eighteen years. Two-hour sessions were held five evenings a week for thirteen weeks and "were conducted by our gentlemen Teachers, at a compensation nearly proportioned to their regular salaries." [25]

In Chicago the first evening sessions were held in the winter of 1856 with a total enrollment of 208. While the use of the building was granted by the city, the teachers were recruited from the day school faculties on the basis of gratuitous service. Not until 1863 was a small appropriation made to cover instructional cost, and not until 1865 was a substantial appropriation made by the Common Council for general support for evening schools.[26]

Similarly timid attempts to organize evening programs to meet the needs of working youths were taking place in the public schools of other major cities across the country. For example, evening courses were begun in Baltimore in 1839 for boys between twelve and twenty-one years of age unable to attend day schools,[27] and in 1856 the age limit was extended to thirty years.[28] In Buffalo evening courses were offered in four schools in 1851 and they proved so popular that the number had increased to twelve by 1859. In that year the program was discontinued, however, largely because of criticism by the opponents of public schools, and was not resumed until 1872.[29] Evening courses appeared in the elementary schools of St. Louis in 1859.[30]

It is clear that these early evening schools would not qualify as programs of adult education in the modern sense. They were established primarily for youngsters who worked during the day; and their curriculum was a repetition of the regular academic courses given during the day. But the fact that the evening school had become an established unit in many public school systems before the Civil War provided the foundation for what was later to become one of the most important institutions for the education of adults in our country.

Colleges and Universities

At the close of the Colonial period there were nine colleges serving the higher educational needs of the new nation. By 1800 an additional fifteen private colleges had been established. All of these institutions had been founded primarily to educate for the ministry and, with the exception of the University of Pennsylvania, they were under strict denominational control. Support came from philanthropic gifts and bequests, denominational grants, and tuition. It is estimated that by 1800 the two dozen colleges in the country had no more than one hundred professors, two thousand students, or property worth over one million dollars.

With the development of nationalism, egalitarianism, and concern for the wide diffusion of knowledge that characterized the first half of the nineteenth century, there emerged an increasing dissatisfaction with these institutions of higher learning. Specifically, they were seen as being too aristocratic in nature and representing the interests of special sects and factions rather than the interests of the state as a whole. Two remedies were attempted. One was to make state universities out of the colonial colleges. Repeated attempts by state legislatures to encroach on the independence of the private colleges ended in 1819 with the Dartmouth College decision by the United States Supreme Court in which it was held that the charter of a college is a contract that a legislature cannot impair. Since this decision guaranteed the perpetuity of endowments, it had the effect of spurring on the founding of private and denominational colleges—182 permanent colleges had been founded by 1861.

The other remedy was to establish new state universities. Precedent for this alternative had been set in 1787 when Congress, in authorizing the sale of land to the Ohio Company, specified that two entire townships of land could be set aside in any state to help endow a university. Eight years later, in 1795, North Carolina established the first state university, followed by Georgia in 1801, South Carolina in 1805, and Ohio in 1809. With the handing down of the Dartmouth College decision there was increasing activity in the creation of state universities—in spite of opposition by the same forces that were opposing free common schools—until by the Civil War twenty-one such institutions were established in twenty states.

The development of a state-controlled system of higher education was further stimulated by a movement that began near the middle of the nineteenth century for federal legislation in support of agricultural and mechanical colleges. A bill was actually passed by Congress in 1858 but was vetoed by President Buchanan. Finally, in 1862 a Land Grant College Act was passed and signed by President Lincoln, making a grant of 30,000 acres of public land to each state for each senator and representative the state had in Congress, to endow a college of agriculture and mechanic arts. This act laid the foundation for the establishment in the next half-century of a pattern of state land-grant colleges which has become one of the principal elements of our public education system and which was later to provide the home base for the most extensive adult education program ever created, the Cooperative Extension Service.

Another development in higher education during this period was the opening of collegiate instruction to women. In 1800 not a single college in the United States would admit women. But starting in 1821 a series of seminaries for women became established, and by 1860 there were sixty-one institutions of higher education for women. About half of these later developed into colleges. Meantime, private colleges started opening their instruction to women (Oberlin in 1833 and Antioch in 1853) and state universities followed suit (Iowa in 1856, Indiana in 1868, and Michigan, Illinois, and California in 1870).

Technical institutions and normal schools also came into being in this era. The founding of the United States Military Academy at West Point in 1802 marks the beginning of a series of wholly technical institutions, the first nonmilitary example of which was Rensselaer Polytechnic Institute, opened in Troy, New York, in 1824. The first normal schools, dating back to 1823, were private schools rated at the academy level. The first public normal school was opened in Lexington, Massachusetts, in 1839, and by the Civil War twelve such schools had been founded in eight states.

The notion that the universities have a contribution to make to the general community, over and above the training of resident students, was glimpsed but hardly seen during the early nineteenth century. As has been already mentioned, Professor Silliman's popular lectures had extended from New Haven to most of the settled regions of the country by mid-century. But these were not perceived as extensions of the university's services so much as the leisure activity of a public-spirited professor. Other professors were recruited, in a similar spirit, by the lyceum movement. Further evidence that the university extension idea was in the air is contained in the following letter written in 1835 by Dr. William E. Channing to Josiah Quincy, president of Harvard:

The education of the people seems to me more and more to be the object to which the college should be directed. This institution has always existed, and exists now, for the people. It trains young men, not so much for themselves, as that they may be qualified to render services to the community; and perhaps they render no higher service than by spreading their own intelligence and giving a higher tone to the public mind. Can not the college do more for this end? I hope it may. If it can furnish a course of philosophical instruction, which can be pursued by a greater number than now pass through college; if it can extend the demand for this higher education by supplying its means, and if it can give a rank to those who enjoy this advantage, it will render inestimable service to the community.

Perhaps the most important inquiry for the friends of the college is, How can it become a popular institution, an object of public interest, without narrowing at all its present course of instruction? Its well being requires that the community should look to it as their friend and benefactor.[31]

Channing anticipated with uncanny vision not only the adult educational potential of university extension but its public relations mission for the university as well. And he foresaw the problem it would present in regard to traditional academic standards.

But these were purely prophetic phenomena. The flowering of the idea of university extension as an operational concept would have to wait until the end of the century.

SUMMARY

Between the Revolution and the Civil War the basic patterns of a new American way of life took shape, with education looming large in the design. The notion that a free society requires an enlightened citizenry became established as an integral element of the national mind. The essential features of a unified, articulated, democratic national educational ladder for children and youth from the primary grades through university became visible. The idea that adults needed education, too, began to be dimly perceived. A number of informal channels of adult education became well established, including daily newspapers, magazines, books and pamphlets, the theater, and local voluntary associations. An experiment in organizing a national program of adult education, the American Lyceum, was tried, and while it did not succeed in becoming established permanently, it left a heritage of concept and method that proved valuable to later institutions. Three permanent institutional forms of adult education became firmly planted. One of these, the local institute or adult school, as represented by Lowell Institute and Cooper Union, became established in only a few large cities. The other two, the library and the museum, spread throughout the nation. A fourth major institutional form, the adult evening school, was just beginning to develop. But the directions were now set for at first gradual and then rapid institutional blossoming of adult education in the next fifty years.

CHAPTER III

⌘

THE MATURATION OF A NATION

AND MULTIPLICATION

OF ITS ADULT EDUCATIONAL

INSTITUTIONS (1866–1920)

THE SOCIAL SETTING

During the years between the Civil War and World War I the United States experienced the kind of physical and intellectual growth that in human beings characterizes the adolescent years.

Its physical proportions expanded to the shores of both oceans and from Canada to Mexico, and in the filling of this space its population swelled from just over thirty million in 1860 to well over one hundred million by 1920. Much of this population expansion was the result of the pouring into this country of wave after wave of immigrants from almost every part of the world—and their integration into a new culture became one of the great adult educational challenges of all time.

The most phenomenal expansion took place in the country's economic system, as well. Although agricultural production increased dramatically to keep up with the appetites of the growing population, it was far outstripped by the explosive growth of industry. Indeed, during this period the character of the nation changed in essence from agrarian to industrial. And with this transformation, the character of American education was forced to change.

As industry grew, so did urbanization. The nerve system of the country became increasingly centered in the cities—the hubs of commerce, communications, cultural opportunities, medical centers, social services, and political power. By the census of 1920 over half the population of the country lived in cities, and a new set of problems and a new way of life rapidly emerged.

Politically the federal government emerged from the Civil War stronger than ever and with a commitment to the development of a powerful, unified nation. Accordingly it adopted policies that favored the development of big business, efficient centralized government, and a general spirit of nationalism. By the advent of World War I, America had become somewhat awkwardly aware that it was no longer a debtor nation, both economically and culturally, but one of the chief creditors and a first-rate power. America was suddenly confronted with the fact that it would have difficulty in avoiding responsibility in world affairs in spite of a traditional determination to do so. Accompanying this development of political power was a process of broadening democratization, as evidenced by the Thirteenth Amendment abolishing slavery, the Fourteenth Amendment conferring citizenship on all persons born or naturalized in the United States, the Fifteenth Amendment prohibiting the states from abridging the right of citizens to vote because of race, color, or previous conditions of servitude, the Seventeenth Amendment making Senators elective by popular vote, and the Nineteenth Amendment extending the suffrage to women.

Religious development was characterized by a steady increase in non-Protestant institutions, especially Catholic and Jewish, the emergence of a "social gospel" that brought the power of the church to bear on social problems, and a liberalizing theological upheaval caused largely by the surge of scientific knowledge—particularly regarding evolution. The growing heterogeneity of American religious life tended to reinforce the determination to maintain the separation of church and state. By 1900 the prohibition against using public funds for sectarian schools and against teaching sectarian religions in public schools had been widely confirmed by state constitutions, statutes, and court decisions.

The intellectual spirit of this era was as expansive as the political and economic. Knowledge broke the bonds of subservience to theology and philosophy as the application of the scientific method to nearly all fields of knowledge produced a mass of new information. With the rapid increase in knowledge came increasing specialization. "Natural history" was split up into botany, zoology, paleontology, physiology, and a number of other "natural sciences." "Natural philosophy" was divided into physics, astronomy, chemistry, geology, mineralogy, meteorology, and other "physical sciences." And out of "moral philosophy" emerged a whole new set of social sciences: history, political science, economics, anthropology, sociology, and psychology. "Useful," "functional," "pragmatic" became the predominant standards for knowledge and science as well as for art, literature, and almost all intellectual pursuits. These forces greatly influenced the character of education.

While the dominating spirit of the adult education movement up to the Civil War had been the diffusion of knowledge, that of the period between the Civil War and World War I might be characterized as the diffusion of organizations. In this period the penchant for joining, which Tocqueville had observed in Americans in the 1830's, achieved a high level of expression. Hardly a year passed without the forming of at least one new organization concerned with social- or self-improvement. Most of the types of institutions providing educational opportunities to adults in our day trace their birth to this era.

DEVELOPMENTS IN INSTITUTIONS

In keeping with the general expansiveness and experimentalism of the times, a number of new institutional forms and methods of adult education were created, and many of the older institutions and methods were expanded and transformed.

Chautauqua

Founded on the shores of Chautauqua Lake in western New York in the summer of 1874, Chautauqua Institution was initially conceived as a pan-denominational normal school for Sunday school teachers. This was the sole purpose in the minds of its founders, Dr. John Vincent, secretary of the Methodist Sunday School Union, and Lewis Miller, a businessman and church layman. But the idea of a summer educational program proved so popular that Chautauqua began to attract participants other than Sunday school teachers and began broadening its program to include every aspect of culture.

In 1878 the first integrated core program of adult education organized in this country on a national scale came into being, the Chautauqua Literary and Scientific Circle. Recalling much of the pioneering work of Josiah Holbrook and the American Lyceum, the "C.L.S.C." was a four-year program of home reading in history and literature carried on in connection with local reading circles. Rebecca Richmond reports that shortly after Dr. Vincent announced this new program, ". . . the multitude of applicants for membership in this new 'every-day college' fairly inundated him. When some order could be brought into the record, in the following fall, there were discovered to be eight thousand four hundred names." [1]

Broadly speaking the readings were organized into yearly cycles, the reading for any given year being the same for all classes or circles. The English year was followed by the American, the continental European, and the classical years. Diplomas were awarded for the successful completion of four years of study and discussion in the local circles. In 1880 a monthly magazine, *The Chautauquan*, was added to the C.L.S.C. program to provide supplementary reading, discussion questions, news about local circles, and inspiration. The magazine was discontinued in 1914 along with the national C.L.S.C. program, but local circles have continued to meet in many parts of the country.

At the same time that the C.L.S.C. program was developing, Chautauqua initiated its summer schools, which in the course of time came to include a Normal School of Languages, a College of Liberal Arts, a School of Speech, a School of Physical Education, a School of Music, a School of Domestic Science, a School of Library Training (organized by Melvil Dewey), a Theater School, and a School of Theology. The summer schools attracted outstanding educators to their faculties and achieved high academic recognition.

While the formal educational program of Chautauqua was thus broadening, so was its informal program. Numerous lecture series, classes, and conferences were conducted on pressing national issues, contemporary literature, and vital economic, political, social, theological, and international subjects. Outstanding choral, symphonic, and operatic concerts were given. America's leading plays were presented. And numerous extracurricular activities enriched the program, including a woman's club, youth groups, sports clubs, and a Bird and Tree Garden Club.

Chautauqua Institution was early imitated with the founding of a scattering of local and regional "Chautauquas," which for the most part adhered quite faithfully to the principles of their model, and with the founding of a commercial Chautauqua Circuit, which brought both entertainment and culture to rural America.

Chautauqua, to this day a thriving adult education institution, is assured a place in history alone by the influence it has had directly on the lives of thousands of individuals. But it merits additional credit for the contributions it has made to other institutions. It pioneered the development of such new forms and methods as the correspondence course, summer school, university extension, and book clubs, which have been adopted by colleges and universities, public schools, and myriad commercial organizations.

Correspondence Courses

While Chautauqua was the first American institution to establish correspondence courses on a regular basis, Noffsinger reports two earlier attempts to do so:

In 1873 an organization was formed calling itself The Society to Encourage Studies at Home. It sought to stimulate the formation of home study groups, prepared guides to reading and conducted a regular correspondence with members. Failure to adapt instruction to the ability and requirements of the students soon caused the society to suspend. Ten years later a Correspondence University, consisting of an association of instructors from various colleges and universities, was founded at Ithaca, New York, stating as its purpose, "to supplement the work of other educational institutions by instructing persons who from any cause were unable to attend them . . . For a variety of reasons the Correspondence University . . . soon died a natural death.[2]

The first correspondence course at Chautauqua was offered in 1879 by William Rainey Harper, then a professor of Hebrew at Yale. The experiment, at first an informal "advice by mail" process, proved so popular that by 1883 several courses were offered under several instructors, with regular assignments and a course fee of ten dollars. The success of the home-study program at Chautauqua inspired Dr. Harper, when he became president of The University of Chicago in 1892, to establish a correspondence division in the extension department of the new university. The idea of education by correspondence gradually spread to other universities and even to some high schools and junior colleges.

Correspondence courses in the universities tended to be extensions of their regular academic courses, taught by the regular faculty through a process of assigned readings, the performance of lessons in writing by the students, and the return of the lessons with helpful comments by the instructors. These courses were usually offered on a regular credit basis, and many universities permitted up to half of the courses in an individual's degree program to be taken by correspondence. The courses could frequently be taken without credit at a reduced fee.

At the same time that correspondence study was growing in the universities it was being discovered and widely exploited by commercial institutions. The first of these began as a course in coal mining instituted in the latter part of the 1880's by Thomas J. Foster, editor of the *Mining Herald* of Shenandoah, Pennsylvania, as a means of improving mine safety through education. The course met such enthusiastic response that other subjects were added and in 1891 this program became institutionalized into the International Correspondence Schools of Scranton, Pennsylvania. By 1920 this largest and best known of all correspondence schools had attained a cumulative enrollment of 2,271,193 students. The success of this pioneering venture stimulated literally hundreds of correspondence schools to be formed by private individuals, partnerships, and stock companies. The great preponderance of the offerings by these private schools was vocational, although a few schools specialized in academic high school and college courses.

Many abuses arose during this period in the development of

private correspondence schools. The chief abuses were high-pressure methods of recruiting students—often with false promises of placement or advancement—shoddy instruction, exorbitant charges, misrepresentation of credits and degrees, and numerous unethical business practices. An especially serious deficiency was the high ratio of drop-outs (in some cases as high as 90 percent) after payment of a large nonrefundable enrollment fee. There is no doubt that the commercial correspondence schools had brought systematic learning opportunities to more adults by World War I than had any previous institutional form of adult education, but they had also introduced practices which cast a shadow across their reputation in many quarters and which set the stage for a wave of reforms in the period ahead.

Agricultural Education

The local and regional agricultural societies, which reached their peak of influence around 1861, began to wane shortly thereafter in favor of farmers' institutes sponsored by state boards of agriculture. The institute movement had begun in Massachusetts as early as 1839, and by 1880 farmers' institutes had been established in twenty-six states, and by 1899 it was estimated that over 300 institutes were being held each year in New York alone and that farmers' institutes were organized in forty-seven states and territories.[3]

Added momentum was given the extension of agricultural education in 1887 with the passing of the Hatch Act, which provided for a system of agricultural experiment stations in connection with the land-grant colleges. In order to disseminate the findings of the research of these stations to the farmers in the field, it became necessary for state funds to be appropriated for extension teaching. True states:

During this period there was a great increase in the avenues of approach by the colleges to the farmers. The wide development of the granges, farmers' clubs, and other organizations gave the agricultural college workers very many opportunities for disseminating information through lectures, public and otherwise. The farmers' institutes grew materially in number and attendance. In a considerable number of States they were directly connected with the land-grant colleges. . . . Legislatures were beginning to make special appropriations for the support of the institutes. County and State fairs became more numerous and the college workers made exhibits or addresses at many of these fairs.[4]

Out of this ferment of rural interaction three large voluntary associations of farmers took shape during this period: the Grange, the Farmers' Union, and the American Farm Bureau Federation. The Grange was founded by Oliver H. Kelley in 1867 as a secret society "to advance education, to elevate and dignify the occupation of the farmer, and to protect its members against the numerous combinations by which their interests are injuriously affected." [5] Officially named "The Order of the Patrons of Husbandry," the Grange had grown to a membership of more than 850,000 by 1875. Its biweekly meetings included an educational program in which the official lecturer of the local Grange conducted a lecture period. Members were frequently asked to come prepared to participate in discussions or present talks on particular topics. In addition to carrying on their own educational programs, local Granges were influential, through representation in a hierarchy of county Granges, state Granges, and the national Grange, in formulating national statements of policy regarding pressing issues of the day.

The Farmers' Union, organized in 1902, also carried on an extensive educational program of its own and worked for the extension of government-sponsored agricultural education. It never attained the size of the Grange, but it exerted great influence, especially in the South and Middle West.

Farm bureaus were organized primarily to assist county agricultural agents during the period from 1911 to 1918. These bureaus were at first connected with chambers of commerce, but they soon became associated with groups of farmers. County bureaus joined together into a state federation in Missouri in 1915, and other states followed suit in quick succession. Representatives from twenty-nine states met in Chicago on November 14, 1919, and launched the national organization, the American Farm Bureau Federation. Started as strictly an educational organization, the Farm Bureau Federation was in post-war years to become one of the most powerful political influences in the country.

Meanwhile extension teaching in the land-grant colleges was greatly expanding. In 1894 the New York legislature appropriated $8,000 to Cornell for "horticultural experiments, instruction, and information" and this was doubled the next year. By 1896 this work had broadened to include: (1) itinerant or local experiments as a means of teaching, (2) readable expository bulletins, (3) itinerant horticultural schools, (4) elementary instruction in nature study in rural schools, and (5) instruction by means of correspondence and reading courses. By 1897 the appropriation was increased to $25,000, an extension division was created at the college, and winter courses for farmers and their wives were offered. The work at Cornell attracted a great deal of attention and by 1900 colleges in several other states had initiated programs more or less modeled after it.

A new development occurred in the first decade of the twentieth century that was to influence the character of agricultural education perhaps more than any other single event. This was the origination of farmers' cooperative demonstration work by Seaman A. Knapp in 1904. Professor Knapp had become convinced that farmers would not change their practices as a result of merely being informed or even as a result of seeing what could be done on farms operated at public expense. He felt that only by having the farmers demonstrate new techniques on their own farms could they be persuaded to change their habits.

The opportunity to test this theory on a large scale came with the boll-weevil invasion of the cotton fields of Texas. A state appropriation of $40,000 was made available to Dr. Knapp and 7,000 farmers agreed to experiment with methods for overcoming the weevil. The demonstration was successful, and in 1906 the General Education Board became interested in cooperative demonstration work as a means of improving economic conditions among farm families in the South and supported its expansion. By 1908 there were 157 agricultural agents in eleven states, of whom 85 were paid by the Board. The demonstration method was becoming perfected, and a corps of extension agents was being trained in its use.

As agricultural education grew in scope and complexity, pressure began to mount for federal leadership of the movement. After several previous attempts at congressional legislation had failed, the Smith-Lever Act was passed and signed by President Wilson in May, 1914, establishing the Cooperative Extension

Service. The act provided that upon the presentation of a satisfactory state plan, each state was to receive $10,000 in federal funds each year, with additional amounts added in proportion to the size of its rural population. The law provided further that each land-grant college would create a separate extension division under a director and that the federal leadership would be provided by a separate office of extension work in the Department of Agriculture.

A memorandum of understanding between the Secretary of Agriculture and the Executive Committee of the Land-grant College Association has been the basis for extension work since the passage of the Smith-Lever Act. This memorandum provided that cooperative extension work in the states should be planned jointly by a State Director selected by the college and satisfactory to the Department, and that all agents should be joint appointees of the colleges and the Department.

As this system developed, the Federal Extension Service built up a highly competent staff of specialists to carry on research, transmit information from the federal office to the states, from the states to the federal office, and from state to state, and to assist with the training of extension workers through field visits, consultation, conferences, and workshops. Each state extension service, in turn, evolved a staff of leaders and specialists to keep county agents up on new developments and help them plan and conduct educational programs. The basic unit of the national system was the county, which typically has been served by a county agricultural agent and often also by a home demonstration agent and a 4-H Club agent. The county staff was responsible to both the land-grant college of its state and the federal Department of Agriculture for the educational program in its county, but it was directly employed by the county government and in the first instance was reponsible to it. The professional staff in the county was aided by volunteer local leaders who helped to develop programs, conduct meetings, hold demonstrations, and get information to their neighbors.

By the end of World War I a strong cooperative extension service had been established in every state and the Cooperative Extension Service had become a recognized addition to our national educational system; in the decades immediately following it was to demonstrate dramatically that adult education could make a difference in the productivity and way of life of a major segment of our population.

Workers' Education

In view of the dominant role that workers' education has played in the adult education movements of the European countries, it becomes especially interesting to trace its difficult struggle for growth in this country.

Workingmen had begun to band together into local unions or "trade societies" in the last years of the eighteenth century, and by the time of Jackson artisans in every craft had organized in the larger towns. An attempt to organize a National Trades Union had been crushed in the disastrous depression of 1837. These early labor unions had been very active in advancing the cause of public schools, public libraries, mechanics' libraries, mechanics' institutes, and lyceums. But their primary concern was the elimination of industrial abuses and the improvement of working conditions, and they left little heritage of workers' education.

For all practical purposes the labor movement as we know it did not become established in this country until after the Civil War. The very year after the surrender at Appomattox, in fact, a loose federation of local unions, city trade assemblies, and national unions that had sprung up during the War was effected under the name National Labor Union. This movement died out in 1872 owing to internal dissensions and was superseded by the Noble Order of the Knights of Labor, which had been founded in Philadelphia in 1869 on the principle that all toilers, skilled and unskilled, organized and unorganized, should band together in one mighty partnership without distinctions of trade or vocation. The Knights rose to a peak membership of perhaps 700,000 in 1886 and then went into a period of decline, largely as a result of the rise of a rival labor body organized according to crafts.

Established in 1881, this body became the American Federation of Labor in 1886. It was organized as a confederation of self-governing trade unions, supervised by a central board of officials. The guiding hand of the AFL was Samuel Gompers, whose own deep distrust of intellectuals probably accounts in large measure for the long reluctance of the AFL to have anything to do with education. Membership in the AFL had grown to over half a million by 1900, and it became the established spokesman for the bulk of skilled labor. But it was not until after World War I that it developed a significant interest in education.

The major activities in the field of workers' education during this period were outside the main stream of labor movement development. In 1895 a residential labor college was established at Trenton, Missouri. Originally called Avalon College, it was renamed Ruskin College in 1900 after the prototype residential labor college in Oxford, England. In 1898 Thomas Davidson, one of the early Fabians, inspired the establishment of the Bread Winners' College in New York City to disseminate knowledge of the classics to workingmen. The Rand School of Social Science, organized in New York City in 1906, was another Socialist venture in workers' education. These were all highly specialized institutions with strong ideological orientation, and they did not produce an extensive development of residential labor colleges such as occurred from similar beginnings in England.[6]

More indicative of future trends were the organization of the Women's Trade Union League in 1903 and the establishment of permanent educational departments by the International Ladies Garment Workers' Union in 1916 and by the Amalgamated Clothing Workers' Union three years later.

Industrial Education

Probably all education within industry began with the institutional form of apprenticeship, and much of the history of industrial education until the twentieth century was concerned with efforts to change and improve this institutional form.[7]

With the rapid expansion of the economy and the increasing complexity of manufacturing processes that occurred following the Civil War, the need for more systematic and widespread facilities for training industrial workers became urgent. A few of the larger industries established their own corporation schools to provide young men with both technical and some general education, often through a combination of classroom and factory work.[8] On the whole, however, these activities were so narrow as to cause one of the first students of industrial education to question their right to be classified as educational:

It is necessary for purposes of record that a report such as this take cognizance of certain educational efforts carried on under the auspices of industrial corporations. Only for the record, however, since most of these efforts are of a technical nature and designed to fit a particular industry. They are part of the industrial process rather than education.[9]

The prevailing attitude among industrialists was that the provision of such basic training was the responsibility of the public schools, with the result that the attention of business leaders was directed primarily to securing legislation to provide federal aid to vocational schools.

The educational activities of trade associations and other industrial voluntary associations are described in a later section.

Colleges and Universities

From the point of view of the advancement of adult education, several important developments occurred in the colleges and universities between the Civil War and World War I. Perhaps the most striking phenomenon was their tremendous growth in numbers. An examination of the founding dates of colleges and universities listed in the Educational Directory of the United States Office of Education indicates that 453 were founded between 1866 and 1920. This expansion almost tripled the number of colleges and universities existing in 1865.

The curriculum of higher education was also undergoing expansion and change. The undergraduate programs put increasing emphasis on English, the physical sciences, the social sciences, and other "modern studies." Graduate instruction was also introduced, with the first Ph.D. degree being offered at Yale in 1861, thus giving this country for the first time universities in the true sense. A part of this development was the emergence of separate professional schools in medicine, theology, engineering, architecture, and other specialties.

An innovation of this period that was essentially a new adult educational form was the summer session. Although Harvard had started a summer school in 1869 for teachers of marine biology, it was the pioneering work of Chautauqua a decade later that exerted the greatest influence on the universities to move in this direction. By 1910 the summer session, usually of six weeks' duration and attended primarily by teachers, had become common in universities around the country.

But the most significant development of this period for the future of adult education was the emergence of the new institutional form, university extension. English universities had begun to engage in extension work early in the nineteenth century, and in 1873 Cambridge University created the first full-fledged extramural organization, a Syndicate for Local Lectures. This development greatly impressed American visitors and they stimulated discussion of the idea in this country. In 1887 Herbert B. Adams, Professor of History at Johns Hopkins University, advocated the development of university extension in the United States at a meeting of the American Library Association. The following year Melvil Dewey, then chief librarian of Columbia University, laid the plan before the Regents of the University of the State of New York, and in 1891 an appropriation of $10,000 was made for the organization of university extension in that state.

Actually, university professors had experimented with extension services in many institutions of higher learning—often in collaboration with libraries—before extension divisions were formally organized. Edward Bemis pioneered library extension work in Buffalo in 1887 by presenting a series of twelve lectures on such contemporary and controversial problems as monopolies, socialism, and labor organization. Richard T. Ely was simultaneously and equally controversially presenting extension lectures on economics and the social gospel from his post as professor of political economy at Johns Hopkins University. In fact, a number of young men who were later to become distingusished leaders of American higher education—E. P. Cheyney, J. C. Freeman, Charles M. Andrews, and Frederick Jackson Turner—took part in the pioneering extension work at Princeton, Harvard, Bryn Mawr, Pennsylvania, and Wisconsin. The fact that they dared not only to lecture off the campus, but to challenge many of the prevailing doctrines of the day, gave extension an early tinge of excitement and at the same time induced opposition to it.

But popular pressure for services from the universities in dealing with real problems could not be resisted. Morton gives several examples of the actual beginnings of some extension programs that illustrate this phenomenon:

A wealthy merchant left a will providing for the establishment of a perpetual fund to be used to bring the resources and leadership of universities into the lives of groups of people in his home community. . . .

A group of elementary and secondary school teachers petitioned a university to arrange study opportunities at times and places which would allow continuing their professional training. . . .

Owners of a machine shop requested a university to give instruction in engineering courses at night so that they and their employees might have the benefit of this training.[10]

In response to these various forces, extension divisions began being formally organized: in 1891 at the University of Wisconsin and the University of Kansas, and in 1892 at The University of Chicago. This last event represents an especially significant milestone in the development of extension in this country. The first president of The University of Chicago, William Rainey Harper, had become imbued with the extension idea in his work at Chautauqua and insisted at the time of the founding of the new university that an extension division be included as one of the five fundamental divisions of the institution.

A national meeting of people engaged in extension work was held in Philadelphia on December 29–31, 1891, under the auspices of the American Society for the Extension of University Teaching, which had been organized the previous year primarily to develop extension centers in the Philadelphia area. The speeches at the conference were given over largly to expressing enthusiasm for the new movement, discussing technical problems, and presenting visions as to its future. Reports from the delegates indicated that by this time some kind of extension work had been started in twenty-eight states and territories. The need for forming a national organization of university extension programs was voiced, and plans for forming a permanent organization were explored, but it was twenty-four years until another national meeting of this kind was held.[11]

The energy and enthusiasm that was generated in the late eighties and early nineties disappeared as suddenly as it appeared.

Woods and Hammarberg give the following reasons for this phenomenon:

Between 1891 and 1906, instead of the anticipated rapid and steady growth, Extension work in the United States declined. Several explanations have been offered. Perhaps the fundamental reason was that the initial enthusiasm was not accompanied by the thorough planning which experience has proved is necessary to initiate and carry on any Extension programme. There was also probably too much dependence on inspirational lectures. The other reasons given might apply today: inflexibility of much university organization; unwillingness to adapt university methods to the needs and training of adults; insistence that programmes adhere to strict university academic standards; lack of financial support; lack of suitable university extension lecturers; inability of university faculty members to carry the extra burden of travel and teaching; greater claims of academic service on college campuses; and development of less expensive forms of popular education.[12]

In 1907 the extension division of the University of Wisconsin was reorganized under the direction of Dean Louis E. Reber and the university extension movement took on a new life. A new spirit was infused into the idea of extension representing a shift away from an emphasis on academic subjects toward an all-embracing concept of the role of the university in serving all of the people of the state in relation to the full scope of life problems—agricultural, political, social, and moral. In his inaugural address in 1904 as president of the University of Wisconsin, Charles R. Van Hise had set the stage for this new era by proposing that the university "should extend its scope until the field was covered from agriculture to the fine arts." [13]

The literature of the formative years of university extension records frequent complaints from extension directors about the opposition being encountered from the university faculties,[14] college presidents,[15] and the tax-conscious public.[16] For example, when a request for a generous appropriation for extension was presented to the Wisconsin legislature in 1909, Rosentreter reports:

This time . . . extension's critics were ready and attempted to sabotage the measure. Some, like Regent G. D. Jones . . . desired to discredit Van Hise for alleged socialistic tendencies. Jones was aided by Regent William D. Hoard, who had sparked the creation of the Farmers'

Institutes, and who was now determined to restore agriculture's waning influence in University affairs. . . . Also among Extension's critics were University professors who deemed its work unworthy, a disgrace to one of the greatest of the state universities. And there were those who had tasted the bitterness of Reber's sarcasm or who otherwise disapproved of him personally.[17]

But the Extension Division also had powerful supporters—including the Milwaukee Merchants and Manufacturers' Association and the Wisconsin State Federation of Labor—and its appropriation was approved.

The founding of the National University Extension Association in 1915, an event which will be treated in detail in Chapter V, stands as a symbol of the establishment of general extension as a permanent element of our national system of higher education. By 1916 this association was able to list twenty-two member institutions with more or less formally organized extension divisions or departments. Morton's survey shows that by 1920 thirty-one universities had "officially established" extension services.[18]

From its earliest stages the program of university extension was highly heterogeneous and unintegrated. The first services to be established were extension classes, correspondence courses, and conference activities. But gradually, in response to particular needs and imaginative leadership, such other "nonacademic" activities were added in various institutions as short-term institutes, traveling libraries, lecture bureaus, publication services, lecture series, and classes at distant points by circuit-riding instructors.

Libraries

By the close of the Civil War the free public library movement had gained a firm foothold, especially in the cities of the North and West. But subscription libraries still outnumbered public libraries two to one. The early traditions of dependence on philanthropic support and local initiative made for slow progress in the development of state support and dictated that the growth of public libraries would be limited largely to the cities. With the expansion of the educational system, and therefore of the reading public and of political stakes in education, momentum began gaining.

In 1875 the state board of education in Rhode Island started to grant sums up to five hundred dollars to existing libraries. Commissions were established in Massachusetts in 1890 and in New Hampshire in 1891 that could make grants of one hundred dollars worth of books to any town library. Within the next decade many other states followed these examples, and under this stimulus many subscription libraries were induced to become public libraries. The state library commissions also attempted to solve the problem of making books available to rural populations by encouraging the establishment of county libraries and making union catalogues and the resources of the state libraries available to them.

The public library movement was thus expanding under its own power when, in the early 1880's it received a stimulant that made previous progress seem static. This stimulant was the contribution of over $41,000,000 to the building of community libraries between 1881 and 1917 by Andrew Carnegie. Having educated himself largely through books, and believing that "the true university of these days is a collection of books," Carnegie offered to finance the building of libraries in those communities that would guarantee 10 percent of the building cost for annual upkeep. By 1917 he had financed the building of 1,679 libraries. In that year the building program was terminated as the result of a survey by Alvin Johnson, a prominent social scientist, which revealed that almost two thirds of the libraries had been built in small towns that were interested more in getting something for nothing than in providing working libraries. Johnson found that the emphasis on buildings as depositories for collections of books had produced architectural monstrosities (often dubbed "Carnegie Renaissance" or "Carnegie Classic"), but, more importantly, had diverted energy and funds from the true adult educational function of the libraries. He concluded that "coverage, an extensive conception, rather than education, an intensive one, came to be an accepted criterion of successful library activity." [19]

It was during this era that a library profession came into being. Except in the larger cities, libraries were largely staffed by well-read ladies whose children had grown and who could spare a few hours a day to keep the books in order. Many of them were volunteers. As libraries increased in numbers and size and as more and more librarians came to look upon their jobs as full-time and permanent, interest started to be expressed in the formation of a professional association. A conference of some eighty persons interested in libraries was held in 1853 at which this idea was explored, and a committee was appointed to draw up plans. But the Civil War intervened, and it was not until 1876 that another conference was held, in Philadelphia, as a result of which the American Library Association was formed.

Starting in 1890 state and regional associations were also organized, and they came to play a significant part in promoting library extension in the states and in developing professional attitudes and standards locally. The profession turned its attention early to systematizing library procedures. It adopted a standard decimal system of book classification that had been developed by Melvil Dewey, librarian of Columbia University; it devised more efficient schemes for cataloguing, storing, and charging out books; and it made studies of other problems of library operation. As specialized knowledge and skills grew, the need for specialized training became increasingly recognized. Schools for library training were organized, starting with the one founded at Columbia by Dewey.

Thus, with a growing professional organization in existence and opportunities for professional training beginning to be offered by the universities, the groundwork was laid for the emergence of the modern library movement.

Public Schools

In the development of a national system of elementary and secondary education, the period between the Civil War and World War I was one of expansion and consolidation. Compulsory attendance through the elementary grades, which had been established by two states (Massachusetts and New York) prior to the Civil War, had been extended to all states by 1918. The public high school movement advanced more slowly. The right of states and local boards to use tax funds to support high schools had been questioned in the courts, but in a series of decisions—the most famous of which was the Kalamazoo case in 1874—the courts laid down a firm legal foundation for the public support of secondary schools. This action, coupled with state legislation providing state aid to local boards in establishing high schools, resulted in a spiraling growth until by the end of World War I almost 2,000,000 youths were enrolled in public high schools.

As the public education system grew in size and complexity, there occurred a prodigious growth in the techniques and agencies of administration, and a movement toward more effective central control. In the large city school systems boards of education began employing skilled administrators as general superintendents to manage the large staffs and appropriations now required to operate the "big business" of education. In rural areas there began to be a movement to consolidate small school districts into larger combinations so as to provide better facilities, equipment, management, and instruction.

The scope and function of state educational administration also increased. By 1880 there was a chief educational officer in every one of the thirty-eight states then in the union, and twenty-four had state boards of education. The responsibilities of the state offices included collecting and disseminating information, advising local officials, apportioning school revenues, certifying teachers, conducting teacher-training programs, carrying on research studies, and making evaluations of local schools.

Not producing the administrative centralization of our educational system—but nevertheless a strong factor in its voluntary integration—was the creation in 1867 of a federal Department of Education for the purpose of collecting such statistics and facts as shall show the condition and progress of education in the several States and Territories, and of diffusing such information respecting the organization and management of schools and school systems, and methods of teaching as shall aid the people of the United States in the establishment and maintenance of efficient school systems, and otherwise promote the cause of education throughout the country. In 1869 this department became the Bureau of Education within the Department of Interior, but its functions remained largely unchanged.

The evening schools during this period began to attract older youths and adults in greater numbers and increasingly took on the character of adult educational institutions. Although this new use of the schools did not gain immediate acceptance, most superintendents who had tried them related satisfactory experiences, and resolutions supporting the idea of evening schools were passed by conventions of the National Education Association starting as early as 1860. By the turn of the century the evening school had become an established fixture in the American educational scene.

Several trends and developments in evening schools during this period are worthy of note:

Evening schools experienced rising enrollment. While national figures on enrollment did not become available until much later, the general trend toward increasing use of the evening schools can be demonstrated by enrollment figures from a sample of cities. In Cleveland, for example, enrollment increased from 135 in 1851 to 1,982 in 1889, 5,031 in 1909, and 11,383 in 1915.[20] In Chicago, enrollment grew from 208 in 1857 to 1,591 in 1865, 6,965 in 1883, 14,530 in 1893, and 27,987 in 1913.[21] Los Angeles evening schools opened in 1887 with an enrollment of 30 students and by 1901 had grown to only 235; but by 1911 enrollment had increased to 3,414, by 1916 to 22,080, and by 1920 to 32,874.[22] This pattern of gradual growth until the turn of the century and then a rapidly rising curve was repeated in most large cities of the country.

The age level of students in evening schools rose. This trend is also established from reports from a sample of cities rather than from national statistics. In St. Louis, for example:

For 21 years previous to 1904–05 the average age of the pupils was 16 years. During the next four years the average age was 17 years. From 1908–09 to 1910–11, the average age was 18 years. The beginning of this increase in age was coincident with the beginning of the enforcement of our compulsory attendance law, and it is possibly thus explained. During the school year 1919–20 there were only 3,561 students below the age of 18 and 8,897 above that age.[23]

The curriculum of the evening schools began to broaden. The curriculum of the early evening schools was limited almost entirely to the basic subjects of the primary grades. There is little evidence that the curriculum broadened significantly until

close to the turn of the century, at which time four directions of
change can be identified: (1) expansion of "Americanization"
programs for immigrants, (2) expansion of vocational courses,
especially in trade and commercial subjects, (3) extension into
secondary and college level subjects with the opening of evening
high schools, and (4) experimental sorties into informal adult
education.

References to special courses for immigrants began appearing
in annual reports in the 1890's. The Cleveland Report of 1898–
1899, for example, refers to:

. . . a considerable number of earnest young men in the city who
honestly wish to supplement their education by further study of the
common branches. This feeling is very marked in connection with a
large and rapidly increasing number of foreigners, largely Italian, German, or Bohemian, who have recently come to this country.[24]

The development of distinctive and massive programs of
Americanization for the foreign-born did not occur, however, until shortly before the United States' entrance into World War I.
The problem of assimilating immigrants was not perceived as
being critical so long as their number was small and they came
overwhelmingly from the countries of northern and western
Europe, which had educational systems and cultural heritages
similar to those of early America. Severe pressure to educate the
foreigners did not appear, therefore, until the volume increased
to an average of almost a million a year, between 1903 and 1914,
and the sources of immigration shifted to eastern and southern
Europe. With this rising influx of less educated and less familiar
nationalities, the public began to become aroused about the
great numbers of unassimilated immigrants.

The pressure was further increased with the passage of an act
by Congress in 1917 adding the requirement of literacy for naturalization. In 1918 Congress authorized the Federal Immigration
and Naturalization Service to cooperate with the public schools
both by sending them identifying information about applicants
for naturalization, and by preparing citizenship textbooks and
supplying these without cost to the schools.

By the end of World War I the education of the foreign-born
had become the dominant activity of the public evening schools.

And whereas in the earlier stages of assimilation the immigrants had simply been amalgamated into the basic courses along with the native students, by the end of this period "Americanization programs became so large that they often overshadowed other adult-education activities. In the minds of many adult education became synonymous with Americanization, and even today some people think of adult education primarily as the education of immigrants." [25] But Clark points out that these programs had become a "special badge of merit" by 1920 which helped bring public acceptance and support to the idea of evening schools for adults.[26]

With the opening of the high schools to evening students the scope and level of instruction available to adults gradually expanded. The process of broadening the curriculum for adult students is well illustrated by the St. Louis experience. The Annual Report for 1895–1896 lists two "higher" courses offered: (1) a commercial course, including higher arithmetic, bookkeeping, English, and penmanship; and (2) a mechanical course, including higher arithmetic, geometry, natural philosophy, and drawing. In 1903 the courses offered were: industrial and mechanical drawing, English for the foreign-born, practical bookkeeping, algebra, geometry, ancient and modern languages, history, stenography, English language and literature, physics, and chemistry.

The evening schools began receiving local and state legislative recognition and support. The evening schools were financed in their early stages in a most tentative and informal manner. In times of financial difficulty the needs of the evening schools were considered subordinate to those of the day schools, and they were the first to be considered for reductions. The "Historical Review" of the Chicago Public Evening Schools, for example, observes that up to 1905–1906 the sessions varied in length from ten to sixteen weeks, and whenever there was a shortage of funds or if attendance dropped the schools were abruptly closed, sometimes on one day's notice. On several occasions they remained closed for the entire year due to the shortage of funds.[27] In spite of their secondary position, the evening schools had nevertheless become widely established as worthy objects of local tax support, at least in principle, by the end of World War I.

State support for evening schools came in several stages. The first was permissive legislation, granting local school districts authority to operate evening schools, and later, adult classes in given subject areas. The Ohio legislature, passed a law in 1840 directing that if twenty-five persons petitioned for an evening course the local board of education should furnish a room and teacher.[28] A Pennsylvania act in 1842 authorized Philadelphia to open schools at night for the instruction of male adults as the comptrollers of public schools may deem necessary.[29] An act passed in 1847 authorized towns in Massachusetts to support schools for the instruction of adults in reading, writing, English grammar, arithmetic, and geography.[30] It should be pointed out that although permissive state legislation began appearing before the Civil War, in many states evening schools were started by local school authorities without express authorization to do so from state legislatures. In fact, permissive legislation has continued to be enacted, in many cases *ex post facto,* until the present time.

A second stage in the development of state support for evening schools was the passage of various mandatory requirements. In some cases these had to do with providing certain required subjects, such as Americanization, or vocational training. Another area of mandatory legislation had to do with teacher certification.

A third, and perhaps more critical stage, was the passage of legislation providing for financial assistance. Although few states started providing direct financial aid for the evening schools until after 1920, several important precedents were set before and after the Civil War. The New York legislature, for example, authorized an appropriation of $6,000 a year for evening schools in 1847 and raised this amount to $15,000 in 1848. The Rhode Island Assembly appropriated $5,000 for public evening schools in 1873. Special provision was made toward the close of this period for co-operative federal-state subsidy of vocational education.

A fourth stage in the development of state support was the provision of state-wide services to local school systems through the state departments of education. This development was just starting to occur at the close of this period. In 1917 a division of evening and continuation schools was created in the State Department of Education in Connecticut, with a full-time supervisor, and in 1919 a Division of Americanization was created; these later were combined into a single department. A supervisor of immigrant education was appointed in the State Department of Education in New York in 1918, and a similar position was created in Delaware in 1919. California established a division of adult education in its State Department of Education in 1920.

The evening schools began to develop differentiated administrative and teaching operations. The administrative status of the early evening schools was usually most informal and often quite confused. In the early stages responsibility for organizing and operating evening courses was often assigned to principals or teachers as extra duty, without extra compensation. This situation was summed up by one of Cleveland's later supervisors as follows:

It was thought, in the early days of the history of the Educational Extension Division, that these schools were sufficiently organized and developed to run of their own accord. They were left to shift for themselves quite at the displeasure and silent protest of the principals, who were at times at a loss to know where and when to deposit money collected for fees, to submit reports, or to look for guidance.[31]

The need for separate planning, coordination, and supervision of the evening programs gradually became recognized. Typically, the process followed was first the assignment of responsibility for the evening schools to one of the assistant superintendents as a peripheral duty. As the load of administrative responsibilities became too heavy for peripheral handling, the evening schools were placed in separate divisions, with distinct staff services. In Chicago, for example:

So numerous and so varied had grown the problems governing the control of the evening schools that on September 22, 1886, Albert R. Sabin was appointed as Supervisor of Evening Instruction for the purpose of bringing uniformity into the system and for acquiring a better knowledge of the wants and necessities of the evening schools.[32]

In Cleveland a supervisor of evening schools was appointed in 1887. His work was "to visit the respective teachers as often as possible, note irregularities, suggest improvements, hold meetings of teachers, and in every way possible aid the superintendent in bringing the schools to a higher level."[33] In 1917 the Cleveland Board of Education created a Division of Educational Extension under an assistant superintendent of schools, with central responsibility for evening programs in both the elementary and high schools.[34] Other cities followed these examples, and with the expansion of the Americanization and vocational programs during the war years separate administrative units for adult education were organized in most of the larger cities of the country.

Vocational education became an established element in the curriculum. Very little attention had been given to educating youth for vocational life until the beginning of this century, in spite of the great growth of industrialization and occupational specialization that had occurred in preceding decades. The first trade school was founded privately in New York in 1881; and by 1900 some half-dozen had been established in other parts of the country. In 1906 Massachusetts created a State Commission on Industrial Education and later provided for the creation of industrial schools; and in 1907 Wisconsin enacted the first trade school law, with New York following in 1909.

With increasing American competition for world trade, however, leaders of commerce, agriculture, and industry began to become concerned lest America's economic position would be at a disadvantage in relation to countries with more advanced systems of vocational education. Through the National Society for the Promotion of Industrial Education, organized in 1906, they began putting pressure on Congress to enact federal legislation supporting vocational education. After repeated failure to secure the passage of the legislation, the proponents of vocational education persuaded Congress to establish a presidential commission, the National Commission on Vocational Education, in 1913, to investigate the desirability of federal aid for vocational education. The Commission made its report in 1914 and strongly urged the adoption of a plan for gradually increasing national aid to the states to assist them in developing a nation-wide system of vocational education.

In 1917 Congress passed the Smith-Hughes Vocational Education Act making available federal funds, to be matched by state funds, to promote the teaching of courses in agriculture, home economics, trades, industries, and commerce in public schools. The Act also created the Federal Board for Vocational Education to supervise this program. As a result of this federal support an expanding curriculum of vocational subjects began being offered in American high schools, and in a number of larger cities separate vocational high schools were established. While this program of vocational education was focused on preparing youth to enter a trade or industrial pursuit, it was open to experienced workers who wished to upgrade their skills and was widely participated in by them.

Junior colleges made an appearance during this period, providing another institutional base for adult education. As early as 1852 President Henry Tappan of the University of Michigan had recommended that the part of the work of the college which was secondary in character should be transferred to the high school.[35] Toward the end of the century President Harper reorganized the college of The University of Chicago into two units, with the freshman and sophomore years becoming a junior college. Several privately owned junior colleges were established before 1900, but the first public junior college that is still in existence was organized in Joliet, Illinois, in 1902. Legislative authorization for the organization of public junior colleges was passed in California in 1907, and that state has led in the expansion of this institutional form ever since. By 1915 there were 74 junior colleges, of which 55 were private and 19 were public.[36] Junior colleges took several forms. Some became units of four-year colleges; others, extensions of high schools; and still others, independent institutions. While all of them were established strictly for the education of youth, they provided a trunk onto which adult educational branches could be grafted.

Voluntary Associations and Agencies

As was seen in the last chapter, a lush growth of voluntary organizations had sprung up in local communities throughout the country before the Civil War. The distinctive development in this aspect of national life following the Civil War was the emergence of national voluntary organizations with local and state chapters.

WOMEN'S ORGANIZATIONS. While the middle of the nineteenth century marked the emancipation of the Negro slaves, it also marked a turning point in the emancipation of women. One of the most pervasive expressions of this phenomenon was the women's club movement, launched with the founding of Sorosis in New York in 1868 by Jane Cunningham Croly "to bring together women engaged in literary, artistic, scientific, and philanthropic pursuits, with the view of rendering them helpful to one another, and useful to society." [37] Within the next three decades women's clubs sprang up in profusion all over the country, often unaware of the existence of similar clubs elsewhere. They took on such names as the New England Club (Boston), the Fortnightly Club (Chicago), the Ebell Society (Oakland), and a number that went by the plain name of "Woman's Club." Much of this quick spread was the result of the work of the Association for the Advancement of Women, founded in 1873 at the instigation of the Sorosis, which held annual Women's Congresses for the twenty-five years of its existence. The need for a representative organization that would weld the clubs together became increasingly apparent, and in 1890 the General Federation of Women's Clubs was founded.

During this period of development the clubs were primarily concerned with cultural self-improvement. Their programs consisted of periodic meetings in which speakers would be heard or readings would be presented on history, philosophy, art, science, and other serious subjects, followed by a question-and-answer period. Some clubs sponsored, in addition, reading circles that met in homes and churches for informed conversation. But shortly after the founding of the General Federation the emphasis shifted sharply from "education for self" to "education for service." Clubs became increasingly concerned with matters connected with education, reformatory schools, sanitation, female labor, dishonesty in public life, township affairs, libraries, and other aspects of public welfare.

The drive for the advancement of the status of women got another powerful organizational voice with the founding in 1882 of the Association of Collegiate Alumnae, which later (1921) changed its name to the American Association of University Women. Its purpose was to engage in practical educational work, and its membership was restricted to women who had received degrees from approved colleges, universities, or scientific schools. The program of the association included the raising of standards of higher education for women; the organization of study groups, for which a national staff provided study guides; and the sponsorship of such community activities as classes for illiterates, concerts, recreational services, war services, and many others.

The women's rights movement was launched in this country in 1848 at a convention in Seneca Falls, New York, following which a number of local and state organizations of suffragists were formed. Not until 1889, however, did they join forces in a national organization, the National American Woman Suffrage Association. After winning the vote in state after state, the suffragists finally suceeded, with President Wilson's support, in inducing the Senate to approve the Susan. B. Anthony Amendment granting woman suffrage on a national scale. Women voted in their first national election in 1920. While the suffrage organizations had been more intent on action than on education, they bequeathed a legacy of practical idealism and valuable experience in organizational management to a successor organization, the League of Women Voters, which was to make an outstanding record in adult education in the period ahead.

Service to the community was a purpose around which a number of additional women's groups were organized, including the Junior Leagues (the first of which was founded in 1901), Altrusa (1917), Quota (1918), and within the next few years, Zonta and the Soroptimists. Nationality, religious, and racial interests formed the basis of other women's organizations, such as the National Council of Jewish Women, the Nation Council of Negro Women, and numerous Swedish, German, Polish, and other nationality groupings. Cultural pursuits bound other women together in such groupings as the Daughters of the American Revolution, music societies, art societies, and literary societies.

YOUTH ORGANIZATIONS. Concern for the continuing education of young men had been a strong motivating force for adult education since its earliest days. The mechanics and mercantile libraries and institutes, the lyceum movement, the early evening schools, and the various forms of vocational training were designed especially to serve young men. Another institution that came into being in response to this force, and that was to exert a considerable influence on the movement, was the Young Men's Christian Association. First introduced into this country from England in Boston in 1851, YMCA's quickly spread to the major cities of the country.

Concentrating originally on prayer meetings and Bible classes, the YMCA gradually extended its purpose to the general intellectual improvement of young men and introduced classes in commercial subjects, languages, public affairs, and literature, as well as public lectures on a variety of subjects. In the period following the Civil War the adult educational work of the YMCA became more practical and expanded rapidly, until by 1895 over 22,000 young men were enrolled in YMCA evening classes in more than 300 cities of the continent.[38]

Until 1892 the educational work of the YMCA's was entirely the product of local initiative and planning, but in that year an education department was formed in the International Committee, and a national secretary was appointed to promote this type of work. The national education department proceeded to develop course outlines and examinations for use in local YMCA's, and to issue certificates to students completing national course requirements. Under this strong direction, the formal adult educational program expanded, especially in vocational and technical subjects, until a peak enrollment of 85,000 students in 491 YMCA's was reached in 1914. In many cities these programs became formalized into separate administrative units— schools, colleges, and technical institutes of various kinds.

Of perhaps more lasting influence in determining the YMCA's role in adult education were the beginnings made during this period in developing group-work methods of informal adult education through the formation of educational clubs, in starting programs of leadership training for volunteer workers, and in initiating the concept of community study as a basis of program planning.

These developments in the YMCA illustrate the emerging role of youth agencies in the field of adult education. Similar developments were taking place in the Young Women's Christian Association as well as in the Young Men's and Young Women's Hebrew Associations.

Organizations for still younger age-groups were also organized, starting with 4-H Clubs shortly after the turn of the century, followed by the Boys Clubs in 1906, the Boy Scouts of America in 1910, and the Girl Scouts and Campfire Girls in 1912. The adult educational role of these youth agencies was limited almost entirely to the training of the thousands of adults recruited to serve as volunteer leaders of groups of boys and girls. A good deal of this training was on the job, as a part of the process of supervision by experienced volunteers or professional workers. But before the close of the period attempts were being made to develop more systematic training through courses, institutes, and manuals.

HEALTH, WELFARE, AND RECREATIONAL AGENCIES. The rapid increase in poverty, disease, crime, and other forms of human suffering that resulted from the industrial revolution and accompanying urbanization soon gave rise to a wave of humanitarianism and reform. Out of this movement was born a wide variety of public and voluntary agencies dedicated to improving the general welfare. And from the beginning most of these agencies discovered that in order to achieve their goals they must engage in the education of adults.

An illustration of the typical dynamics at work in these times is given in the following account of the establishment of the first public health service in Manhattan:

In America young Stephen Smith was assigned in 1863 to typhus duty on Blackwell's Island. He traced one hundred cases to a single house in the city where Irish immigrants got free quarters and were living in appalling filth. He called upon the city authorities to close the "fever nest," but they refused. Smith brought his indignation and knowledge to the Citizen's Association, then fighting Tweed and civic corruption in New York. Peter Cooper, its president, welcomed Smith and the idea of a crusade for better health. The doctor became secretary to the Association's Council of Hygiene and helped initiate a survey of living conditions in New York. Dorman B. Eaton, public-spirited lawyer who had observed health services at work in Europe, framed the first American health law with "teeth" in it and under this the Metropolitan Board of Health began to function in 1866.[39]

The success of this experience stimulated similar crusades in other localities and in 1872 these activities were amalgamated into a country-wide cooperative effort with the founding of the

American Public Health Association. Through research, legislative action, prefessional development, publications, and a variety of programs of health education, the association spearheaded a national movement for the improvement of public health that had tremendous influence on the general health standards of the country.

This attack on the general problem of health was followed by the formation of a series of giant organizations to work on more specific health problems: the American Red Cross in 1881, the National Tuberculosis Association in 1904, and the Social Hygiene Association, the National Safety Council, and the American Cancer Society in 1913. All of these agencies perceived the education of adults to be a central mission and employed similar means toward this end: organization of local societies, the publication of pamphlets and other literature, reportage of research, production of exhibits, charts, posters, and plays, and provision of speakers to other organizations.

A parallel mushrooming of organizations to tackle social problems took place. Perhaps the first institutional form for this purpose was the relief society or charity organization formed strictly to give relief to the poor. Starting in Buffalo in 1877, these gradually became transformed into family service agencies which placed emphasis on prevention and rehabilitation, working directly with individual families through "friendly visitors" and, later, professionally trained case workers. By 1911 these local agencies had grown to a sufficient number to warrant their being federated through a national organization, the Family Service Association of America. While these agencies carried on their educational work primarily through individual counseling, many of them conducted educational programs for groups and engaged in general community education.

Another institution that spread throughout the country during this period was the settlement or neighborhood center. Originated in London with the founding of Toynbee Hall in 1884, the settlement movement was transplanted to this country with the establishment of the Neighborhood Guild (now University Settlement) in New York City by Stanton Coit in 1886. The most famous of these institutions, however, is Hull House, founded in Chicago by Jane Addams and Ellen Gates Starr in 1889. In 1911 a

National Federation of Settlements was organized. The aim of the settlements was to work with their neighbors in a depressed area and help them to learn how to live together and to secure good living conditions. Their programs from the beginning included social action, but their main work was educational, through individual counseling, clubs, teams, classes, councils, and committees.

Another cluster of agencies concerned with social problems was organized under the auspices of religious organizations. The charity work traditionally carried on by the Jewish synagogues began to be coordinated into the United Hebrew Charities in the late 1870's. Orphanages, Jewish Community Centers, vocational adjustment bureaus, and other agencies were established to serve the unique needs of the Jewish communities. In 1917 a number of these became federated nationally with the founding of the National Jewish Welfare Board. A similar development took place in regard to Catholic agencies, with national leadership provided by the National Conference of Catholic Charities founded in 1910 and the National Catholic Welfare Conference founded in 1919.

Another facet of this general trend toward social improvement was the recreation movement. The first municipally sponsored playground was opened in Boston in 1886, and by 1900 ten cities had followed Boston's example. The greatest growth, however, occurred following the organization in 1906 of the Playground and Recreation Association of America (later renamed the National Recreation Association). Under its leadership there ensued a great expansion of community recreation efforts under the sponsorship of public, tax-supported managing authorities, such as recreation commissions and boards, park departments, school boards, and welfare divisions. Within the next few decades there appeared in communities throughout the country an abundance of playgrounds, playfields, parks, forests, golf courses, swimming pools and beaches, community centers, field houses, clubs, and camps. Although the programs conducted in these facilities emphasized leisure-time activity engaged in for its own sake, many of them included organized instruction in sports, music, drama, crafts, the dance, and other cultural and social activities.

ECONOMIC ORGANIZATIONS. While the earliest forms of voluntary organizations to further economic interests—the labor unions and agricultural societies—continued to grow during this period, the increased complexity of economic activity that followed the industrial revolution gave rise to a number of other economic organizations.

One of the most pervasive forms was the trade association, the first industry-wide example of which was the American Iron and Steel Association (later renamed the American Iron and Steel Institute), founded in 1855. By the end of World War I hundreds of such associations had been organized. Initially the primary function of these organizations was to keep their memberships informed of state and federal legislation and to combat impending laws when they were deemed to be unfavorable to their industries. But gradually their programs broadened to include research and education. Their educational programs were directed both to the public—with interpretation of their industries through pamphlets, textbooks, and the mass media—and to the employees of their member firms, for whom they conducted courses, institutes, and conferences and published instructional materials.

Two powerful national organizations more broadly representative of business and industry came into being during this period: the National Association of Manufacturers, in 1895, and the Chamber of Commerce of the United States, in 1912. Both of these organizations, along with their local and state affiliates, developed educational programs similar in format to those of the trade associations but much broader in scope and substance.

Among various attempts to organize on the basis of consumer interests, including consumers' leagues, buyers' clubs, and taxpayers' associations, the most successful was the consumers' cooperatives. Building on the Rochdale principles of the strong movement established in England in the middle of the century, a number of consumers' cooperatives were established in this country, especially among rural and immigrant populations. In 1915 they became federated into the Cooperative League of the U.S.A. An essential element of the cooperative idea was the carrying on of a continuous educational program on the facts and principles of cooperation and "cooperative democracy" through membership meetings, study circles, pamphlets, films, and magazines.

FRATERNAL ORGANIZATIONS AND SERVICE CLUBS. Self-improvement clubs, for many years exclusively for men, have a tradition that goes far back into American history. Franklin's Junto is an early prototype; the lodges of the Masons appeared in America about 1730; and the Sons of Liberty, organized in the early 1760's, had branches throughout the colonies and exerted a powerful influence on public opinion prior to the American Revolution. The nineteenth century witnessed the organization of an amazing variety of local men's groups—political clubs, debating clubs, and informal discussion clubs on the more serious side; and sports clubs, marching societies, and card clubs in a lighter vein. The first category tended to have certain common characteristics: they drew their membership almost exclusively from the middle class and typically had the dual purpose of self-improvement for their members and service to their communities. Most of them met at lunch or dinner, and almost all of them had some focal interest—literature, music, art, public affairs, public speaking, economics, and the like.

Perhaps the most striking development of this period was the creation of various national networks of clubs of several types. One type was the secret fraternal order, patterned after the early nineteenth century prototypes, the Masons and Odd Fellows. Best known examples of this type were the Knights of Pythias (1864), the Benevolent and Protective Order of Elks (1868), the Knights of Columbus (1882), and the Loyal Order of Moose (1888). Another type was the businessmen's service club, of which Rotary (1905), Exchange (1911), Optimists (1912), Kiwanis (1915), Lions (1917), and Civitan (1920) were preeminent. A third type was the multiplicity of laymen's organizations, ladies' aid societies, sisterhoods, and service societies of Catholic, Jewish, and Protestant religious institutions. A fourth type was the veterterans' organizations, of which the Grand Army of the Republic (1866), the United Confederate Veterans (1889), the Veterans of Foreign Wars (1899), the United Spanish War Veterans (1904), and American Legion (1919) were examples.

Although most of these fraternal orders were men's organizations, many of them created auxiliaries for their womenfolk. At the same time that the programs of the majority of them were strongly flavored with fellowship, self-protection (through insurance, legislation, and so on), recreation, ritual, and service, all of them had strong undertones of self-improvement through educational activities.

Hill's assessment of the educational value of the work of men's organizations can probably be applied to fraternal organizations in general:

Certainly we must recognize that it is most uneven in character. In general it lacks coherence and careful organization, although we have seen that in a number of cases both exist to a considerable degree. A large amount of men's club activity is thin, and some of it dull and monotonous. Nevertheless, it has a definite importance as an existing phase of education, and great potentialities for development.

No one who studies the clubs in action can help but feel that they reach an important group in our population, bringing something of value, even where this is vague and general, to hundreds of thousands who otherwise might have much less. The clubs give mental, and, to an extent, aesthetic and skill stimuli to a million men.[40]

PARENT EDUCATION ORGANIZATIONS.   The education of parents in child development and family living had been a concern of many of the women's clubs, Chatauqua reading circles, mothers' clubs, and other self-improvement groups that emerged early in this period. In 1888 the Society for the Study of Child Nature (which later became the Child Study Association of America) was organized to assist these groups with scientific information and study materials, but it did not seek to organize them into a movement. This task was left to the organizing zeal of Alice Birney and Phoebe Hirst, co-founders of the National Congress of Mothers (later to become the National Congress of Parents and Teachers) in 1897. The objects of the National Congress were stated in its bylaws as being:

To promote the welfare of children and youth in home, school, church, and community.

To raise the standard of home life.

To secure adequate laws for the care and protection of children and youth.

To bring into closer relation the home and the school, that parents and teachers may cooperate intelligently in child training.

To develop between educators and the general public such unified efforts as will secure for every child the highest advantages in physical, mental, social, and spiritual education.

The means employed for achieving these objectives included membership meetings with speakers, demonstrations, and discussions; school visitations, study groups, literature, and service projects of various sorts. Although the original organization was largely composed of women and was looked upon with some suspicion by school people, it gradually gained the participation of fathers and the support of educators. Its strength lay in the closeness of its identification with neighborhood schools and in the caliber of its volunteer leadership at city, county, district, state, and national levels.

A number of parent associations were organized independently of the National Congress, particularly in private schools and in New York City. And, of course, parent education was a frequent activity in a number of other voluntary organizations, such as women's clubs, which were established for more general purposes.

PUBLIC AFFAIRS EDUCATION AGENCIES. Although many voluntary organizations included concern for the education of adults in public affairs among other cares, a few came into being exclusively for this purpose. The American Academy of Political and Social Science (1889) and the Carnegie Endowment for International Peace (1910) are examples of agencies established to provide research and informational services to other organizations. Other organizations, such as the National Civil Service League (1881) and the National Municipal League (1894), were created to promote efficiency and democratic procedures in government through research, publications, conferences, and other educational means. America's emergence as a world power toward the end of this period induced the organization of a number of groups concerned specifically with international relations. The largest and strongest of these was the Foreign Policy Association, established in 1918, which carried on an extensive program of forums, study groups, and publications through local world affairs councils and other study groups.

Another group of agencies came into being at this time with a primary concern for intercultural education and the protection of civil rights. Some of them carried on their work with particular minority groups. Examples of this group were the National Association for the Advancement of Colored People (1909) and the Urban League (1910), which worked especially on behalf of Negroes; and the American Jewish Committee (1906) and the Anti-Defamation League (1913), which worked especially on behalf of the Jewish community. Other organizations, such as the American Civil Liberties Union (1920), had the general population as their target and concern. All of these organizations engaged in action projects, but also carried on education through meetings, publications, study groups, speakers' bureaus, and other means.

PROFESSIONAL SOCIETIES. One of the striking characteristics of this era was the widespread concern for the differentiation of professional roles and the raising of professional standards. A sampling of professional societies that came into being will illustrate this trend:

American Medical Association, 1847
National Education Association, 1857
American Institute of Architects, 1857
American Dental Association, 1859
American Public Health Association, 1872
National Conference of Social Work, 1873
American Library Association, 1876
American Bar Association, 1878
American Psychological Association, 1892
American Nurses Association, 1896
American Home Economics Association, 1908
Speech Association of America, 1915

The adult educational role of these professional societies was twofold: (1) providing in-service educational opportunities to their members through publications, conferences, short courses, and other means, and (2) providing educational stimuli and resources to other groups and the general public regarding their special field of interest through publications, speakers, the mass media, and other means.

MISCELLANEOUS ORGANIZATIONS. The organizations categorized above account for probably only a fraction of the total voluntary associations in this country with adult educational programs of some sort that came into being during this era. Looking at the national scene as a whole, they were without doubt the major organizations in this field. But in every local community there emerged, in addition, myriad other groups with educational purposes. Some of them were organized around particular interests: garden clubs, stamp clubs, drama groups, music groups, and literary circles. Others were organized according to nationality groupings: German, Swedish, Polish, etc., clubs and societies. Others had as their base some common need: organizations for the handicapped, the aged, the widowed, and the alcoholic. Perhaps the most numerous, but the most difficult to locate, were the completely autonomous friendship or social groups.

Religious Institutions

As has been previously indicated, the adult educational role of the churches was traditionally limited largely to indoctrination in the precepts and tenets of particular faiths. And this continued to be the chief characteristic of religious adult education during this period.

For example, in the Catholic Church the chief instrument for the education of adults continued to be the pulpit and the liturgy. But MacLellan points out that "from 1885 to 1900 the development of the Reading Circles was rapid and widespread," and in 1889 became formally organized with the founding of the Reading Circle Union, the object of which was to:

. . . encourage the diffusion of sound literature and to instill a love of good reading into the hearts and minds of the Catholic masses; to give those who pursue their studies after leaving school an available opportunity to follow prescribed courses of the most approved reading; to enable others who have made considerable progress in education to review their past studies, and, particularly, to encourage individual home study in systematic Catholic lines . . .[41]

And in 1892 the Catholic Summer School of America was established:

. . . to enable those whose occupation did not allow them to attend the University courses regularly to derive as much benefit from the Summer School lecture as from attendance at a regular university. It aimed to arouse in the minds of its students a thinking spirit and an abiding interest in profound questions, mundane and metaphysical, which dealt with man's past, present, and future.[42]

Although the adult educational work of synagogues and temples remained fairly traditional during this period, they did step out into positions in many communities in pioneering the development of highly intellectual public forums. The Sinai Temple in Chicago, for example, launched its first series of lectures in the fall of 1914 and rapidly gained a national reputation as a champion of free speech in the Chicago area.

In the Protestant churches there was only slightly greater creativity during this period. Interdenominational national conventions of Sunday school leaders had been meeting intermittently since 1832, and at the Fifth National Convention in 1872 a plan for International Uniform Lessons was adopted which had far-reaching consequences in both the expansion and the fixation of religious education in this country.

Additional consolidation of the Sunday school movement was promoted with the establishment of various national and international organizations. William Rainey Harper founded the American Institute of Sacred Literature in 1889 in an effort to communicate critical and historical scholarship to adults in the form of popular Bible study, summer schools, extension courses, and weekly institutes. The League for Social Service was organized in 1898 to provide a clearinghouse for social information as well as to conduct extension work for social education through providing study outlines and lecture services. Other organizations included the Religious Education Association (1903), the World Sunday School Association (1907), the International Sunday School Association (1907), the Sunday School Council of Evangelical Denominations (1910), and, through a merger of the latter two, the International Council of Religious Education (1922).

It should be pointed out, too, that Chautauqua was essentially a training center for Sunday school teachers, and that many of its Literary and Scientific Circles were organized under church auspices. On the whole, however, the religious institutions themselves did not experience the kind of dramatic development of institutional forms for the education of adults that characterized other institutions.

Museums

A number of new museums were established during this period in the fields of art, history, natural history, and science, for one of the frequent expressions of public spirit by the new class of industrial titans was the endowment of a museum, usually named in honor of the donor. The development of museums educationally is described by Low in these words:

Education and museums were first linked together seriously in 1870. In that year, when charters were granted to three of our present largest public museums, education was a constant byword of the founders. However, the exigencies of collecting and the tribulations of fund-raising soon contrived to relegate fulfillment of the educational ideal to some later date. Subsequently, during the first decade of the present century, when active education was finally recognized as one of the functions of museums, staffs consisted primarily of research scholars having little or no interest in popular education. . . . Furthermore, the education which did slowly take its place as a museum function was conceived essentially as the education of the child and not of the adult.[43]

The principal methods developed by the museums for education were the guided tour, exhibitions, publications, loans, talks, and organized classes or lecture series. With the founding of the American Association of Museums in 1905 an instrumentality was created for the continuous improvement of educational practices and the coordinated planning of methods of study to meet popular needs.

SUMMARY

The dominant theme of this period of development in the American adult education movement was "multiplication." The period opened with hundreds of institutions engaged in the education of adults, but it closed with thousands.

A number of new institutional forms of adult education were either created or became firmly established—correspondence schools, summer schools, university extension, residential labor colleges, evening schools, junior colleges, settlement houses, social service agencies, parks and recreation centers, and, most prolifically of all, national voluntary associations.

A few new methods were created: the demonstration method pioneered by the Cooperative Extension Service, the short course, the home study course, the conference, and the short-term institute. Visual aids appeared in simple form.

The general character of adult educational content shifted from general knowledge to several pin-pointed areas of emphasis—vocational education, citizenship and Americanization, the education of women, civic and social reform, public affairs, leisure-time activity, and health. Adult education was clearly in tune with the needs of this era of industrialization, immigration, emancipation, urbanization, and national maturation.

This period also witnessed an increasing participation by government in the development of adult educational opportunities. At the federal level this was evidenced by the establishment of a Department of Education, the passage of the Smith-Lever Act creating the Cooperative Extension Service, and the passage of the Smith-Hughes Vocational Education Act. At the state level it was evidenced by the passage of permissive legislation in a number of states and the provision of direct financial aid in a few, and the establishment of service bureaus for adult education in the departments of education in three states. At the local level it was evidenced by increasing support for evening schools, libraries, museums, and county agricultural extension work.

The big tragedy of this period was that following the Emancipation Proclamation and the ending of the Civil War adult education was not used as an instrument of national policy to equip the freed slaves to enter the main current of American life on a massive scale—as was done a quarter of a century later with the waves of European immigrants. Gehring and Venable have documented that (1) during the period 1862-1870 nearly 10,000 teachers—mostly from New England—worked intensively to instruct freedmen and poor whites in reading, writing, arithmetic, and religion; (2) this work included the efforts of the Freedmen's Bureau and over seventy voluntary charitable associations; and (3) between $5 million and $6 million were expended for this purpose.[44] But obviously the effort fell far short of what was needed.

CHAPTER IV

⌖

THE DEVELOPMENT

OF INSTITUTIONS

FOR THE EDUCATION OF ADULTS

IN THE MODERN ERA (1921–1961)

THE SOCIAL SETTING

A kaleidoscopic presentation of American society from 1921 to 1961 would show changing patterns in rising tempo in population, technology, economic conditions, international relations, social arrangements, communications, philosophical and religious ideas, and government. It was an era that moved from crisis to crisis. And it was the era of greatest expansion and innovation in adult education to date.

The characteristics of the population of the United States probably underwent more drastic changes than any major nation has experienced in a similar period of time in history. The total population increased in size by over one third: from almost 106,-000,000 in 1920 to over 178,000,000 in 1960. It changed from an almost even balance between rural and urban to predominantly urban: from 51.2 percent urban in 1920 to 69.9 percent urban in 1960. It grew somewhat older: from a median age of 25.3 years in 1920 to 29.5 years in 1960.[1] The ratio of foreign-born to native population declined: from 13.2 percent in 1920 to 6.9 percent in 1950.[2] And the level of education of the population rose: as one of America's leading educators observes, "An outstanding social achievement of this century has been the raising of the general education level of the American people. . . . The typical young adult of today completes four years of high school, while the chances are that his father had less than a year in high school and that his grandfather did not go beyond grade school." [3]

The nation's economic changes were no less drastic. In broad strokes, during this era the United States experienced the dislocation of World War I, followed by ten years of unprecedented prosperity, then the ten-year catastrophe of the Great Depression, then the dislocation of World War II, followed by a period of technological development and economic expansion the scope and limits of which are still not discernible. Perhaps the central characteristic of this economic trend has been bigness. For example, the total estimated national wealth more than quadrupled between 1920 and 1960; but even more significantly it became more evenly distributed among the income classes. The labor force became more skilled—shifting sharply away from the unskilled toward the skilled occupations; it became more productive —output per man-hour in manufacturing almost doubled; and it became highly organized into powerful trade unions, the largest of which was the AFL-CIO, organized in 1955 with a total membership in excess of 15,000,000.

The change in the government's role in the economy was especially marked. With the collapse of the economy in 1929 and the landslide victory of the Roosevelt administration in 1932, the traditional laissez-faire policy regarding government's role in economic affairs was reversed. The government undertook to restore prices through loans and regulations and to control the credit structure, banking, and currency. It sought to stimulate employment, expand purchasing power, provide relief and social security, and improve living conditions. The notion that the federal government has a responsibility to take initiative in providing for the minimum welfare of all the people became so firmly rooted during the Roosevelt era that it became accepted in the later platforms of both parties.

Radical social changes accompanied these economic changes. One of the most striking of these changes was the urbanization of life in general. With the improvement of transportation and mass communications, most of the amenities of life that were once available only in the cities became almost equally accessible to rural people, and the difference between rural and urban life began to disappear. Other changes with special implications for adult education included a generally higher standard of living, a broader distribution of luxury goods and services, a more autonomous role for women, greater mobility—both geographical and social, a marked improvement in health conditions, the wider acceptance of recreation as a desirable social function, the expansion and coordination of welfare services, and the reduction of racial and religious discrimination.[4]

The revolution that took place during this era in the world of things was matched by that which took place in the realm of ideas. In the natural sciences this revolution produced an entirely new conception of the nature of matter and the structure of the universe. The rigid, stable, and relatively simple world of Newtonian physics was shattered by Einstein's theory of relativity. The conception of matter as a system of organized energy and electromagnetic fields of force, the theories of quantum physics, and advances in biology, physiology, chemistry, and mathematics not only revolutionized science and technology but opened up new frontiers of exploration regarding the nature and meaning of life itself. These reorientations to nature produced tensions in theological and philosophical thought between scientifically- and nonscientifically-oriented schools of thought. The social sciences reacted by becoming both more scientific—in the sense that their methods of data collection and measurement became more objective and precise—and more concerned with the application of social science to the real problems of life.

The arts flourished in America in the decades after World War I. As Commager explains it, "economic convulsions at home and political, social, and moral convulsions abroad brought a reconsideration of the significance of America, a search for what was valid in the American past, sound in the American present, encouraging in the American future." [5] Modern literature, drama, poetry, music, dance, and fine arts were concerned both with finding and describing the realities of America and twentieth century civilization, and with criticizing and changing it. Indeed, the creative artist had more direct access than ever before to the minds of all men, through the mass media of newspapers, magazines, radio, and television, and the mass distribution of paperback books. Because of the economics of the mass media, artists were tempted to create for the lowest common denominator of the mass audience. Without doubt, some of our finest talents were warped and wasted in this process. On the other hand, more Americans than in any previous period in history were exposed to important ideas, experienced excellent art, and witnessed significant events.

These changes in society were replete with implications for the further institutional development of adult education in the modern era. What would be the effect on the field of the expansion of the population, especially in the upper age brackets; of the increasing concentration of the population in urban centers; of the rising educational level of the population; and of the declining volume of immigrants? How would the field react to the rising income, shrinking work-week, increasing need for skill, and growing organization of the labor force; to the radically changing economy; and to the changing role of government in the economy? What would be the response of the adult educational institutions to the social, intellectual, and cultural changes that were so drastically transforming the society these institutions were designed to serve? These questions can best be answerd by describing the developments that occurred in the various institutions responsible for the education of adults.

INSTITUTIONAL DEVELOPMENTS IN ADULT EDUCATION

Business and Industry

A distinct shift toward a broader conception of the role of industry in the continuing education of its workers began to occur in the 1920's. Indeed, the assertion was made at the Congress for the Study and Improvement of Human Relations and Conditions in Industry in June, 1928, that "the most significant fact in American industrial and professional life at present is this steady transformation of industry and the professions into educational institutions." [6]

But the depression of the 1930's reduced business activity—and especially its educational activity—to a minimum. Then a number of forces were stimulated by World War II and the attendant industrial expansion that caused an upsurge of education in industry. These forces included the greatly increased level of skill required as a result of automation and mechanization; the shortage of broadly educated and flexible executive talent; and the increasing acceleration of technological change. Perhaps a more subtle force was also at work as well—a shift in attitude on the part of management away from regarding employees only as instruments of production toward regarding them as human beings.[7]

As a result of these forces, the following significant developments took place in education in business and industry especially during and since World War II:

The number of companies providing educational opportunities for their employees greatly increased. In their study of the educational programs of 349 corporations in 1957, Clark and Sloan found that 296, or 84.8 percent, of them carried on some sort of educational activity requiring regular attendance on the part of the participants.[8] Brody had estimated in 1948 that only "fifty percent of the large corporations employing three thousand or more people have established training programs."[9]

Professional leadership for industrial education tended to become increasingly differentiated. At first, the educational function was merely a secondary aspect of the line operations—an extra duty of the master craftsmen, foremen, supervisors, department heads, and executives. Then as personnel management became differentiated as a function, responsibility for training tended to become subsumed under it. Later there was a tendency for departments of training, personnel development, or employees' education to become separated out as independent units responsible to top management. In some instances this general training function was further subdivided into training of first-line workers, training of foremen, training of office workers, and developing executives.

The subject matter of industrial education broadened and deepened. In the corporations studied by Clark and Sloan orientation programs were conducted by 93.2 percent of those carrying on educational activities, managerial development by 90.5 percent, human relations training by 85.4 percent, technical and professional training by 67.9 percent, and general education by 15.8 percent. The ranking of offerings for the various classifications of employees was as follows: foremen and supervisors 92.5 percent, junior executives 77.7 percent, technical and professional workers 70.6 percent, and senior executives 53.7 percent. A large part of these programs consisted of isolated courses. But an increasing number of industries were developing integrated programs, defined by Clark and Sloan as "a systematic plan involving formal or informal instruction, usually both, and designed for some specific end determined by the corporation . . . [which] may be managerial and supervisory development, or, in the technical field, a specialized program for graduate engineers." [10] In some cases, this integrated program included an elaborate and continuous process of individual counseling.

Perhaps the most far-reaching development, however, was the sortie of business and industry into general education—a territory previously reserved for educational institutions. For the general run of workers, this program of general education included off-hour, tuition-free courses in such subjects as leisure-time activities, business machines, communication, economics, elementary school subjects, engineering, high school subjects, human relations and psychology, managerial and supervisory courses, manufacturing and production, mathematics, office subjects, physics and chemistry, research, and salesmanship.[11] For the executive groups, a variety of programs of liberal education were carried on either directly within the company or in cooperation with a university. Of this development, one observer comments:

These programs indicate that business, industry, and academia have committed themselves to a third phase of in-service education for the new era. If the first phase was the provision of specific technical training either in company-owned schools or outside, and if the second phase can be considered the broadened over-all business-management education in the manner of the Harvard Advanced Management Program or the University of Chicago Executive Program, then the third phase is the development of the liberal arts programs we see mushrooming all over the country.[12]

Industry began providing facilities designed exclusively for education. For example, the International Business Machines Corporation erected huge educational buildings in proximity to each of its seventeen main plants to be used for job-related training during the daytime and general education during evenings. In addition, IBM established a resort-type training center for executives on a mountainside in Endicott, New York. Facilities on a similar scale were constructed by General Motors, General Electric, Corning Glass, Ford Motor, Socony Mobil Oil, and other companies.

Industry developed increasingly closer cooperation with formal educational institutions. At the same time that corporations were expanding their own company-operated educational programs they discovered how to make better use of the established educational institutions. At the college level, company-sponsored educational programs generally followed four patterns: (1) courses offered on the company premises by university faculty members and under the jurisdiction of the university; (2) courses held on the university campus but attended exclusively or predominantly by company personnel; (3) a rotating plan in which the employee alternates between the campus and the company plant; and (4) courses taken in the regular program of a university, the tuition for which is refunded. Below the college level similar patterns were developed by some companies with city school systems. No doubt this trend was greatly accelerated during World War II by the cooperative experience between industry and education—under the stimulus of government—in the Training Within Industry and Engineering, Science, and Management War Training programs.

The growth of adult education in business and industry has been so spectacular since World War II as to cause two responsible scholars to assess its potential in these glowing terms:

It is possible that we are now witnessing, in the educational activities of American industry, the birth of a third great educational force of far-reaching consequences. For, just as the first [the university] has perpetuated learning, and the second [the American free public school system] has provided the bulwarks for democracy and for a free economy, so this third innovation is adapting civilization to a new technological era, the ultimate consequences of which stagger the imagination. Nor is this merely an adjustment to mechanical wonders. It is an integration of new technical skills with revitalized human relationships, envisaging a world augmented not only in material comforts but, far more important, in spiritual values.[13]

Colleges and Universities

A number of changes took place in the American institutions of higher education during the years following World War I that influenced in various ways the development of their roles in the education of adults. For one thing, colleges and universities grew enormously in size—their student bodies, faculties, and physical plants were multiplied by six between 1920 and 1960. In the area of educational program, the universities greatly enlarged the number of specialized studies provided and at the same time engaged in a variety of experiments to determine the core curriculum that would provide their students with a basic general education. Perhaps a more subtle but far-reaching change occurred in the relationship of the universities with the nonacademic community. Under the stimulus of two world wars, a depression, and an explosively expanding economy following the last war—as well as under the stimulus of the universities' own need to broaden their base of financial support to meet rising enrollments and costs—their linkages with the outside world were vastly increased. Their research facilities were used more and more, under contract, by industry and government; their faculties were increasingly called on to provide consultation and "brain trusts" for government, industry, labor, and community organizations; and their publication departments increasingly moved from strictly academic to commercial markets.

From the point of view of adult education, the effect of these developments was to bring the university into closer relationship with the people. In this sense, the total university system was in a process of extension. But specific services to the community beyond the campus tended to be assigned to separate administrative units: those directed primarily at the rural population in the land-grant colleges were assigned to the Cooperative Extension Service (which will be discussed in the next section); while those directed to the general community were assigned to divisions of "university extension" or "general extension." Several trends during the period following World War I can be discerned in the general extension movement:

The size of enrollment increased, both absolutely and relatively. The Biennial Survey of Education indicates that enrollment in "extension and correspondence" in all institutions of higher education rose from 101,662 in 1920 to 843,923 in 1952.[14] But Morton estimates that in the year 1951–1952 50 to 60 million people participated in one or more of the short-term activities of the seventy-six member institutions of the National University Extension Association, with more than a million and a half taking part in organized and continuing instructional programs.[15] Indeed, in a number of urban universities the enrollment of adult students grew so much faster than that of youth that the student body of the extension program became larger than the student body served by all other units of the university combined—in numbers, if not in student hours. Few universities had yet taken cognizance in their policy and administrative structures of the fact that in the last few years their constituency had shifted from one composed primarily of full-time youthful students to one composed predominantly of part-time adult students.

The scope of services for the education of adults was greatly broadened. Where the original extension programs had consisted primarily of extension classes and correspondence courses, with occasional conferences, lecture series, and traveling libraries, during the period following World War I a rich variety of new services was inaugurated. Houle and Nelson identified twenty-one major kinds of university adult education that had come into being by 1956, including such nontraditional forms as short courses, radio and television programs, community development programs, alumni education programs, and a wide variety of services and publications for clubs, associations, and other special groups.[16]

There was a tendency toward the development of a broader and uniquely adult curriculum. Although the notion that the extension curriculum should be built around the real-life problems of adults and society (rather than around the academic organization of knowledge) was inherent in the "Wisconsin Idea," which was introduced in the first decade of the century, this notion only gradually became translated into practice. Morton's study of the subject-matter fields with which university extension services were concerned in 1952 showed that over half the total offerings were in academic subjects, but that approximately 30 percent of all university conference activities were in some field of business administration, 16 percent were concerned with questions dealing directly with "the public interest and welfare," 12 percent were concerned with improvement of government services, 10 percent involved problems of professional education, and 9 percent dealt with engineering problems.[17]

A concern that intensified among university adult educators after World War II—largely as a result of their experience with veterans under the "G.I. Bill"—was the creation of a uniquely adult curriculum. This concern had two aspects: (1) finding some way to organize adult learnings into a sequence in which past self-education is integrated with a plan of organized instruction so as to produce a unified, cumulative but individualized outcome of general education; and (2) finding some symbol that would give recognition to the achievement of this outcome. Endeavors in the first area of concern centered around inventing equivalency measures for equating experiential learnings with course credits[18] and devising special sequences of courses and other learning experience or defining "core curriculums" for adults.[19] In the second area of concern special certificates and degrees ("Associate of Arts") were experimented with, but to date there has been no agreement on standard degrees especially for adults.[20]

There was a tendency toward centralization of the administrative responsibility for extension activities. In spite of opposition at times from other departments, extension divisions or evening colleges were established in an increasing number of universities to coordinate all work with adults by these institutions. Of the fifty-three university extension divisions included in the Morton study, for example, twenty-two were established between 1920 and 1947.[21] Potential conflict between the responsibility of academic departments for the maintenance of standards and the responsibility of the extension divisions for administrative efficiency and the satisfaction of adults in terms of their unique needs was dealt with by different universities in different ways. In some cases full responsibility for course organization was retained by the academic departments, with the extension divisions having responsibility only for scheduling, promotion, and administration. In other cases these responsibilities were shared through such devices as joint committees and joint staff appointments. The problem of centralization was even further complicated in a number of state universities by virtue of the creation of separate but equal divisions for general and agricultural extension.

Extension staffs tended to grow in size, stature, and differentiation of role. In contrast to the part-time staff arrangements characteristic of earlier stages, Morton found that by 1951–1952 the administrative staffs of university extension organizations usually consisted of a chief officer and seven to ten associates. About two thirds of the staff members had rank and tenure in the extension organization itself and about one third in instructional departments. Almost all administrative officers in extension were employed on the same financial basis as other officers of the university having similar responsibilities. A substantial proportion of the staff members had advanced degrees.[22]

A variety of practices regarding instructional staffs for extension programs appeared. Some universities developed a core extension faculty composed of teachers who devoted their full time to work with adults; others relied primarily on the part-time service of resident faculty members for extension work; others recruited most of their instructors from the outside community; and still others tried to maintain a balance from all these sources of talent. Morton found that essentially the same standards governed selection of instructional staff members primarily engaged in extension services as were applied to resident instructional staffs. Where an instructor's primary responsibility was for university extension services, there was a tendency for emphasis to be placed on the importance of having an attractive personality and some experience in dealing successfully with adults. It was becoming increasingly recognized, however, that adults are different from youths as learners in many ways, and that teachers who are specially trained to work with adults produce better educational results than those who know how to teach only young people. Accordingly, an increasing amount of energy began to be channeled into in-service faculty training.[23]

Universities spent increasing amounts of money and an increasing proportion of their total budgets on university extension operations. From the beginning, extension activities were expected to be self-supporting to a greater degree than most other university programs—probably because of underlying attitudes on the part of the faculties and administrations that they were an "extra" service of the universities and that adults are able to pay for what they get. Morton found that more than 60 percent of the expenditures for university extension activities came from payment of fees by those using the services in 1951–1952, although "the proportion of support . . . coming from universities' appropriated funds seems to have been somewhat greater during the last decade than it was before that time." [24] In Dyer's study of evening colleges 96 percent reported that year in and year out their income is greater than their expenditures, and that most of them must turn any excess of income over expenditures over to the general funds of the institution at the end of the year. [25] Nevertheless, extension was gradually gaining an increasing share of the total university budget. In 1930 only 35 percent of the university extension organizations were allotted 5 percent or more of their universities' total budgets, but by 1951–1952 this proportion had climbed to 40 percent. [26]

Although the general financial picture steadily improved, extension work still remained one of the more financially precarious elements of our higher education system. It was frequently the first point of scrutiny and reduction in university budgets submitted to economy-minded legislatures or boards of trustees. In quest of more stable sources of support, many extension administrators consciously devoted substantial proportions of their energies to developing special services to industry, government, and community agencies that would be income-producing. A number of leaders of the university extension movement believed that university extension could not make the impact on society of which it was capable until it received the same kind of cooperative state and federal support that had been provided to agricultural extension since 1914. Bills providing for this kind of support were introduced into Congress repeatedly but unsuccessfully.

There was a tendency for the physical facilities for university adult education to expand and become increasingly differentiated. This trend manifested itself in various ways in the different types of space used for extension programs:

Office facilities. In their early stages, extension programs were almost always administered from whatever space could be spared —often from the offices of the faculty members assigned part-time to extension work, and in at least one instance from space under the grandstand of the football stadium. But as extension work grew in size and importance it began operating from separate and permanent offices. Morton reports, for example, that approximately one third of the extension organizations in his study had moved during the last ten years into new building space, "most of which was constructed for their specific needs." [27]

On-campus facilities. Originally all extension activities were conducted in space used also for activities for regular students. But as extension gained in size and stature, an increasing amount of space was set aside exclusively for the use of adults; for example, when Purdue University built a new Memorial Center an entire wing was earmarked for adult programs.

Off-campus centers. Most state university extension divisions early sent faculty members out from the university to hold classes in rented or contributed space in schools, community agencies, and commercial property in distant parts of their states. During World War I the University of Wisconsin inaugurated a new solution to the problem of serving distant constituents by establishing a permanent Extension Center in Milwaukee, with its own building and a core permanent faculty. Some urban universities even established branch centers in nearby suburbs.

Off-campus facilities of other agencies. In its endeavor to take the university to the people, university extension made increasing use of nonuniversity facilities. Morton found, for example, that in 1952 over half the extension classes being carried on by the institutions in his study were conducted in public school buildings.[28] But many extension activities also took place in hotels, business offices, industrial plants, YMCA's, churches, libraries, and other nonacademic settings.

Residential centers. One of the most notable developments in physical facilities in the modern era was the erection of buildings designed specifically to enable adults to live and study together for extended periods of time. Pioneered by the continuation center erected on the edge of the campus of the University of Minnesota in 1936, this trend was accelerated by three forces: (1) in a number of universities facilities erected on or near their campuses during World War II by the military services for the training of military personnel were turned over to the universities at the end of the war and converted into residential centers; (2) the Kellogg Foundation inaugurated the policy in 1951 of making large grants to universities for the erection of "Kellogg Centers of Continuing Education"; and (3) an increasing number of country estates were donated or bequeathed to universities for conversion into residential centers.

There was a tendency to develop a methodology geared to the unique characteristics of adults as learners. With a growing body of research findings regarding the differences between adults and undergraduates as learners, and spurred on by the creative work in methodology by agricultural extension workers and non-academic adult educators, university extension personnel became increasingly experimental in their teaching practices. The adult constituency was used increasingly in the cooperative planning of programs through involvement in advisory committees, community surveys, interest surveys, and curriculum committees. The classroom procedures of lecture and recitation were increasingly displaced by group discussion, cooperative projects, role playing, case study, and other highly participatory techniques. Motion pictures and other audio-visual aids came into increasing use, and indeed many extension divisions established substantial bureaus for the production and distribution of instructional aids and materials. A number of experiments were inaugurated to discover creative ways to use radio and television in the instructional process, either alone or in conjunction with reading and group discussion. Provision for guidance and counseling services for adult students was made in a number of universities and evening colleges. One of the most original developments of this era was the conversion of the entire community into a classroom through community development programs sponsored by several universities, in which the process of solving community problems was utilized for broad-scale continuing education of the adults involved in the process. Finally, concern increased for improving the techniques of evaluating the outcomes of adult learning, and for the first time a concerted research attack on this problem was launched under the direction of the Center for the Study of Liberal Education for Adults.[29]

Not all college-level adult education that emerged was provided by organized extension divisions and evening colleges. A study conducted by James Crimi in 1953 showed that of 404 independent liberal arts colleges responding to his questionnaire, 233 reported some kind of adult education program serving a total of almost 45,000 adults.[30]

Cooperative Extension Service

The central theme in the development of agricultural extension work after World War I was the movement away from a narrow concern for the farmer primarily as a producer of food and fiber toward a broad concern for farmers and their families as whole human beings. The extension service "has always held high those objectives which help people attain: greater ability in maintaining more efficient farms and better homes; greater ability in acquiring higher incomes and levels of living on a continuing basis; increased competency and willingness, by both adults and youth, to assume leadership and citizenship responsibilities; and increased ability and willingness to undertake organized group action when such will contribute effectively to improving their welfare." However, its program during the early years was almost exclusively vocational in character.[31]

But as the needs of rural people changed, so did the extension program. Before and during World War I the emphasis had been primarily on improving farm production, the success of which is at least inferentially attested to by the fact that in 1910—just prior to the creation of the Cooperative Extension Service—31 percent of all gainful workers in the country were engaged in producing food and fiber for themselves and for the remaining 69 percent of the population. Whereas in 1950 11.6 percent of the labor force produced enough for themselves, for the remaining 88.4 percent, and for an expanded export trade—and still had a large surplus left over.[32] Following World War I, with the problem of production diminishing in importance, the emphasis gradually shifted to problems of marketing and conservation.

During the depression years the extension service was called on to manage state and federal emergency rural relief and farm programs, responsibilities which gradually were shifted to newly created specialized agencies such as the Soil Conservation Service, the Farmers' Home Administration, and the Rural Electrification Administration. During World War II similar emergency responsibilities, including government war-bond sales-promotions, scrap-materials drives, the investigation of claims for agricultural deferment, and the entire war emergency farm-labor program, were added to the tasks of the extension service. While these emergency activities diverted energy from the central educational mission of the extension service, they also added to its prestige and its "reality orientation." And, as Brunner observes, the service found that in dealing with the complicated directives of these emergencies "the best results were obtained by using educational methods, explaining the what, how, and why of any given policy." [33]

In fact, these experiences helped to accelerate a trend toward broader and deeper concern with basic economic, social, and civic issues which had been initiated by pioneering experimental programs in some of the states earlier. For example, Brunner reports that rural discussion groups were organized in Wisconsin in the 1920's, that the Agricultural Adjustment Act of 1933 gave further impetus to the consideration of public issues, and that before World War II "over 100,000 groups of farm men and women were spending winter evenings discussing public questions." He further observes that "the materials prepared for this activity, though dealing with controversial issues, gave well-balanced facts and opinions supporting all major points of view." [34] Drama, music, and art groups were also initiated by the extension service during this period.

By 1950 only about one third of the efforts of county extension workers were directed toward more efficient production of crops and livestock, about one fourth to providing services to rural organizations and training voluntary leaders, and much of the balance toward improving social relationships, helping make social adjustments, and developing cultural values among rural people.[35]

On several occasions the leaders of the Cooperative Extension Service conducted deep reevaluations of its objectives and program, with resulting shifts in focus to take into account the social and economic changes affecting the people it serves. Such a process produced the adoption of the "farm and home unit approach" in 1954, in which farm families as units were assisted in determining long- and short-range goals, analyzing resources, analyzing present farm and home problems, learning to solve problems, developing written plans, determining progress toward achievement of plans, and reviewing and revising plans. By 1960 a total of 74,253 families were engaged in this program.[36]

A similar process produced a "Statement of Scope and Responsibility" in April 1958, which charted the course for agricultural extension work in the decade ahead. The statement identified societal changes that required emphasis in the following nine areas of program: (1) efficiency in agricultural production; (2) efficiency in marketing, distribution, and utilization; (3) conservation, development, and use of natural resources; (4) management on the farm and in the home; (5) family living; (6) youth development; (7) leadership development; (8) community improvement and resource development; and (9) public affairs.[37]

In sheer size, agricultural extension grew to mammoth proportions. On July 1, 1958, there were one or more paid workers in each of the 3,152 counties in fifty-one states and territories of the United States. The roster of employees at all levels included 14,812 individuals—the largest single adult educational faculty in the world. The size of the "student body" is indicated by the fact that 15,600,000 families were assisted in adopting improved farming or homemaking practices in 1960. A corps of trained volunteer leaders was developed that by 1960 numbered 1,276,201 men and women.[38] The total Cooperative Extension Service budget of the year 1958–1959 was just under $145,000,000—about 44 percent coming from federal appropriations, 34 percent from state sources, 21 percent from county funds, and 1 percent from nonpublic sources.[39]

In the development of methods and materials uniquely tailored for the education of adults, agricultural extension's contributions were especially outstanding. It pioneered in the invention of techniques for producing and evaluating actual changes in practices. It perfected the techniques of home visitation and result demonstration as the most effective instruments of change—although as the educational level of the rural population rose, increasing use was made of group meetings and mass media. Without doubt it went farther than any other agency in developing procedures for systematically involving its constituency in the program-planning process through the use of a variety of types of committees and councils. It refined procedures for preparing and pretesting such materials as teaching aids, staff-training manuals, leaflets, reports, digests and reports of educational research, and subject-matter publications at readability levels keyed to particular audiences. But perhaps its most far-reaching contribution was the development of methods for the systematic evaluation of educational activities. Finally, it set the pace for the entire adult educational field in the collection of reliable statistics; its annual report of "Extension Activities and Accomplishments" was the most comprehensive statistical report of adult educational participation yet available.

The Cooperative Extension Service also set an example for the entire field in regard to the in-service training of professional and volunteer workers. Many states adopted the policy of paying staff members while on study leave. The National Agricultural Extension Center for Advanced Study at the University of Wisconsin served as a national resource both for research on administrative and supervisory problems and for advanced training of professional workers. One of the most highly valued functions of the county extension agents was the training of voluntary local leaders to assist in carrying out the extension program. In 1960, for example, leader-training meetings accounted for 13 percent of all meetings held by the county agents. Fifty-nine percent of these meetings were to train leaders of adult work and 41 percent for leaders of youth work.[40]

As the ratio between rural and urban populations shifted in favor of the latter, so did the composition of extension's constituency. For example, during the period 1957–1960 there was a decrease of about 7.5 percent in the number of farm families, an increase of 89.8 percent in the urban, and an increase of 38.5 percent in rural nonfarm families reached by the extension program. The constituency in 1960 was composed of 23.8 percent farm, 20.9 percent rural nonfarm, and 55.3 percent urban people.[41]

During its first forty-five years of existence the Cooperative Extension Service provided key leadership in bringing about a virtual revolution in the farming habits of the rural population of America. But it also stimulated radical changes in such other aspects of rural living as child raising, food preparation, health practices, citizenship participation, and cultural activities. Indeed, the rural adult educators of America provided a demonstration that adult education—when in step with technological progress—can make a difference in the life of a nation.

Foundations

Although foundations had previously supported particular activities related to the education of adults, especially in the libraries and agricultural extension, the general field of adult education was discovered as a worthy object of support by the Carnegie Corporation of New York in the early 1920's. And although in subsequent years numerous other foundations contributed to specific adult educational ventures, the vast bulk of foundation support for adult education in this country came from three foundations.

THE CARNEGIE CORPORATION. When Frederick P. Keppel came to the presidency of the Carnegie Corporation of New York in 1923, one of his first acts was to persuade the trustees to include adult education and the arts in their list of interests, which until then had consisted of education at the college and university level, research (especially medical), libraries, and support of related foundations formed by Mr. Carnegie. Mr. Keppel had been impressed by the adult educational developments in Europe—particularly in Great Britain—following World War I, and he was disturbed that very little information existed about adult education in the United States. The initial undertaking of the Carnegie Corporation in regard to adult education was, therefore, fact finding.

Between November 1925 and March 1926, the corporation convened four regional meetings of adult education workers from a variety of agencies to obtain facts about adult education in cross section and to assess opinion regarding what would be required to develop a strong adult education movement in this country. The principal outcome of these meetings was the formation of the American Association for Adult Education at a conference held in Chicago on March 26 and 27, 1926.

The numerous grants made by the Carnegie Corporation through the AAAE during the next fifteen years for both data-collection and experimental action programs are described in Chapter VI. In the period from 1924 to 1941, when it discontinued its support of the AAAE, the Carnegie Corporation contributed a total of $4,850,000 to the support of adult education.

After 1941 the corporation continued to make a few grants each year in this field—"for community development, for education in international affairs, for conferences, institutes, and leadership training"—but adult education no longer appeared as a separate category in its annual reports. The total value of grants having some relationship with the education of adults during the period 1942–1958 was around $4,000,000.[42]

THE KELLOGG FOUNDATION. In 1939—fifteen years after the first adult education grant was made by the Carnegie Corporation —the W. K. Kellogg Foundation changed its Articles of Association, which had previously designated children and youth as the sole beneficiaries of its services, to read, "for the promotion of the health, education, and welfare of mankind."[43] With this broadening of policy the term "continuing education" began to appear with increasing frequency in the Foundation's programs, policies, and budgets. Operating under the basic policies of (1) promoting the use of existing knowledge rather than furthering basic research, (2) favoring self-help projects in which the recipients contribute their own time and resources, and (3) keeping foundation-supported projects flexible and abreast of changing social and economic conditions, the Kellogg Foundation put early emphasis on agriculture, dentistry, hospital administration, medicine and public health, and nursing. A number of the projects in these areas of concern to which it made grants contained elements of adult education, but in 1945 it began reporting certain activities explicitly under the categorical heading "continuing education."

Projects in this category included experimentation in fundamental education, in-service training in nursing, journalism, and agricultural reporting, agricultural extension, and the the improvement of graduate education in adult education. But by far the greatest contribution of the Kellogg Foundation to the advancement of adult education was in subsidizing the erection of Kellogg Centers of Continuing Education on college campuses. Following the completion of the prototype center at Michigan State University in 1951, grants were given for similar centers to the University of Georgia, the University of Chicago, the University of Nebraska, and the University of Oklahoma. During the period 1945–1959 the Kellogg Foundation reported grants totaling approximately $20,000,000 for continuing education projects in this country and abroad.[44]

THE FUND FOR ADULT EDUCATION.   In 1951 the Ford Foundation established the Fund for Adult Education as an independent organization administered by its own board of directors with responsibility for activities dealing with "that part of the total educational process which begins when schooling is finished." This phase of the educational process was considered to have as its aim "the expansion of opportunities for all adult men and women to continue their education throughout life in the interests of mature and responsible citizenship," bearing in mind that "in today's world civic responsibilities are political, economic, and social in scope." It was against this background that the Fund for Adult Education conceived its special task as that of lending support to programs of "liberal adult education for free citizens in our free society." [45]

In carrying out its purposes the Fund for Adult Education pursued several emphases: (1) It made grants during the period 1951 to 1957 totaling $11,666,291 to underwrite the establishment of educational radio and television facilities and to stimulate program development. (2) It liberally subsidized the development of materials, courses of study, audio-visual aids, and experimental procedures for liberal education by a number of educational institutions, ranging from individual universities to the

Great Books Foundation, the Center for the Study of Liberal Education for Adults, and the American Library Association. (3) It assisted selected colleges and universities, public schools, libraries, and national organizations to inaugurate and operate programs to test a variety of approaches to the liberal education of adults. (4) It carried on experimental discussion programs and developed a variety of materials under the direction of its own staff. (5) It supported the coordination of resources and stimulation of ideas in adult education through projects of the Adult Education Association, its own Test City Project, and other national, regional, and local organizations. (6) It sponsored an extensive program of scholarships and fellowships for leaders of adult education and the mass media. (7) It subsidized a number of fact-finding and research studies and their resulting publications. (8) In its concluding years it supported programs concerned with the development of civic, industrial, and organizational leadership. During the ten years between its creation in 1951 and its termination in 1961, the Fund for Adult Education received from the Ford Foundation a total of $47,400,000, which it disbursed to adult educational institutions or expended on projects administered by its own staff.[46]

SUMMARY. Adult education was thus the beneficiary of contributions totaling over $76,250,000 in the modern era from these three major foundations, and of additional millions from smaller philanthropic institutions. Foundations provided a large share of whatever risk capital was available to the field for experimentation and new developments, added substantially to its physical plant, greatly expanded its literature, strengthened its leadership, and encouraged it to discover its basis of unity as a discrete dimension of our national educational enterprise.

Government Agencies

Under pressure from the need for massive re-education or continuing education of adults created by the emergencies of two world wars, a depression, explosive postwar economic expansion, and the rapid enlargement of the role of government, the adult educational activities of governmental agencies grew on many fronts, especially the following:

In-service and off-duty educational opportunities for governmental employees and their families.   At the federal level every agency developed a variety of activities for the orientation of new workers, the upgrading of experienced workers, executive development, and other programs similar to those described previously in business and industry. Several agencies, including the Departments of Agriculture, State, and Commerce, established their own graduate schools. The status of in-service training as a function of governmental agencies was greatly improved with the passage on July 7, 1958, of the Government Employees Training Act. Section 2 of the Act, on "Declaration of Policy," states:

1. That, in order to promote efficiency and economy in the operation of the Government and provide means for the development of maximum proficiency in the performance of official duties by employees thereof, to establish and maintain the highest standards of performance in the transaction of the public business, and to install and utilize effectively the best modern practices and techniques which have been developed, tested, and proved within or outside of the Government, it is necessary and desirable in the public interest that self-education, self-improvement, and self-training by such employees be supplemented and extended by Government sponsored programs. . . .[47]

An implementing executive order directed that each department head shall review periodically the training needs of his employees, formulate plans of action to meet these needs, establish necessary training programs, stimulate and encourage employee self-development, and make use of the training facilities of other departments.

Many federal agencies also provided extensive opportunities for off-duty education. The largest and most varied of these programs was described in detail in the first study in depth of the adult educational role of a federal agency, *The Armed Services and Adult Education*.[48] The study surveyed and evaluated the activities of the Information and Education Division, Army Service Forces; the Educational Services Section, Training Activity, Bureau of Naval Personnel; and the Education Section, Welfare Division, Special Services Branch of the Marine Corps. Types of activities sponsored by these agencies included direct individual and group instruction, post-hostility schools, orientaton and information activities, library services, literacy training, and guidance and counseling services. The United States Armed Forces Institute (USAFI) was established in Madison, Wisconsin, in 1942, to provide a variety of services to the military and civilian personnel in the armed forces, including correspondence courses, group study guides, resident center programs, tests of general educational development, achievement tests, and educational and vocational advice. In the year 1956–1957 there were a total of 503,787 enrollments in the off-duty programs of the armed forces at an expenditure of federal funds totaling $10,878,673.[49]

In-service training and off-duty educational opportunities were also provided by a number of local and state governmental agencies, but no systematic data regarding them exist.

Educational programs operated directly by government for selected segments of the public. In emergency situations requiring resources beyond the reach of established educational institutions the federal government occasionally established and operated programs directly, usually in cooperation with local or state institutions. For example, the federal government provided large programs of continuing education for the unemployed through the Works Progress Administration, the National Youth Administration, the Civilian Conservation Corps, and other emergency programs. Governments at all levels provided educational services for special populations for whom they have special responsibility, such as inmates of prisons, residents of public housing projects, the families of inmates of mental institutions, the populations of Indian reservations, and the patients in veterans' hospitals. During wartime the federal government sought to alleviate the manpower shortage by sponsoring programs of training within industry and to alleviate food shortages by carrying on programs to educate housewives on the use of substitutes.

The activities of the Cooperative Extension Service and the armed forces constituted the largest educational programs operated directly by government. But programs of great significance were operated by the Public Health Service and the Office of Civil and Defense Mobilization. The United States National Commission for UNESCO in the State Department sponsored a nationwide program of "Citizen Consultations" designed to obtain the advice of informed citizens on programs related to international activities of the United States in the fields of education, science, and culture. The commission supplied background papers and supplementary materials on certain current topics and requested the citizen groups to hold discussions and to report back their findings and recommendations. The International Cooperation Administration must be included in any listing of governmental agencies active in the education of adults, although the public it served was outside of this country. It maintained a faculty of over 6,000 American specialists in fifty-eight different countries to carry on educational programs in agriculture, forestry, health and sanitation, community development, the industrial arts, engineering, and public administration.

Research, statistical, materials, and advisory services. The federal government operated the largest publishing establishment in the world, the Government Printing Office. Many municipal and state governmental agencies also published free or low-cost instructional and informational materials, especially in subject areas having to do with natural resources, agriculture, home management, economics, and civic affairs. In fact, governmental agencies became the richest single source of supply for instructional materials in the education of adults.

Statistical services were also common activities of many local, state, and federal agencies, often in connection with more basic research activities. Most directly related to adult education were the research and statistical services of the Office of Education of the Department of Health, Education, and Welfare, which worked in close collaboration with the Bureau of the Census in providing basic statistics. In the Current Population Survey of October 1957 these two agencies started collecting systematic data about participation in adult education, but on only a limited scale.[50] Other federal agencies providing research and statistical services which are relevant to adult education were the National Science Foundation, the Department of Agriculture, the National Health Institutes, the Bureau of Standards, the Atomic Energy Commission, and the Public Health Service.

Although almost every federal agency provided advisory services to local and state governments as well as private agencies and individuals, the one most directly concerned with adult education was the Adult Education Section of the Office of Education. A distinguished precedent of service by the U.S. Office of

Education to the adult education field—especially the public school segment of it—was set by L. R. Alderman, who served as Principal Specialist in Adult Education from 1925 to 1942. But its distinction was a function of the man, not of the office, for the role itself was accorded relatively low status in the division responsible for secondary education in the Office of Education.[51] A significant symbol of the growing importance of adult education was the establishment of an Adult Education Section in 1955 to achieve the following purposes:

1. To help Americans become more aware of the importance of life-long learning and of what it can do to solve many of their problems.
2. To assist in identifying national trends and problems that have implications for adult education.
3. To encourage adult educators and the public generally to accept adult education as an integral part of their regular educational programs.
4. To help bring about greater clarity of purpose and policies, more communication and co-operation among adult education groups, and better co-ordination among both public and private agencies in the use of resources.

In working toward these objectives the section developed programs of research, consultative services, publications, and an information clearinghouse. Its special areas of interest were statistics; education of the aging, the foreign-born, young adults, and leaders and teachers of adults; fundamental and literacy education; community development; education for public affairs and leisure time; and intergroup and human relations education.[52]

Financial support.   The two programs that received the largest direct financial assistance jointly from local, state, and federal governments—agricultural extension and vocational education—are described in detail elsewhere in this chapter. Certainly the adult education programs of public schools, libraries, museums, and tax-supported colleges and universities must also be included in any listing of the objects of governmental financial support. The emergency education programs of the depression years, the veterans' educational programs of World War II and the Korean conflict—especially the G.I. Bill of Rights—the grants-in-aid to rural libraries provided by the Library Services Act of 1956, and most recently, the still-to-be-realized potentials of the Defense Education Act of 1958, all represented a substantial contribution to the financial resources of adult education by the federal government. A recent study of the use of federal funds in education estimated a federal expenditure of at least $87,000,000 for adult education in 1956–1957, as compared with $21,000,000 in 1948–1949.[53]

Policy leadership. Enviable examples of leadership by national governmental bodies in providing policy direction to the adult education movements in their countries have been contributed by the United Kingdom in the report of the Adult Education Committee of the British Ministry of Reconstruction in 1919,[54] and by Canada in the "Massey Report" setting forth the findings of the Royal Commission on National Development in the Arts, Letters, and Sciences, in 1951.[55] Both of these policy statements made a strong impact on the course of the development of adult education in their respective countries in both governmental and nongovernmental agencies.

Adult education in the United States did not enjoy similar leadership on such a broad scale from its government, although the subject was mentioned obliquely in the reports of such distinguished bodies as the National Advisory Committee on Education in 1931, the Advisory Committee on Education in 1936, the President's Commission on Higher Education in 1947, the first Hoover Commission in 1949, and the President's Committee on Education Beyond the High School in 1957. For example, in 1947 the President's Commission on Higher Education proposed the following statement of policy regarding the role of adult education in institutions of higher education:

An expanded program of adult education must be added to the task of the colleges. This is a vital and immediate need, because the crucial decisions of our time may have to be made in the near future. Education for action that is to be taken, for attitudes that are to be effective, in the next few years must be mainly adult education.

. . . .

The colleges and universities should elevate adult education to a position of equal importance with any other of their functions. The extension department should be charged with the task of channeling the resources of every teaching unit of the institution into the adult program.[56]

The President's Committee on Education Beyond the High School included the whole field of adult education in its investigation, and concluded: "It is important that attempts be made to appraise the whole development of adult education in terms of what it is trying to do and how well it is succeeding. The needs must be analyzed if resources are to be planned to meet the needs. But the true proportions and potentials of the movement are unknown." [57]

It summarized its findings and stated its principal recommendation regarding adult education as follows:

In its consideration of the broad field of adult education, the Committee has noted great needs for more information, for better definition and organization of programs, for clearer relationships between the many kinds and levels of adult education, and for answers to a number of specific questions. In the face of such needs, substantive recommendations would be premature. The Committee strongly recommends, therefore, that as a very important next step in this field the Secretary of Health, Education, and Welfare organize and call a working conference or series of conferences for the purpose of considering and proposing how best to go about solving the problems of adult education.[58]

This description of only the better documented activities, incomplete as it is, suggests the enormous and growing role that government agencies at the local, state, and federal levels were performing in adult education. It also clearly indicates that there was pressing need for more adequate information about the adult educational activities of governmental agencies, perhaps for better coordination of them in their adult educational roles, and certainly for more positive policy leadership, at least from the federal government.

Voluntary Health and Welfare Agencies

As was indicated in Chapter III, a varied assortment of health, welfare, and recreational agencies had been established at the local, state, and national levels by the end of World War I. Since that time these types of agencies have continued to multiply. The services of these agencies were described by one observer in the following classifications:

1. Services to individuals and families, provided by such agen-

cies as family service associations, visiting nurse associations, hospitals, clinics, settlement houses, and health agencies.

2. Services to groups and individuals in groups, provided by such agencies as recreation and informal education agencies, church-centered agencies, and youth agencies.

3. Services to agencies and communities by such agencies as welfare federations, united funds, health councils, and community councils.

The "educational component" of these services, according to Hoffer, consisted of: informal education (formal instruction in classes, clubs, and special interest groups); social work (social case work, social group work, and community organization); staff and volunteer training (in-service training, institutes and workshops, conferences); education of the public; and recreational activities.[59]

A comparison of the descriptions of adult educational activities of national health and welfare agencies in the *Handbooks of Adult Education* for 1934, 1936, 1948, and 1960 indicates the following major trends during this era:

The adult educational activities of the health and welfare agencies tended to become broader in scope and less remedial in nature. This shift in the case of health agencies was noted by another observer in these words:

Many voluntary health agencies are accepting a broader approach to their educational efforts. This reflects the newer goals which are now recognized by the health agency. In these larger health goals there is recognition of the relationship between optimum health for the individual and community planning, especially as it relates to raising the health standards of the community.[60]

Bruno cites as evidence of the shift in the general field of social work the fact that the national coordinating organization for the field "even changes its own name from time to time, not because it does not know its own mind but to recognize a change in the concept of the broad field whose spokesman it is." [61] The change in name was from National Conference "of Charities and Corrections" (1873) to "of Social Work" (1917) to "on Social Welfare" (1956).

While the program descriptions of the various agencies in the series of Handbooks show an increasing variety of educational activities being offered to the public, clearly the dominant emphasis in the period since World War II was a rapid expansion in the training of volunteer adult leaders.[62]

The adult educational function in health and welfare agencies became increasingly differentiated. With the expansion of their adult educational activities, health and welfare agencies gained an increasing consciousness of their adult educational roles. While the 1934 and 1936 Handbooks listed only a handful of these agencies, by 1960 their status in the adult educational field warranted the listing of twenty-two in the Handbook for that year. In the earlier Handbooks only one agency (the YMCA) was identified as having an officer specifically responsible for adult education; but in 1960 almost every agency specified an office carrying a title such as "Director of Public Education," "Director, Health Education Department," "National Training Director," or "Director, Adult Program Services Department."

Health and welfare agencies became increasingly active in cooperative endeavors with other agencies of adult education. At the local level, health and welfare agencies played increasingly important roles in the adult education councils. For example, thirteen of the sixty-three member agencies of the Adult Education Council of Greater Chicago were in this category.[63] And as will be shown later, several adult education councils received substantial support from local welfare councils. At the national level, the role of the health and welfare agencies in the general adult educational field is symbolized by the fact that almost a third of the organizations participating in the Council of National Organizations in 1961 were from this category.

Independent and Residential Centers

In contrast to the development of adult education in European countries, where residential colleges and folk schools became highly important institutional forms, their counterparts in the United States—independent adult schools and residential centers—remained a largely peripheral institutional form. The independent center, both residential and nonresidential, was one of the few institutional forms, however, which was created expressly for the education of adults free from control by institutions that were established for other purposes.

A wide variety of nonresidential centers came into being after World War I, especially during the depression years. Some of them were general in purpose and completely autonomous, including the Boston Center for Adult Education, the Cambridge (Massachusetts) Center for Adult Education, the Baker-Hunt Foundation in Cincinnati, and the Watkins Institute in Nashville.

Other independent centers were established as general-purpose and semiautonomous institutions in that they were controlled by citizen boards but held their programs in public school facilities and were subject to some policy influence by the school boards. Examples of this type of center are the Junto in Philadelphia, the Mott Foundation in Flint, Michigan, and a number of adult schools in New Jersey.

Still other centers were established as autonomous but special-purpose institutions. Examples include the numerous nonprofit art centers, music schools, drama workshops, and crafts studios that can be found in most large cities and in many small art colonies around the country.

Independent residential centers were established in this country under the influence of both the Chautauqua Institution and the Danish folk schools. A number of them had affiliation of some sort with larger institutions, such as universities or labor unions, but maintained a considerable degree of autonomy in their policy control. A historical list of this type of center would include the Pocono Peoples College at Henryville, Pennsylvania; the Opportunity School at Berea, Kentucky; the American Peoples Schools at Gladden, Missouri; the Bryn Mawr Summer School for Women Workers in Industry; the Hudson Shore Labor School; the Opportunity School of South Carolina; the Lisle Fellowship; the National Training Laboratory in Group Development at Bethel, Maine; the American Assembly at Arden House, Harriman, New York; and the Residential Seminars on World Affairs.[64]

In addition to Chautauqua Institution, outstanding examples of completely unaffiliated independent residential centers include: the John C. Campbell Folk School, Brasstown, North Carolina; Highlander Folk School, Monteagle, Tennessee: the

Penland School of Handicrafts, Penland, North Carolina; Pendle Hill, Wallingford, Pennsylvania; the Aspen Institute of Humanistic Studies, Aspen, Colorado; the Cold Spring Institute (for the aged), Cold Spring-on-the-Hudson, New York; and the Clearing, Ellison Bay, Wisconsin.

In spite of their small numbers, independent and residential centers have contributed importantly to adult education in this country in experimenting with new approaches to the education of adults and in meeting the needs of particular populations. But, in the view of two students of their history, "the odds in today's society seem to be against any major development of residential adult education which does not have the money, personnel, facilities, and prestige of the institutionalized agencies of our culture." [65]

Labor Unions

The labor movement in this country did not start realizing its educational potential until the Great Depression shocked it into action. Until that time the dominant institution in workers' education was the resident labor school, although a few unions—especially those in the garment industries—had pioneered the establishment of union-operated educational programs.

Even the Workers Education Bureau, which later was to become the official educational arm of the organized labor movement, had its genesis outside the union structure. Organized in April 1921 to serve as a national clearinghouse of information and guidance in workers' education, it derived its principal support during the new decade and a half from the contributions of individuals and foundations, especially the General Education Board and the Carnegie Corporation.

Three events occurred, roughly a decade apart, which had the cumulative effect of starting labor unions on the road to becoming educational institutions: the Great Depression, World War II, and the merger of the AFL and CIO. The impact of the depression years is assessed by one pioneer labor educator as follows:

The New Deal brought a new beginning for American Labor, and radical changes in workers education activity. Education became a recognized function of the unions. There was a rapid expansion in staff and program among those unions which had traditionally been concerned about education. Many of the new unions established education departments. The UAW wrote into its constitution a dues allocation for education. Older unions saw education as an aid in training new local leadership.[66]

The workers' education program of the Works Progress Administration during its brief existence demonstrated the feasibility and need of a mass program of continuing education for workers. It also trained and gave experience to a large cadre of teachers and leaders of adult educational activities, many of whom were absorbed into the unions when the WPA dissolved.

World War II and its immediate aftermaths produced several consequences for workers' education. Perhaps the most significant was the greater stability of the labor movement that resulted from the recognition of the right of collective bargaining, so that unions were able to turn some of their energy from fighting to serving. Labor's attention began to focus increasingly on the community problems affecting the welfare of workers, as evidenced by the formation of the CIO Community Services Committee and the AFL Labor's League for Human Rights. Furthermore, the many experiences the unions acquired in working with established educational institutions, especially universities, in war training programs set a pattern of cooperative relations that persisted and further developed after the war.

The merger of the American Federation of Labor and the Congress of Industrial Organizations in 1955 eliminated much of the interunion competition that had previously drained a good deal of the energies and finances of the unions, and at least some of these conserved resources were made available for education. The amalgamation of the education departments of the two federations brought new strength and integration to the labor education program at the national level, and made possible the appointment of a number of full-time education directors at the local level, where previously neither of the federations could support such a separate function.

The chief characteristics of the labor unions as an institutional form for the education of adults might be summarized as follows:

OBJECTIVES. The labor movement was for a long time in tension between two philosophical poles regarding its adult educational role. On the one hand, there were union leaders who held that the union's educational objectives should be derived exclusively from the needs of its members as workers and as union members. Programs based on these objectives were limited to vocational training, labor history and economics, union management, and the like. On the other hand, there were union leaders who held that the union's responsibility extended to objectives derived from the needs of its members as whole human beings and as units of the total community. Programs based on these objectives included the entire range of educational subjects. The trend following the merger appeared to be toward the latter position.

Mire found in his survey of the educational programs of unions that their objectives could best be classified according to the functional roles of the various populations they served:

Programs for the line and staff employees of labor organizations were directed toward the objectives of improving their skills in collective bargaining, union administration, and community leadership, as well as developing knowledge and understanding of government, economics, and international affairs.

Programs for local union officers tended to have similar objectives, but at a more elementary level and with greater emphasis on managing relationships with the rank-and-file membership.

Programs for labor education specialists tended to focus on three problems: (a) how to stimulate demand for education among the members, (b) how to recruit and develop good teachers, and (c) how to develop programs with continuity so as to achieve long-range results.

Programs for the rank-and-file members included the objectives of improving the individual's ability to participate in group efforts, increasing his understanding of protective labor and social security legislation, and "education for better living" (consumer education, educational programs for wives, and cultural education).[67]

A fifth population grouping—the general public—was also a concern of many labor union educational efforts, especially through the mass media. The principal objective in regard to this population was the development of an understanding of labor's aims and policies.

PROGRAM. The program that was developed to achieve these objectives tended to emphasize the traditional content of unionism, including collective bargaining, grievance procedure, labor history, political action, and economics.[68] But Mire found an increasing concern in union programs for education aimed at the development of the human personality, consisting of such subjects as sculpture, ceramics, music appreciation, painting and drawing, sports, health, and the liberal arts.[69]

METHODS. The early labor union educational programs relied almost exclusively on formal classroom methods—reading assignments, lectures, and recitations—almost as if in search of academic respectability. But gradually the unions adopted methods more appropriate to adult learners, including debates, role playing, open forums, panel discussions, conferences, seminars, discussions based on specific readings, and radio and television programs. Several international unions established large audio-visual departments that produced and distributed some of the most creative educational materials in the field of adult education.

ORGANIZATION. The adult educational function was increasingly differentiated in the union organizational structure. In 1955 the unions employed an estimated two hundred full-time adult education specialists, and uncounted hundreds of volunteer leaders served on educational committees and leading groups. Mire identified five levels in the organizational structure of union education:

1. The Department of Education of the AFL-CIO, the function of which was described by its director as follows:

The role of the AFL-CIO Department of Education in all of this activity is to assist affiliated organizations in developing their own educational programs. In addition, the Department has responsibilities in public education, vocational education and apprenticeship training, with the liaison jobs these imply. . . . A special effort is made to inform our entire membership on the aims of the AFL-CIO itself.[70]

2. International and national unions, about fifty of which established departments of education in their national headquarters. A few locals of these unions also had full-time staff

members directing educational activities, but the vast majority of local programs were conducted by volunteer local union education committees.

3. Regional organizations, examples of which were the Southern Labor School, the Rocky Mountain Labor School, and the Union Leadership Academy.

4. State-wide federations affiliated with the AFL-CIO, at least fifteen of which had full-time staff members assigned to education.

5. Local federations, including central labor unions, industrial union councils, and labor education councils.

RELATIONSHIP WITH OTHER ORGANIZATIONS. Labor unions established a variety of relationships with other organizations, both public and private, in developing their educational programs. Especially close relationships were established with universities. Mire found, for example, that seventeen universities maintained year-round programs of classes, week-end or summer institutes, conferences, and workshops planned with and for labor groups, and that a number of others rendered limited services to unions, ranging from evening classes to occasional institutes and conferences. Liaison between unions and universities became institutionalized with the founding of the Inter-University Labor Education Committee in 1951, and its reorganization in 1957 as the National Institute of Labor Education with the purpose "to expand the scope and volume of labor education and to improve and enlarge the co-operation between labor and nonlabor agencies in the field of education." [71] Close relationships were also established by unions with a number of other organizations concerned with the education of working people, including the American Labor Education Service, the American Library Association, the Joint Council on Economic Education, various religious labor committees, councils of social agencies, youth organizations, and race relations organizations. Organized labor was especially concerned over the role of the government in providing for the educational needs of working people, and for years urged the creation of a federal Labor Education Service.

As of 1961, the multimillion membership of the organized labor movement constituted the single most underdeveloped constituency of adult education in the United States.

Libraries

The year 1924 appears to mark a distinct turning point in the library's role as an adult educational institution. In that year William S. Learned's *The American Library and the Diffusion of Knowledge* proclaimed the type of informal educational agency needed by the adult population and advocated the concept of the library as a "community intelligence center." [72] When the President of the Carnegie Corporation called the first conference on adult education in June, 1924, the librarians participating were already aware of the challenge and eager to meet it.[73] Perhaps the best possible measure of this readiness is the fact that within a month after this conference the Executive Board of the American Library Association appointed a Commission on the Library and Adult Education "to study the adult education movement, and the work of libraries for adults and for older boys and girls out of school, and to report its findings and recommendations to the ALA Council." [74]

The report of the commission, issued in 1926, enunciated a philosophy and set forth directional guide lines which exerted a powerful influence on the development of the library as an adult educational institution. It made three principal recommendations:

First of all, and on its own responsibility, the library owes consulting and advisory service, supplemented by suitable books, to those who wish to pursue their studies alone, rather than in organized groups or classes. Such a service, which can function effectively only through a specially trained and well-educated personnel, will offer advice in the choice of books. and will assist students through the preparation of reading courses adapted to their age, education, taste, and previous experience. . . .

In the second place, there is the obligation to furnish complete and reliable information concerning local opportunities for adult education available outside the library. Persons desiring class work in any particular subject, stimulus from discussion groups or lecture courses, cultural development through opportunities obtainable in the local art museum or elsewhere, should naturally turn to the public library for information, descriptive circulars, or trustworthy advice.

Thirdly, the library should recognize as a fundamental duty the supplying of books and other printed material for adult education activities maintained by other organizations.[75]

The commission also recommended the creation of a permanent board, and in October 1926 the ALA Council brought into being the Board on the Library and Adult Education to encourage research, stimulate activity, and provide leadership within the profession in the area of adult education. In its first few years the board received financial support from the Carnegie Corporation and had its own executive assistant at ALA headquarters, but during the depression its income was greatly reduced, and through much of its life until it was discontinued in 1957 it persisted on the volunteer energies of a few dedicated librarians.

TRENDS IN LIBRARY ADULT EDUCATION. Largely under the leadership of the Adult Education Board a number of substantial developments took place along many fronts in the public library's performance of its adult educational role:

The library staff functions were internally reorganized with the establishment of the Reader's Advisor Service. Starting in 1926 in seven large libraries, this service spread until by 1935 it was generally accepted across the country. Specialist "reader's advisors"—the first distinctly adult educational role established in the library field—prepared tailored reading lists for individual patrons and provided continuous guidance in sequential programs of reading. The backbone of this service was the "Reading with a Purpose Series" published under a Carnegie grant by the American Library Association between 1925 and 1933. The series covered sixty-seven subjects, with introductory essays written by experts.

By 1939 it had become widely recognized that a reader's advisory service was not a panacea for the library's proper role in adult education. Accordingly, larger libraries began developing well-qualified staffs to carry on broad programs of adult educational activities, and by 1954 almost 11 percent of the libraries of the country had established separate divisions for carrying on their adult educational work.[76]

The library movement exerted strong pressure for the improvement of books and materials for adult use. In July 1925 the Commission on the Library and Adult Education appointed a Sub-Committee on Readable Books, which determined that books for the adults who make up the bulk of the constituency of adult education should possess five characteristics: simplicity of language, nontechnical treatment, brevity of statement, fluency, and literary merit. It proclaimed a great need for the development of a "new type of writer" who can "serve as liaison officer, interpreting to the man of little education the results accomplished in the scholar's study or the scientist's laboratory." [77] The sub-committee later published a pamphlet, "First Books in Many Subjects," and in 1943 its chairman, Rudolph Flesch, published his book, *Marks of a Readable Style*.

The Adult Education Board participated in several other activities sponsored by the ALA directed toward improving materials, including a study of reading habits that resulted in the publication of *The Reading Interests and Habits of Adults* by William S. Gray in 1929; the publication of *What People Want to Read About* by Douglas Waples and Ralph Tyler in 1931; and the establishment in 1935 of an advisory bureau on readability at Teachers College, Columbia University, under the auspices of the American Association for Adult Education. Most of these activities were largely supported by grants from the Carnegie Corporation.

Efforts were made to improve communication within the library profession regarding library practice in adult education. A bulletin, "Adult Education and the Library," was published from 1924 to 1930 with a wide readership both within and outside the library field. After this bulletin was discontinued the *ALA Bulletin* carried periodic articles on adult education. Many pamphlets, reading lists, monographs, and study reports were also published by the ALA under the leadership of the Adult Education Board.

The library shifted from a largely passive to a very active role in serving the educational needs of adults, and in so doing greatly broadened the range of its activities. Whereas the role of the library was once almost exclusively one of providing books and materials when asked for them, occasionally with some advice about their use, in 1954 a total of thirty-seven services were identified in the course of surveying the adult educational activities of libraries. They were arranged into six categories, as follows:

1. Supplying (displays; exhibits; book collections; reading lists; films; recordings; physical facilities).

2. Planning (initiating and cooperating in community-wide programs).

3. Advising and Counseling (program-planning assistance to other organizations and community leaders; assistance to other libraries).

4. Training (of individuals in story-telling and book-reviewing; of discussion group leaders, of program-planners, of librarians in use of adult educational techniques and audio-visual aids).

5. Informing (about adult educational activities in other agencies; about films and other resources; about library services).

6. Doing (presenting book reviews; conducting activities based on books, films, recordings; conducting or using educational programs on radio and television; producing materials for adult learning; studying adult education needs and resources).[78]

It is clear that in the modern era the library moved from the status of an adult education resource toward that of an adult education operating agency, that it moved from perceiving its constituency as consisting of individuals toward perceiving it as the total community, and that it moved from regarding its function as custodial toward regarding it as educational.

The changing adult educational role of the libraries was increasingly taken into account in the training of librarians. The Commission on the Library and Adult Education recommended in 1926 that library schools be requested to consider the advisability of establishing special courses of instruction in adult education work for librarians. Lectures in adult education were introduced in the library schools of Columbia University and Simmons College in 1937, and in the same year the Graduate Library School at the University of Chicago presented an institute on adult education. But as late as 1954 Stevenson reported that "a recent appraisal of library school catalogs revealed only sixteen schools offering opportunities for study in adult education, and these were chiefly the philosophy of adult education, or, work with the individual reader. Practically nothing in theory or methods of working with groups is being offered." [79]

FUND FOR ADULT EDUCATION GRANTS. If the year 1924 marked one clear turning point in the development of the library as an adult education institution, the year 1951 marked another turning point hardly less distinct or significant. In that year the Fund for Adult Education began making a series of grants to the American Library Association which greatly affected the adult educational activities of the libraries of the country.

The first of these grants was for the American Heritage Project, which between 1951 and 1955 enabled the American Library Association to assist libraries throughout the country to organize local groups to discuss political, economic, and social problems in the light of the basic documents that make up the American heritage. A number of lay leaders were recruited and given extensive training in both state and national conferences.

Another grant was made in 1952 to finance the survey of adult education activities in public libraries that has been previously referred to. In addition to providing valuable information that was used for long-range planning by the profession, this survey had the effect of causing librarians throughout the country to become more conscious of their adult educational potentials and responsibilities as a result of the very process of having to think through answers to the probing questions that were asked.

By May 1953 the load of administering these projects and the rising volume of adult educational activities they helped to stimulate had grown so heavy that the ALA established an Office for Adult Education in its headquarters, with the Associate Executive Director of the ALA as its head. Another grant from the Fund for Adult Education made it possible to assemble a competent staff to give technical assistance and leadership to the library field in its expanding adult educational program.

In July 1953 another grant was made for a Subgrant Project to stimulate adult educational activities in libraries. Libraries from all over the country were invited to submit projects to initiate new programs or develop existing ones; as a result subgrants were made to twenty libraries in nineteen states.

In 1954 a grant was made to enable the ALA to convene a representative group of leaders from library schools and practicing librarians to discuss the training needs of librarians working with adults and to recommend steps that should be taken by the library schools and the profession better to meet these needs. The report of this conference, held at Allerton Park, Illinois, charted a new course for pre-service and in-service training for adult education workers in the libraries.[80]

In 1955 a grant was made for a five-year Library-Community Project to assist local libraries to develop long-range adult education programs based upon the analysis of community needs. Under this project subgrants were made to eight state library extension agencies, each of which undertook: (1) to provide services to librarians, trustees, and lay leaders on a state-wide basis to increase their knowledge and skills in library adult education through publications, workshops, and institutes; and (2) to designate one local library as a pilot library to conduct an intensive experiment in community study which would involve librarians, library trustees, and citizen leaders in assessing the educational needs, interests, and resources of their community and determining the library's role in the light of this assessment. The staff of the Library-Community Project provided consultant services to libraries and library schools in all the states, and conducted an extensive program of in-service training workshops.

In 1957 an evaluative study of the effects of these projects was made under another grant from the Fund for Adult Education. The conclusion of this study was that "the ALA Adult Education projects supported by the Fund for Adult Education have had far-reaching and significant effects not only upon the libraries which participated in the projects, but upon the entire public library field. The ALA projects have produced more skilled professionals, stronger adult education institutions, and a profession better able to define its role in adult education and more willing to accept its responsibilities in the total adult education field." [81]

DELINEATION OF ROLE.   A final step in the process of delineating and conferring status on the adult educational function of the library was taken in 1957 with the reorganization of the Adult Education Board into the Adult Services Division, with its own office and secretary at ALA headquarters.

A parallel growth of strength in the adult education function started taking place at the state level, where an increasing number of state library extension agencies established full-time staff positions in adult education. This development was greatly helped by the assistance, stimulation, and financial support provided these agencies through the ALA projects, but it was accelerated by the passage of the Library Services Act in 1956. Through matching funds provided under this act, the state library extension agencies encouraged rural libraries to cooperate in establishing larger units of service and placing increased emphasis on services to adults.

Mass Media of Communications

The mass media of communications performed an educational function from their inception, whether those who managed them were conscious of an educational purpose or not. The mere act of transmitting information is in a limited sense an educational activity. But traditionally the mass media have served only as aids to learning, not as agencies providing programs of learning. The mass media could therefore hardly qualify as an institutional form for the education of adults until they undertook to develop programs organized specifically for educational purposes. The progress made by the principal mass media—printed materials, audio-visual materials, and broadcasting—in this direction was one of the more significant adult educational achievements of the modern era.

Certain aspects of this progress occurred differently in the various media, while other aspects were the result of the use of the media in combination.

PRINTED MATERIALS. The wide range of aids to learning encompassed by this medium can be illustrated by the categories developed by Houle in describing the kinds of print which adult educational agencies use. They included: (1) specially published materials (manuals, newsletters, lesson plans, discussion guides, pamphlets, information sheets, journals, and research reports, produced by agencies and organizations primarily for their own members or clientele but sometimes also for the public); (2) textbooks prepared for children and young people (widely used in the adult educational programs of schools and universities); (3) special textbooks for adults (largely limited to the fields of elementary English, Americanization, vocational courses, and correspondence courses); (4) government publications; (5) sponsored materials (such as health education materials distributed by insurance companies and money-management materials prepared by banks); and (6) general books and magazines (in many cases accompanied by discussion outlines or study guides to permit their use in group situations).[83] For the purposes of this survey a seventh type of printed material should be added to this list, the newspaper.

There were several noteworthy approaches to increasing the usefulness of printed materials for adult educational purposes in this era:

Gaining a better understanding of the adult as a reader. A series of studies beginning in the twenties investigated the reading interests and habits of adults and the effects of reading on their development.[84] The results of these studies helped the producers of materials to increase the appeal and educational value of their products.

Improving the readability of printed materials. Stimulated by the research on the adult as reader and the rise of the "basic English" movement, increasing effort was devoted to making printed materials more readable—and therefore, presumably, more useful in the education of adults. As early as 1925 the American Library Association appointed a Sub-committee on Readable Books that published lists of books meeting minimum criteria of readability, and in 1935 it joined with the American Association for Adult Education in sponsoring the establishment of the Readability Laboratory at Teachers College, Columbia University. Under the direction of Lyman Bryson this laboratory produced eleven books for the laymen ("The People's Library," The Macmillan Company, 1939–1940). The development of readability tests, formulas, and principles by such investigators as Rudolph Flesch, Edgar Dale, and Wilbur Schramm made it increasingly possible for writers and publishers to produce materials on serious subjects within the comprehension of "average readers."

Improving the reading ability of adults. Although the effect of this approach was on the reader rather than on the materials, it had the consequence of increasing the educational usefulness of printed materials. Short courses designed to increase the reading speed and comprehension of adults spread with increasing acceleration in the military services, business and industry, libraries, public schools, universities, and elsewhere.

Making good books more readily available to the adult reader. Great strides forward in this direction were taken by the library movement by virtue of the growth in the number of local libraries, especially branch libraries; the improvement of technical library procedures; the introduction of "bookmobiles"; and the development of consolidated rural libraries. But without doubt the single greatest advance in this direction in modern times resulted from the expansion of the "paperback" book trade, which made books of high educational value available at low cost in drugstores, airports, supermarkets, and bus depots across the nation.

Presenting sequential materials in newspapers and magazines. As the managers of the daily and periodical presses gained greater consciousness of their educational roles, they engaged in a variety of experiments in an effort to find out how these roles could be better performed. One approach was to provide comprehensive treatment of a single subject in a single issue. For example, the editorial page of the *St. Louis Post-Dispatch* frequently probed a particular issue in depth by presenting an editorial, a cartoon, reprints of editorial opinions from other newspapers and magazines, and letters to the editor on its editorial page. Leading magazines, notably *The Atlantic Monthly, The Reporter,* and the *Saturday Review,* sometimes devoted entire issues or supplements to a multidimensional presentation of a major issue. Another approach was to present a linear series of articles on a given topic. For example, Austin C. Wehrwein of the *Milwaukee Journal* won the Pulitzer Prize in 1953 for a series of twenty-five articles on Canada; and George Beveridge of the *Washington Evening Star* won the prize in 1958 for a series on "Metro, City of Tomorrow: What It Will Be Like." *Life* published several series-in-depth on such subjects as geology, religion, anthropology, and the arts. The *Saturday Evening Post* inaugurated an outstanding series in 1958 on "Adventures of the Mind."

Stimulating the use of printed materials for study and discussion by groups. The pioneering work done by the lyceums, Chautauqua, and the correspondence schools in the preparation of materials for study and discussion bore the fruit in the modern era in the "coordinated course." Houle called this phenomenon "a new educational idea which may, in time, prove to be as important for the mass development of adult education as the textbook was for the spread of elementary and secondary schools." [84]

The coordinated course was an integrated sequence of units, usually planned to extend for a given period of time, in which educational objectives are defined, materials and methods are selected in the light of these objectives, and assistance is given to leaders (in the form of either printed guides or face-to-face training, or both) in guiding a group in the study and discussion of the materials. The idea of the coordinated course was widely adopted by industry and the armed services for job training and by many national voluntary organizations for leadership training. It also provided the base for the organization of general programs of adult education, such as those of the Great Books Foundation, the American Foundation for Continuing Education, and the Fund for Adult Education experimental discussion project.

The idea of the coordinated course was also adapted to the use of newspapers and magazines for study and discussion. For example, a number of newspapers cooperated with the Foreign Policy Association in the "Great Decisions Program" inaugurated in 1955, in which columns and editorials printed weekly by the newspapers supplemented pamphlets, bibliographies, and other materials provided by the association for use by self-organized adult discussion groups in the study and discussion of major current issues of foreign policy. A number of popular magazines, notably *Reader's Digest, Parents' Magazine,* and *Newsweek,* maintained educational bureaus to provide discussion guides and other assistance to groups wishing to make use of these periodicals for systematic study and discussion.

AUDIO-VISUAL MATERIALS.   Audio-visual materials were usually used as supplemental aids in learning experiences organized primarily on the basis of some other medium of communication. For example, the phonograph recording was used in music appreciation courses in which the principal methods of instruction were lecture and discussion. Charts, tapes, motion pictures, film strips, models, exhibits, and other forms of auditory and visual presentation were similarly used, especially in connection with the educational programs of the libraries, museums, Cooperative Extension Service, industry, and armed services. A number of institutions established specialized bureaus to develop, produce, and distribute these materials.

However, perhaps the most significant development in modern

times—in terms of the use of the mass media in adult education—
was experimentation with the packaging of complete instructional programs using audio-visual recordings. The earliest experiments in this direction were the production of sequential
courses of language instruction by commercial phonograph record companies. Later, the film forums that sprang up around
the country in the 1930's developed thematic programs in which
the showing of motion pictures was followed by discussion. During World War II complete courses of instruction by motion picture were widely used by the armed forces and industry, especially in job-training programs.

BROADCASTING. The emergence of broadcasting as an instrument for the education of adults was almost completely a post-
World War I phenomenon. And it occurred in two dimensions,
commercially sponsored broadcasting and educationally sponsored broadcasting.

Although the first commercial broadcasting license was issued
to Station WBZ in Springfield, Massachusetts, in 1921, several
privately owned stations had experimented with systematic radio
broadcasting before that time. Indeed, the broadcasting of the
1920 election returns by the Westinghouse Station KDKA at
Pittsburgh is frequently cited as the starting point in building a
mass audience for commercial radio in this country.[85] The discovery of this new medium by the advertising industry occurred
in 1922, and the number of radio stations began to increase daily
until they ran into the hundreds. Out of a series of four conferences held by Secretary of Commerce Herbert Hoover, plus legislative acts and court decisions, a set of policies had emerged by
1924 that defined the "American system" of radio broadcasting
based on private ownership under government supervision.

The early radio programs were mostly haphazard potpourris
of phonograph recordings, hasty talks, and amateur singers, with
little impact of an educational nature. But with the founding
of the National Broadcasting Company in 1926, the organization
of the counry's radio stations into several network systems began,
and with it came more responsible broadcasting. Under the
guidance of an Advisory Council (with committees on agriculture, church activities, education, labor, music, and women's
activities), NBC embarked on an extensive series of public serv-

ice broadcasts that included operas, dramas, concerts, lectures, news, and weather. With the establishment of the National Advisory Council on Radio in Education in 1930, educators and representatives of the radio industry were brought together for the first time to work toward the better use of radio for educational purposes. Under the stimulation of grants from the Carnegie Corporation and John D. Rockefeller, Jr., the Council prepared twelve series of programs on such subjects as "Psychology Today," "American Labor and the Nation," "Art in America," and "Economics in a Changing Social Order." The economic depression of the mid-1930's brought an end to this promising experiment, although several of the cooperating organizations continued to produce programs of high quality which were used by some stations as "sustaining programs."

But by 1935 the principle was well established that a substantial proportion of radio broadcasting time should be devoted to public service and educational programs. The major networks established educational staffs and entered into cooperative relationships with many educational institutions in producing educational programs. For example, from 1935 until the industry was reorganized with television at its center, NBC presented such programs as a Music Appreciation Hour, the National Farm and Home Hour, the University of Chicago Round Table, Town Meeting of the Air, Tales from Opera, the NBC Home Symphony, and periodic dramatizations of the classics. The Columbia Broadcasting System carried such educational programs as the American School of the Air, operatic and symphonic concerts, Science Service, the Columbia Public Affairs Institute, the Columbia Workshop, and "Invitation to Learning" moderated by the pioneer adult educator, Lyman Bryson.

Many local stations provided substantial periods of free time for educational presentations by such organizations as the Cooperative Extension Service, labor unions, libraries, public schools, colleges and universities, medical societies, health agencies, and safety councils. In the late 1930's and early 1940's a number of frequency-modulation stations were established that provided continuous programing of classical music, news, public affairs discussions, and other serious material.

One of the principal obstacles in the exploitation of commercial radio for adult education was the ineptitude of educators in using the medium. In an effort to remove this obstacle local stations and the networks cooperated with universities in conducting radio workshops, the earliest of which was established in Chicago in 1935 by the University Broadcasting Council. A more truly national center was established in 1936 at New York University in cooperation with the Federal Radio Project of the U. S. Office of Education, NBC, and CBS.

Educational radio experienced even greater difficulty. The first experimental radio license was issued to an educational institution, St. Joseph's College in Philadelphia, in 1912, and the University of Wisconsin was sending music and lectures over the air in 1917. Broadcasting licenses started being issued in 1921, with universities lining up side-by-side with commercial applicants for permits. The major part of the brief history of educationally owned stations was summarized by Hill in this single paragraph:

. . . The early rush of colleges to get broadcasting licenses had brought 73 institutions into the field by the end of 1922. The interest continued in 1923, with 39 obtaining permits, and in 1924, with 38. In 1925 and 1926 there were more than 100 educational stations active in radio, or about one-seventh of the full number. It is impossible to fix a set number, for colleges were constantly securing and relinquishing licenses, and the total varied from month to month. But with 1927 there began a steady decline, and by 1929 there were but 62 educationally owned broadcasting stations.[86]

Hill attributed this decline to the fact that radio became a business requiring expensive equipment and talent, and the university administrators and trustees were not willing to invest sufficient funds in it to compete with commercial stations.

By 1930 a number of educators had come to feel that the commercial interests which dominated the air waves were inherently unfriendly to the development of educational broadcasting and that therefore the battle lines between commercial broadcasters and the educators should be sharply drawn. Accordingly, they organized the National Committee on Education by Radio under a five-year grant from the Payne Fund. The first program of the new committee was the promotion of a policy requiring the setting aside of 15 percent of the total broadcasting frequencies for educational service. A bill to this effect was introduced into Congress by Senator Fess of Ohio in January, 1931, but it was solidly opposed by the broadcasting networks, station owners, and the Federal Radio Commission, and it was never reported out of committee. A second attempt to force the establishment of this policy—in hearings before the newly constituted Federal Communications Commission in 1934—also met with failure, but it produced a new mechanism for bringing about cooperation between commercial broadcasters and educators, the Federal Radio Education Committee.

Thirty-eight publicly owned radio stations survived the competition of the 1930's. The largest of these was the state-owned station WHA in Madison, Wisconsin, of which Hill observed that technically it occupies a position with regard to the people of Wisconsin roughly paralleling that of the British Broadcasting Corporation with regard to the British people. The demonstration by the publicly owned stations of the ability of educators to serve the common welfare in ways that commercial broadcasters cannot was to be an important factor in the shaping of policies regarding the distribution of television channels following World War II.

In 1945 television came out of the laboratory and into the market place. The Federal Communications Commission began allocating channels to those who applied in much the same way that radio station licenses had been issued a generation before. But by 1948 the commission discovered that the number of channels available had been miscalculated, and it postponed further allocations until it had had time to study the situation. This delay enabled educators to marshal their forces and develop strategies for getting a share of the channels reserved for noncommercial use and for preparing the educational field to make use of them.

On the suggestion of the National Association of Educational Broadcasters (which, having been organized in 1925, had experienced the consequences of uncontrolled distribution of radio frequencies), the American Council on Education sponsored the formation of the Joint Committee on Educational Television in 1951. Composed of representatives of seven of the most powerful national educational organizations[87] in the country, the

JCET was in a position to speak with authority regarding the interests of educators. Fortunately, almost simultaneously a large national foundation threw its resources into the battlefield when the Fund for Adult Education made several substantial grants: (1) to the Joint Committee on Educational Television to enable it to provide general information and technical and legal assistance to educational institutions and to appear as party of record in hearings before the FCC; (2) to the National Association of Educational Broadcasters to make a series of monitoring studies of the fare being broadcast by commercial television stations and to develop a series of new types of radio programs to demonstrate what could be done by educators given adequate resources; (3) to station WOI-TV at Iowa State University, the only educational station then telecasting, to experiment in programing; and (4) to FM radio station KPFA in Berkeley, California, to discover what it might about the financing of educational television.

With the JCET leading the attack, the forces of education made a strong case before the Federal Communications Commission, and on April 14, 1952, the commission set aside 242 channels (later increased to 258) for educational television. Four national organizations—the American Council on Education, the Joint Committee on Educational Television, the National Association of Educational Broadcasters, and the newly organized National Citizens Committee for Educational Television—embarked cooperatively on a concentrated program to convince and help educational and community organizations to make plans for the establishment of noncommercial stations and to prepare teachers to make use of this new tool. The Fund for Adult Education made offers in the fall of 1952 of grants-in-aid (in amounts of $100,000 to $150,000) for the construction of stations. Beginning in May 1953, when the University of Houston's KUHT-TV began telecasting, noncommercial stations were founded at an increasing rate until by the end of 1960 sixty-two stations were on the air.

Local stations have developed according to three patterns of organization: (1) single-agency stations, in which the college or school board holding the license underwrites the station financially, allowing other educational groups to participate in station programing; (2) state-wide network stations, in which a state educational agency or TV authority is the licensee and the station is financed by state funds; and (3) community stations, in which educational, cultural, and civic organizations in the community band together in a nonprofit corporation, establish a station, and direct its operation.

A new element was added to the educational television picture, which had been missing from the educational radio picture, with the establishment of the Educational Television and Radio Center in Ann Arbor, Michigan (later moved to New York City) under a grant from the Fund for Adult Education in the fall of 1952. This center linked together programmatically, although not electronically, all of the educational television stations in the country. It acquired programs by kinescope and tape from a variety of sources, but especially from the educational stations themselves, and made them available to all cooperating stations. It also gave grants-in-aid for the production of outstanding programs and assisted local stations in engineering, recording, training, research, and publicity. Largely as a result of the influence and assistance of this national center, the range and quality of educational programs produced by the educational stations were greatly superior to those provided by the earlier educational radio stations.

One of the major social inventions to emerge in the early years of educational television was the "telecourse" for credit. A survey made in 1958 revealed that 117 educational institutions offered 464 credit courses by television in that year.[88] Typically, these courses were offered at a standard fee for those wishing credit and at a reduced fee for those wishing to audit. Both groups then received a syllabus and other materials, and the credit students submitted lessons for correction by instructors and took examinations. Non-credit enrollment was several times the size of the credit enrollment.

At the same time that educational television was thus mapping out a new and respected place for itself, commercial television was demonstrating greater educational responsibility than had been true of the early radio industry. Both NBC and CBS experimented with credit courses, "Sunrise Semester" by CBS and "Continental Classroom" by NBC. All networks presented documentaries of significant events, high-level discussions of public affairs, instructional programs in the appreciation of the arts, and editorial comment on the news. The commercial industry was also more supportive of the educational stations than was true in the days of radio. Many local commercial stations contributed equipment and talent to help educational stations get started, and in 1957 NBC set aside a fund of many millions of dollars to finance a series of daily half-hour programs that was made available to educational stations either live or by kinescope. But for the most part, the directly educational efforts of the commercial television industry were relegated to the "intellectual ghetto" of Sunday afternoon.

COMBINED MEDIA. Without question the most promising development in the use of the mass media as an institutional form for the education of adults was the combining of the several media together with group discussion into an integrated learning experience. One of the pioneering ventures in this direction was the Community Education Project operated by the San Bernardino Valley College, California, with financial support from the Fund for Adult Education. The evolution of this program was graphically described in the 1955-1957 Report of the Fund as follows:

In 1953 the Community Education Project began to develop programs around two of the series of records produced by the National Association of Educational Broadcasters—first *Ways of Mankind*, then *Jeffersonian Heritage*. A newspaper printed specially prepared supplementary readings on the theme. A commercial radio station broadcast the recordings. One thousand people in 97 groups met to listen and then discuss issues raised by the articles and the broadcasts. Most of the groups met in homes.

After using these radio programs, the Community Education Project began the creation of its own dramatic radio-discussion programs. One mass media discussion program entitled *The Living Generation* was the result of the cooperation of the county libraries of Riverside and San Bernardino; six commercial radio stations that serve the Inland Empire; and two newspapers with valley-wide coverage. . . . These radio programs have included not only scripts and original music but also supplementary reading materials, bibliographies, participants' manuals, and special manuals for discussion leaders. . . .

A system of leadership training has evolved. Residential conferences have been used, both for the intensive training of leaders and for general interpretation of the aims and purposes of the Community Education Project. The Project has incorporated leadership training into almost every activity it has sponsored. As the San Bernardino Valley is transformed into a "classroom," thousands of people learn the facts about issues and problems, and, in turn, discuss these matters in an extended "town meeting." [89]

Experiments of a similar character were conducted in Sioux City, Iowa, Salt Lake City, Yellow Springs, Ohio, and other communities. When Eugene Johnson, the architect of the San Bernardino project, moved to Washington University in St. Louis in the mid-1950's he added another dimension to the demonstration of the power of mass media in combination. He instituted the St. Louis Metroplex Assembly, which operated twice a year, each time for a period of six to ten weeks. Each evening program consisted of three units: (1) a half-hour presentation of the issue of the week on television; (2) a one-hour discussion by the more than two hundred listening groups, the findings and questions of which were telephoned in to the station; and (3) a concluding half-hour television discussion. The groups were also serviced with discussion guides provided by the Civic Education Center of Washington University, reading lists of books available from the public library, and newspaper articles appearing before the television program each week.

The nature of the relationship between the mass media and education had changed for the better late in the modern era. The educators learned much more successfully how to make use of print, audio-visual materials, and broadcasting for educational purposes. And the personnel of the mass media became increasingly conscious of their educational responsibilities and roles. A significant contribution was made to this latter development by the institution in 1953 of Leadership Training Awards to persons employed in the mass media. In establishing this program the Fund for Adult Education identified the following purposes: to increase the number of gifted, well-prepared persons in the media; to help improve the quality of training; to promote an understanding of the basic unities beneath the several media; and to encourage persons in the mass media to think of themselves as educators.[90]

Although the number of people in the mass media who saw

themselves as having an educational role was still small and although few of them associated with the organized adult education movement, the direction of movement and the accelerating pace of movement of the mass media gave cause for hope that they were in the process of emerging as a major institutional form of adult education.

Museums and Art Institutes

The number of museums continued to increase after World War I; the American Association of Museums boasted some 800 members in 1961, and there were untold numbers that did not belong. But at the beginning of this period very few of them perceived education to be a central function—and certainly not the education of adults. The traditional view that the museum is a building containing collections of objects and a staff to study and maintain them was tenacious. When a museum did undertake to conduct an active program of education, it was likely to be a program that would please the staff and reflect their professional interests rather than please the public and take into account their interests. The dominant spirit of the program usually tended toward stiffness and formality, with guided tours and lectures organized according to academic principles.

This view began to change, however, as a result of the economic pressure brought on by the depression of the 1930's. As contributions from wealthy patrons diminished, museums became increasingly dependent upon public support. Accordingly, the "curriculum" of the museums began to broaden. Exhibits were redesigned so as to arouse interest, develop an understanding of scientific principles, explain phenomena of contemporary significance, and in other ways be more educative. Where art institutes had previously limited their instructional programs almost exclusively to the preparation of professional artists, they now began offering informal courses in art appreciation and avocational drawing and painting. Planetariums around the country added "Sputniks" to their displays and scheduled special programs explaining the phenomenon within weeks after the Soviet satellite went into orbit.

The methods used by museums also became more varied and

experimental. Informal courses, in which lectures are followed by group discussion, were introduced. Ways were invented for enabling the museum visitor to participate in the educational venture, by manipulating devices, asking questions of experts through intercommunication systems, and the like. Services to outside groups and institutions were expanded and made more available, including the loan of teaching materials and exhibits, program consultation, and the provision of speakers. Increasingly, representatives of the community were brought into the process of planning the museums' own educational programs.

The advent of educational television provided museums with the opportunity to go out into the community to a greater extent than ever had been anticipated. Many museums grasped the opportunity by joining other community institutions in sponsoring community stations, and others cooperated with single-agency stations in producing programs.

Proprietary Schools

As was indicated in Chapter III, the private correspondence school movement had grown to enormous proportions by the end of World War I. It was estimated that in 1925 the money expended in fees to profit-making correspondence schools was in the neighborhood of $70,000,000. In the first major study of this institutional form, published in 1926, Noffsinger found that:

> There is no official list of private correspondence schools because there is no method of registration, official or unofficial, but careful examination has resulted in the compilation of a list of 300 active private correspondence schools; probably there are fifty more. New schools are founded every year; at least a fourth of the 300 now listed were founded in the last five years. These are organized as a rule by men who were at one time salesmen or minor officials of the older, well established and prosperous schools. Seeing the possibilities of quick and easy profits if certain tactics were adopted, these men have decided to make the most of them for themselves.[91]

The study also found that about 80 percent of these schools were owned or controlled by private individuals, and the balance by partnerships and stock companies. A few of them specialized in elementary school, high school, and college courses. A large percentage of these were "diploma mills" which awarded spurious degrees in return for large fees and little work. The vast majority of correspondence schools, however, specialized in vocational subjects—some of them offering a wide range of subjects and others limiting their scope to a single vocation. The legal status of private correspondence schools in most states was that of business enterprises, not of educational institutions, so that they operated almost entirely free of any governmental supervision or restrictions.

Noffsinger concluded his study in 1926 with this scathing indictment:

> Unfortunately the majority of correspondence schools are not well equipped and still less conscientiously conducted. A large proportion of them are not conducted as schools at all. They are commercial enterprises designed to make quick and easy profits. Many of them are in the shady zone bordering on the criminal. A large proportion of those who enroll in correspondence courses are wasting time, money and energy or even are being swindled. . . . On the other hand, there is also a small minority of correspondence schools which, although the making of profit is their first consideration, a dangerous situation at best in education, do none the less give value received and can show a record of concrete benefit to thousands of students.[92]

Correspondence schools were not the only forms created to exploit the hunger of adults for self-improvement. A wide variety of private schools—some of them holding classes in store fronts, others in office suites, and others in elaborate custom-built plants—came into being parallel to the correspondence schools and with many of the same virtues and vices.

In the face of rising criticism several steps were taken to improve the situation:

Many of the private schools took steps on their own initiative to improve their standards. A number of them changed their organizational structure from individual ownership to a non-profit corporation and brought respected educators to serve on their boards. They toned down high-pressure selling practices, raised the qualifications required of their faculties, adjusted their fee scales, and introduced other measures to improve the quality of their services.

Many states passed legislation tightening the restrictions on private schools and in a number of instances put them under the supervision of the state departments of education.

Three types of private schools formed federations to police their own fields. The first of these, the National Association and Council of Business Schools, was organized in 1912 primarily as an informational and promotional agency. Increasing criticism of business school practices forced growing concern for raising standards, and in 1951 the Council established the Accrediting Commission for Business Schools, which was recognized by the U. S. Commissioner of Education as a national accrediting agency. The National Home Study Council was organized in 1926 to raise the standards of the correspondence schools and employed its chief critic, John S. Noffsinger, as its executive director. Its efforts were concentrated on the persuasion of the school owners and the publication of a directory listing the schools meeting its minimum standards. In 1956 the National Home Study Council also established an accrediting commission recognized by the U. S. Commissioner of Education and began publishing a *List of Accredited Home Study Schools*. The third federation was the National Council of Technical Schools, which was incorporated into the accrediting processes of the Engineering Council for Professional Development.

Except for a brief flurry of new private schools of questionable ethics that came into being following World War II in an effort to exploit the G. I. Bill of Rights, the trend in proprietary schools was decidedly toward greater educational responsibility.

Public Schools

In contrast to the excellent statistics available on the development of elementary, secondary, and higher education, the statistical picture of adult education in the public schools was grossly inadequate. The Biennial Surveys of Education did not start reporting the number of teachers and pupils in "part-time, continuation, Americanization, evening, and adult schools" until 1939. In 1948 Kempfer was able to find only nineteen state departments of education that collected comprehensive data on general adult education in their school systems.[93] Therefore, students of public school adult education are largely limited in regard to statistical sources to estimates based on the observations of national leaders, a few sample surveys,[94] and linear studies of particular state and local school systems.

Given these limitations, the main developments of public school adult education in the modern era seem to be the following:

The number of schools providing adult education programs continued to increase and the total enrollment continued to rise. Early estimates of the number of public schools with adult educational offerings and their total enrollment vary widely. Dickerman observed that in 1916 slightly over half a million students were enrolled in public evening schools.[95] Cartwright estimated that in 1924 the number of adults enrolled in public schools programs was 1,000,000.[96] Frederick P. Keppel, in opening the national conference on adult education sponsored by the Carnegie Corporation in Cleveland in 1925, stated that studies made by the corporation indicated that "the evening and other part-time schools total more than 200,000 in enrollment." [97] For the same year the NEA Department of Immigrant Education estimated that 325,000 students were enrolled in classes in adult elementary education.[98] By the mid-1930's estimates were ranging between 1,000,000 and 1,500,000, and by the early 1950's, between 3,000,000 and almost 5,000,000.[99] But the most reliable statistical measure of growth in enrollment in the post-war period was provided by a comprehensive study made by the U. S. Office of Education in 1958, which showed an increase from 2,682,786 in the year 1946-1947 to 4,373,054 in 1956–1957.[100]

The growth in volume of public school adult education enrollments was a result both of expansion within school systems with established adult education programs and of extension of adult education to new school systems. The NEA study of 1952, for example, found that between the 1947–1958 and 1950–1951 school years enrollments increased 37.2 percent in large cities (where adult education programs were established early), 87.7 percent in medium cities, and 100.3 percent in small cities. But adult education was still predominantly a service of the larger school systems.

Another striking characteristic of the growth of public school adult education in this period was the great variation among the states. In the survey made by the U. S. Office of Education for the year 1956–1957, for example, it was found that in the eleven states that provided substantial leadership and state aid for general adult education an average of 4.8 percent of the total population was enrolled in adult schools, while in the states providing some leadership and state aid the ratio dropped to 1.4 percent and in the twenty states providing no state aid the ratio was 1.2 percent. During that year 3.1 percent of the total adult population was enrolled in adult education in the public schools of the thirty-seven states for which figures were available, with a range among the states from 0.2 percent in Mississippi to 8.7 percent in California.[101]

Without question, even considering the unreliability of the statistics, the era following World War I was one of great expansion in public school adult education.

The curriculum of public school adult education continued to broaden. At the opening of the modern era, public school adult education had essentially a three-part curriculum: regular academic subjects, Americanization courses, and vocational courses. In the middle 1920's and early 1930's two forces emerged that exerted a strong influence in the direction of an almost explosive broadening of the curriculum of public school adult education. The first was the widespread adoption of a "need-meeting" doctrine of curriculum building. The notion that the curriculum of adult education should be determined by the needs and interests of the students gained wide currency in the literature of adult education from 1925 on. For example, Eduard Lindeman wrote in 1926:

The approach to adult education will be via the route of *situations*, not subjects. Our academic system has grown in reverse order: subjects and teachers constitute the starting point, students are secondary. In conventional education the student is required to adjust himself to an established curriculum; in adult education the curriculum is built around the student's needs and interests. Every adult person finds himself in specific situations with respect to his work, his recreation, his family-life, his community-life, et cetera—situations which call for adjustments. Adult education begins at this point. Subject-matter is brought into the situation, is put to work, when needed. Texts and teachers play a new and secondary role in this type of education; they must give way to the primary importance of the learner.[102]

Similarly, forceful statements of the doctrine of need-meeting appeared with great frequency in the two periodicals of the field, the NEA's *Bulletin of Adult Education* and the American Association for Adult Education's *Journal of Adult Education,* as well as in the writings of Overstreet, Dewey, and Kilpatrick.

With the encouragement and legitimization of this philosophical spirit and the added impetus of increasing state aid and pressure for quantitative expansion, the public school adult education curriculum began breaking out of its traditional boundaries. The greatest bulges occurred in avocational subjects, especially the arts and crafts, and in such personal development areas as public speaking, vocabulary building, creative writing, and home and family relations.

This trend also received a strong nationwide boost with the entrance of the Federal Emergency Relief Administration (and its successor, the Works Progress Administration) into the field of adult education in 1933. Initiated primarily as a relief measure for unemployed teachers, the FERA made federal funds available for projects by state and local educational authorities in six subject fields: literacy education, general adult education, parent education, workers' education, vocational education, and vocational rehabilitation.

When the Works Progress Administration took over the program in 1935 it sponsored a number of special projects that further contributed to the broadening of the public school programs, including a Writers' Project (which contributed new textual materials), a Radio Project (which contributed transcripts of educational radio series), an Art Project (which contributed instructors in the arts and crafts as well as art collections and displays), and music and theater projects (which made their contributions to the cultural enrichment of the schools and other community agencies). One of the most far-reaching frontier programs of this constellation was a nationwide experiment in public forums sponsored by the U. S. Office of Education under the leadership of John W. Studebaker, who had conducted the prototype of this movement in the Des Moines public schools. At its peak, adult civic education through forums took place in thirty states under the auspices of forum committees created by the state departments of education.

Grattan credits the federal relief program with introducing "thousands of people to adult education for the first time, spreading the idea to groups of people and to geographical areas that hitherto had never been able to experience it and judge its utility." [103] But even more significant effects were the broadening of the curriculum and the freeing of the adult schools' methodology from the shackles of traditional classroom procedure, particularly through the extension of the discussion method.

The new flexibility of the public school adult education programs was well illustrated by their rapid adjustment to the new needs occasioned by the advent of World War II. Within months after the attack on Pearl Harbor schools around the country were offering emergency courses on national defense, training for war industry, rationing, and other timely subjects.

Well before the end of the war attention began turning toward gearing the curriculum to the needs of returning servicemen and war workers who would be going back to peace-time pursuits. The passage of the Servicemen's Readjustment Act of 1944, popularly known as the G.I. Bill of Rights, and the Korean G.I. Bill in 1952, gave tremendous impetus to the back-to-school movement of returning veterans.

The effect of these veterans' educational programs on the curriculum of the public schools was threefold: (1) they impelled the schools to place greater emphasis on counseling; (2) they increased enrollments in vocational and academic subjects (since many veterans wished to complete the requirement for a diploma); and (3) they influenced the schools toward greater flexibility in dealing with older students. Many schools established veterans' institutes, in which the veterans were grouped separately and provided with enriched or accelerated instruction. Many schools gave credit toward a diploma for educational experiences in the armed forces, especially on the basis of results of the General Educational Development Test.

In the early 1950's the curriculum trend toward meeting all the interests of all the people started to come under attack. In the spring of 1951 the California Senate created an Interim Committee on Adult Education to conduct "a study of adult education in California, including federal, state and local regulations, finances, administrations, programs and financial responsibility" in regard to the public schools. During the ensuing year the committee conducted hearings in which much of the public school program, especially the avocational courses, was defined as "frills" and therefore disapproved as an object of state aid by some legislators, taxpayers' groups, and individuals. Strong support for the need-meeting approach to curriculum building came from the public school adult education administrators and teachers, a number of adult students, and many voluntary association leaders.

In its report to the senate the committee stated that:

In determining the recommendations to be made, the committee recognizes and concedes there is nothing "bad" about the adult education program insofar as the types of classes are concerned. Rather, it must agree with many of those who testified that the various courses are all "good."

But the decision for this committee to make was not whether or not such things are good but whether or not such programs were essentially a part of the public school program and within the practical abilities of the State to provide assistance.[104]

The committee made a total of fourteen recommendations for tightening controls and clarifying objectives, but its principal recommendation regarding curriculum was as follows:

A state-supported adult education program should have as its primary objectives the development of a literate and productive society. To this end, the State has a responsibility to assist the public schools in providing adults with the opportunity to attain education necessary for individual literacy, citizenship and productiveness. Classes which are recreational or social or predominantly for entertainment or leisure time activities should not be conducted.[105]

While the Senate voted overwhelmingly for a heavily restrictive bill, the California Teachers Association brought its powerful influence to bear on the side of the adult educators in the Assembly and less restrictive compromise legislation was passed. The programs of the adult schools were modified somewhat—if only, in many cases, to changing the titles of the courses by giving them more educationally respectable labels.

Similar attacks occurred in several other states, the most serious of which took place in New York in the spring of 1958. Without the thorough hearings which characterized the California incident, the New York legislature suddenly cut the amount of money in the Executive Budget for adult education in half, from $4,400,000 to $2,200,000. The National Association of Public School Adult Educators conducted an investigation of this action and reported that it resulted from this sequence of events:

A television program featuring skin diving and fencing classes of one local school caught the attention of at least one legislator who, not knowing that recreational courses do not receive state aid in New York, felt that these courses were an inappropriate expenditure of taxpayers' money. In checking other programs he found similar courses and used these to convince other legislators that tax monies were being misspent on adult activities.[106]

The State Department of Education reacted to this attack by issuing a new set of regulations governing adult education. It raised the average daily attendance required for an individual class to be eligible for state aid, required that all classes must bear "educational titles," and prohibited adults from taking courses in fine arts, homemaking, and similar subjects more than once. The effect of these regulations on the state's public school program for adults was to cause fees to be raised, small courses (mostly in the "serious" subjects) to be dropped, course titles to become more academic in flavor ("Star Gazing" became "Basic Astronomy"), and enrollment to decline. At about the time the new regulations were issued the Board of Regents of the University of the State of New York, under whom the State Department of Education operates, appointed an Advisory Council on Adult Education "to assess the State's efforts in adult education and to prepare a guide for future development of these efforts." The council transmitted its preliminary report on October 13, 1959, stating its conclusion that:

. . . we do not believe that the public schools should be expected indiscriminately to meet all adult needs in their multifarious expressions. We think that those in charge of adult education should analyze the needs and only undertake to meet those that clearly involve creative educational values which are not otherwise available in the communities of our state.

. . . .

Founding our position on the truth that a society is only as sound and fine as the people composing it, we believe that adult education, wisely directed, can make a tremendous contribution to sustaining and raising the quality of the citizens of the State of New York. This, we think, can best be done by providing intelligently for their functional educational needs on the job, in the home, and as citizens and by crowning the structure by offering sound opportunities for them creatively to cultivate their mental, moral and spiritual talents as individuals.[107]

While pressures of a negative nature were thus being exerted on the public schools to narrow their curriculum, pressures of a positive nature were also being exerted, if not to narrow it, at least to deepen it. The moving force in this endeavor was the Fund for Adult Education, which through a series of grants to the National Association of Public School Adult Educators financed a program of conferences and demonstration projects aimed at enlarging the "liberal education" content of the public school adult program.

It is still too early, of course, to assess whether the effect of these forces is great or little, permanent or temporary. But without question the long-run trend in the public school adult education curriculum since World War I was toward covering an ever-lengthening band of the spectrum of adult needs, interests, and concerns.

The methodology of public school adult education was increasingly adapted to the unique characteristics of adults as learners. Following the widespread adoption of the discussion method in the 1930's came a marked expansion in the use of audio-visual aids and nonclassroom forms of activity in the 1940's. Kempfer found, for example, that informal activities were reported by the school districts he surveyed in 1947–1948 in the percentages indicated in Table 2.

The NEA study in 1950–1951 showed that during the preceding five-year period forums, workshops, informal group discussion, and panel discussion were the methods showing the greatest increase in use, while lectures and correspondence courses actually decreased in popularity.

TABLE 2

Percent of Public School Districts Reporting
Informal Adult Education Activities, 1947–1948

Activity	Percent
Exhibits to the public	44.4
Film showings	24.0
Training-within-industry programs	21.2
Workshops or short institutes	14.3
Community center activities	12.4
An open forum	12.3
A concert series	11.9
A lecture series	11.8
Adult guidance services	11.8
Civic education discussion groups	11.5
Directed visiting and observation	10.3
Radio broadcasts for adults	7.7
Film forum discussions	4.9
Training for community leadership	4.4
A little theater	4.0
Radio listeners' groups	1.4

Source: Homer Kempfer, *Adult Education Activities of the Public Schools*. Report of a Survey, 1947–1948. U. S. Office of Education Pamphlet No. 107. Washington, D.C.: Government Printing Office, 1949.

Another strong methodological trend was toward increased participation by the adult students in the activities of the adult education programs. For example, there occurred a marked expansion in the use of citizens' groups in the planning processes of the adult schools and of students in planning, conducting, and evaluating particular learning experiences.

The administrative responsibility for adult education in the public school systems became increasingly centralized and differentiated. It is not known how many full-time directors of adult education (or evening schools) had been appointed by city or county school systems by the end of World War I, but a strong force in this direction was exerted by the tremendous expansion of Americanization and vocational programs that developed during the decade centered around 1920. Subsequent advances in this direction occurred as a result of the expansion of the public school program during the depression years and following World War II.

The trend toward increasing differentiation of the adult educational role in the school systems met with considerable controversy and resistance. Some of this opposition came from outside the schools, but a good deal came from within the educational family itself—over such issues as use of teachers' time and energy, conflict in the use of facilities, division of the budget, academic standards, and teacher certification. But resistance to the establishment of a separate adult educational role did not prevent its spread throughout the country. In 1961 the National Association of Public School Adult Educators estimated that there existed about 500 full-time city directors of adult education and about 3,500 part-time directors or supervisors—and its own membership, composed of school personnel with a primary assignment in adult education, had grown to 5,600.

A parallel, although later-starting, trend toward differentiation of the adult educational function occurred at the state level. While state supervisors of evening schools or immigrant education had started appearing in state departments of education in 1917, responsibility for assisting local communities in the development of general adult education programs was more often grafted on the job description of the Director of Vocational Education, an office established in many states to oversee the disposition of funds received in the states under the several vocational education acts. But an increasing number of states established the special position of director of adult education and assigned it such functions as: collection of statistics; organizing of conferences for state-wide planning and leadership training; certification of part-time teachers of adults; accreditation of adult schools; establishment of standards; allocation of state funds; preparing and publishing resource materials; consulting local school officials concerning program planning, teaching methods, and administrative problems; and otherwise providing leadership for the public school adult education program of the state. By 1960 this position had been established, at least on a half-time basis, in twenty-five states and Puerto Rico.

The public school adult education program received increas-

ing support from local and state tax funds. The precedents in state aid to adult education set before World War I in a few pioneering states were adopted gradually by an increasing number of states in the next few decades. By 1930 twenty-one states had made some provision for state aid for the education of adults, but only seven had provided aid for fields other than Americanization and literacy education.[108] In his 1952–1953 survey, however, Olds found that only ten states could be classified as having "considerable" state aid, and that the remaining thirty-eight had to be classified as having "little or no aid."

The methods of apportioning state aid varied widely among the states, but most of them employed one or more of the following practices:

1. Reimbursement on the basis of clock hours of attendance in classes for adults (average daily attendance).

2. Allocation of a prescribed sum for the instructional cost per class session.

3. Reimbursement of the actual costs of the program.

4. Provision of specific grants for instruction or administration.

5. Matching funds for approved classes.

While there appeared to be little tendency toward standardization of policies and practices among the states in providing state aid to adult education in the public schools, and while this source of support fluctuated sensitively with the general economic and political climate, the general trend in the amount of state aid provided nationally was decidedly upward. The 1958 study by the U. S. Office of Education revealed that state aid for general adult education increased in the ten-year period from 1946–1947 to 1956–1957 from $5,419,433 to $17,927,651.[109]

Local school systems derived support for their adult education programs from a variety of sources. Olds found that in 1952–1953 these sources together totaled an estimated $79,040,000 and that the school districts were arranged as in Table 3 according to their chief source of support.

While many problems remained to be solved to put the national public school adult education program on a sound financial basis, clearly the fact that the public had a stake in the continuing education of adults, and therefore a responsibility for its financing, was becoming increasingly accepted in this country.

TABLE 3

EXPENDITURES BY SCHOOL DISTRICTS GROUPED
BY CHIEF SOURCE OF SUPPORT

School districts grouped by chief source of support	Number of districts	Total expenditures for adult education
Veterans Administration payments	1,920	$22,270,000
State and federal aid for vocational education	1,307	6,370,000
Fee or tuition payments	761	3,220,000
School district or local tax funds	771	20,720,000
State aid for general adult education	741	11,720,000
No single source predominant	533	14,740,000
School districts without adult education	10,984	
Total	17,017	$79,040,000

Source: Edward Olds, *Financing Adult Education in America's Public Schools and Community Councils,* p. 19. Report of the National Commission on Adult Education Finance. Chicago: Adult Education Association, 1954.

Public school adult education programs became increasingly related to the rest of the community. In its early stages of development, public school adult education's constituency consisted almost exclusively of the individuals who came to its buildings for course instruction. In the modern era this constituency increasingly came to be made up of the total community.

One evidence of this trend was the growing extent to which public school adult education activities took place outside of school buildings. Kempfer found, for example, that in 1947–1948 13 percent of all districts with adult education activities reported using other public buildings; 7 percent, factories and stores; 6 percent, homes; 6 percent, church buildings; 4 percent, club rooms; 2 percent, settlement houses; 1 percent, museums; and 4 percent, other places such as camps, libraries, parks, playgrounds, and swimming pools.[110] Another evidence was the increasing use of public school facilities by outside organizations—often with the adult education staff providing program assistance. For example, in a survey conducted in 1958 in preparation for a national conference on architecture for adult education, a sample of 204 adult education leaders named high schools as the place where their programs most frequently took place. Of these only 43 were high school personnel, 36 were from colleges and universities, 28 from community centers, 4 from business and industry, and 3 each from libraries and labor unions.[111]

Religious Institutions

The Protestant and Catholic churches, and to a somewhat lesser degree the Jewish temples and synagogues, continued to lag behind many other institutions in the expansion and differentiation of adult education well into the modern era. A number of factors which influenced the churches toward modernization of their educational programs and methods can be identified, but one student of these institutions suggests that the most compelling was that their members began to fulfill their needs in associations other than the church, with the result that the church sensed a threat to its claim on its members. Accordingly, this observer concludes, "many churches re-evaluated their approach to the individual and, in order to keep members in the church, began educating them not only for 'life in heaven' but also for 'action on earth.' "[112]

Because the institutions of the three major faiths created different forms for the education of adults, their development in the modern era can best be described separately.

DEVELOPMENT IN PROTESTANT CHURCHES. The differentiation of an adult educational role in the Protestant church structure occurred very gradually and spottily. At the local level, a few of the very largest churches established the position of director of adult work or assigned a minister to this function. At the denominational level, the trend was more marked but still far from universal.

At the national interdenominational level, an attempt to build a unified adult program for American Protestantism was made with the founding of the United Christian Adult Movement under the auspices of the International Council of Religious

Education in 1936. This movement's most concrete contribution was the launching of a "Learning for Life Program" which kept the lights of thousands of churches burning on week-day nights. The program provided study materials for a variety of elective courses grouped under seven main headings: (1) The Bible and Life; (2) Personal Faith and Experience; (3) Christian Family Life; (4) Church Life and Outreach; (5) Community Issues; (6) Major Social Problems; and (7) World Relations. The International Council had a position in which adult work was combined with other functions from the early 1930's until it was reorganized as the Division of Christian Education in the newly formed National Council of Churches of Christ in the United States of America in 1950. In this new federation of some forty denominations a Department of Adult Work was established within the division, with a staff headed by a Director of Adult Work.

While the Bible remained the focus of most adult educational activities in the Protestant churches and uniform lesson plans were used as the primary resource in many, there was a distinct trend away from the traditional lecture-recitation format. Deffner found that "there is basic loyalty to 'fundamentals'—the basics of doctrine and belief—but mostly through discussion techniques, an inductive approach and a practical application of Scripture to the daily lives of the members." [113] Week-day courses available in churches across the country included such secular subjects as: preparation for marriage, child development, dancing, handicrafts, politics, drama, literature, music, economics, and many others. A large number of churches sponsored public affairs programs and a variety of social action projects. The programs of the various men's and women's clubs, couples' clubs, oldsters' clubs, and other auxiliary organizations frequently contained substantial educational content.

A development that occurred in the decade of the 1950's with special significance for the emerging role of the Protestant churches in the education of adults was the broadside introduction of group techniques into the educational activities of the churches, accompanied by massive programs to train lay and professional leaders. For example, starting in the early 1950's several denominations instituted nationwide programs of workshops for leadership training in group methods. The launching of one of these was described in the *International Journal of Religious Education* as follows:

> During the last few years the church has begun to awaken to the transforming power which can be released in groups when certain conditions are met. An ambitious training program has been sponsored by the Protestant Episcopal Church. Within a five-year period, about 3,500 of their clergy and directors of Christian education are being trained at two-week laboratories on "The Church and Group Life." [114]

In 1956 the National Council of Churches' Department of Administration and Leadership inaugurated an annual "Protestant Laboratory on Group Development" at Green Lake, Wisconsin, and by 1959 several hundred "graduates" of these summer sessions were busy conducting leadership workshops in their respective denominations.

Several of the denominations supplemented these face-to-face training programs with new periodicals and other training materials. For example, in 1945 the General Board of Education of the Methodist Church started publishing the monthly *Adult Teacher;* and in 1957 the Board of Christian Education of the Presbyterian Church in the United States of America inaugurated the quarterly *Westminster Adult Leader,* as well as a new series of "Adult Leadership Leaflets."

At the state level a pioneering series of experiments was conducted in Indiana by Indiana University and Purdue University in cooperation with five denominations in that state in an endeavor to discover ways to improve the educational quality of the adult educational activities of the churches.[115]

Probably a major turning point in the development of Protestant churches as institutions for the education of adults occurred with the convening of two workshops on the Christian education of adults at the University of Pittsburgh in 1958 and 1961. Sponsored jointly by the School of Education of the university and the Department of Adult Work of the National Council of Churches, these workshops brought together over eighty denominational leaders and a dozen nationally known secular education specialists to re-examine the assumptions on which adult educational practices in the churches were based and to propose ways in which the churches can improve their services to the estimated

14,190,000 persons enrolled in their adult church school departments.[116]

DEVELOPMENTS IN CATHOLIC CHURCHES. As has been true of many adult education institutions, war produced one of the major innovations in Catholic adult education. In 1917 the National Catholic Welfare Council was founded to "promote the spiritual and material welfare of the United States troops during the war . . . and to study, co-ordinate, unify, and put in operation all Catholic activities incidental to the war." In 1919 the Council was transformed into a permanent organization to serve as the official agency of the Hierarchy of the United States for the promotion of broad religious, educational, and social interests of the American people. The NCWC carried on an active program of publications giving the Catholic view on current questions and issues, helped Catholic immigrants, and sponsored Catholic lay organizations. Of these latter, the National Council of Catholic Men conducted programs through the mass media explaining Catholic teachings on religion, economics, sociology, and international affairs; and the National Council of Catholic Women acted through 12,000 local affiliates in the presentation and discussion of important issues, with emphasis on problems in the fields of education, community welfare, family life, and parenthood.

Among the most extensive adult educational programs under Catholic auspices were those sponsored by the Social Action Department of the NCWC. They included a Catholic Conference on Industrial Problems, Social Action Schools for priests, Catholic Labor Schools, and an Institute on International Relations. NCWC also stimulated a continuous program of study groups by providing an article and discussion outline in each month's issue of its periodical, *Catholic Action*. The Confraternity of Christian Doctrine additionally promoted religious discussion groups for adults and religious education of children by parents in the home.

In the Catholic scheme of things in this country a high degree of autonomy was exercised by each local diocese in carrying out the directives of the Encyclical Letters (especially *Christian Education of Youth, Christian Marriage,* and *Reconstruction of the Social Order* by Pope Pius XI and *The Condition of Labor* of Pope Leo XIII) and the program of the American Hierarchy and its national agencies. In the final analysis the character and extent of adult education in any community was dependent upon the interest and skill of its priests. Accordingly, there was a wide variation across the country in Catholic adult education. For example, the Sheil School of Social Studies, which operated successfully in Chicago for several years after World War II, remained purely local, while the Cana and Pre-Cana Conferences, which also originated in Chicago in 1944 for education on marriage and family life, spread by osmosis to many other dioceses.

In 1955 a small group of priests, nuns, and lay people interested in Catholic adult education began meeting in connection with the annual conferences of the National Catholic Education Association. In June 1958 this group was formally organized as the National Catholic Adult Education Commission. It immediately launched several projects designed to assemble current information about Catholic adult education (*A Handbook of Catholic Adult Education*); improve communications among Catholic adult educators (annual conferences), and between Catholic and other adult educators (participation in the Religious Education Section of the AEA); and upgrade the skills of Catholic adult educators (summer workshops and leadership training schools).[117]

DEVELOPMENTS IN JEWISH RELIGIOUS INSTITUTIONS. Much the same kind of tension between traditionalism and modernism that affected Protestant adult education characterized the growth of adult education in Jewish synagogues and temples. There tended to be agreement among all types of synagogues that Jewish adult education should be concerned with four basic aims: (1) psychological reassurance for the individual Jew, reducing self-doubt and even self-hatred; (2) fostering an intelligent loyalty to the Jewish community; (3) restoration of the traditional Jewish ideal of "learning for its own sake"; (4) drawing members closer to their synagogues and making prayer and worship a significant part of their lives. But in the matter of precedence among these aims there was considerable difference between the Orthodox, Conservative, and Reform groups. According to Rabbi Feldman:

Orthodox Jews emphasize the information and training necessary for the full observance of traditional Jewish laws, customs and observances. Reform Jews, on the other hand, emphasize 'cultural' Judaism rather than observances; problems of relationships between Jews and non-Jews, and problems of ethics and character building. Conservative Jews generally stand midway between the Orthodox and Reform ideologies, balancing observance and adult education for 'culture,' and emphasizing the importance of understanding Jewish history.[118]

In methods of programing, adult education tended also to depend on a difference among types of synagogues. Orthodox congregations favored the classroom type of program involving intensive study based on texts. Reform temples leaned toward large meetings featuring lectures, debates, and recitals, with opportunity for audience participation. Conservative synagogues mixed the two. A program pattern that was adopted widely in the Conservative and Reform synagogues was the Congregational Institute of Jewish Studies, sponsored by a single synagogue or cooperatively by several congregations and community agencies. An institute met one evening a week for from six to thirty weeks, with the first hour devoted to small study groups on Hebrew, Bible, Jewish history, and other basic subjects, and the second hour to a major lecture series attended by all participants in the earlier classes. Many synagogues also offered series of morning or afternoon classes for women.

A good deal of the responsibility for Jewish adult education was carried by the national Jewish lay organizations, such as the American Jewish Congress, B'nai B'rith, and Hadassah. For example, among the fastest growing programs in adult Jewish education were the Institutes of Judaism sponsored by B'nai B'rith, in which groups of individuals gathered at isolated resorts for several days of intensive study with Jewish scholars.

Although the Jewish religious institutions were traditionally permeated with an educational atmosphere, little was done to differentiate their adult educational function. The situation was assessed critically by two contemporary Jewish adult education leaders as follows:

In the typical synagogue, adult education enjoys a marginal status only. Though all congregations have a special budget and a special committee for child education, few have such a budget or committee for adult education. If there is an adult education committee, it has a low priority rating. Rarely does a trained director administer the program, and the instructional staff is seldom specially qualified. In nearly every case, the rabbi directs all activities, but his seminary courses have overlooked the field of adult education almost entirely, and the growing literature and increasing professionalism in the general field are virtually unknown to him.[119]

Today, however, the sad reality is that much of what passes for adult study is not worthy of the name. Some of it might better be called indoctrination or promotion of specific Jewish causes or specific branches of Judaism. There is a wide range of interpretation on what aspects of Judaism to teach and for what purpose, and in certain areas there is too much unselective clinging to tradition for its own sake with too little thought about its relevance today.[120]

Both critics saw hopeful signs. Lily Edelman, from the vantage point of a lay organization, B'nai B'rith, saw a growing number of Jewish leaders, rabbis, and professional educators coming to realize that adult Jewish education would do well to divorce itself from the narrow partisan or sectarian approach and to align itself with the forces of liberal adult education. Rabbi Feldman, from his vantage point as the director of the Department of Adult Education of the New York Jewish Education Committee —which was established in the early 1950's to carry on action-research in Jewish adult education—made the following assessment:

Definitely a leaven is at work in Jewish education and congregational life that should end the years of neglect. Rabbis and educators in many places are beginning to think, talk and act in terms of professionalism rather than provincialism. We are in the midst of transitional years which will lay the groundwork for a vigorous, healthy program of congregational adult Jewish education.[121]

Voluntary Associations

The basic pattern of voluntary organizations had been established by 1920, but the formation of new assocations continued in the modern era. Of the ninety-two voluntary associations (separated out from health and welfare agencies) listed in the 1960 *Handbook of Adult Education in the United States,* fifty-nine were founded before the end of 1920 and thirty-three came into being afterward. Some of these new associations reflected the

152   THE EMERGENCE OF INSTITUTIONS

development of new professions (such as the American Management Association, the American Personnel and Guidance Association, and the American Physical Therapy Association); others, the development of new institutions (such as the American Association for the United Nations, the Association of University Evening Colleges, and the National Association of Educational Broadcasters); others, new special concerns (such as the Gerontological Society, the Muscular Dystrophy Association, and Planned Parenthood); and others, new patterns of relationship (such as the National Health Council, the National Association of Intergroup Relations Officials, the National Home Study Council, and the Council of National Organizations of the Adult Education Association).

Certain general trends and developments can be discerned in this complex institutional setting that have special relevance to the education of adults.

Voluntary associations tended to broaden the scope of their adult educational activities. Most voluntary associations came into being to advance a cause of some sort—the correction of a social evil, the conquest of a disease, or the improvement of the status and condition of a minority group (women, Negroes) or of a professional or occupational group (physicians, librarians, teachers, agricultural extension agents). Accordingly, in its early stages of development a voluntary association typically centered its educational activities around building up its own organizational strength (orientation of members, training of leaders, interpretation to the public) and promoting its cause (propaganda, social action). As it became established as an organization and achieved some progress toward advancing its cause, the voluntary association turned an increasing amount of attention toward the development of its members and of the community on an ever-broadening scale. [122]

The adult education function in voluntary associations tended to become increasingly differentiated. In 1920 very few voluntary associations had identified a separate adult educational role in their organizational structures. For example, of the eleven representatives of voluntary associations who attended the Carnegie Conferences preceding the formation of the American Association for Adult Education in 1925–26, only four possessed titles that in any way suggested concern with adult education. But in the ensuing years, and especially after World War II, an increasing number of associations established first committees in many cases, and then departments with full-time staff to provide leadership specifically in adult education. In the directory of national organizations of the 1960 *Handbook,* of the ninety-two voluntary associations listed, fifteen were wholly adult educational organizations, with professional adult educators as chief executives, and twenty-five had distinguishable adult educational positions with such titles as director of education, continuing education services director, director of program development, and national training director. In other organizations, many with paid staffs combined the adult education function with other functions in a more general office, and many without paid staffs assigned this function to an adult education committee.

With increasing differentiation of the adult education function, voluntary associations engaged in an expanding program of specialized leadership training for the leaders of adult educational activities. A study conducted in 1959, revealed that twenty-two out of thirty-three national associations surveyed were conducting intensive in-service training programs for their professional and volunteer workers in adult education methods.[123]

The increased differentiation of function also enabled voluntary associations to focus their publications more directly on adult educational targets. These materials included journals and house organs, leadership manuals, informational pamphlets and leaflets, research reports, study guides, and many other types of publications. The total distribution of these publications was enormous: one study found a circulation of around two million periodicals and pamphlets by voluntary associations in Minnesota alone.[124]

The voluntary associations became increasingly active in co-operative endeavors with other agencies of adult education. While the frequency of joint sponsorship of such activities as adult education week and program planners' institutes was increasing at the local level, this trend was most marked at the national level. Especially close alliances were established between local and state units of voluntary associations and their public school and university extension services, which served as resources in the development of materials, the planning of programs, the securing of speakers, and the training of leaders. Voluntary association leaders were also appearing in increasing numbers at meetings of the local adult education councils and state adult education associations.

But the greatest impetus to the expansion of interassociational cooperation—and, indeed, to the upgrading of the adult educational programs of voluntary associations in every respect—came with the establishment in 1952 of the Council of National Organizations by the Adult Education Association, the program of which is described in detail in Chapter VII.

SUMMARY

During the forty years between 1920 and 1960—under the stimulus of two world wars, a great depression, and a rapidly accelerating pace of change in technological, economic, political, and cultural affairs—adult education became an integral part of the American way of life. Whereas before 1920 the term "adult education" did not appear even in the professional educational vocabulary, by 1960 this term was widely used as a symbol of a significant aspect of the national institutional system. Indeed, during this period the variegated activities for the education of adults began to become organized into an adult educational field.

PART TWO

THE SHAPING OF A FIELD
OF ADULT EDUCATION

CHAPTER V

❦

THE DEVELOPMENT
OF COORDINATIVE ORGANIZATIONS
WITHIN SEGMENTS
OF THE FIELD (TO 1961)

One of the phenomena that occurred in the course of the growth of adult education in this country that greatly affected the task of developing an integrated movement was the emergence of organized groupings within various segments of the field. Some of these groupings became established before the notion of a national movement of adult education had even been envisioned; others came into existence after the founding of a national coordinative association, but without reference to it. Not many of them perceived coordination to be one of their aims; indeed, the central purposes of most of them centered around fellowship, self-protection, and professional development. But since their existence and activities tended to establish communications, loyalties, sense of responsibility, and cooperation within the boundaries of particular segments of the field, they did in fact produce some degree of segmental coordination.

Three categories of segmental groupings have appeared in the field of adult education: (1) institutional groupings, (2) subject-matter groupings, and (3) geographical groupings.

INSTITUTIONAL GROUPINGS

The institutional settings in which adult education developed provided an obvious and natural basis for segmental organiza-

tion. Within each institutional setting could be found some degree of specialization of aims, structure, clientele, and methods
that produced problems different from those of other institutional settings. Some of these specialized problems could be dealt
with more effectively when treated separately by those working
in the respective institutional settings than when treated in
connection with general problems of the larger field. There was a
natural tendency, in addition, for the persons working in a given
institutional setting to derive special personal satisfactions from
associating with people working in other institutions in the same
setting. Thus, there were both functional and psychological reasons for the formation of institutional groupings of adult education workers.

Business and Industry

The earliest interinstitutional organizations to appear in this
segment of the field were general-purpose organizations with
only a peripheral concern for adult education.

The National Association of Manufacturers was organized in
1895 as a federation of manufacturing companies (in 1959 its
membership consisted of 21,000 companies) to represent industry to the public and to government. Its education department has sponsored meetings between manufacturers and educators to consider common concerns in the education of adults
(especially in vocational and economic matters), has produced
a variety of educational materials, and has conducted special
workshops and seminars for representatives of member companies, particularly in the area of political action. The NAM
has not attempted to provide machinery for intercommunication among adult education workers in industry as a separate
group. But its identification with the general field is indicated
by the fact that it was one of the original participants in the
Council of National Organizations and the NAM's Director of
Education served as one of the early presidents of that organization.

The Chamber of Commerce of the United States was organized
in 1912 "to protect, strengthen, and improve the private business
system and to translate economic growth into human progress."

Its membership in 1959 consisted of 22,000 individual business-men and 3,400 organizations, including local chambers of commerce. The education department of the U. S. Chamber has developed special projects, sequences for study groups, and other activities for local and state chambers of commerce to consider. It has also sponsored summer institutes for executives of local chambers. The U. S. Chamber was also an early participant in the Council of National Organizations of the AEA.

The *American Society of Association Executives* was organized in 1920 to provide a mechanism through which the executives of trade associations could work together on common problems. It has sponsored an annual conference and periodic regional meetings for its 2,000 members and local affiliates. It has not been closely related to the national coordinative organizations in the general field of adult education.

The *American Society of Training Directors* has been the one organization in this segment of the field which has specifically served people performing adult educational roles. It was established in 1945 to provide the usual services of a professional society for training directors in business and industry and staff members of industrial training centers in universities. Its program has included an exchange service, a directory, annual conferences, basic and advanced institutes, regional conferences, seminars, and workshops. It has published a monthly magazine, the *Journal of the American Society of Training Directors* with materials of both a scholarly and a practical nature. In 1959 it had almost 4,000 members and sixty-eight local chapters. Although it has not been active as an organization in any of the national coordinative organizations, some of its individual leaders were active in the Adult Education Association, and one of them served as president for one year and as treasurer for several years.

Colleges and Universities

The first general meeting on university extension was held in Philadelphia on December 29 to 31, 1891, under the auspices of the American Society for Extension of University Teaching. Almost one hundred delegates came from twenty states, almost

exclusively in the northeastern section of the country. The con-
veners of the meeting had a preconceived plan for creating a
General Society of University Extension to serve as a bureau of
information about university extension for the entire country.
They had a plan of representation in a general council consisting of one representative besides the president of each college, together with the state superintendents of public instruction.[1] Enthusiasm for the plan was expressed at the meeting,
but leadership to implement it did not emerge and no subsequent meetings were held. But later two coordinative organizations did emerge which exerted powerful influence on this
segment of the field.

The *National University Extension Association* came into being as a result of a second national conference on university
extension held in Madison, Wisconsin, on March 10 to 12, 1915.
A constitution was adopted on April 13, 1916, which provided
that "the purpose of this Association is the establishment of an
official and authorized organization through which colleges
and universities and individuals engaged in educational Extension work may confer for their mutual advantage and for the
development and promotion of the best ideals, methods, and
standards for the interpretation and dissemination of the accumulated knowledge of the race to all who desire to share in its
benefits." The constitution further provided that membership
be limited to "colleges and universities of known and recognized
standing whose sole aim is educational service," and that "the
principle of representation in this Association shall be institutional rather than official or individual." [2] Twenty-two universities became charter members of the new association, and
by 1959 its membership had grown to eighty institutions.

The program of the NUEA has consisted primarily of conferences, committee work, and publications. The *Proceedings* of
its annual meetings document the leadership that the association
has provided in helping the general university extension movement to mature in philosophy, structure, administrative practices, professional standards, instructional methods, and relationship to the outside community. Its committees have been
instrumental in stimulating research and in influencing many important developments in the field, including the establishment

of the United States Armed Forces Institute; the Engineering, Science and Management War Training Program; the National Film Council; the Educational Film Library Association; and audio-visual, radio, and television services in various universities. It has published a monthly *NUEA Spectator,* the *Proceedings* of its conferences, and periodic reports of studies.

The *Proceedings* of the NUEA reflected an awareness from the very beginning of a relationship to and responsibility toward the general field of adult education that is unique among segmental organizations. For example, in the first meeting there was a report on the relation of extension departments to discussion clubs, local leadership, and state medical societies. In the 1922 *Proceedings* appeared a discussion of cooperation with the agricultural extension movement; in 1923, with the Workers' Education Bureau, the National Academy of Visual Instruction, and local community organizations; in 1925, with public and state libraries and the United States Bureau of Education. While the NUEA was not officially represented at the founding of the American Association for Adult Education in 1926, Leon J. Richardson, extension director of the University of California, was chairman of the National Executive Committee and presided at the founding meetings.

The NUEA played an active role in connection with the founding of the Adult Education Association. It was one of the five national organizations which co-sponsored a national conference on adult education in Detroit on April 23–26, 1946, which set in motion the forces that resulted in the founding of the AEA in 1951. The NUEA also gave strong leadership in the founding of the Council of National Organizations of the AEA in 1952, and its delegate was elected the first chairman of the council.

The *Association of University Evening Colleges* emerged in 1939 as an offshoot of the Association of Urban Universities, which had been organized in 1915. Membership in the AUEC grew from the thirty-three charter members it possessed in 1939 to one hundred and twenty-eight institutions in 1959. With its growth in size came growth in structure and program. Committees were organized that conducted numerous studies, furnishing data for the improvement of instruction, teacher selection and training, curriculum building, services to the community, and promotion of evening college education. Other committees worked on television education, education-industry relations, research, and liberal education.

Although in its early years the AUEC tended to be primarily concerned with the internal problems of its segment of the field, as it matured its concerns broadened. In 1949 it accepted an invitation to membership on the Joint Commission for the Study of Adult Education. And its leaders were active in the formation of the Adult Education Association in 1951 and the Council of National Organizations in 1952.

But one of the crowning achievements of the AUEC was the establishment in 1951 of the *Center for the Study of Liberal Education for Adults* under a grant from the Fund for Adult Education. The center has had three major areas of interest: improving university programs of liberal education for adults, developing improved methods of teaching and discussion leadership, and building a climate of understanding and support for liberal adult education in the colleges and universities and in the general public. Its program has included four types of activity: a research program conducted by the staff, a clearinghouse for collection and distribution of information, a series of publications, and conferences and consultation. The center sponsored a series of leadership conferences that brought leaders of adult education work in the evening colleges and university extension divisions together, often with representatives of other segments of the field, to consider needs and strategies for future development. Its publications, which have included *Notes and Essays* (a series of pamphlets on problems and issues in liberal adult education); *Reports* (including research studies, surveys, and program descriptions); a *Clearinghouse Bulletin;* and various discussion guides, have been widely used both inside and outside the college and university segment. By virtue of the leadership it exerted and the communications lines it established, the center has become one of the principal coordinative agencies within the college and university segment. It has accepted responsibility for relating its work to the larger field of adult education, as evidenced by its involvement of representatives of other segments in its conferences, by the extent to which it has made its publications available to the general field, and by the extent to which it has entered into such activities of the Adult Education Association as the Council of National Organizations, conferences on architecture and residential adult education, and the work of the Commission of Professors of Adult Education.[3]

Cooperative Extension Service

The Federal Extension Service has operated as the principal coordinative agency for the vast agricultural extension system in this country—by virtue of its services, not through any coordinative authority. Its extensive leadership training workshops, statistical reports, monthly *Extension Service Review*, reports of educational research, and miscellaneous training materials and program guides have provided educational leadership, have opened communications lines, and have contributed cohesiveness to its segment of the field. Through its close policy ties with the American Association of Land-Grant Colleges and State Universities, the Federal Extension Service has maintained close liaison between agricultural extension and the larger institutional field of which it is a part. Indeed, this relationship has tended to be valued most highly by extension workers, so that when they have had a choice of attending a meeting of this association or of a general adult education organization, they usually have chosen the former.

Professional relationships in this segment have been maintained through four professional societies: (1) Epsilon Sigma Phi fraternity, to which all extension workers with ten years or more experience are eligible to belong; (2) the National Association of County Agricultural Agents; (3) the National Association of County Home Demonstration Agents; and (4) the National Association of 4-H Club Agents. All of these societies have organized district and state chapters, and their programs have featured meetings and periodical publications.

The Cooperative Extension Service as a whole has not been especially closely related to the general adult education movement. But certain key leaders of the federal staff have occupied important posts on the executive committee and various program committees of the Adult Education Association, and the county agents' and home demonstration agents' associations have participated in the activities of the Council of National Organizations.

Foundations

Although three foundations were highly active in supporting adult education and numerous others demonstrated a peripheral interest in the field, there was no evidence of any relationship among the foundations concerning their role in the field up to 1961.

Government Agencies

A number of government agencies have been active in the field of adult education, and a considerable number of employees in the various departments have worked full-time in it, but no permanent mechanism has been established for inter-agency coordination or communication. *Ad hoc* committees were established to coordinate the various government agencies in relation to particular activities, such as the White House Conferences, but these dissolved with the passing of the event for which they were created. With the creation of an Adult Education Section in the U. S. Office of Education in 1955, a resource was brought into being which at least potentially could serve a coordinative purpose.

Health and Welfare Agencies

Three organizations have provided coordinative services in the field of health and welfare, and a fourth has served the field of voluntary health agencies.

The National Conference on Social Welfare (formerly the National Conference of Social Work) has conducted annual forums since its founding in 1874. In these forums social workers and interested lay citizens have come together to discuss the problems and methods identified with the field of social work and immediately related fields. Its group work and community organization sections have been especially concerned with matters related to the education of adults. Although it has not separated out the adult education function in social welfare for focal treatment, it has evidenced its awareness of relationship to the field of adult education by participating in the Council of National Organizations of the AEA.

The *National Social Welfare Assembly* was organized in 1945 as the central national planning organization for social welfare. Its membership consisted in 1959 of 110 individuals (nominated by 43 affiliate national voluntary organizations, 14 federal agencies, and 5 associate groups) and 83 members-at-large (elected). It has pursued its objective of facilitating more effective operation of organized social welfare through the studies, reports, and projects of its committees and divisions. Its interests have touched the field of adult education most closely at the points of young adult education, group work, health education, and service to the aging. The assembly has not, however, participated officially in any activities of a national coordinative adult education organization.

The *National Association of Social Workers* was formed in 1955 as the result of a merger of seven separate professional groups from different areas of social work practice. The conference, committee, and publication activities of the NASW have chiefly been concerned with the strengthening and unifying of the social work profession and improving social work practice. It has established no mechanism for dealing with the adult educational concerns of social workers, and its only indication of interest in the general adult education movement has been to send observers occasionally to the meetings of the Council of National Organizations of the AEA.

The *National Health Council* was established in 1921 "to help the national health agencies work more effectively together and with others in the cause of health improvement of the nation." Its program consists of forums, conferences, and publications, and its membership consists of sixty-seven affiliated national voluntary health organizations. It has shown no awareness of a relationship to the general adult education movement.

Independent and Residential Centers

No organization has emerged outside of the Adult Education Association itself for the coordination of this institutional grouping.

Labor Unions

The *Workers' Education Bureau of America* was organized in 1921 as the first attempt to coordinate the adult education work of the labor union movement. The purpose of the new organization was "to collect and disseminate information relative to efforts at education on any part of organized labor; to coordinate and assist in every possible manner the educational work now carried on by the organized workers, and to stimulate the creation of additional enterprises in labor education throughout the United States." Membership was open to all trade union bodies, cooperative associations, and labor education enterprises.

During its first two years the WEB was a service agency to organized labor, rather than an agency of organized labor, and it derived its financial support principally from the contributions of individuals. But in 1923 the American Federation of Labor constituted the WEB the official agency for carrying on workers' education efforts for its own members, and a year later it started appropriating moderate funds for its operation.

The program of the WEB included the publication of books and pamphlets, conferences and institutes, a news service, radio talks, correspondence courses, and consultation services. The WEB was active in the process of founding the American Association for Adult Education, and its secretary and director, Spencer Miller, Jr., was a prominent member of its leadership circle during most of its existence. Between 1926 and 1933 the American Association for Adult Education made grants to the WEB totalling $99,000 for general support, publications, and institutes.

When the Congress of Industrial Organizations was organized in 1938, it established a Department of Education. While it provided many of the same services for the CIO unions that the WEB provided for the AFL unions, it placed special emphasis on staff training in political and social action. The CIO Education Department did not participate in the activities of the AAAE nearly as actively as the WEB, but it was much more active in the formation of the Council of National Organizations of the AEA from 1951 on.

It is truly remarkable, in view of the rather sharp difference in educational philosophy between the AFL and CIO educational departments, that they were able to come together into a single department when the parent organizations were merged into the AFL-CIO in 1955. In the politics of the merger, however, the top office in the new education department was given to the AFL, and the continuing tensions within the staff over their differing conceptions of the role of workers' education may account for the relative inactivity of the department in the general adult education movement.[4]

The *Department of Education of the AFL-CIO* was established to encourage, assist, and support educational programs of local unions, trade councils, city central bodies, state central bodies, regional agencies, and national and international unions. It has maintained an extensive film library, produced and distributed a large volume of materials (including the monthly *AFL-CIO Education News and Views*), provided staff consultation, and conducted resident summer schools and special institutes. Its annual conferences have served as the principal meeting place for the paid and volunteer educational leaders in the trade unions of this country, and as the instrument through which they have spoken to the public regarding the educational issues of the day. Except for rather apathetic participation in the activities of the Labor Education Section of the AEA, which has brought together persons interested in workers' education from a variety of institutional settings, it has not related itself closely with the general adult education movement.

The *American Labor Education Service* was organized in 1927 as a loose federation coordinating the activities of workers' summer schools, but later broadened its purpose to that of cooperating with local and international trade unions "in stimulating educational programs among trade unionists, emphasizing dem-

onstration and experimentation in the field of labor education."
The program of the ALES has placed special emphasis on the
sponsorship of summer schools for white collar workers and on
the development of materials and institutes on public affairs.
Eleanor Coit, its director since its founding, has given consistent
and active leadership in the affairs of both the American Association for Adult Education and the Adult Education Association of the U.S.A.

The *National Institute of Labor Education* has exerted a
coordinative influence between the labor movement and the
labor education specialists in various universities. In 1951 the
Inter-University Labor Education Committee was established to
administer a grant from the Fund for Adult Education for the
purpose of widening the scope of labor education activities in
the areas of foreign affairs, economics, and community participation. Through its program of studies, conferences, and experimental projects, the IULEC demonstrated the value of a
mechanism for continuing university-trade union cooperation,[5]
and in 1957 the National Institute of Labor Education was
founded with the endorsement of the Executive Council of the
AFL-CIO, from which it derives substantial support. The major
purpose of the NILE has been to expand the scope and volume
of labor education and to enlarge the cooperation between labor
and nonlabor agencies in the field of education. It is too early,
of course, to assess the effects of this new organization, but from
the outset it has made a point of relating itself closely to the
coordinative agencies of the general field.

Libraries

The *American Library Association* has served as the principal
coordinative agency or the general library field. The first mech-
anisms created by the ALA for the coordination of the adult
education work of the libraries were the *Commission on the
Library and Adult Education* (1924–1926) and the *Adult Education Board* (1926–1957), the activities of which have been
described in Chapter IV. But these were both administrative
operations, and in 1927 the first mechanism was established for
the facilitation of a membership grouping in this area of inter-

est. In that year the *Adult Education Round Table* was formed, with responsibility to plan and conduct meetings at the annual conference in which librarians with a special interest in adult education could meet together. In 1944 the Round Table became the Adult Education Section of the Division of Public Libraries, and in 1950, with the merger of the Division of Public Libraries and the Library Extension Division, the Adult Education Section became the Adult Education Committee. In 1952 the committee was again granted section status in the Public Libraries Division. Obviously, the librarians were having difficulty in finding the right place for this burgeoning new function in their social system.

The *Adult Service Division,* established in 1957 as a result of a general reorganization of the ALA structure, accorded full divisional status to adult education alongside such other central library functions as Children's Services, Library Administration, Reference Services, Library Education, Resources and Technical Services, and Young Adult Services. With a full-time headquarters staff and a membership that grew to four figures, this new division has carried responsibility "for those library services designed to provide continuing educational, recreational, and cultural development for adults in all types of libraries. This responsibility has included the identification and evaluation of library materials which are useful in adult services (except reference); the stimulation of the production and use of such materials; and the identification of the principles involved in their selection and use." The division has had specific responsibility for: (1) continuous study and review of the activities assigned to the division; (2) conduct of activities and projects within its areas of responsibility; (3) synthesis of the adult educational activities of all units within ALA; (4) representation and interpretation of its type of activity in contacts outside the profession; (5) stimulation of the development of librarians engaged in adult education; and (6) planning and development of programs of study and research for this type of activity for the total profession.

From the beginning of the modern era the library profession has been increasingly cooperative with other segments of the field. From her examination of the reports of the Adult

Education Board of the twenties and thirties, Stevenson identifies examples of cooperation between the ALA and such organizations as the League of Women Voters, the Congress of Parents and Teachers, the National Education Association, the National University Extension Association, the U. S. Office of Education, and others, on projects, publications, conferences, lists, and other activities.

But from the point of view of the general coordination of adult education, the fact that the ALA has given continuous and active leadership in the formation and operation of the American Association for Adult Education, the Adult Education Association of the U.S.A., and the Council of National Organizations is of particular significance. Carl Milam, the executive secretary of the ALA at the time of the founding of the AAAE, was a member of its first Executive Board. Grace Stevenson was the sixth president of the AEA in 1957–1958 while serving as deputy executive director of ALA. Librarians have been prominent in the leadership circles of both organizations in many other capacities. The ALA was one of the five national organizations constituting the Joint Commission for the Study of Adult Education in the late 1940's, and John Cory, Executive Secretary of the ALA, served as chairman during much of its life. When the AEA was organized in 1951, the ALA contributed office space for the new organization's headquarters staff during its first year. Many other evidences could be cited to show that the library profession, while achieving increasing coordination in its own segment of the field, succeeded in bringing that segment into increasingly closer relationship to the rest of the field.

Mass Media of Communications

Early attempts to establish coordinative services in regard to adult education by radio through a National Advisory Council of Radio in Education, a National Committee, and the National Association of Educational Broadcasters have been described in Chapter IV. Of these, the only organization to survive to the present time is the last, the NAEB.

Established in 1925, the *National Association of Educational Broadcasters* has served three coordinative purposes: (1) as a professional association for men and women engaged in educational broadcasting; (2) as a programing network, distributing tape-recorded programs to member stations; and (3) as the trade association of educational institutions operating radio and television stations, closed-circuit television operations, and radio and television production centers. Its membership in 1959 consisted of 460 individuals and 324 institutions. Between 1951 and 1961 the NAEB received generous support from the Fund for Adult Education for projects designed to improve the quality of educational broadcasting through the production of experimental programs, the conducting of workshops and conferences, and the awarding of scholarships. It has become increasingly closely related to the general adult education movement, especially through its participation in the Council of National Organizations of the AEA.

Several abortive attempts to develop similar coordinative services in regard to audio-visual and motion picture operations in the field of adult education were made in the decade following World War II. These included the Educational Film Library Association,[6] the Joint Committee on Film Forums,[7] the Commission on Motion Pictures in Adult Education,[8] and the Film Council of America.[9] But apparently this specialized service was too peripheral a concern of adult education workers to warrant a separate coordinative organization.

The *Joint Council on Educational Television* (which was organized in 1951 as the Joint Committee on Educational Television) has provided an effective coordinative service in the field of educational television. A federation of ten national organizations, the JCET has served as a source of information on TV channel allocations and government regulations and actions regarding educational TV; has published regular reports on the status of educational TV; has provided consultative service to groups planning to establish educational stations, including information on legal, technical, and engineering matters; has maintained legal representation for educational TV in Washington; and has represented educational TV in matters concerning the total national development of the television art. It has not established any official relationship with the AEA or the Council of National Organizations.

In the area of printed materials no equivalent coordinative organization has emerged so far as the adult education function is concerned, although the American Book Publishers Council, as the trade association of commercial publishers, has cooperated with the American Library Association on projects concerning the use of books in adult education. On the whole, the producers of books, newspapers, and magazines have remained outside the organized field of adult education. Their adult educational roles have been so ill-defined that a coordinative function has not even been considered.

Museums and Art Institutes

The *American Association of Museums* has served as the sole coordinative organization for this segment of the field since the association's founding in 1905. Its annual meetings have dealt with topics of interest to each type of museum represented in the association, including history, art, and science museums, college and university museums, children's museums, national and state park museums, planetariums, and industrial museums, as well as to such professional groupings as museum librarians, registrars, preparators, superintendents, and other specialists. It has also sponsored regional conferences and published an annual *Museums Directory*, a monthly *Museum News*, and miscellaneous leaflets, bulletins, and books.

As was pointed out in Chapter IV, the museums have lagged far behind most other institutions in differentiating their adult educational function. At the local level they have moved into varying degrees of relationship with other agencies of adult education, but at the national level there has been little evidence of identification with the general adult education movement.

Proprietary Schools

The three coordinative organizations that have served this segment of the field—the *National Association and Council of*

Business Schools, the *National Home Study Council,* and the *National Council of Technical Schools*—have already been described in some detail in Chapter IV. The first two of these organizations have identified themselves quite closely with the general adult education movement through their participation in the Council of National Organizations of the AEA.

Public Schools

The *National Education Association* has served as the coordinative organization for the professional employees of the public schools for over a century. Organized in 1857 as the National Teachers' Association, it amalgamated in 1870 with the American Normal School Association and the National Association of School Superintendents and changed its name to the National Education Association. This event also inaugurated a complex conception of organizational structure in which the NEA serves as an umbrella under which three types of organizational elements cluster: (1) departments, which are semi-autonomous professional societies organized according to functional roles (elementary school principals, secondary school principals, classroom teachers, and others); (2) committees and commissions, which make studies, maintain liaison, or conduct programs in large areas of professional interest cutting across departmental lines (such as educational policies, legislation, professional standards); and (3) divisions, which are headquarters staff groupings to provide specialized services to the entire organization (such as accounts, membership, publications, and press and radio relations).[10]

In view of the fact that the adult educational function had begun to be differentiated in public schools before the turn of the century, it seems surprising that no professional grouping of adult educational workers appeared in the NEA until the *Department of Immigrant Education* was authorized by the Representative Assembly in 1921. Originally the membership of this department came from the administrators (and a few teachers) of the then-flourishing Americanization programs. But in 1924 the leaders of the department decided that its title should be broadened to include those working with native illiterates, and the name was changed to *Department of Adult Education*. With the founding of the American Association for Adult Education in 1926 the destinies of these two organizations became so intertwined that subsequent developments in both of them are treated together in Chapter VI.

In 1945 a *Division of Adult Education Service* was established to provide staff service to carry on the NEA's interest in adult education in the public schools over and above the activities of any membership organizations for public school adult education workers that might exist. The division served as an instrument for providing consultation services to schools and other agencies and as a headquarters for membership organizations of public school adult educators.

In 1951 the Department of Adult Education was dissolved and its membership was absorbed into the newly created Adult Education Association of the U.S.A. But shortly thereafter a new membership organization came into being, the *National Association of Public School Adult Educators,* which was so closely related to the AEA that developments in these two organizations are described together in Chapter VII.

As will become clear in the next two chapters, the public school segment of the adult educational field experienced difficulty in differentiating itself clearly from the general field—a fact that created special problems in the development of a coordinated field.

Religious Institutions

Beginnings were made in developing coordinative organizations among the Protestant denominations through the Department of Adult Work of the Division of Christian Education of the National Council of Churches, and among Catholic adult educators through the National Catholic Adult Education Commission, which are described in Chapter IV. No similar trend toward national organization has appeared in regard to the adult educational function in Jewish religious institutions, although the Department of Adult Jewish Education of B'nai B'rith has provided services to the Orthodox, Conservative, and Reformed Jewish congregations. While the Religious Education Association has for many years served as a meeting place for persons of all faiths who are concerned with the general area of religious education, it has never identified adult education as a separate concern. Indeed, the first national attempt at an interfaith approach to problems of religious adult education was the initiation of special interest meetings on this subject at the annual conferences of the AEA in the late 1950's.

Voluntary Associations

While some voluntary associations have joined with health and welfare agencies in the coordinative activities of the National Conference on Social Welfare and the National Social Welfare Assembly, no mechanism has ever been established for the coordination of voluntary associations as such.

SUBJECT-MATTER GROUPINGS

Since most full-time adult education workers are employed in roles of general supervision or administration, they have not tended to identify strongly with particular subject-matter areas. Accordingly, subject-matter groupings have never been a prominent feature of the organized adult education movement in this country.

A relatively small number of people, however, have worked full-time on their subject specialty in the education of adults. For this group, membership in a subject-matter grouping has been equal in importance to their membership in an adult education organization. In some cases the chief result of this duality of interest has been conflict within the individual as to where he will invest his time, energy, and money. But where there has been a clustering of adult education workers in a given subject-matter society, the effect has often been to tend to bring that society into closer relationship with the adult education movement. This phenomenon has occurred especially in the case of several departments of the NEA, including the American Association for Health, Physical Education, and Recreation, the Music Educators National Conference, and the Speech Association of America; and in the case of such other subject-matter organizations as the

Society of Public Health Educators, the Gerontological Society, and the American Vocational Association. On the whole, however, the cooperation between these general subject-matter organizations and the national adult education coordinative organizations has been at the level of exchanging observers at conferences, reprinting articles, and distributing materials.

GEOGRAPHICAL GROUPINGS

Early in the development of the organized adult education movement in this country it was recognized that if there was to be an effective coordination of resources for the education of adults, the primary loci of that coordination would have to be the local, state, and regional geographical units in which the vast bulk of adult educational services originate. Accordingly, a variety of patterns of organization at these levels has been attempted.

Local Coordinative Organizations

It is difficult to determine when or where the first local adult education council came into being, since many of them started as program-operating agencies and only gradually became transformed into coordinating organizations. The earliest to be mentioned in the literature is the Institute for Social Relations founded by the Civic Federation of Dallas in 1919. This institute carried on a program that included a library, an open forum, and classes in such subjects as social hygiene, history of religion, history of philosophy, dramatics, and democracy, largely in cooperation with other community organizations—especially "non-academic professional associations." [11] When the Carnegie Corporation made a grant through the AAAE in 1927 to provide general support for the institute from 1927 to 1933, the director of the AAAE assessed the Dallas group as "possibly the best of the community organizations for adult education." [12]

A somewhat similar program was inaugurated in 1924 in Chicago with the founding of the Chicago Forum (incorporated in 1925 as the Chicago Forum Council) for the stated purpose of promoting understanding and good will in the community by bringing people of different groups into friendly association with each other for discussion of problems related to the public welfare. In 1929 its name was changed to the Adult Education Council of Chicago and its purpose was amended to include the encouragement of cooperation among educational agencies in raising the general level of intelligence and culture. Until 1929, however, its program consisted almost entirely of presenting internationally famous speakers each Sunday at Orchestra Hall.

The city that is usually credited with being the site of the first full-fledged adult education council is Cleveland, where the Adult Education Association of Cleveland was formed in 1924.[13] Although its main program consisted of organizing study groups, it undertook from the outset also to suggest study programs to clubs and other organizations and to disseminate information about the adult educational opportunities throughout the city. In 1927-1928 it engaged in a comprehensive study of the cultural needs of the city and of the opportunities for further cooperation among the various agencies in meeting these needs.

In rapid order new councils (or "conferences") were formed and received Carnegie grants for studies and experimental programs in Buffalo (1925),[14] Brooklyn (1929),[15] and New York City (1932). Additional councils were organized without Carnegie support in Pittsburgh (1932), Toledo (1933), Schenectady (1930), Milwaukee (1933), and Richmond (1933).[16] In 1934 a Carnegie grant was given to the Adult Education Council of Denver as "the first large city council to be organized by and conducted from a public library." [17]

Interest in local coordination had grown to such a point by 1934 that the AAAE assembled delegates from sixty communities in a special conference following its annual meeting in May "to hear reports on typical community enterprises . . . ; to review the technical organization and procedures of community and state surveys; to consider questions of leadership, the mobilization of community resources, the interchange of ideas in a community, and the functions of community councils; and to discuss practical problems of organizations." Pressure was put on the AAAE at this meeting to take a more active part in organizing and strengthening local councils, but the executive committee "felt that too little was known about the present operating scope of existing urban and state groups to embark upon any considerable program of direct assistance, even assuming such an action on the part of a national association to be wise." Instead, the AAAE assigned a staff member as a field representative to collect information about and provide consultative assistance to local councils.

In 1937 the AAAE financed the establishment of an *Inter-Council News Letter* which was published quarterly through a pooling of the services of the Denver, Cincinnati, and New York councils. The *News Letter* reported the activities of local, state, and regional councils and gave an annual directory of the councils known to be in existence each year. During 1949 and 1950 the *News Letter* was incorporated into the *Adult Education Journal* as a special section of that quarterly publication, and thereafter news about local councils was treated as part of the general "News of the Field" in the *Journal,* then in *Adult Education,* and since 1952, in the AEA's *Adult Leadership.*

During the era of the AAAE (1926–1951) local councils proved to be elusive and volatile. Where the 1934 *Handbook* is able to list eleven councils in local communities or counties, the 1936 *Handbook* listed twenty-three, and the 1948 *Handbook* was down to twelve, but the 1949 Directory of Adult Education Councils in the *Inter-Council News Letter* was able to identify twenty-eight.[18] It is interesting to note that eight of the eleven councils listed in 1934 appeared in the 1949 list, while only ten of the twenty-three councils in the 1936 list were in the 1949 list. While these discrepancies are partly the product of inadequate information-getting procedures on the part of the list builders, they also indicate that some of the local councils brought into being in the enthusiasm of the early 1930's did not last long, and others went through periods of dormancy.

The founding of the AEA and the Fund for Adult Education in 1951 introduced another period of activity in the establishment of local community organizations. In 1951 the Fund for Adult Education launched its Test Cities Project, in which a dozen medium-sized communities more or less evenly distributed geographically over the country were selected "to discover whether or not these communities are interested in experimenting with new approaches to the development and coordination of adult education on a community-wide basis." The project had two specific purposes: "(1) to test old, and invent new, methods of stimulating and integrating adult education activities at the community level; and (2) to determine the extent to which Fund-supported programs are useful educationally to various groups and various segments of the population within the community." [19] Three-year grants, in diminishing amounts, were made to groups in the dozen communities who organized "councils" to sponsor the project. While some latitude was allowed to local groups in determining their programs, all were expected to organize experimental discussion groups to test the use of the Fund's study-discussion package programs and were urged to involve the mass media of their communities in the program. In actual practice, the majority of the "test cities" felt a greater pressure on them to serve as salesmen for the Fund's package programs than to provide coordinative services, with the result that with the withdrawal of funds from the Fund for Adult Education most of them went out of existence as councils and their program-promotion functions were transferred to individual institutions under the Fund's "Test Centers" project inaugurated in 1955.

The Adult Education Association undertook to assist local councils primarily through field consultation. Its most ambitious undertaking in this regard was an Area Organization Project, described later in this chapter. The AEA also resumed the sponsorship of meetings of leaders of local councils at its 1956 annual conference and published materials designed to help local community organizations become more effective.[20] These activities presumably had little effect on the total number of councils, since the invitation list for a meeting of local council leaders at the 1959 AEA annual conference contained twenty-seven councils.

Typically, local adult education councils have attempted to serve the needs of five constituencies as follows:

1. The needs of the "consumers" of adult education for information about educational opportunities available to them and for assistance in making choices about them. The means councils have used for meeting these needs include counseling, directories of educational activities, "adult education week" visitation programs, announcements in the mass media, and news letters.

2. The needs of individual adult education workers for fellowship, personal growth, identification with larger causes, assistance in the solution of practical problems, and information about trends and developments in the larger movement. The means councils have used to meet these needs include monthly membership meetings; training workshops; the sending of delegates to state, regional, and national meetings; visitations by national leaders; consultation; and news letters.

3. The needs of adult educational agencies to assess total community needs, plan together, be informed about the plans and activities of one another, bring about a better understanding of their programs on the part of the public, and influence certain community policies. The means councils have used to meet these needs include interagency planning meetings; information-exchange meetings and publications; joint promotion and interpretation campaigns; community surveys and studies; program directories; social action activities; and interagency projects (such as the sponsorship of "adult education weeks").

4. The needs of the community-at-large for adequate assessment of its adult educational needs, adequate interpretation of their implications, adequate information about existing resources, and effective use of resources in meeting its needs. The means councils have used in meeting these needs include the creation of community advisory councils; community surveys and studies; directories and other informational publications; experimental projects to test new approaches to community need-meeting; and joint planning activities.

5. The needs of the national movement for liaison with the adult education programs of local communities and their participation in the determination of national policy. The means councils have used in meeting these needs include providing opportunities for national leaders to meet with local leaders; keeping the national coordinative organization informed about local needs, activities, and plans; taking responsibility for interpreting national goals, activities, and plans to local leaders; and sending delegates to national meetings.

The chief obstacle to the achievement of stability and effectiveness in local councils, as well as to their extension to other cities, appears to have been their difficulty in obtaining financial support. Olds found that in 1954 only six of the sixteen councils not in the Fund for Adult Education's Test City Project had budgets of $5,000 or more per year, three had budgets of approximately $12,000, and one (New York) had a budget of about $34,000. All councils derived some income from membership dues and individual contributions, but these were the chief sources of support in only two of the councils with budgets of $5,000 or more (New York and Denver). Three received substantial support from the community chest (St. Louis, Cleveland, and Cincinnati), one of which (Cleveland) was a functional unit of the Welfare Federation supported entirely by the community chest. Several councils received substantial services or income from host institutions. For example, the Cincinnati, Denver, and Milwaukee councils were provided headquarters space by their respective public libraries; Denver received large contributions in addition from the public school system and the University of Denver; the Springfield, Massachusetts, council received both headquarters space and staff service from the public schools. Two councils derived substantial earnings from their own services: Chicago, from the operation of a commercial speakers' bureau and the publication of a directory of local colleges; and New York, from a year book containing paid advertisements, special money-raising events, and service fees.[21]

The statement often appears in the literature that the adult education council movement in this country was launched under the handicap of foundation nurture which prevented local councils from developing strong local financial roots, so that when foundation support was withdrawn they collapsed. The record does not support such a generalization. Of the eight local community organizations that were given direct subsidies by the American Association for Adult Education in the late 1920's and early 1930's (Buffalo; Cleveland; Denver; New York; Brooklyn; Dallas; Leonia, New Jersey; and Radburn, New Jersey), the first four have survived to the present day and are among the strongest councils in the country; and the last four were highly specialized experimental projects intended to produce new knowledge or programs, not new councils primarily.

So far as financing local councils is concerned, Olds concluded from his study:

The ideal pattern, towards which some communities are heading, would seem to be major support by the public school system, the local college or university, and the public library system with some support coming from the Community Chest in recognition of services rendered member agencies, and membership dues paid by private individuals. Denver appears to be coming close to this pattern and each council illustrates it to some degree.[22]

But difficulty in financing has not been the only obstacle to the development of strong local councils in this country. Confusion of purpose and structure stands out as another. Each of the five constituencies of local councils imposes unique organizational requirements which few councils have delineated in their structure: (1) The meeting of the needs of the consumers of adult education involves the establishment of liaison with major groupings within the socio-economic substructure of the community and with the mass media to an extent not yet achieved by any council. (2) The meeting of the needs of the individual adult educators requires an associational structure with a high degree of cohesiveness. Most councils have provided the associational structure through individual memberships, but few have succeeded in overcoming the prior institutional loyalties of their members to the extent required for high cohesiveness. (3) The meeting of the needs of the adult educational agencies requires a mechanism for the official representation of the individual agencies in a process of joint planning. This, of course, is essentially what is meant by "council," a body composed of representatives of organizations. While all councils have made provision for organizational members, few of them have established machinery for them to deliberate as representatives of their organizations. In most councils, the role of individual member and the role of organizational representative have not been delineated; the council function has been confused with the associational function, with the result that little joint planning has been accomplished. (4) The needs of the community-at-large require the involvement of the power structure of the community in the policy structure of the council. Yet the policy-making bodies of most councils have been composed almost entirely of paid workers on the firing line of adult education—dedicated persons but low in the power and influence structures of their communities. Beginnings have been made in remedying this situation, notably in Chicago and St. Louis, by adding influential citizens to the boards of directors. (5) The meeting of the needs of the national adult education movement requires some mechanism for tying local councils into a network of intercommunication, joint planning, and policy influencing with state, regional, and national coordinative organizations. No such machinery has ever been established, and it is unlikely that it will be—or can be—until local councils become more universal among the cities of the country.

Coordinative functions are also performed by more general-purpose community councils and councils of social agencies, and through informal relationships among adult education workers. The suggestion has been made that attempts to maintain specialized adult education councils should be discontinued and that their functions should be taken over by general community organizations. To this proposal Kotinsky replies as follows:

> There is in fact no need for an either-or position. The two types of organization are closely related, but do not substitute the one for the other. Community organization is, in effect, among other things a program of adult education; the council is an instrument for encouraging the free play of intelligence among adult educators in devising and implementing all the programs of adult education in the community.[23]

The record of experience to date seems to indicate the following: (1) the needs of the five constituencies of coordinative organizations exist in every geographical area populous enough to support organized adult educational services, and (2) these needs are generally not met or are met inadequately, except when they are the explicit and primary concern of an organization.

State Coordinative Organizations

The first comprehensive state-wide coordinative organization to be recorded in the literature was the California Association for Adult Education, organized in 1927 to "give form and impetus" to the adult education movement in that state and to render service to existing educational agencies in three ways:

> 1. By giving assurance through repeated experimentation that adults, whatever their previous education, are able to study even profound subjects if properly presented.

2. By promoting education in the arts, social studies, literature, and science so successfully that all skepticism concerning the interest of adults in cultural development may be dispelled and proof given that Americans will continue their education without the promise of improving their earning capacity and applying what they learn directly on their jobs.

3. By carrying on demonstrations in various communities throughout the state, and developing suitable methods for teaching adults, using every possible approach to arouse people's interest in continuing their education.[24]

During its first two years the work of the California association was financed by private contributions supplemented by fees for lectures given by the director, Lyman Bryson. But starting in 1929 the Carnegie Corporation, upon recommendation of the AAAE, made a series of grants totalling $19,000 for a three-year period to support the association's program. Under the philosophy that its chief purpose was to "promote and strengthen whatever was already in the field, and to undertake experiments which might be of value to existing groups if they turned out successfully," rather than "to create a super-organization, or to impose itself upon any established effort," [25] the association conducted a variety of experimental discussion groups, forums, library clubs, broadcasts, and institutes on "serious" subjects.

With the expiration of the Carnegie funds, the diminution of support from private contributions owing to the depression, and the loss of the services of its illustrious director, the program of the association was drastically curtailed in the autumn of 1932. The last project developed by the director before this curtailment was a plan for the creation of a state office of adult education, to be organized as follows:

It was to be manned by a small staff, the members of which should be state employees, responsible to the president and regents of the University but not under the same regulations as members of the University staff nor subject to faculty committees. Policies of the bureau were to be determined by the Board of Directors of the Association, and the Association was to be expanded to include many nonscholastic bodies.[26]

Some objections were raised to this plan on the score of the danger of standardization of adult education and the dominance of the university in its operation, but enthusiasm for it was generally quite high among organizational leaders and educators throughout the state. It failed to obtain legislative appropriations principally because of the economy-mindedness that came with the onset of the depression, and it therefore was never implemented. But it remains as a model of a state-supported general coordinative organization, and this may still be the best ultimate solution to the problem of state-wide coordination of adult education.

Other state organizations came into being during the 1930's and 1940's. Four were listed in the 1934 *Handbook*, seven in the 1936 *Handbook*, and eleven in the 1948 *Handbook*. In the 1950's, largely under the stimulus of the AEA's Area Organization Project, there was another flurry of organization that brought the total of state councils, committees, or associations up to twenty-seven.

The constituencies served by state organizations have been essentially the same as those served by local councils, except that their "community" has been the total state, and the agencies with which they are concerned were the state-wide educational institutions and associations and state-wide voluntary organizations. The organizational structures created to serve these constituencies have varied considerably. Some state organizations have been associations of individual members; others have been councils of agency representatives; others have been committees of interested adult educational leaders; and others have been simply annual conferences. The majority of them have been combinations of the association and council forms of structure, with the confusion of role between individual member and agency representative alluded to above in relation to local councils being typical. The work of state organizations has been accomplished primarily through the voluntary energies of dedicated members, although one, Pennsylvania, attempted to support a part-time paid executive. On the whole the state organizations that have demonstrated the greatest strength and stability are those in which headquarters services have been provided by a state institution, such as the state library, state university, or state department of education.

The programs of state organizations have universally emphasized intercommunication among adult education workers, primarily through conferences and newsletters. Two states, Indiana and Michigan, have experimented with the substructuring of their states into districts or regions in an attempt to bring about closer relationships and better communications among adult education workers in different communities. Other activities by state organizations have included the conducting of state-wide surveys of adult educational needs and resources, the sponsorship of training institutes, the publication of directories of agencies and their programs, the stimulation of research, the conducting of experimental projects, and the facilitating of joint planning among state-wide agencies. A few, notably Michigan, have undertaken to exert influence on state legislatures for enlarged support of public adult education.

Financially, state organizations have typically been subsistence-level operations. Except for the temporary support of the California association by the Carnegie Corporation, foundations have not perceived them as being fruitful objects of support. Accordingly, they have been almost wholly dependent on contributed services from state agencies and small membership dues. In 1956 the Adult Education Association inaugurated a Joint Membership Plan designed to strengthen the financial position of state organizations. Under the Joint Membership Plan all members of the national organization in a state were automatically incorporated into the membership of the state association, with 20 percent of all dues collected in the state being returned to the state organization. The state organization served these members with publications and conferences, and took responsibility for membership recruitment and maintenance in its state for the national organization. Perhaps of even greater ultimate significance, under this plan the state association became an official constituency and organic element of the national organization, in that it elected the representatives of its state to the Delegate Assembly of the national organization. By 1959 seventeen state organizations had affiliated with the AEA under this plan, with a total of 2,500 joint members. For the first time in the development of adult education in this country a link was being established between the state and national coordinative functions.[27]

Regional Coordinative Organizations

The existence of a Pacific Northwest Association for Adult Education was noted in the 1934 and 1936 *Handbooks,* with this description appearing in the latter:

Membership consists of individuals and organizations interested or engaged in adult education in Idaho, Montana, Oregon, Washington, and Alaska; purpose is to foster interests of adult education in Pacific Northwest through conferences and discussions; annual conferences held successively in each of 4 states.[28]

But not until 1937 was the idea of regional organization given serious consideration across the nation. In that year the American Association for Adult Education, with subventionary grants from the Carnegie Corporation, sponsored a series of thirteen regional conferences in Minneapolis, Spokane, Trenton, Cincinnati, Denver, Boston, Lake Geneva, Wisconsin, Chapel Hill, North Carolina, Los Angeles, St. Louis, Toledo, Pittsburgh, and Dayton. These conferences were assessed to be successful for two reasons: "they provide opportunities for the intensive discussion of local problems; and they make possible the participation of a large number of persons active in adult education who can not afford to spend the time and money necessary to attend a national conference held in a distant city." [29] Accordingly, the AAAE contin ued to sponsor regional conferences for the next several years— seven were held in 1938, eleven in 1939, and fifteen in 1939-1941. After this year the AAAE discontinued its financial support of these conferences, but several of them continued on their own.

Out of this experience four formally organized regional organizations emerged: (1) the Southeastern Adult Education Association, (2) the Missouri Valley Adult Education Association, (3) the Mountain Plains Adult Education Association, and (4) the Southwestern Adult Education Association. The Pacific Northwest Association had gone into a state of dormancy by 1951. The activities of these regional organizations have been limited almost exclusively to the holding of annual conferences, with the exception of the special projects described later.

The most comprehensive development of regional organization was attempted through the Area Organization Project carried on by the Adult Education Association under a grant from the Fund for Adult Education between 1952 and 1955. The objectives of the project were (1) to increase the competence of adult educators through more effective conferencing and organizational service; (2) to strengthen existing adult education councils and associations and to help create new organizations where they are needed and desired; and (3) to spread adult education beyond its present boundaries, and to involve the not now identified adult educators in the movement. The first undertaking of the project was to collect information about exising patterns of relationship and feelings of need among adult educators through questionnaire surveys and a series of twelve regional exploratory conferences. On the basis of the findings of these activities, the project next engaged in three regional projects, in which (1) the Missouri Valley association undertook to determine what kind of services a regional office might give to adult educators, and how such services could be supported; (2) the Mountain Plains association undertook to develop a system of interconsultation among the communities and between the states of its regions, and to provide specialized training for community consultants; and (3) the Southeastern association undertook to establish better communications among the nine states in its region, using its annual conference as a focal point. As a result of these projects, the programs of the three regional associations were greatly strengthened, several state associations and local community adult education councils were brought into being, and a series of recommendations were formulated to guide future policy development on the part of the national organization. In addition, several documents were published containing factual information and technical suggestions of use to coordinative organizations at all levels.[28]

SUMMARY

Clearly, there has been a tendency toward the development of substructural organization within the field of adult education. The natural process of clustering adult educational workers and organizations into systems of relationship has tended to define the field in terms of three dimensions: an institutional dimension, a subject-matter dimension, and a geographical dimension. But this process has been far from uniform and is far from complete. The organization of subgroupings has progressed much further within the institutional and geographical dimensions than it has within the subject-matter dimension. But within each dimension some subgroupings are much more highly organized than others, and glaring gaps in substructural organization occur in all of the dimensions. Most importantly, the relationship of these various parts to one another and to the whole field of adult education has not been systematized and made clear.

CHAPTER VI

☸

STRIVINGS FOR

A NATIONAL ORGANIZATION FOR

ADULT EDUCATION, 1924–1961

EMERGENCE OF THE IDEA

There was apparently little awareness of a need for a comprehensive national organization to serve the total field of adult education prior to 1924. Statements were made in meetings as early as 1892 regarding the importance of cooperation among agencies, but they referred to relationships between particular agencies, not to the coordination of the whole field.[1]

Credit for introducing the vision of a unified field of adult education belongs overwhelmingly to one man, Frederick P. Keppel. Shortly after he assumed the presidency of the Carnegie Corporation of New York in 1923, Keppel became disturbed by the paucity of information about adult education in this country and by the fact that "though many national bodies deal with different parts of the field, there is no agency that concerns itself with the problem of adult education as a whole ." [2]

Keppel appointed a committee of distinguished citizens to advise the Carnegie Corporation whether "a comprehensive study of the present situation might be made" in order to provide the corporation with "a guide for such grants as it might be in a position to make from year to year in this field." [3] The advisory committee members prepared a series of statements setting forth their views on what kinds of studies were needed,[4] and arrived at a consensus that the Carnegie Corporation should sponsor: (1) a general study to "call attention to the most significant en-

190

terprises in each branch of Adult Education"; (2) intensive studies "of some few parts of the whole problem"; and (3) scientific
studies, such as "a study of the psychology of the learning process
in terms of different age levels." The early perception regarding
the role of a national organization can be discerned from this
further proposal:

> Some form of independent organization, composed of competent and
> responsible men and women, shall be set up, who shall thereafter make
> themselves responsible for recommendations to the Corporation regard-
> ing grants in the field of Adult Education, and under whose direction
> and control such grants as may be voted by the Corporation shall be
> administered.[5]

A series of conferences was then called to consider the organization of a new national organization for adult education.[6] The
first of these was a national conference held in Cleveland on October 16–17, 1925, which was attended by forty-two individuals
from a wide variety of agencies and institutions. Following an extensive exploration of the meaning of adult education, a number
of descriptive reports as to what various individual agencies were
doing in adult education, some discussion of the purposes and
possible tasks of a national organization, and considerable expression of hostility toward profit-making adult education enterprises,
the conference agreed to proceed with the formation of a national organization and tentatively adopted a constitution as a
basis of organization.[7]

Regional conferences were then held in New York City (December 15, 1925), San Francisco (February 8 and 9, 1926), Nashville (February 19, 1926), and Chicago (March 24, 1926). At
each of these meetings "unanimous endorsement was given the
proposal for the formation of a national association, and a committee of seven was appointed to attend a national meeting formally to inaugurate such an association." [8] It should be noted,
however, that this "unanimous endorsement" was not achieved
without some reservations being voiced. For example, in the New
York meeting Leroy Bowman, a lecturer in sociology at Columbia University, stated:

> I think the thing that is most helpful to us is not to start out with
> some preconceived idea, not even that we are all reformers. Instead of
> an organization or association of any kind, I think it might be more

worth while occasionally to get together in conferences of this kind, with no idea of something to "get across," but so that we can realize that the other fellow has something of value and that we need his point of view. . . . It seems to me that the function of a group like this is to get together and have conferences and not to try for an organization. The less of it the better! [9]

The opposing point of view was stated by Will Durant, then the director of the Labor Temple School in New York: "I'm amazed at the hostility of Mr. Bowman to organization. How can we get anywhere unless we organize? I protest against the notion that we must have no organization." [10] Obviously this was the prevailing sentiment, for at the National Conference on Adult Education and Organization Meeting of the American Association for Adult Education held in Chicago on March 26, 1926, the twenty-three delegates representing the four regional conferences voted unanimously for the constitution establishing the AAAE.[11]

THE AMERICAN ASSOCIATION
FOR ADULT EDUCATION

Setting

Several general observations can be made about the setting of the founding of the American Association for Adult Education which seem to have special significance in the light of subsequent developments:

1. The delegates to all the conferences preceding the founding meeting were selected by the Carnegie Corporation and attended by invitation of the corporation as individuals; they brought with them no commitment from any constituency and felt no obligation to report back to any constituency.

2. The individuals selected by the Carnegie Corporation were overwhelmingly people of personal distinction who had little direct contact with the day-to-day operation of adult educational programs. Consequently, the practitioners in general, and the public school practitioners in particular—the most numerous single group in the field,—were under-represented.

3. There was little knowledge—indeed, considerable misinformation—about the field with which they were concerned, with resulting insecurity about judging which were the critical elements in it; in fact, there were almost phobic attitudes toward the profit-making agencies of adult education, and these agencies were expressly excluded from membership in the association.

4. From the very beginning anxiety was expressed over the dominant influence of a foundation in the preparations for establishing a national organization which presumably would be responsible to a whole field. One delegate at the New York Regional Conference, for example, raised the question regarding the new association's having power to recommend who would get grants from the Carnegie Corporation by asking, "Shouldn't we be very careful in doing things that might seem to indicate control through subsidies or grants? We should be careful, I think, not to lay ourselves open to the fear, on the part of friends and enemies both, that we are getting into a goose step—that control would follow a subsidy." [12] And the elaborate ritual that attended the invitation of the Carnegie Corporation's representatives to join the founding meeting of the AAAE had the effect of highlighting their dominant influence:

Chairman Richardson: I cannot finish these introductory remarks without expressing a word of gratitude to an organization that has assisted us in holding these conferences and in taking the necessary steps in order to get on with our first business. I refer, of course, to the Carnegie Corporation of New York. . . . I am wondering, therefore, if I should express the sentiment of this organization if I were to be allowed to appoint a committee to invite Mr. Keppel and his associates to join our meeting this morning. Does any one want to make a motion to authorize me to take this action?

Mr. Victor I. Cartwright: I so move.

The motion was seconded and carried.

Chairman Richardson: The motion has been made, seconded, and carried unanimously. I shall ask Mr. Bestor, Mr. Snell, and Miss Richardson if they will proceed as a committee and invite Mr. Keppel and his associates to join our meeting. Our business will be suspended for three or four minutes until our guests arrive.

Mr. F. P. Keppel, Mr. Nathaniel Peffer, and Mr. Morse A. Cartwright joined the conferees.

I should like to say to Mr. Keppel and his associates that a very friendly expression has recently been passed by this body, and I hear a desire expressed for a word from Mr. Keppel if he cares to give it to us at this time.

Mr. F. P. Keppel: . . . I am very glad to be able to say that the trustees of the Carnegie Corporation . . . authorize me to say that an association founded in this way can be assured not of luxurious or extravagent support, but of a reasonable minimum. . . . The appropriation for overhead will cover five and one-half years.[13]

5. An early precedent was set for delegating responsibility for the important decisions to executive committees; there was very little involvement of the delegates themselves in the preparatory work or the founding of the association.

Purposes, Goals, and Policies

The purpose of the new association was stated in Article II of its constitution as follows:

Its object shall be to promote the development and improvement of adult education in the United States and to cooperate with similar associations in other countries. It shall undertake to provide for the gathering and dissemination of information concerning adult education aims and methods of work; to keep its members informed concerning the achievements and problems of adult education in other countries; to conduct a continuous study of work being done in this field and to publish from time to time the results of such study; to respond to public interest in adult education and particularly to cooperate with community group activities in this field, in the formation of study groups whether within or without regular educational institutions; and in other ways to cooperate with organizations and individuals engaged in educational work of this nature in the task of securing books and instructors; and to serve in such other ways as may be deemed advisable.[14]

These general objectives were translated into more specific goals and operating policies that varied with the stages of development of the organization.

The central goal in the minds of the founders in 1926 had been "to embark upon a five-year period of experimentation designed to indicate whether or not the idea of adult education was one worth the expenditure of a considerable amount of time, energy, and money." [15] At the end of only three years the executive board concluded that "adult education has come to be, not only through formal agencies but through adaptation of the programs of huge informal agencies for education and culture, an integral part of the educational life of America." The association therefore proceeded to shift its attention to the development of "certain undeveloped sub-fields where it seemed that further expansion, experimentation, and demonstration were needed," namely, rural adult education, alumni education, and radio.[16]

Meantime, certain fundamental organizational policies were being determined. One had to do with "fending off attempts on the part of various special pleaders to enlist the new movement under their special interest banners." This policy of independence had its final test when the support of the Carnegie Corporation was withdrawn in 1941 and proposals for merger and other forms of joint activity were made by the Department of Adult Education of the NEA. At that time, "after long debate and most careful consideration on the part of the Executive Board, the Association again declined to link itself with any special form of adult education . . . and reiterated its desire to continue to serve as a clearinghouse for information for all types of adult education."

Another policy made early in these formative years was to resist all pressures for "the formation of a final and somewhat rigid definition of adult education" by which certain adult activities partially of an educational nature would be excluded from the field. The only exclusion permitted was "adult education for profit."

A third policy decision had to do with "the degree to which [the Association] should propagandize for the idea of adult education," with the policy being established that "the main task of the new organization was to interpret, explain, and clarify, and only in a limited degree to propagandize for adult education."

A fourth policy decision concerned the relationship of the association to local, state, regional, and other national organizations. The policy adopted was one of "unwillingness to superimpose the forms which adult education might take in various sections of the country" and of avoidance of "taking measures of initiation, particularly where other existing organizations could be induced to undertake the necessary first steps."

A fifth policy decision resulted in 1930–1931 from an "apparent conflict . . . between those who felt that the trend of the movement should be in the direction of practical vocational instruction and those who felt that cultural considerations should be dominant." The association came out with "a conception of a nicely balanced ideal program of educational opportunities for the adult in which recognition was given both to vocational and to cultural needs, and to recreational needs as well."

In the early 1930's the association's goals were adjusted to the problems of the depression, such as the role of adult education in the relief of unemployment, vocational readjustment, racial discrimination, and pressure to expand the activity of the federal government. During this period it also gave major emphasis to the extension of the open forum movement and the stimulation of local community organizations for adult education.

During this period there evolved a new policy whereby the association performed the role of "constructive critic" of the field, indeed, of society, through the annual reports of the director. Whereas the early annual reports had been limited almost entirely to discussions of internal organizational matters and reports of field activities, starting with the 1931–1932 report, the director began devoting an increasing number of the opening pages of successive annual reports to hard-hitting editorializing on a variety of subjects. In 1931–1932 it was the "acute mental colic on the part of some of the educators," whose educational thinking was lagging behind economic thinking in regard to the problems of the depression. In 1932–1933 it was the "unparalleled transfer of democratic rights and privileges to the executive arm of the government," a theme continued in 1933–1934 with added invectives against both the "die-hard conservatives" and the "one-time liberals" who have become "radical extremists," both of which groups, according to the AAAE's director, confuse the role of adult education in social change.

During 1935–1936 the policy of the AAAE's playing a role of constructive critic was re-examined and the "wise decision" was made "not only to continue the policy of lending emphasis to high standards of performance in adult education but also, through careful study, to indicate ways and means by which low standards of performance could be raised and acceptable programs improved." Accordingly, a five-year program of studies in the "Social Significance of Adult Education" was launched.

With the outbreak of war in Europe in 1939, the director presented a memorandum on policy "which called for a partial curtailment of the program of social significance studies and a devotion of a large part of the resources of the Association to several emergency services relating to the national program of defense by that time initiated by the Federal government." These policies were adopted, and a program developed for stimulating local groups across the country to discuss matters which would increase "the preparedness of the American mind for war." By 1943–1944 the association's immediate program goals were shifting over to postwar problems, especially the readjustment of returning military personnel.

In 1945–1946 the executive board appointed a "Committee on Future Policy of the Association" which reported the following year. Its principal recommendation regarding goals was that "the Association must establish direct contact with the consumers; it must find means whereby it can assist them to create within their communities an environment conducive to the development of their own adult education programs." [17]

Membership

The AAAE's perception of its field was reflected in a membership policy which for the first fifteen years limited affiliation to those individuals and organizations "who have a direct and usually a professional interest in adult education." [18] Under this policy the rolls of the association grew from 192 charter members in 1926 to 500 in 1927, 850 in 1928, and 1,000 in 1930. Membership was maintained at about this level during the depression years, but by 1941 had reached 1,500.

When the Carnegie Corporation discontinued its support of the AAAE in the spring of 1941, the role of membership in the organization's life suddenly took on new significance. For one thing, the association was increasingly dependent upon income from membership dues, so that sheer size of membership for the first time seemed to have inherent value. With additional efforts being given to membership campaigns, the roster grew to a peak of 3,000 in 1946 but then shrank back to about the 2,500 level for the remainder of the life of the association.

Even more fundamentally, the increasing dependency of the association on its membership brought changes in the role of the membership in the policy-making and program-operating functions of the organization. During most of the life of the association the membership remained in an essentially passive role as an organizational element. Its function was primarily to receive the publications of the association and keep informed. Only those who attended annual meetings, at which the quorum was twenty-five members, had any formal opportunity to influence the policy of the association; and this opportunity was limited almost entirely to approving a single slate of nominees for office. One consequence of the revolt of the early 1940's, therefore, was the revision of the constitution to provide the greater participation by the members in elections.[19]

Organizational Structure

OFFICERS.   The constitution provided for a president, a secretary, and a treasurer to be elected by the executive board from its own members, and as many vice presidents as the executive board deemed it advisable to elect. By providing for such close control, the founding fathers of the AAAE assured that the top leadership of the association would be stable and of high quality. Indeed, the roster of presidents, as shown in Table 4, is a "Who's Who" of the intellectual leadership of the time.

It will be noted that James E. Russell served as president of the association continuously during the first five years of its existence. In March 1930 he addressed a letter to the executive committee stating his belief "that some alteration should be made in the articles of the constitution in order to provide for participation and recognition of a larger number of members of the Association in the business of its government," and that "it would be desirable to change the presidency from year to year, or at two-year periods. . . ."[20] In accordance with his wishes, the constitution was changed, creating the position of Chairman of the Association, "who would serve as Chairman of the Council,

TABLE 4

Presidents of the AAAE

James E. Russell	1926–1930
Newton D. Baker	1930–1931
Felix M. Warburg	1931–1932
Dorothy Canfield Fisher	1932–1934
Edward L. Thorndike	1934–1935
Charles A. Beard	1935–1936
Everett Dean Martin	1936–1937
William Allen Neilson	1937–1938
John H. Finley	1938–1939
Alvin Johnson	1939–1940
Harry A. Overstreet	1940–1941
Harry W. Chase	1941–1942
Alexander Meiklejohn	1942–1943
Austin H. MacCormick	1943–1944
Lyman Bryson	1944–1946
Alain Leroy Locke	1946–1947
Harvey N. Davis	1947–1948
Hans Kohn	1948–1949
Morse A. Cartwright	1949–1950

of the Executive Board, and of the Executive Committee," and "would be a more or less permanent official who, with the Director, would be responsible for continuity of policy, etc." Russell was appointed to this new post and occupied it continuously until 1936, when he became Honorary Chairman. He remained in the post until his death in 1945, at which time the offices of both chairman and honorary chairman were discontinued.

There was similar continuity in the other offices.

THE COUNCIL. The constitution provided for a council as follows:

There shall be a Council of not more than one hundred persons, elected at the Annual Meeting of the Association. This Council shall be responsible to the Association for the conduct of its work. It shall meet once each year, at a time to be fixed by itself, and, also, at such other times as the President shall call a meeting. At its Annual Meeting, this Council shall:

1. Elect an Executive Board of eighteen from its own numbers, whose

task shall be to direct the executive and administrative work of the Association, and to elect members of the Association.

2. It shall elect a Membership Committee whose task it shall be to submit to the Executive Board all nominations for active membership.

3. It shall elect a Nominating Committee whose task it shall be to submit at the Annual Meeting of the Council nominations for members of the Executive Board.

The council's functions were limited almost exclusively to approving the reports of the nominating committee. Real issues of policy were quickly delegated to the executive board until 1948, when the survival of the organization became an issue and the annual meetings of the council began to be allotted more than a few minutes in the conference schedule.

THE EXECUTIVE BOARD. In addition to the provisions for the election of an executive board by the council, the constitution specified that it shall have general charge of the affairs and work of the association. This board was, in fact, the true governing body of the association, although it delegated much of its responsibility to a smaller executive committee. The following, for example, are the minutes in full of the executive board's meeting of May 23, 1929:

A meeting of the Executive Board was held, Dean Russell presiding. The Board voted to endorse all actions of its Executive Committee taken at the Third Annual Meeting and at subsequent meetings held during the year. The Board accepted the report of the Nominating Committee which recommended the re-election of the present officers of the Association.[21]

This appears to be quite typical of the minutes of the board meetings until the mid-forties, when the board began making major decisions itself.

The policy of continuity of leadership that prevailed throughout the association was applied with special force to the membership of the executive board, twelve members of which enjoyed tenures in excess of ten years.

COMMITTEES. The constitution provided for a membership committee and a nominating committee, and in addition the executive board created additional committees on publications, the council, international relations, research, and annual meetings. In 1929 additional committees were created on community projects, public school relations, and reading habits study; in 1930, one on university cooperation; in 1931, one on art and museum cooperation; in 1932, committees on cooperation with industry and labor, Negro education, parent education, and rural education; in 1933, one on techniques of discussion; in 1934, committees on recreation and science; but between then and 1937 all committees were dissolved except those on membership, nominations, annual meetings, and adult reading.

In the annual report for 1939–1940 it was explained that "in the light of possible need for emergency services, the list of standing committees is much longer than is usually the case," and eighteen committees are identified. The number grew to twenty-two the next year and in 1941–1942 the categories were again reorganized as follows:

Professional Groups and Libraries
Workers' and Social Service Groups
Agricultural Extension and Rural Interests
Colleges and Schools of Education
Forums and Radio
Community Organizations and Councils
University Extramural Relations
Learned Societies and Museums
Public Education Systems

Committees were ignored in subsequent annual reports until the report of the Committee on Future Policy in 1946, which urged the enlistment of the rank-and-file members in the work of the association through the creation of committees on (1) leadership, (2) methods, including adult psychology and interests, (3) materials, (4) bibliography, (5) promotion, (6) training facilities, and (7) legislation.[22] With the resignation of the director and other organizational crises, the recommendations were allowed to remain largely unimplemented.

Obviously, the AAAE did not in its lifetime discover how to involve the population of its field in carrying on its work through committees.

Staff. Within a month after the founding of the association the executive board appointed Morse A. Cartwright executive director. The fact that he had previously been the assistant to the president of the Carnegie Corporation, and had attended all the preliminary conferences in that role, enabled him to take the helm with a continuity of experience. This fact also served as a persisting symbol, however, of the paternalistic relationship between the corporation and the association.

The role of director, as it emerged, was defined in terms of positive policy leadership. Repeatedly the formula, "The Executive Board took formal action approving the recommendations of the Director as to policy and program . . ." [23] or its equivalent appears in the minutes. The director's own perception of his role regarding the total movement is brilliantly illuminated by the following statement made at the Niagara Falls meeting in 1940:

> Since 1927 it has been the self-imposed annual duty of the Director of the American Association for Adult Education to present to the membership and to the public at large, through the medium of the Annual Meeting, certain of his views as to the progress of the adult education movement in the United States and in other countries of the world. This is a task that has gladly been undertaken by the Director, who has felt it no less than his obligation to apprise the adult education leadership of the country both of achievements and of losses in the rapidly developing concept of adult education, particularly in this country.[24]

Morse Cartwright served full time as executive director for sixteen years (1926–1941), and then as the unpaid director for an additional nine years (1941–1949) as part of his responsibility as executive officer of the Institute of Adult Education at Teachers College, Columbia University. The headquarters of the association was moved from Teachers College to Cleveland College, and Herbert C. Hunsaker, Dean of Cleveland College, served as acting director of the association for the remaining two years of its life, 1949–1951.

During its lifetime the association employed the services of forty-seven other persons in staff roles. Most of these staff members were primarily concerned with the collection and dissemination of information; a few of them during the first ten years directed experimental field projects; and two of them in later years were assigned to provide field consultation. Almost all of them were on temporary two-year contracts.

Program

The AAAE's principal instrument of program development was its recommendatory power to the Trustees of the Carnegie Corporation. Its program role was one, therefore, primarily of planning and coordinating activities for other organizations and funneling resources to them. Its own direct program was limited largely to conferences and publications, with a minimum amount of field service. The major aspects of its twenty-five year program can be broadly summarized as follows:

RESEARCH AND PUBLICATIONS. This category accounts for the lion's share of the association's energy and resources. The AAAE commissioned and subsidized a wide variety of studies, most of them descriptive but some of them experimental. A large proportion of these studies resulted in books, some published by commercial publishers and distributed through trade channels, and others published by the association and distributed free or at greatly reduced rates to its own members.

In addition to these directly sponsored publications, the AAAE and Carnegie Corporation contributed to various other projects that resulted in publications, including teaching aids by the New York University Service Bureau for Adult Education; a series of books and pamphlets by the National Theatre Conference; reading lists by the American Library Association; special publications of the World Association for Adult Education; a Bronze Booklet series by the Associates in Negro Folk Education; numerous publications of the Employment Stabilization Research Institute of the University of Minnesota; numerous reports of the New York Adjustment Service for the Unemployed; books, pamphlets, and periodicals of the National Occupational Conference; *The Peoples Library* series produced by the Readability Laboratory at Teachers College, Columbia University, and published by The Macmillan Company; and six volumes in the *Workers Bookshelf* published by The Macmillan Company in cooperation with the Workers Education Bureau of America.

But the publication that without doubt made the most far-reaching impact was the association's quarterly journal. Published from February 1929 to October 1941, under the title *Jour-*

nal of Adult Education, the quarterly adopted as its model the "quality" magazine. Although it carried a section for reports of experiences from the field—"On the Firing Line"—and a section on news about the field and about the AAAE, most of its pages were devoted to highly literary book reviews and feature articles on general cultural issues, philosophical topics, social problems, and adult educational aims. Its stable of fairly regular authors included such members of the intellectual elite in addition to the AAAE's presidents as James Harvey Robinson, L. P. Jacks, Scott Buchanan, William H. Kilpatrick, Nicholas Murray Butler, Stuart Chase, Elmer Davis, Archibald MacLeish, Allan Nevins, and others of similar stature.

In January 1942, the name was changed to *Adult Education Journal,* a new series of volume numbers was begun, and a new policy was announced that "places chief emphasis upon news from the adult education field, accompanied in each case by two or three feature articles, book reviews, special announcements, and an editorial page." [25] Its format and size were also simplified and reduced, partly as the result of wartime restrictions on paper. The stature of the authors of its feature articles also changed, with men of letters giving way to professional adult educators. In the fall of 1950 this journal was combined with the *Adult Education Bulletin* of the NEA Department of Adult Education into a new bimonthly journal, *Adult Education,* that began a new series of volume numbers which was continued by the Adult Education Association of the U.S.A.

During the year 1940–1941 the association engaged in an experimental Emergency Defense Program that had two purposes: (1) the stimulation of groups for the study and discussion of national and international issues, and (2) the production of study and discussion materials for the use of these groups. The first purpose was pursued through the publication of a quarterly, *Community Councils in Action,* which was supported by the activities of two field representatives who traveled around the country assisting in the organization of study groups, especially under the auspices of community councils. In pursuance of the second objective, two types of materials were produced: (1) a series of eight issues of *Defense Papers,* each of which presented six to eight short articles on such topics as foreign relations, defense, morale, postwar planning, and civil liberties, followed by questions for discussion and suggested sources of further information; and (2) a series of twelve *Defense Digests,* each of which took up one subject, such as freedom of assembly, housing, the nation's health, and other national problems, and presented a more detailed exposition of it, followed by aids to discussion, including questions, readings, films, and radio programs. The program was discontinued as a result of the withdrawal of support from the Carnegie Corporation after a demonstration of less than a year, and no systematic evaluation of the project could be made.

CONFERENCES. The principal conferences of the AAAE were its annual meetings. These tended to reflect the same view of the field and its needs and to provide generally the same types of content as the publications. The general sessions presented outstanding intellectual leaders on such subjects as "The Obligation to Be Intelligent," "The Philosophy of Adult Education," "Religion and Adult Education," "Adult Education and Public Opinion," "Adult Education and Employment," "The Arts and Adult Education," and "The Radio as a Means of Adult Education." [26] The section meetings were largely organized around occupational and subject-matter interests, although there was some greater freedom to introduce groupings around such mundane operating problems as "Financing Adult Education," "Adult Education Publicity," and "Community Needs." The conferences also frequently included demonstrations of motion pictures, folk dancing, dramatics, and singing.

The AAAE sponsored occasional special conferences, such as a series of conferences on philosophy of adult education under the leadership of L. P. Jacks in 1928, a conference on alumni education at Vassar in 1935, and a conference in New York, in 1936, of librarians, publishers, and educators on the production of readable books.

EXPERIMENTS AND DEMONSTRATIONS. The association's policy placed chief emphasis on experiments and demonstrations until 1935–1936, at which time emphasis was shifted to the study of the social significance of adult education. A large number of relatively small allotments were made to a wide variety of institutions during the first ten-year period for the testing of such new approaches as forums, alumni clubs, adult education councils, community-wide organization of adult education—for example, the Radburn, New Jersey, experiment—new materials for literacy education, traveling libraries, and vocational guidance centers.

NATIONAL COOPERATION. The AAAE's leaders viewed cooperation with other national organizations as being a specific element in the association's program. Each annual report devoted a section to describing its cooperative activities, which ranged from attendance at the conferences of other organizations by staff or executive board members to the joint sponsorship of projects with such organizations as the American Library Association, the National Education Association, and numerous local councils, universities, and other institutions. The AAAE clearly was perceived by its leaders as one among many organizations, each with specialized functions—the function of the AAAE being to advance the general concept of adult education through stimulating other organizations.[27] This approach was greatly aided by the association's recommendatory power to the Carnegie Corporation, by virtue of which it obtained a number of grants for projects sponsored by itself and other national organizations. While this situation, no doubt, made it easy for the AAAE to establish cooperative relations with a number of organizations, it also tended to place other organizations in a relationship of dependency toward the AAAE.

There is no evidence that the leaders of the AAAE ever considered the establishment of a mechanism for joint planning with other organizations until such a proposal was made by the NEA Department of Adult Education in 1942. After a series of informal discussions were held with leaders of a number of "subfields" of adult education in the fall of 1943, the executive board rejected the proposal.[28]

Actually, the AAAE did join with four other national organizations in sponsoring a multiorganizational conference in Detroit on April 23 to 26, 1946. But this action proved to be the first step in the formation of a new organization rather than the launching of a new policy of multilateral relationships on the part of the AAAE itself.

INTERNATIONAL COOPERATION. From its inception, the leaders of the AAAE expressed deep interest in adult education in other countries and undertook to develop cooperative relationships with adult education leaders around the world. Within months after the founding of the new association it sent a delegation to the conference of the World Association for Adult Education (founded in 1918) in Frederiksborg, Denmark, August 14 to 17, 1926. Immediately it arranged for a grant of $5,000 from the Carnegie Corporation to the World Association to underwrite a world conference and an expanded publication program. Subsequent grants for these purposes totaling $31,000 underwrote the expenses of an American delegation to the first World Conference on Adult Education at the University of Cambridge in August 1929, and the cost of publication of the *International Handbook of Adult Education* in 1929 and the *Proceedings of the World Conference* in 1930. The AAAE continued to send delegations to the meetings of the World Association until 1938, when the impending outbreak of World War II caused the World Association to cease functioning.

The AAAE also arranged for Carnegie Corporation grants for the support of institutional programs, fellowships, and student exchanges in Canada, Australia, New Zealand, and Newfoundland. When the State Department created the U.S. National Commission for UNESCO in 1946, the AAAE was one of the original fifty national organizations selected to form its nucleus. It sent a delegation to the first postwar International Conference on Adult Education sponsored by UNESCO and held in Elsinore, Denmark, in June 1949.

TRAINING. The AAAE identified the training of adult education leaders early as one of the high priority needs of the field. In keeping with its general policy of stimulating others in preference to directly operating programs itself, it supported several training projects in existing institutions. The first of these was a series of four teacher training courses in adult education instituted at the beginning of the academic year 1926–1927 under the joint auspices of the New School for Social Research in New York and the People's Institute of New York. A number of demonstration centers were set up by the People's Institute for testing different approaches to the teaching of adults, especially the approach of book-based discussion.

In the summer of 1927 a summer-session course for public school teachers of adults was inaugurated at Teachers College,

Columbia University, under the sponsorship of the State Department of Education, and in 1929 this program was broadened through a subvention by the Carnegie Corporation to include a general adult education course. In 1931 this course was incorporated into the regular program of Teachers College.

In 1933 a grant of $6,000 was made to Teachers College on the recommendation of the AAAE for twelve fellowships in adult education. And for the year 1934–1935 a second grant of $15,000 was made "partly for the purpose of financing new or renewed fellowships, partly to make possible the appointment to full professorship on the Teachers College faculty of a specially qualified person who could devote himself to the further development and critical evaluation of the adult education teacher training experiment." [29] Lyman Bryson was selected for this pioneering assignment, the first professor of adult education and architect of the first graduate degree program in this field of specialization. In 1935 the first Doctor of Philosophy degrees in adult education were awarded to Wilbur C. Hallenbeck and William H. Stacy.

The AAAE also supported a number of other experimental approaches to specialized training for adult education workers, including grants-in-aid to students in the Division of General Graduate Studies in Yale University for special projects in adult education, a project for the training of leaders in workers' education by the Hudson Shore Labor School, a summer seminar in adult education leadership at Claremont Colleges in California, a service and research bureau in adult education in the Division of General Education of New York University (which prepared bulletins and other aids for teachers), and a variety of local experiments—especially through adult education councils—in the training of discussion leaders. Its final act in this area of work was cooperation with Teachers College, Columbia University, in establishing an Institute of Adult Education in that institution under a ten-year grant of $350,000 from the Carnegie Corporation in 1941. [30]

Finance

The AAAE received and disbursed grants made by the Carnegie Corporation for special projects, studies, and support of other organizations, and these grants appeared as a part of the general budget of the association. The AAAE's own operation was almost entirely subsidized by the Carnegie Corporation. For example, in the fiscal year ending September 30, 1929, grants from the Carnegie Corporation totalled $86,900, while the AAAE's earned income amounted to $3,770—slightly over 3 percent of its total income. In 1939, the last "normal" year before Carnegie support was discontinued, earned income amounted to $5,544, which was about 8 percent of the total income of $69,591 —an increase of five percentage points in ten years.

With the cessation of direct Carnegie support, the AAAE became dependent upon another creation of the foundation, the Institute of Adult Education at Teachers College, Columbia University. From 1941 to 1949 the institute provided headquarters facilities and staff service for the association, along with some subsidy for annual meetings and publications. In the fifteen years during which the association was directly subsidized by the Carnegie Corporation, it gave little attention to expanding its own means of self-support. Little energy was devoted to broadening the membership base of the association until the last years of its life, and the largest amount ever derived from membership dues was $5,358 in 1948.

There is strong evidence that the leaders of the AAAE did not in fact—until its closing years—view the association as being more than a temporary instrument of the Carnegie Corporation for developing and strengthening other agencies of adult education. This assumption is expressed clearly in the following statement in the Annual Report for 1935–1936:

. . . the Association should be pledged to examine its position and the general situation of adult education in the United States four years hence, and to determine at that time whether or not its responsibilities, either in whole or in part, can be assumed by other organizations and institutions after 1941. Within five years the present apparent lag between leadership and needs may well have been overcome and the functions of the Association, including that of serving as constructive critic, may be found capable of transfer elsewhere. If the Association, within a period of fifteen years, could succeed in working itself out of its job, then its officers, board and staff might well congratulate themselves and retire from the field with easy consciences. The Association should welcome the time, if and when it arrives, at which it truthfully can be said that its parts are greater and stronger than the whole.[31]

That this was also the assumption of the Carnegie Corporation is evidenced in the following statement issued at the time it voted to discontinue further support of the AAAE:

After extended study and discussion of all the considerations involved, the Corporation Committee now believes that the Corporation can best serve the cause of adult education during the next decade by providing funds not for the continuation of the program initiated in 1925 and developed to date, but for the establishment of a limited society, institute, or other organization devoted to intensive study of the opportunities, problems, materials and methods of adult education and to the training of leaders and competent workers.[32]

The fact that the AAAE failed to take advantage of its fifteen-year period of subsidization to develop its own ability to survive seems, therefore, to be irrelevant to an evaluation of its financial experience; its own conception of its mission did not include self-perpetuation.

THE NEA DEPARTMENT
OF ADULT EDUCATION

When the Department of Immigrant Education (later renamed the Department of Adult Education) was established by the National Education Association in 1921, its membership was limited to workers in the public schools and its purpose was to serve their individual needs. Therefore, when the American Association for Adult Education came into being in 1926, the NEA Department was strictly a segmental professional association.

But in 1927 the NEA Department took two actions that had the effect of moving it away from the role of a strictly professional society of public school adult educators toward a more general coordinative role. The first of these actions was to redefine its membership to include "all those educators who instruct adults from beginning English classes to evening high school and general evening classes in special subjects, all under public auspices." But it attached a broad meaning to the final clause: "Such educational activities under public auspices resolve themselves into two classes: (a) Those subject to direct public school administration, and (b) Those which lend themselves readily to coordinative and cooperative effort—such as normal schools, colleges and universities, libraries, art galleries, and museums." [33]

The second action was to approve a report by its Commission on Coordination in Adult Education, appointed in 1926, which recommended that the NEA Department accept responsibility for bringing about better coordination of adult educational activities under public, institutional, and private auspices at the national level and that it encourage state departments of education and local school systems to provide similar coordination at the state and local levels. It proposed that this coordination be achieved through (1) conferences "representing all reputable and recognized organizations engaged in educational service among adults"; (2) surveys "for information and guidance"; and (3) centralized information clearinghouses. The report further proposed recognition of this principle:

That education for adults is a desirable form of education extension under public auspices, and that the chief responsibility for the education of adults as well as children is public. To supplement the service of public education agencies, private and quasi-public initiative, enterprise and effort are needed. But in the extension of all three forms of educational service among adults common ideas, ideals; cooperative, coordinated effort; and clearly defined notions of interdependence and inter-responsibility are desirable. [34]

The commission went on to welcome "the organization and establishment of the new American Association for Adult Education, which with allied local, state, or sectional associations or councils may materially advance the possibilities of mutual effort and cooperation."

The coordinative ambitions of the department were made even more explicit in a resolution adopted in 1928 providing "that the Department of Adult Education of the National Education Association shall function as an agency for the coordination of means and the study and solution of problems in the field of adult education." [35] Clearly, the department was moving closer and closer in its interpretation of its role to the constitutional purpose of the American Association for Adult Education, a movement that culminated with the amendment of the department's constitution on June 29, 1938 providing: "The purpose of the Department of Adult Education of the National Education Association shall be to promote adult education of all kinds in the United States and to insure continuity of purpose and effort in the development of an effective national program." [36] In membership, also, the department moved increasingly in the direction of duplicating the membership of the AAAE. Under liberalized eligibility provisions adopted in 1927, an increasing number of representatives of such other public institutions as colleges, universities, and libraries joined the department. In 1928 the department again broadened its eligibility provisions to provide that "membership in this Department shall be open to all who are actively engaged or interested in adult education work, upon the payment of an annual membership fee of one dollar." [37] At the annual meeting that year the president was able to report that "forty-two libraries throughout the country have enrolled as member organizations," and in January 1940, that "the National Education Association's Department of Adult Education enlarged its membership from 2233 to 3760 in its 1938–39 year and thus became the pre-eminent organization of the profession." [38] Although the membership rosters of the two organizations were never completely cross-checked, there is evidence that by 1951 fully half of the total memberships of the two of them belonged to both.[39]

In spite of this growing confusion of role and overlapping of membership, there is little evidence in the literature of conflict and tension between the two organizations for many years. The annual reports of the director of the AAAE repeatedly alluded to the cooperation between the two organizations. The director of the AAAE and various members of the Executive Board of that organization appeared on the programs of the annual meetings of the NEA Department and served on its editorial board. It is interesting to note, on the other hand, that the name of a public school adult educator appeared in the roster of the Executive Board of the AAAE first in 1931–1932 and not again until 1937–1938.

On the whole, by the end of the 1930's, the difference in character—if not in purpose—between the two organizations had begun to clarify. While the AAAE emphasized the theory, philosophy, and national prestige of the adult education movement, the NEA Department stressed practice, social action, and relationship building. The department's periodical (*Interstate Bulletin*, 1927–1934; a section of the *Adult Education Journal*, 1934–36; *Adult Education Bulletin*, 1936–1950) gave primary attention to such practitioners' needs and interests as personnel news, articles and experience reports on teaching techniques, subject-matter fields, professional development, administration, and proposals for legislation. Its conferences tended to have a similar practical flavor.

During the 1940's the tension between the two organizations started coming out into the open as a result of several forces. Competition for members intensified as both organizations came increasingly to see their contituencies as consisting of the same population, and especially as the AAAE became increasingly dependent on income from membership fees following the termination of support from the Carnegie Corporation in 1941. Complaints increased from individual members over their having to pay dues to two organizations, attend two conferences, and read two periodicals in order to receive comprehensive service. Accordingly, at the June 1942 convention of the NEA Department, representatives of the two organizations agreed to the appointment of a joint committee to explore ways to bring about closer cooperation.

The joint committee unanimously recommended that as soon as arrangements could be made the two organizations meet jointly at their national conferences, publish a single journal, and conduct a joint membership campaign. These recommendations were approved by the Executive Committee of the Department, but the following month the Executive Board of the AAAE approved only the recommendation for a joint national meeting "as soon as transportation restrictions would permit," and made all other proposals conditional upon the holding of the joint national meeting.

In March 1944, the AAAE's Executive Board rejected an alternative proposal for a joint publication and a combined membership campaign; after this action the President of the NEA Department turned over his office and closed off further negotiations with these embittered words:

Our new officers should know well the record of the past two years and the efforts which were made to achieve a working relationship between the American Association and the Department. Thus armed with a more realistic understanding of what "cooperation" means, they can get on with the tasks for which this Department is peculiarly fitted. With direct election of national officers, with decentralized control and administration through elected regional officers, and with eleven active state and regional associations for adult education already affiliated with the Department and other applications on file, this Department is in a unique position to give expression to the grass roots opinions and judgments of those teachers and community leaders who alone give substance to what we call adult education in the United States.[40]

But what the NEA Department perceived as overtures for cooperation, the AAAE's leadership apparently perceived as threats of annexation, according to the following interpretation of the AAAE's director:

Attempts to cause the Association to abandon its broad conception of the adult education field and to adopt in its stead some specialized (and therefore limited) form of adult education recurred occasionally in the years that followed, though no really insistent demand was made until 1941 and 1942 when—after the withdrawal of Carnegie Corporation support—proposals for absorption were made by officers of the Department of Adult Education of the National Education Association. These were followed by proposals of merger and other forms of joint activity. After long debate and most careful consideration on the part of the Executive Board, the Association again declined to link itself with any special form of adult education—in this case, public school adult education—and reiterated its desire to continue to serve as a clearinghouse for information for all types of adult education.[41]

This atmosphere of mutual distrust prevented further discussions of cooperation until after the war. Then, in Detroit on April 23–25, 1946, the AAAE kept its 1943 promise to the NEA Department and participated in a joint conference with it and the National University Extension Association, the Educational Film Library Association, and the Board on the Library and Adult Education of the American Library Association.

The major outcome of the Detroit meeting was the formation of a Joint Committee for the Study of Adult Education Policies, Principles, and Practices composed of representatives of the five participating organizations. In October 1946 the joint committee held its first meeting and identified the needs of the field to which a national coordinative organization should address itself.[42] It is interesting to compare these needs with those identified at the Carnegie Conferences in 1925–1926 and to note how markedly the emphasis had shifted from information gathering toward more positive developmental action.

In 1948 the name of the joint committee was changed to the Joint Commission for the Study of Adult Education, and it turned its attention to trying to interest established research institutions in undertaking studies of some of the adult educational problems it had identified.

In October of that year the Executive Committee of the NEA Department authorized a constitutional amendment to be submitted to its membership regarding changing the name of the department, and a preliminary ballot indicated that the membership favored "The Adult Education Association of the National Education Association of the United States." In its meeting on March 21, 1949, the Executive Board of the AAAE passed a resolution stating that it "deprecates and sincerely regrets the impending action of the Department of Adult Education of the National Education Association of the United States in changing its name to one so closely approximating that of the American Association for Adult Education, believing that such action inevitably will lead to greater confusion both in the United States and in dealing with adult education internationally."[43] The NEA Department agreed to hold off submitting a final ballot to its membership for approval of the constitutional amendment until after the next meeting of the Joint Commission, on the understanding that "certain readjustments on the national adult education scene might result in the coming year and that the possibility existed of working out a program which would lead to a more fully integrated adult education profession."[44]

Accordingly, the Joint Commission met in May 1949 under tension and pressure to produce and came out with three recommendations: (1) that the Joint Commission be enlarged to include other organizations with a primary interest in adult education; (2) that the AAAE and the NEA Department consider the creation of a joint committee to explore the possibility of greater collaboration in their efforts; and (3) that the Joint

Commission's committee on research undertake a study "of the kind of over-all organization that would come closest to meeting the expressed needs of adult educators in our country." The first opportunity to test the sentiments of the field at large regarding these recommendations occurred at the annual meeting of the NEA Department in October 1949, with results reported as follows:

> At this meeting the sense of urgency was established; the goal of one, over-all organization—rather than two, distinct groups—was articulated; the principle of broad, professional involvement with the formulation of decisions relating to unification . . . was clearly demonstrated as one, unfailing principle of sound decision-making.[45]

Within the next two days both the AAAE and the NEA Department adopted identical resolutions creating a joint committee to make recommendations "regarding the establishment of one over-all adult education organization adequately representative of the entire adult education field."

This event, perhaps tied in with the retirement of Morse Cartwright as executive director of the AAAE on May 9, 1949, marked a distinct turning point in the relationships between the two organizations. As the 1950 Progress Report of the Joint Committee stated, the first meeting was convened in December of that year in a spirit of mutual trust and concern, with the focus of its attention not on "merger," "absorption," "amalgamation," or "federation," but on the positive task of "making plans for a new kind of adult education organization that can meet the needs of the adult education field, unify existing leadership, and provide an executive channeling of service between local, state, regional, and national adult education programs." [46]

A progress report presented to the annual meeting of the AAAE in May 1950, met with such enthusiasm that the conferees urged the joint committee to expedite its work to the end that a national convocation might be held in 1951 for the purpose of achieving a new organization. Accordingly, the joint committee hurriedly arranged for a six-day workshop to be held in August 1950 at Sarah Lawrence College to develop a detailed plan of organization for the new association.

The twenty-seven adult education leaders who attended this workshop, representing a broad geographical and institutional cross section of the field, started with the assessment of needs and operating principles previously formulated by the joint committee and spent six creative and intense days projecting their implications into "far-reaching, excitingly novel" proposals for the organizational structure, administration, and program of the new association.[47]

In September the joint committee presented these recommendations with its endorsement to the Joint Commission for the Study of Adult Education, which in turn presented them to the governing bodies of the AAAE and the NEA Department and the latter approved them in October. An autonomous National Organizing Committee was appointed immediately and the joint committee was dissolved. As a visible symbol of the new unity, the two journals of the AAAE and NEA Department were combined into a new bimonthly publication, *Adult Education.* In February 1951 the Joint Commission for the Study of Adult Education met with representatives of several national organizations to discuss plans for the formation of a Council of Organizations. In April the members of the AAAE and the NEA Department participated in a mail ballot in which they approved the dissolution of the two organizations in favor of the new association, elected delegates to the founding assembly, and gave their reactions to a first draft of a constitution for the new association. Then, on May 13, 14, and 15, 1951, some 200 elected delegates met at Columbus, Ohio, and founded the Adult Education Association of the U.S.A., with the executive boards of the AAAE and the NEA Department simultaneously voting to dissolve their organizations (the AAAE transferring its library, office equipment, and treasury of some $10,000 to the new association).

THE ADULT EDUCATION ASSOCIATION
OF THE U.S.A.

Setting

In contrast to the highly formal atmosphere and procedures which characterized the founding meeting of the AAAE in 1926, the founding assembly of the AEA operated according to a complex pattern of committees, subcommittees, task forces, and caucuses in which the delegates were deeply involved in the decision-making process. While the general spirit was one of good will and optimism, an underlying resentment against absent ghosts of the past strongly influenced the deliberations.

Several general observations about the preparations for the founding of the AEA can be made which seem to have special significance in the light of subsequent developments.

1. The pendulum was swung to the opposite extreme from the AAAE's policy of planning from the top down by an elite in an effort to have the new organization built from the bottom up. All delegates were elected rather than being hand-picked, but few of them in fact represented organized constituencies, since few state associations were then in existence. Accordingly, delegates were responsible only to the high abstraction of "all the members in their states," and in practice most delegates spoke only for themselves.

2. The founders of the AEA were considerably more secure in their understanding of the character of the adult education field for which they were organizing than had been the case with the founders of the AAAE—thanks, of course, to the knowledge of the field accumulated by the AAAE in the intervening twenty-five years. As a result, the founders of the AEA were aggressive— although with an underlying attitude of experimentalism—in planning an organization that would provide positive services to the field, where the founders of the AAAE placed their emphasis on information gathering.

3. While the founders of the AEA gave considerable attention to the "needs of the field" as a basis for organizational planning and operation, they were highly self-conscious about their procedures for membership involvement, participation in decision making, communication, and self-evaluation. Indeed, the AEA was launched in a rather introspective mood which set its tone for many years. Related to this mood was what amounted to almost a compulsion to be creative, experimental, and "different" in its organizational philosophy and operation.

4. All planning for the new organization was based on the assumption that it would start out with a relatively small membership and limited resources, and therefore would operate on a

very small budget, with the major services being contributed by related national organizations. Accordingly, a concept of staff service teams operating out of decentralized headquarters was devised. Great enthusiasm was expressed for this "novel form of organization and operation," in which coordination would be achieved by developing teamwork among the agencies and staffs presently engaged in rendering significant national services and in which "the new association would itself be a team operation —service teams working with an executive committee—with an elected president functioning as expediter of the team operations and as spokesman for the organization as a whole between executive committee meetings." [48]

5. The "field" of adult education for which the new association was to perform a coordinative function was perceived as being a rather random, unsystematized scattering of individuals (it was not clear how organizations fitted into the picture) with certain common interests that were described as follows in the report of the Sarah Lawrence College conference:

> In addition to an interest in improving their common methodology and providing for leadership training, adult educators have a growing sense of the social significance of their calling and a desire to develop adult education on a scale adequate to bridge the gap between the competence of the adult community to deal with its personal and social problems and the growing seriousness of these problems in the present-day world.
>
> These common concerns provide the basis in interest and in need for a national association.[49]

Especially was there confusion over where the public school adult educators fitted into the structure of the field.

Purposes, Goals, and Policies

The general purpose of the AEA is stated in its constitution as follows:

> The purpose of the Association shall be to further the concept of education as a process continuing throughout life by affording to educators of adults and to other interested persons opportunities to increase their competence; by encouraging organizations and agencies to develop adult education activities and to work together in the interests of adult

education; by receiving and disseminating education information; by promoting the balanced development of educational services needed by the adult population in the United States; and by cooperating with adult education agencies internationally.

A comparison of this statement of purpose with that of the AAAE indicates that the later organization put greater emphasis on development of the competencies of individual adult educators and encouraging adult educational agencies to work together, while the earlier organization emphasized the collection and dissemination of information. Both organizations professed a primary concern with the general advancement of the adult educational movement, and both expressed a concern for international cooperation.

Numerous attempts were made in resolutions of the Delegate Assembly of the AEA, in a series of long-run plans of development, and in interpretive statements in the annual reports, to translate these general purposes into specific operational goals.[50] While these statements contained variations in emphasis and priority, the operational goals that governed the policies of the AEA during its first eight years are well summarized in the following formulation from the five-year plan of 1957:

1. Raising the level of competency of workers in the field of adult education.
2. Increasing public understanding of adult education and support for it.
3. Strengthening relationships between organizations on all levels.
4. Deepening and extending knowledge about adult education.
5. Encouraging the innovation and refinement of specialized institutions and subject areas.
6. Strengthening the organizational structure and core services of AEA.

Two factors made it difficult for the AEA to find an acceptable focus for its limited energies during its first eight years. The first factor was the duality of the AEA's organizational nature. On the one hand, the AEA was a membership organization seeking to serve the needs of individuals and organizations paying their dues to it. To a large extent the AEA's immediate organizational and financial strength depended upon its being perceived by present and potential members as directly—and to some extent, selfishly—useful to them. On the other hand, the AEA was a social institution with responsibility to society for advancing the adult education movement in general. Its ultimate organizational and financial strength depended upon its ability to affect the expansion of the basic resources for the education of adults, especially in local communities. While these two ends were not contradictory, they presented competing pressures at any point of time on the use of the resources of the AEA.

The second factor which complicated the goals and policies of the AEA, as well as almost every other aspect of its early operation, was the creation of the Fund for Adult Education by the Ford Foundation in the months just preceding the founding of the AEA. While all the preliminary planning for the AEA had been based upon the assumption that the new association would be wholly dependent upon its own earned income and the contributed services of related organizations for its basic operation, and so would function as a catalytic coordinative agency rather than as a centralized operating agency, the AEA was suddenly confronted—at the very conclusion of the founding assembly itself—with the possibility of obtaining substantial financial support from the Fund for Adult Education. There was some sentiment within the original executive committee against accepting general support from the new foundation because it would present the risk of the AEA's becoming the "foundation instrument" they perceived the AAAE to have been. But the majority sentiment favored making these additional resources available for work in the field, and a formula was worked out by which general organizational support was not provided directly but was incorporated in various items in project budgets.

This event also complicated the AEA's assumption that its goals would arise exclusively out of the needs and interests of its members and the general field of adult education. The Fund had its own goal—the promotion of liberal adult education—and quite properly (assuming the wisdom of this prior decision) sought to limit its grants to activities that would further this goal. While it interpreted the meaning of "liberal education" quite broadly at first and justified supporting grants for the strengthening of the general adult education field so as to provide a more solid base for the advancement of liberal education, it put increasing pressure on the AEA to focus the emphasis of activities supported by the Fund on the four subject areas which it identified as encompassing liberal education: (1) national affairs, (2) world affairs, (3) economic affairs, and (4) the humanities. The AEA was thus confronted with the choice of either emphasizing those goals that conformed to the interests of the Fund in order to obtain financial support that would enable it peripherally to serve other needs of the field, or rejecting support from the Fund in order to keep itself free to respond purely to the needs of the field, but with few resources with which to serve these needs. The AEA responded to these conflicting pressures by constructing projects that would have enough flavor of "liberal education" to satisfy the requirements of the Fund, but with sufficient general services to meet some of the more operational needs of the field. This solution proved to satisfy neither set of requirements and was a prominent factor in preventing the AEA from achieving an integrated goal structure during its first eight years.

The leaders of the AEA responded to the many pressures on the organization to render services beyond its means by engaging in a series of direction-finding projects, most of which involved study and discussion by the members.[51] But the most comprehensive direction-finding study was made by an outside agency, the Bureau of Applied Social Research of Columbia University, in 1958–1959. This study showed a surprising amount of agreement among the adult educators queried regarding the priority order of eleven possible goals for the AEA. About four fifths of the respondents to a questionnaire specified the two most important activities for a national coordinative organization to be "to conduct and promote research related to adult education and adult leadership" and "to disseminate practical techniques of adult education and leadership." A smaller number of respondents to depth interviews also rated research as the first priority but gave second place to "field service to build up regional state, or local adult education organizations." [52] At the end of 1961 the AEA was still trying to translate the findings of this study into operational goals.[53]

Membership

The AEA inherited 2,160 members from the AAAE and the NEA Department of Adult Education, many of whom had belonged to both organizations. Membership was opened to all individuals or organizations engaged in or interested in adult education upon meeting requirements determined by the delegate assembly, and these requirements never went beyond specifying dues, except in the case of national organizations, which were screened through a special committee of the Council of National Organizations. From the beginning the AEA's policy was to develop as large, varied, and active a membership as possible.

By the end of the first year membership had grown to 3,297, and by June 1954 to slightly over 5,000. At that time the membership committee embarked on a one-year massive experiment to test the "readiness for membership" of various population groupings by means of a large-scale direct-mail campaign conducted by a commercial promotional agency. As a result of this effort, which was liberally subsidized by a grant from the Fund for Adult Education, the membership soared to a total of 13,480 in June 1955, with an additional 5,299 subscribers to the magazines. When the massive promotional mailings were discontinued the membership rolls began gradually to diminish, since drop-outs were not replaced as aggressively as they had been recruited. Attempts were made to replace "mass recruitment" with "personalized recruitment" through the organization of state membership coordinators and through the adoption in 1957 of a joint membership plan with state associations. But membership continued to decline and by the end of 1961 was at the 3,500 level.

One of the objectives of membership development at the outset had been to "broaden the base" of the AEA's liaison with society by bringing into its membership a wider diversity of occupational representation than either the AAAE or the NEA Department had attracted. The results of analyses of the characteristics of the membership made in 1952, 1956, and 1958, as summarized in Table 5 show that the proportion of representatives of educational institutions did decline in relation to those from religious institutions and social welfare and voluntary organizations.

TABLE 5

OCCUPATIONAL DISTRIBUTION OF AEA MEMBERSHIP
IN 1952, 1956, AND 1958

Institutional Affiliation	1952	1956	1958
College or University	25%	15%	19%
Public school	21	8	15
Library	10	3	5
Government	11	10	9
Church or religious	3	16	11
Business or industry	5	6	4
Labor union	1	1	1
Social, health, youth serving, welfare, civic, fraternal, or other voluntary organization	16	30	24
Other, unknown, or none	8	11	12
	100%	100%	100%
Base of %	(1828)	(6945)	(1840)
Size of membership at time	(3163)	(12,935)	(5656)

Sources: Adult Education Association, *Annual Report for 1956;* Edmund deS. Brunner, *et al., The Role of A National Organization in Adult Education,* p. 79. New York: Bureau of Applied Social Research, Columbia University, 1959, (duplicated).

Organizational Structure

OFFICERS.   The constitution originally provided that the officers would consist of a president, a first vice-president, a second vice-president, and a secretary treasurer. All officers were to be elected for one-year terms directly by the membership. Later the office of president-elect was substituted for one of the vice presidencies (1955) and the office of secretary-treasurer was divided into two offices, with the treasurer being elected by the executive committee rather than by the general membership

(1956). In contrast to the relative stability of the AAAE's officer group, the AEA's officers seldom served for longer than one term (although the office of secretary-treasurer rotated somewhat less rapidly). Also in contrast with the AAAE's roster of distinguished public figures, the AEA's officers tended to be active workers in the field.

In contrast also to the honorary nature of the AAAE's elective offices, the AEA's elected officers carried executive responsibility; indeed, the constitution provided that "the President shall serve as principal officer of the Association and as its spokesman and representative to the public."

THE DELEGATE ASSEMBLY. The constitution provided for a delegate assembly of not fewer than 150 members, which was vested with "all powers of the membership of this Association, except those expressly reserved to the members." It was assumed by the founders of the AEA, in keeping with their democratic theory of organization, that the delegate assembly—being the organ closest to the membership—would be the true legislature of the association. Specific responsibility for overseeing elections, determining the place and nature of conferences, establishing program policies, fixing dues, adopting budgets, and evaluating the effectiveness of the organization was given to it. Elaborate precautions were taken to assure that too much power was not delegated to the executive committee and staff. But for a group that met for only a day or two at the conclusion of a national conference the load proved to be too heavy to carry, and gradually the delegate assembly itself assigned increasing amounts of its responsibility to the executive committee, reserving to itself only broad direction setting for the organization.

Special problems were encountered in attempting to compose a delegate assembly that would be truly representative of the "grass roots" membership of the organization and would be free of any suspicion of control by a small group. Originally nominations were obtained through a nominations ballot mailed to the entire membership—so as to avoid possible control by a nominations committee. However, this proved to be so cumbersome and expensive that it was dropped in favor of state nominating committees made up of previously elected delegates plus officers of state associations where they existed. This process still failed to provide a visible constituency for the delegates to represent and be responsible to, and so the policy was adopted of having existing state associations take full responsibility for obtaining the nomination and election of the quota of delegates for their states.

But even under the most ideal circumstances of nomination and election, the delegate assembly was not able to become fully representative of the membership. The basis of representation —except for ten delegates-at-large nominated by the Council of National Organizations—was purly geographical, thus making representation of occupational, clientele, institutional, and subject interests a matter of chance. A prime consideration in obtaining nominees to stand for election was their ability to get their way paid to the meeting, thus assuring a preponderance of administrative personnel with travel budgets. And many duly elected delegates found it impossible to give the time to stay through a full session of the delegate assembly after attending preceding conferences for up to a week.

The Brunner study found dissatisfaction with the composition and operation of the delegate assembly to be general among the membership. Although from the perspective of time the compulsion of the founding fathers toward democratic control may seem to be excessive—almost an over-reaction to the control by an elite of the AAAE—their actions were the result of a deep sense of educational obligation, as the following passage from the literature of the day indicates:

> Adult educators, collectively, are more keenly concerned with the development of active adult citizenship than are any other single group. They have a unique opportunity, as a group, to experiment with functional approaches to organizational structure in the operation of their own professional organization—particularly at this moment in its formative period. The Adult Education Association can, and should, be the *avant-garde* in evolving a dynamic pattern of organization which genuinely implements democratic values and which can have meaning for the whole society.[54]

The basic theory and design of the delegate assembly seem sound enough in themselves, but they apparently assumed a degree of development in the substructure of the adult education field that simply did not exist.

Executive committee. The constitution provided for an executive committee consisting of the officers, the past president, representatives of subdivisions (CNO and NAPSAE), and fifteen elected members (elected by regions). Originally the powers of the executive committtee were largely limited to executing policies established by the delegate assembly, but specific powers such as determining the place and character of the conferences and adopting the budget were increasingly delegated to the executive committee, until the smaller body became the principal policy-making organ of the association.

In contrast to the executive board of the AAAE, the average tenure of executive committee members was around three years. In fact, the rapidity of rotation of the membership of this body was a strong factor in the lack of stability of the policy structure of the association. With almost half of the membership changing each year, the obstacles to maintaining continuity in planning and policy making proved almost insurmountable.

The council of national organizations. Where the AAAE had limited itself to one-to-one relationships with other national organizations concerned with the education of adults and had expressly rejected the notion of multilateral cooperation as a proper function for a coordinative organization, the founding fathers of the AEA assumed that the new organization would have to do something about the need for communication and cooperation among national organizations. There was considerable difference of opinion in the preplanning meetings as to where national organizations should fit into the structure of the new organization. Strong sentiment was at first expressed in favor of their occupying a key position in the basic policy-making structure, and the proposal was made that a delegate assembly consisting of representatives of the individual members function as a sort of "house of representatives," with a council consisting of representatives of national organizations functioning as a sort of "senate." But the fact that many organizations could not by their bylaws participate in any other organization which could take action that would be binding on its member-organizations proved to be an insuperable obstacle to this proposal. Some sentiment existed, in fact, in favor of the new organization's being constructed entirely as a council of organizations, without any individual membership, but this proposal was also rejected.

It was not until almost a year after the founding of the AEA, in February 1952, that agreement was reached among a substantial number of organizational representatives to form a Council of National Organizations of the Adult Education Association of the U. S. A. Two sets of needs were identified as justifying the creation of the CNO: (1) the need for exchange of information by means of a clearinghouse on programs, materials, publications, studies, techniques, and methods of participating organizations, and (2) the need for discovering possible areas of cooperation among participating organizations in developing and maintaining new program services. The purpose of the CNO was defined as being "to afford an opportunity for national organizations voluntarily to confer, plan, or work together more effectively on problems of common concern in adult education."

Eligibility for participation in the CNO was defined as follows in its Operating Procedures:

National and international organizations, including government or inter-government agencies, meeting all the following criteria, are eligible to become Participating Organizations:

a. those interested in the general philosophy and basic purposes of the AEA of the USA which have a constituency,—individual, group, or institutional;

b. those actively concerned with and contributing to the educational improvement of the adult population;

c. those dedicated to broadly acceptable social goals;

d. those who maintain standards of integrity and factual accuracy in their educational materials;

e. those which are not essentially partisan political organizations;

f. those which are not established primarily for profit.

Under these criteria a wide heterogeneity of organizations affiliated with the CNO—reaching in number as high as 125, but averaging around 100 during most of the first ten years. They included professional associations (National University Extension Association, American Dental Association, National Association of County Agricultural Agents), direct service or membership organizations (American National Red Cross, Association of Junior Leagues of America, General Federation of Women's Clubs, YMCA), government agencies (U. S. Armed Forces Institute, U. S. Office of Education, Federal Extension Service), and a miscellany of special-purpose resource agencies (American Iron and Steel Institute, Consumers Union, Foreign Policy Association). A special affiliation, "business associate," was also created (Household Finance Corporation, Standard Oil Company [N.J.]).

The program developed by the CNO in its first ten years falls naturally into several classifications: (1) annual conferences in which emphasis has been placed on identifying national problems and trends to which the educational programs of national organizations should be related and on identifying common problems on which they wish to work together; (2) special conferences around problems on which particular clusterings of organizations wish to work together (such as improving organizational leadership, dealing with controversial issues, and improving the use of mass media for educational purposes); (3) exchange of information and materials (through distribution of materials packets containing examples of the publications of various organizations, the publication of a periodical newsletter, and the facilitating of interorganizational consultations); (4) action projects, in which interested organizations work jointly on particular problems (such as training workshops on mass media skills and the development of manuals of practice for newsletters and other instruments of national-local communication); and (5) the clarification and interpretation of the role of national organizations in the education of adults (through conferences, the stimulation of research, publications, and publicity).

The relationship of the CNO with the AEA was a complicated one from the very beginning. Constitutionally defined as an "organ" of the AEA and charged with the responsibility of being the official and exclusive instrument for relating the AEA to the many national organizations concerned with the education of adults, the CNO at the same time demanded and was granted a high degree of autonomy. But there was a good deal of vacillation between considering the CNO as an integral part of the AEA and therefore entitled to support from the AEA's general funds, and considering the CNO as a semi-independent organization with complete responsibility for self-support. CNO representatives participated actively in the conferences, policy-making bodies, and committees of the AEA, and vice versa, but this participation was the result more of interpersonal relations than of integrated organizational machinery and was therefore largely subject to the choices of the personalities involved at a particular time.

Toward the end of the year 1959 the relationship between the AEA and the CNO entered a period of transition. With mutual agreement between the leaders of the two organizations, the CNO incorporated as an autonomous organization under the new title, "Council of National Organizations for Adult Education." Arrangements were being made for separate financing of the CNO independently of the AEA budget. The nature of the relationship between the two organizations in regard to policy-making and coordination of program still remained to be defined.

THE NATIONAL ASSOCIATION OF PUBLIC SCHOOL ADULT EDUCATORS. According to the original plan of organization of the AEA, public school adult educators were absorbed into the general membership, but provision was made for them to meet and work separately on problems unique to the public schools through a "self-governing organ" of the AEA, a Council of Public School Adult Education Administrators. The NEA Division of Adult Education Service agreed to serve as the secretariat of this new council, while continuing its more general services to the AEA.

It was pointed out in the 1951 meeting of the Council of Public School Adult Education Administrators, however, that the public school workers did not yet have a "home base" from which to relate to the rest of the field as did other occupational groupings (the librarians had the American Library Association, and so on). Accordingly, a plan was presented to the 1952 Delegate Assembly of the AEA for the establishment of a National Association of Public School Adult Educators which would be affiliated with the AEA but would also be free to establish affiliations with other organizations. Under the constitution of this new association, which was approved by the AEA Delegate Assembly, the membership in the NAPSAE was limited to "administrators, supervisors, and teachers in Public School Adult Education," but prior membership in the AEA was not required.

The new constitution also authorized the NAPSAE to assess membership dues, but provision was made for the assessment of AEA members to be at a lower rate. In 1953 the NAPSAE voted to seek affiliation also with the NEA, and in 1955 it became a department of the NEA. Perhaps the sharpest symbol of the changing relationship between the AEA and the NAPSAE was the fact that until 1957 the AEA sought and received foundation grants on behalf of the NAPSAE for special projects concerning public school adult education, but subsequently the NAPSAE sought and received grants independently.

While in some respects the relationship between the national coordinative organization and the public school segment of the field was similar to what it was prior to the 1951 reorganization, in crucial respects it was different: (1) Membership in the NAPSAE was limited to persons employed by public schools or state departments of education, and thus the danger of rivalry between it and the AEA for membership from the general field was eliminated. (2) The role of the NAPSAE was constitutionally limited to serving the public school field, and thus it was precluded from having pretensions to become the professional society for the general field that characterized the earlier NEA department. (3) Representation of the public school field in the policy-making structure of the AEA was assured by a constitutional provision that the President of the NAPSAE shall *ex officio* be a voting member of the AEA Executive Committee. (4) The policy of holding their annual meetings jointly was adopted by both the AEA and the NAPSAE.

The program adopted by the NAPSAE for serving its segment of the field included these elements: (1) Annual conferences, held in connection with the annual national conferences of the AEA, and occasional special conferences on particular problems. (2) A series of periodical publications (*Techniques for Teachers of Adults, The Pulse of Public School Adult Education, Swap Shop for Administrators, Public Relations Idea File,* and *The Public School Adult Educator*). (3) A program to expand and strengthen adult education services in state departments of education through subsidies for the initiation of such a service, field consultation, and meetings of state directors of adult education. (4) A program to stimulate local school systems to broaden their curriculums, particularly in the liberal arts, including training workshops, pilot demonstrations, and the production of materials. (5) A program to increase public understanding of public school adult education. (6) The exertion of continuous influence on the other public school groupings in the NEA constellation to broaden and deepen their support of adult education. (7) The stimulation and sponsorship of needed research about public school adult education. (8) The mobilization of support for state and federal legislation in support of public school adult education.

The role of the NAPSAE in the organizational structure of the AEA was confused from the beginning. Constitutionally, the NAPSAE occupied a semi-autonomous position as an "organ" of the AEA similar to that of the CNO. But the NAPSAE was different in character from the CNO in that it was in fact a professional society for workers from a single segment of the field rather than an instrument of interorganizational cooperation and it was, indeed, one of the participating organizations in the CNO. The image that it was something more than a segmental organization—and was therefore entitled to some special place in the power structure of the AEA—arose, of course, out of the historical fact that its predecessor NEA Department of Adult Education did increasingly become a generalized organization defining its constituency as the same field being served by the AEA's predecessor organization, the AAAE. The halo effect of this historical situation has without doubt greatly impeded the placing of the public school group in an appropriate and realistic position in the new organizational structure of the field.

OTHER SUBDIVISIONS. The constitutional provision for the creation of any other subdivisions that the delegate assembly or executive committee may authorize has resulted to date in three additional elements in the organizational structure: (1) committees, (2) commissions, and (3) sections. These organizational subdivisions were perceived by the AEA leadership as being the principal devices for actively involving large numbers of members in the operation of the organization, and accordingly at various stages in the organization's history they proliferated into highly complex patterns. In fact, the servicing and coordinating of the numerous committees, commissions, and sections that evolved during the first ten years occupied a substantial portion of the time, energy, and financial resources of the executive committee and staff.

Committees of several kinds were used, including: (1) standing committees to operate the internal organizational machinery (Nominations and Elections, Committee on Committees, Commissions, and Sections, Membership and Public Relations, Conference Planning, and so on); (2) standing committees to oversee aspects of the program (Field Development, Social Philosophy, Legislative Policy, International Relations, Publications, Professional Development, and so forth); and (3) special or *ad hoc* committees to carry on particular terminal studies or projects. Except for committees of the last type operating under foundation grants on special projects, most of the committees had to operate without funds for meetings, information gathering, reporting, or other activity, and all of them were under the policy of rotating membership. As a result, their performance was highly uneven, their degree of activity being determined largely by the dedication and resourcefulness of their membership at a given moment.

Commissions, the membership of which remained constant and could include members other than those of the AEA, were employed to carry on some special, immediate program of limited action. During its first ten years the AEA established highly productive commissions on finance, architecture, civil defense, literacy education, and graduate education.

Sections developed originally out of special interest meetings held—often at the request of interested members—in connection with the annual conferences. At first they were set up as simply additional committees, but by 1954 it was recognized that "the labelling of these groupings as 'committees' tended to confuse them with the operating committees, and to muddy their role in the AEA structure," and a new category of subdivisions was established, "Special Interest Sections."

It was visualized that the sections would function primarily at the national conference. Some sections, however, were active the year around and undertook to provide some service for the general organization. In consequence, increasing pressure was brought to bear to raise the status of the sections in the organizational structure, with more assistance from the headquarters staff in membership recruitment, communication, and program operation, and a larger share of budgetary allocations. Small allotments for postage and supplies started being made to the sections from the general budget, and in 1957 a systematic procedure for including sectional affiliation by all members was incorporated into the basic membership processes. An indication of the dormant potential that apparently had existed for some time in this new organizational instrument is provided in the tabulation of affiliations with sections as a result of the first all-member canvass in 1956-1957 in Table 6.

TABLE 6

SECTIONAL AFFILIATIONS OF AEA MEMBERS IN 1956–1957

Community Development	734
Home and Family Life	690
Young Adult Education	404
Research and Evaluation	333
Public Affairs	280
Residential Adult Education	170
Rural Adult Education	170
Professional Development	154
Labor Education	135
Education for Aging	121
International Affairs	105
Financing Adult Education	103
Education of the Foreign-Born	66
Fundamental and Literacy Education	65
Music in Adult Education	33
Liberal Adult Education	30

Source: Adult Education Association, *Annual Report, 1957, Adult Leadership,* VII (May 1958), 27.

STAFF. The definition of the role of staff in the AEA organizational structure was strongly influenced by two factors: (1) the over-reaction of the founding fathers to the definition of the role of the executive director of the AAAE as one of positive policy leadership, and (2) commitment in the pre-planning stages to the notion of contributed staff-service teams operating out of decentralized headquarters. As a symbol of the unique role assigned the chief staff officer, his office was given the title "administrative coordinator," and his original assignment was as half-time "coordinator of administrative committees" and half-time "director of the publication project."

As foundation grants were received for an increasing number of projects, as the volume of activities increased, as the size of the supporting staff grew, and as the complexity of the organizational structure multiplied, the need for central management functions to be performed was increasingly recognized and the administrative coordinator was gradually relieved of collateral duties. However, it was not until early 1957—after a series of crises in staff relations growing out of the ambiguous definition of responsibility and authority of the chief executive officer—that the office was retitled "executive director" and the job description was revised to invest the office with managerial authority. During the period of liberal support of the AEA by the Fund for Adult Education the staff grew to a total of twelve professional workers and eighteen clerical workers, and when this support was discontinued early in 1957, the positions of all but two professional and eight clerical workers were abolished and many of the functions previously performed by paid staff were transferred to volunteer officers and committee chairmen.

While the majority of the staff workers employed by the AAAE were concerned with the collection and dissemination of information, the majority of the AEA's staff workers were concerned with field consultation, project operation, and publications; and while the former were largely generalists with established reputations in the field, the latter were largely specialists in the early stages of their career development.

Program

The AEA's program developed during its first ten years largely in response to pressures from the field and to the interests of the Fund for Adult Education, not according to any long-run plan of sequential development. Rather elaborate working papers proposing long-run plans for the consideration of the AEA's delegate assembly in 1953, 1955, and 1957 were given only cursory attention in the deliberations of that body.

In general, the AEA's program evolved through the following developmental phases: (1) internal organization and testing of possible program alternatives (1951–1952); (2) rapid expansion, particularly in publications, field service, fact finding, conferences, and interorganizational cooperation (1953–1955); (3) stabilization of these programs and expansion of special interest programs (1955–1956); (4) contraction of all program to a "self-supporting base" (1957–1959); (5) replanning on the basis of a deep reassessment of needs and resources (1959–1961). Within this developmental context, the AEA's principal program activities during its first ten years can be summarized as follows:

PUBLICATIONS. The bimonthly journal, *Adult Education,* which was begun in 1950 as a result of the amalgamation of the AAAE's *Adult Education Journal* and the NEA Department's *Adult Education Bulletin,* continued to be published by the AEA and in the fall of 1954 was enlarged in format and made a quarterly. Until this time *Adult Education* was the general membership publication of the association—its house organ, with a varied content that included organizational news, reports of experience, summaries of research, reviews of professional literature, and a variety of articles on general concerns of the field. In May 1952 the AEA also began publishing a monthly magazine, *Adult Leadership,* under a special grant from the Fund for Adult Education. This magazine was originally conceived as an instrument for establishing communication between the AEA and the large numbers of part-time leaders and teachers of adults and full-time professionals in other fields who carry secondary adult educational responsibilities and were largely outside the AEA membership. The contents of *Adult Leadership* therefore emphasized practical solutions to "the real problems of groups and leaders"—and, indeed, were organized according to the principles of design of a leadership training workshop.[55]

Adult Leadership was also conceived in part as a device for broadening the AEA's membership base, on the assumption that many of its subscribers would move up the scale from selfish interest in learning about techniques to altruistic interest in advancing the cause of adult education. But when it was recognized that there were approximately three times as many subscribers to *Adult Leadership* as there were members of the Association, the functions of the two periodicals were redefined. Starting in January 1954, *Adult Leadership* became the official house organ of the AEA and therefore the publication that went to all members, with *Adult Education* being reserved for professional members. Accordingly, the contents of both periodicals were changed— *Adult Leadership* carrying the news of the field, reports of experience, and articles of general interest (with about half its pages initially reserved for the leadership training materials it had previously featured); and *Adult Education* carrying materials concerning theory, philosophy, research, professional literature, and other subjects of primary interest to adult education specialists.

Interestingly, where the role of the director and executive board served as the primary focus of controversy among the contending special interests in the power struggle within the AAAE, the role of the periodicals largely served this purpose in the first few years of the AEA. The mission of *Adult Leadership* to recruit a broad new population, essentially of lay leaders, to the membership fold was never accepted by many of the members already in the fold; and it was seen by some as imposing a doctrine of "group dynamics" or "methods and techniques as ends" upon the members. Others, especially the new recruits from noneducational institutional settings, perceived the early contents of *Adult Leadership* as providing them the only useful service available by the AEA, and this group vigorously criticized the later changes in its editorial policies toward more substantive issues.[56] In retrospect, it seems clear that many of these difficulties in constructing instruments of communication for the field arose out of the fact that the structure of the field was itself in the process of metamorphosis, a condition which, indeed, the AEA helped to induce. Tensions over communications policies were probably partly a reflection of resistances to these changes and partly a reflection of confusion as to the true nature of the functional population groupings within the field and their differentiated needs and interests.

The AEA also produced or sponsored a series of "Leadership Pamphlets," three anthologies of early articles in *Adult Leadership* in the form of "Leaders' Digests," numerous reports of committees, conferences, and special interest sections, and a number of books and monographs.

CONFERENCES. The AEA placed a high value on "conferencing" as a method for solving organizational problems, rendering service to the field, and accomplishing educational objectives. It devoted a good deal of attention in its publications and at conferences themselves to exploring new conference techniques and to training its members to participate more effectively in conferences. Indeed, in the sense that studies and publications were the heart of the AAAE's program, conferences were the heart of the AEA's program.

Its annual conferences were complex mosaics consisting of various combinations of the following elements: (1) preconference sessions of the NAPSAE, the CNO, often the AEA Executive Committee, and frequently of special groups such as the State Directors of Education; (2) general sessions featuring outstanding public or professional leaders, usually on societal issues and their implications for adult education; (3) discussion groups to feed back to succeeding general sessions the reactions of the participants to preceding general sessions; (4) work groups to develop specific recommendations to the delegate assembly; (5) meetings of the special interest sections—and, often of other subgroupings of the participants; (6) problem clinics, technique and audio-visual aid demonstrations, and other "training activities"; (7) exhibits and field trips; (8) social, fellowship, and recreational activities; (9) sessions of the delegate assembly; (10) postconference meetings of the executive committee and, on several occasions, of other groups (such as a community relations training workshop). As a matter of policy the annual conferences rotated around the country so as to equalize the travel factor as much as possible. Attendance at them ranged between 500 and 1,000 participants.

The AEA also conducted or cosponsored a variety of conferences on special problems. The series of conferences on regional problems sponsored by the Area Organization and Conference Project between 1952 and 1955 has already been described. Other specialized conferences included: two international conferences on residential adult education; a national conference on architecture for adult education; two national conferences on the role of adult education in business and industry; one national conference on the role of labor unions in adult education; a national conference on philosophical issues; two national conferences on the problems of local adult educational councils; and various special conferences sponsored by the NAPSAE and the CNO.

FIELD SERVICE.   The major attempt to develop a comprehensive field service was made under the aegis of the Area Organization and Conference Project. At the conclusion of this project a permanent Field Development Program was visualized, and a professional worker was added to the staff to give leadership to the establishment of this area of service as a part of the core program of the AEA. With the lessening of support from the Fund for Adult Education after a little over a year, however, this service proved too expensive to maintain as a staff function, and it was carried on through the volunteer efforts of a Field Services Committee.

The general approach of the AEA to field service was from the beginning highly permissive, with emphasis on developing local initiative rather than organizing the field from above. During the operation of the Area Organization and Conference project the major service consisted of providing expert consultation in the planning and conducting of fact-finding activities and conferences and in direct training in the skills of community consultation. With the loss of staff service in this area of work, however, AEA's field service program shifted during 1957 from emphasis on national consultative services to a series of mutual self-help projects. Small grants were made to state and regional associations to enable them to conduct studies, inaugurate new services and publications, sponsor conferences, and otherwise strengthen their organization and program. As budgetary support for field services continued to diminish, the load of responsibility for providing such services fell increasingly on the elected officers.

In spite of this large expenditure of energy over a period of eight years, it is doubtful if the "field" moved very far in its organizational development. There were a few more state associations, but all of them were still unstable, precarious, subsistence-level operations, with only the most tenuous ties to one another, to substructures within their states, or to the national organization. On the whole, the relationship of state associations with the national organization was a dependent one; they looked to it for financial help and "big name speakers," and tended to resist both consultation and meaningful organic relationship. Local councils and regional associations were, for the most part, even less well developed and more precarious. It is clear that "the field" awaited a workable theory of organization and a pattern of inter-relationships to give it a workable structure.

OTHER. Although these are the major categories of the AEA's program as developed by 1960, a full accounting would include additional activities. It sponsored some research, including the study of adult education finance and the field studies of the Area Organization and Conference Project already referred to, but it did not give the emphasis to research that characterized the AAAE. It made some effort to interpret the adult education movement to the public through publicity campaigns, the passing of resolutions, appearances of its officers on television, and the like, but these were halfhearted in comparison with the aggressive standards of most national organizations. It sought to bring influence to bear on state and national policy, as in urging (successfully) the U. S. Office of Education to establish an Adult Education Section and in protesting (unsuccessfully) the reduction of appropriations for public school adult education in several states, but it did not attempt to organize a really effective lobby. It continued the tradition started by the AAAE of encouraging the expansion and improvement of graduate training in adult education through its Commission of Professors of Adult Education, and it included an element of training in many of its conferences, publications, and other activities, but it saw its role to be primarily that of stimulating training emphases in other organizations rather than providing training opportunities directly. It participated in cooperative activities at the international level, including holding membership on the U. S. National Commission for UNESCO, sponsoring exploratory meetings with adult educators from other countries concerning the establishment of some form of international organization, and sponsoring exchange-of-persons programs, but it did not take aggressive leadership roles internationally.

Finance

The founders of the AEA resolved that in contrast to the AAAE, the AEA would not be dependent on any single source of financial support, and plans were laid out for the AEA's major services to be provided by "associated organizations." But within hours after the founding of the AEA, negotiations began with the newly created Fund for Adult Education and a substantial subsidy for the new organization was soon forthcoming. Although services already agreed to by the NEA, the ALA, Cleveland College, and Cooper Union continued to be contributed for a year or more (in the case of the NEA, until 1957), further attempts to obtain contributed services from associated organizations were abandoned. Consequently, this method of operating a national coordinative organization on a self-supporting basis and its attendant theory of administration were never tested. The AEA entered into a dependent relationship with the Fund for Adult Education on the basis of a new theory—the theory that by using foundation grants as capital investment to build up the membership and program resources of the AEA it would be in a better position to carry on at a higher level of income-production of its own after the outside funds ceased.

The dependency relationship of the AEA with the Fund for Adult Education was different in one important respect from that of the AAAE with the Carnegie Corporation. The AAAE was the "chosen instrument" of the Carnegie Corporation for all of its activity in the adult education field; all grants for adult education were made by the corporation on the recommendation of the AAAE and were disbursed through it. In contrast, the AEA was only one of a number of adult educational organizations and institutions competing for the largesse of the Fund for Adult Education. Indeed, in some respects the Fund for Adult Education was itself a competing—or at least duplicating—agency, in that it directly provided services and operated programs (for example, it sponsored conferences on community development under its Test City Project, and its staff rendered a large amount of field service in the form of speeches, publications, and consultations), that would be appropriate to a national coordinative organization. In this sense, the Carnegie Corporation put the power of its money behind the unification and coordination of the adult education field whereas the Fund for Adult Education used its money-giving power in ways that had the effect of increasing competitiveness within the field and fragmenting it.

The Fund for Adult Education made grants to the AEA totaling about $1,500,000 during the AEA's first eight years. The largest proportion of this amount was for publications, including the subsidization of *Adult Leadership* between 1952 and 1958 and varying degrees of subsidy for other publications. Substantial amounts were also granted for "general support" of the AEA as an organization between 1953 and 1958. Several study projects were liberally supported, including those on adult education finance, architecture, *Adult Leadership,* the AEA membership, and the overview of research. Several developmental projects by the CNO and the NAPSAE, and to a modest extent the "core services" of those organizations, received support. The support of early experimentation in the development of field services through the Area Organization and Conferences Project has already been described, and in the same category might be placed the annual grants of $8,000 begun in 1954 to subsidize the office of the presidency of the AEA so that its incumbent would be able to travel more freely.

The AEA leadership was highly conscious from the beginning of the importance of building up its own sources of financial support against the day when foundation support would be reduced or withdrawn. It justified the expenditure of considerable amounts of money and energy in enlarging its membership and in developing profitable publications largely on this basis. The measure of the AEA's progress in this direction is indicated by the fact that during its first year its earned income was $19,848 and by 1958 earned income had risen to $103,888. The AEA's leaders recognized, however, that maintenance of earned income at this level was predicated on being able to render services sufficiently valuable to retain a stable volume of members and that this, in turn, required a relatively high level of expenditures. At what point these two correlates will stabilize in balance is yet to be determined.

One of the consequences of an organization's being wholly dependent on income from membership dues and publications sales is that it is under pressure to limit its efforts to producing those services which are most visibly useful to the members. In the case of a professional society this consequence presents no conflict. But in the case of a coordinative organization, such as the AEA, which inherently carries some responsibility for the general development of its field, the interests of the members as individuals and the needs of the field may not always be perceived as the same. Especially in a relatively new field with a rapidly rotating membership, it is difficult to interpret abstract needs of the field in such a way that the members are willing to give financial support to services aimed at building the field rather than meeting the needs of members.

Recognizing this problem, the AEA made two attempts to develop sources of outside support that could be used for general services to the field. A Committee on Development, consisting of past presidents, explored a number of possible avenues for obtaining contributions from individuals, organizations, and corporations in 1953 and 1954, but their informal testing of interest proved discouraging. In 1954–1955 a professional fund-raising firm was engaged to organize a comprehensive contributions campaign, and after an intensive study of the situation it concluded that the AEA did not have either a type of membership that could be used for fund-raising or sufficiently challenging goals to attract large contributions.

By 1960, therefore, the AEA's leaders had become committed —or, perhaps, resigned—to the principle of self-support. Three courses of action were laid down for increasing the organization's own income: (1) substantial increases in membership dues were voted by the delegate assembly to take effect January 1, 1960; (2) plans were made to increase the volume of income-producing publications through volunteer energy; and (3) a campaign to solicit financial contributions from the AEA's members was launched.

SUMMARY AND ASSESSMENT

A third of a century of striving for the achievement of a national organization that would unify the national adult education movement produced some notable progress but left considerable distance to go.

In the twenty-five years of its existence the American Association for Adult Education succeeded in establishing adult education as a respectable field of study and practice and a widely recognized area of social concern. By enlisting the energies of the most illustrious figures of the day in interpreting the meaning of adult education it caused a connotation of significance to be attached to the symbol "adult education." By virtue of this fact, the field of adult education itself acquired a sense of mission and a feeling of self-respect which enabled it better to tolerate the growing pains of adolescence and which attracted to it practitioners of increasing stature.

The numerous studies and publications sponsored by the AAAE, the NEA Department, and the AEA have provided a solid foundation of scholarship that has greatly enhanced the stability of the field of adult education and has advanced the quality of its content and methodology, the soundness of its planning, and the fruitfulness of future research.

All three organizations were highly influential in the development or strengthening of certain special institutional resources for adult education, especially in the areas of community organization, library adult education, workers' education, training, professional education, and adult education in voluntary organizations.

The AAAE in particular effected the establishment of a broad image of adult education, by resisting pressures to place its stamp of approval on conceptions of the field that would limit it to a narrow range of institutional settings and subject areas. The AEA continued and extended this undertaking, with the consequence of increasing the difficulty of integrating and interpreting the field but also of preventing its development from being arrested at a primitive stage.

All three organizations contributed substantially to the development of a sense of cohesion and professionalism in the field —the AAAE primarily through its constant pleas for quality performance and high standards appearing in the *Journal,* the annual reports of the director, and the programs of its national conferences; the NEA Department primarily through its relationship-building and practical technique-building publications and conferences; and the AEA primarily through its experiments in involving members in organizational operation and its leadership-training activities.

In meeting the needs of the field for coordination the contributions of the three organizations were distinctly different. The AAAE did not perceive itself as a coordinative organization and consciously avoided organizing itself so as to encourage even voluntary coordination on the part of the individuals and agencies in the field. But by its very existence the AAAE set in motion forces which induced a demand for coordinative services from a national organization. It attracted to its membership a number of individuals and organizational representatives who gradually came to see themselves as a collectivity with certain common needs and aims that required a national organization (as contrasted with a service center) for satisfaction. The discoveries about the nature of the adult education field made by the AAAE through its numerous studies added to the pressure for greater coordination. Because of them the field came to be seen as a whole, and the interrelatedness of its parts came to be better understood. In a sense, the AAAE largely created a need for the coordination of the adult education field which it itself largely resisted.[57]

The NEA Department of Adult Education probably added to the confusion about the nature of the adult education field and its coordinative needs by vacillating between serving only a segment of the field and serving the general field. But in the long run this very action perhaps helped to clarify the field by sharpening the issue of role delineation between segmental and general organizations. And certainly the Department, by championing the needs of individual practitioners and local communities and the concept of membership involvement in decision making, insured the possession of the adult education movement by "the grass roots" rather than by an intellectual elite.

The AEA was the first organization actually to test various ways to try to bring about coordination of the field of adult education. Although the machinery it established was still functioning inadequately, the fact is that in the 1950's more joint planning took place than in the preceding quarter century. And the very squeaks and groans in the machinery were revealing new insights about the nature and needs of the adult education field.

Several critical problems remained to be solved before a viable national coordinating organization for this complex field could be achieved.

First and foremost, the true structure of the existing field of adult education needs to be understood and a model of its desired future development needs to be constructed—a task undertaken in the next chapter. Then a structure must be created for a national coordinating organization in which the present reality and future requirements of the field are adequately reflected.

Once an adequate structure is built, ways must be found to make it operate efficiently, and the experience of past organizations in this field suggest that certain peculiar difficulties must be overcome in this regard. One is the difficulty of involving large numbers of individuals with a wide variety of agency interests over a broad geographical spread in the month-to-month work of a national coordinative organization. Such obstacles as difficulty in communications, the expense of face-to-face meetings, and the competition of other interests for time and energy must be hurdled. A second difficulty is that of identifying the functions of a coordinative organization that are appropriate for delegation to committees and that are of interest to members. The record of both the AAAE and the AEA indicates that the involvement of elements of a social system in relevant coordinative activities is difficult if the structure of the social system is not clear and realistic.

And most importantly, the problem of financing must be solved. Since society is the chief benefactor of the coordinated use of adult educational resources, perhaps such societal sources of funds as foundations, taxes, or contribution campaigns should be depended upon. But until these sources are developed a national organization is dependent upon membership dues from practitioners in the field. And it is probably axiomatic that people who pay dues expect personal services, not coordination.

PART THREE

THE NATURE AND FUTURE OF
THE ADULT EDUCATION
MOVEMENT

CHAPTER VII

☸

THE CHARACTERISTICS AND

DYNAMICS OF ADULT EDUCATION

AS A FIELD

CHARACTERISTICS OF THE FIELD

The fact that it has been possible to describe the evolution of adult educational institutions in the preceding chapters within relatively clear boundaries is evidence enough that there has emerged in our country a discrete and definable field of adult education. The fact that this new field is still in the process of evolving does not invalidate its identification as a field, but only imposes the requirement to define it in dynamic rather than static terms. In the historical perspective of its development to 1961, certain characteristics seem most sharply to reveal the true personality of this adolescent field:

The adult education field is highly expansive and flexible. As has become clear in the preceding chapters, responsibility for the education of adults was not vested in a limited number of institutions in this country, as was the tendency in European countries, but was accepted by a growing number and variety of institutions. In sociological terms, adult education is an open system which any institution may enter at a time and under conditions of its own choosing. As a result, the institutional sponsorship of adult education in this country has expanded continuously and rapidly, although unevenly; and the end of this process is not yet in sight.

As the institutional sponsorship of adult education has grown and changed, so has the clientele of the field. Although the actual size of adult education's student body at various points of time cannot be accurately verified, owing to the lack of systematic methods of reporting participation, a reasonably reliable indication of the rate of growth is provided by a series of estimates of participation that were based on similar techniques of calculation. These estimates are shown in Table 7. The estimates for 1924 and 1934 were made by Morse A. Cartwright, director of the American Association for Adult Education;[1] the estimate for 1950 was made by Paul L. Essert, executive officer of the Institute of Adult Education at Teachers College, Columbia University;[2] and the estimate for 1955 was made by this writer[3] while serving as executive director of the Adult Education Association of the U. S. A. These estimates do not take into account the fact that some individuals may participate in more than one type of activity. But they do indicate that the volume of adult education in this country more than tripled between 1924 and 1955.

A census of participation in adult educational activities that is statistically more defensible was made in the October 1957 Current Population Survey of the Bureau of the Census. This survey showed that 9,212,000 individuals, or about 8 percent of the adults in the United States "participated in adult education classes at some time during the preceding year."[4] Admittedly this was a highly conservative estimate, since it excluded a number of activities—such as groups and classes in religious institutions—that are adult educational in purpose and effect. Unfortunately, since this was the first tabulation by the Bureau of the Census, there is no basis of comparison with earlier years.

Because of this constant diffusion into new areas of the population and of the institutional structure of the country, the adult educational field has confounded those who want to define it within fixed boundaries. And the fact that certainly less than half of the adult population was encompassed within the field in 1960 suggests that a spirit of expansiveness will continue to characterize the field for a long time to come.

The adult educational field is taking the shape of a multidimensional social system. The component parts of the field have tended to become organized into patterns of goals, needs, interests, status and power relationships, values, loyalties, and

TABLE 7

ESTIMATED PARTICIPATION IN ADULT EDUCATION, 1924-1955

Type of Program	Enrollment (in thousands)			
	1924	1934	1950	1955
Agricultural Extension	5,000	6,000	7,000	8,684
Public Schools	1,000	1,500	3,000	3,500
Colleges and Universities	200	300	500	1,500
Private Correspondence Schools	2,000	1,000	1,000	1,000
Educational Radio and Television	500	5,000	6,000	5,000 e
Libraries	1,200	1,000	1,500	1,961
Men's and Women's Clubs	1,000	1,000	— d	1,525
Parent-teacher Associations	15	60	— d	350
Religious Institutions	150	200	— d	15,500 f
Business and Industry	100	60	— d	750
Labor Unions	13	15	— d	850
Armed Forces	— a	— a	250	388
Health and Welfare Agencies	— b	— b	— b	6,500
Others c	4,681	6,156	10,000	2,000
Total	14,881	22,311	29,250	49,508

a Not in operation in 1924 and 1934.

b This item included under "Others" by Cartwright and Essert.

c Includes: Alumni Education, Community Organization, Negro Education, Prison Education, Recreation, Settlements, Special Schools, Theaters, Vocational Rehabilitation, and Museums.

d Essert included these items in "Others."

e This decline does not reflect fewer listeners, but limitation of the later figure to formal enrollment in "telecourses."

f Adult Sunday School classes are included. This drastic increase is caused by growth of adult educational activities in churches and synagogues and by improved reporting procedures.

channels of communications, according to the following dimensions:

The institutional dimension. As has previously been shown, a wide variety of institutions has undertaken to provide educational activities for adults. In Chapter V it was seen that these institutions tended to develop segmental coordinative organizations according to the following specific system of categories: (1) business and industry; (2) colleges and universities; (3) Cooperative Extension Service; (4) foundations; (5) government agencies; (6) health and welfare agencies; (7) independent and residential centers; (8) labor unions; (9) libraries; (10) mass media; (11) museums and art institutes; (12) proprietary schools; 13) public schools; (14) religious institutions; and (15) voluntary associations.

The adult educational function has been much more highly developed and differentiated in some institutional categories, such as colleges and universities, libraries, and public schools, than in others, such as government agencies, mass media, and museums. Also, within each category certain institutions are more advanced in their adult educational service than in others; for example, large public school systems tend to be more advanced than small ones. And there are wide variations in the degree of development of segmental coordination among the several institutional categories; for example, no coordinative organizations have yet appeared for foundations, government agencies, independent and residential centers, or voluntary associations. Clearly, the institutional dimension is not a fully matured substructure of the field, but it is farther along in its development than any of the other dimensions.

The subject-matter dimension. As was indicated in Chapter V, few adult educational workers are specialists in particular subject fields, and so interest in different subject-matter areas has not been a prominent basis of substructuring of the field in the past. The recent experience of the AEA with Special Interest Sections based upon differentiation according to what might more accurately be called "program areas" suggests, however, that this may be a dimension with great potential for future development. A typology of program areas in adult education that was developed by this writer for the 1960 *Handbook of Adult Education in the United States* provides at least a starting point for the systematic development of this dimension. That typology includes the following program areas: (1) academic education; (2) education for aging; (3) community development; (4) creative arts; (5) economic education; (6) fundamental and literacy education; (7) health education; (8) home and family life education; (9) human relations and leadership training; (10) intergroup education; (11) liberal adult education; (12) public affairs education; (13) adult recreation education; (14) science education; and (15) occupational education.

The geographical dimension. The fact that adult educational workers and organizations have tended naturally to organize on the basis of their identification with local communities, states, and regions was also documented in Chapter V—as was the fact that this development has been highly uneven around the country. In most national coordinative organizations serving other fields and in previous thinking about the coordination of the adult educational field, the substructuring of a field according to a hierarchy of geographical units has been assumed to be a prerequisite of effective coordination. But except for some minor concessions to this idea in the AEA's joint membership plan, the geographical dimension has not been an integral part of the national coordinative machinery of the adult educational field.

The personnel dimension. Within the total population with which adult education is concerned are two general types of persons: those who provide educational opportunities (the leadership group) and those who partake of the educational opportunities (the consumer group).

The leadership group includes three subpopulations, which Houle describes as the "pyramid of leadership."[5] At the base of the pyramid is the largest group, the volunteer leaders of myriad group activities with an educational purpose. In the middle is a smaller group of persons who, as part of their paid employment, combine adult educational functions with their other duties. At the top of the pyramid is the smallest group, those who have a primary concern for adult education and basic career expectations in this field. Repeated evidence was cited in Chapter IV indicating that there is a strong trend in the field toward the increasing differentiation of the roles of these professional adult educational workers in their various institutional settings.

The consumer group in the adult educational population dimension is less easily described,[6] but, as it has already been pointed out, this group is rapidly growing in size, variety, and educational level. Both the leaders and the consumers of adult education have a stake in the nature and quality of the adult educational enterprise, and both should presumably be involved in the decision-making processes of the field. In actual practice, however, the consumers have seldom participated beyond the level of local institutional program planning, with the result that the coordinative efforts at the local, state, regional, and national levels have on the whole been deprived of the wisdom, experience, support, and influence of this most numerous—and potentially powerful—element of the field.

The adult educational field is a highly interactive social system. The various dimensions of the field intersect and interact with one another at many points. Each of the program areas in the subject-matter dimension, for example, is composed of persons from a variety of institutions; to give one illustration, specialists in home and family life are found in the institutional settings of business and industry, colleges and universities, agricultural extension, government agencies, health and welfare agencies, public schools, and religious institutions. Each geographical substructure includes persons from both the institutional and subject-matter dimensions. And within each of the first three dimensions—institutional, subject-matter, and geographic—there are or could be consumers and persons from every level of the leadership pyramid. Indeed, this is a social system in which each individual typically has multiple memberships, each membership affecting the others in conflicting, supplementing, or reinforcing ways. Usually an individual is a member first of his institutional group—"first" in the sense that he usually feels this to be his primary identification. Even this membership is often multiple, though; a director of a labor education program in a university feels identified with both union and university groups. An ndividual may also be secondarily identified with a subject-matter grouping, as in the case of the public school adult education director with a special interest in developing programs for retired persons. This same individual might be the president of his local community adult education council, a member of the executive committee of his state adult education association, the program chairman of his regional association, and a delegate to the Adult Education Association of the U. S. A., demonstrating the possibility even of multiple geographical memberships. Finally, an individual adult educator will be identified with one of the levels of the pyramid of leadership, and his interests will vary greatly according to the level to which he belongs.

The adult educational field is in the process of developing a distinctive curriculum and methodology. In the early stages of the development of the field, both the curriculum and the teaching methods of adult education were directly borrowed from the traditional schools for youth, the assumption being that what was good education for youth was good education for adults. But with experience, adult education practitioners discovered that adults differ from youths as learners in several important regards. For one thing, adults come into a learning experience with both more experience and different kinds of experience than youth, with the consequence that adults are ready for different kinds of learnings than youth and are able to contribute greater resources from their experience to the learning transaction. In the second place, adults tend to enter into a learning experience as a means to help solve particular life problems they have actually confronted whereas youth tend to regard learning experiences as preparation for the future, so that adults tend to have clearer and more immediate purposes for learning than youth. Finally, adults tend to have less time available for learning activities than youth, so that adult students typically cannot tolerate as heavy a load of homework but on the other hand are under pressure to make efficient use of every minute.[7]

As these differences became increasingly recognized the programs offered to adults tended to be constructed less and less on the basis of traditional academic principles of subject organization and more and more on the basis of the problems of individuals and of society; and even in the traditional educational institutions the curriculum for adults burst out of the academic boundaries. New institutional forms were created, including the continuing education center, the training laboratory, the community college, the coordinated course, the college of general studies, and others, in order to better fit the needs of adult learners. The methodology of adult education tended to move away from traditional classroom methods in favor of methods that would make greater use of the experience of the adult learners, such as group discussion, role playing, case method, book-based discussion, the unstructured group method, and various combina tions of methods in workshops, conferences, and institutes. By 1960 adult education had become quite different from youth education in both form and substance.

Adult education is becoming an increasingly clearly delineated field of study and practice. Verner points out in his study of the literature of adult education that "the growing maturity of a field is represented by the changing character of its literature. . . . The literature of adult education is rapidly moving out of the phase of impressionistic propaganda and intuitive reports into more carefully structured research." [8] The large volume of studies published by the AAAE between 1924 and 1950 was more than impressionistic propaganda and intuitive reports. This body of descriptive literature was probably more responsible than any other factor for establishing the adult educational field as a respectable and definable field of study. And the later publications of the AEA, which were concerned primarily with translating the findings of the social sciences into improved adult education practices, had a somewhat similar effect in establishing adult education as a discrete field of practice. But Verner's assertion that the literature of the field is moving in the direction of more carefully structured research is supported by Brunner's review of this aspect of the field, which indicates that the education of adults is becoming an increasingly frequent object of research both in the adult educational field itself and in the related disciplines.[9]

Equally sharp evidence of the growing delineation of the field is provided by the emergence of specialized training for adult educational practitioners. The widespread institution of in-service training programs for both paid and volunteer adult educational workers in the various institutional settings was documented repeatedly in Chapter IV. But probably of even greater ultimate significance is the emergence of adult education as a respected field of professional graduate study. Initiated at Teachers College, Columbia University, in 1935, programs leading to advanced degrees in adult education had spread by 1960 to fourteen other universities in the United States and Canada, and some kind of professional study was offered in over fifty universities.[10]

GENETIC PRINCIPLES

An analysis of the circumstances under which adult educational institutions emerged and survived or changed, as described in the preceding chapters, suggests certain genetic principles that seem to guide the development of this field and that may help to illuminate its character.

The institutions of adult education typically emerge in response to specific needs, rather than as part of a general design for the continuing education of adults. The institutions for the education of children and youth—elementary schools, high schools, junior colleges, technical institutions, and colleges and universities—had their genesis in a broad conception of general education that predicated a continuing process of learning with unity, sequence, integration, comprehensiveness, and articulation. The institutions for the education of adults came into being without reference to any such grand design. Rather, the developmental process of the adult education movement in this country has been one largely of *need-meeting.* When the new nation needed the former colonial subjects to be quickly converted into citizen-rulers, adult educational activities came into being for this specific purpose. When the agrarian population needed quickly to be taught the skills required by the industrial revolution, mechanics' institutes, apprenticeship programs, private vocational schools, and other institutional forms were invented to serve this need. When a flood of immigrants needed to be "Americanized," special programs were devised to meet this need. And so on through history, adult education's role has been one of responding to the needs of individuals and of society as they arose.

This characteristic has caused adult educational institutions as a whole to be more sensitive than most educational institutions to the changing pressures of society for service. If adult education has missed its cue at times, as it did in failing to provide for the intellectual emancipation of the slaves after the Civil War and in failing to prepare our citizenry for the role of world leadership forced on this country by World War I, its record on the whole reflects a high degree of sensitivity to social needs.

The developmental process of adult education tends to be

more episodic than consistent. In a sense, adult education has thrived on crises, since needs are greatest and clearest then. Similarly, it has tended to retrench in periods of placidity. The crisis of the American Revolution produced a rash of informal institutional forms for the education of adult citizens, and it was followed by a twenty-five-year adult educational plateau. The onset of the industrial revolution and the accompanying secular enlightenment stimulated another flurry in which a number of institutions were founded for the diffusion of knowledge among the adult population, including lyceums, public libraries, museums, agricultural societies, and evening schools. Then followed two decades of minimal development, until the crisis of industrial expansion and urbanization that followed the Civil War produced perhaps the most fertile period of institutional development of all—with the appearance of chautauquas, correspondence courses, labor schools, university extension, evening high schools, and a profusion of voluntary organizations and social agencies. The curve of growth tended to level off somewhat during the peaceful years around the turn of the century, except for meeting the crisis of increasing waves of immigrants. Then the succession of twentieth century crises—two world wars, a great depression, and a technological revolution—produced rapid growth all along the front.

Institutional forms for the education of adults tend to survive to the extent that they become attached to agencies established for other purposes. Few instrumentalities created expressly for the education of adults have been able to persist for very long independently of other institutions. For example, the two major national programs organized exclusively for the education of adults, the lyceum movement and the chautauqua movement, endured for only a few years as national programs; but many of the adult educational activities they developed, such as study-discussion groups, extension lectures, and correspondence courses, were adopted by such other institutions as evening schools, university extension, and voluntary agencies. A few exceptions to this generalization can be cited. On the national level a number of private correspondence schools catering primarily to an adult clientele have managed to persist as independent institutions. And at the local level such agencies as the Cooper Union in New

York, the Lowell Institute in Boston, the Junto in Philadelphia, and perhaps a few others, have survived independently.

But the great bulk of the institutional forms for the education of adults that have survived have become attached to some host institution. The agencies that have principally served as hosts for adult education are of three types: (1) those that were created for the education of young people, such as schools, colleges, and youth agencies; (2) those that were created to serve the general community, such as libraries, museums, settlement houses, and community centers; and (3) those that were created to achieve other than educational goals but use adult education as a means for achieving these goals, such as labor unions, business and industry, government agencies, cooperatives, voluntary associations, and prisons.[11]

Adult educational programs tend to emerge with a secondary status in the institutional hierarchy. Because the institutional forms for the education of adults that have survived are for the most part attached to institutions established for other purposes, these programs tend to be perceived as secondary or peripheral functions in their respective social systems. Some of the consequences of this phenomenon are pointed out by Clark as follows:

Peripheral programs within multiprogram organizations typically have low status and little power, and, in consequence, are insecure . . . they have low priority in the budget and frequently must pay their own way; central administrators forget they exist as attention goes to basic functions; and, when retrenchments are in order, the unimportant programs are severely curtailed.[12]

Adult educational programs tend to gain stability and permanence as they become increasingly differentiated in administration, finance, curriculum, and methodology. In their early stages of development most adult educational programs are hardly distinguishable from the other activities of the sponsoring institution. In the public schools, for example, the early activities for adults were administered and financed within the framework of the day school administrative and policy structure and borrowed their subject matter and teaching methods from the day school. So long as this condition persisted the evening schools were highly vulnerable to administrative whims and were not very attractive to their adult constituency. As they developed administrative structures and programs geared more directly to the unique characteristics of adults as learners they tended to become more stable and attractive. In earlier chapters are cited several examples of programs that went into serious decline when they failed to become differentiated in terms of the unique needs of adults, including the early correspondence schools, early university extension programs, and the formal educational program of the YMCA. But Chapter IV documents the growing strength of the adult educational programs in business organizations, colleges and universities, libraries, religious institutions, voluntary associations, and other institutions as the adult educational units in them became increasingly differentiated.

The institutional segments of the adult educational field tend to crystallize into organized substructures without reference to any conception of a general adult educational movement. Indeed, the notion that all the various adult educational activities might add up to some composite entity that might be thought of as a national program of education for adults was not even conceived before the Carnegie Conferences in 1924. But by that time segmental organizations had been formed in the areas of agricultural extension, health and welfare, labor, library work, museum work, public school adult education, and university extension. Even after the establishment of the American Association for Adult Education segmental organizations came into being totally without relationship to it in the fields of evening college work, business and industry, the mass media, and religious education.

A CONCEPTION OF THE DEVELOPMENTAL PROCESS OF THE FIELD

Much of the planning for the coordination of adult education in the past has been based inferentially on the assumption that it is a field that is fully in existence. The practice, for example, of basing current program plans and organizational policies on the findings of surveys of the current perceptions of those in the field as to what services they want and need assumes a fully developed field. Admittedly current perceptions have to be taken into account and contemporary needs have to be met, but unless they are placed in the context of some sense of direction of development of the field, there is danger that the field will become fixated at an immature stage of development.

The picture presented in the preceding chapters is that of a social system in the early stages of development. Comparison with the ages of related fields, as symbolized by the founding of national organizations to coordinate their fields, makes this fact clear. Compared with the 85-year-old library field (the American Library Association was founded in 1876), the 88-year-old social work field (the National Conference on Charities and Correction was founded in 1873), and the 104-year-old public school field (the National Teachers' Association was founded in 1857), the adult education field was a 35-year-old infant in 1961 (the AAAE was founded in 1926). And as was true of these related fields when they were thirty-five years old, many of the difficulties of the adult educational field depicted in Part II—such as vagueness of definition, unevenness of development, confusion of roles, lack of focus in aims and direction, inadequacy of communication, and general instability of the social system—are perhaps merely symptoms of this youthful stage of development.

The direction of the developmental process of which the adult educational field is now in an early stage would be toward a unified field in which (1) each component part is developed to its full potential and has a clearly defined role; (2) all component parts subscribe to a core of common aims, are in communication with one another, and plan cooperatively in regard to mutual objectives; and (3) the field is coordinated by a national organization which is truly representative of the component elements of the field.

THE DYNAMICS OF THE FIELD AS RELATED TO ITS COORDINATION

The Need for Coordination

The need for the coordination of the adult educational field has been widely expressed in many ways, with the direction of movement over the course of time being in general from a narrow to an increasingly broad conception of the need.

At the founding of the AAAE the need was conceived primarily in terms of the pooling of information, with only overtones of concern for the integrated planning of the total adult educational enterprise.

Keppel emphasized the need for "advice to communities as to how they may organize and co-ordinate what they already have, and how, if necessary, they may supplement it in order that the citizens of that community may have available a well-balanced educational ration." [13]

W. S. Bittner, pioneer university extension leader, emphasized the need for integration of learning, pointing out that "segmental efforts at adult education do not have any long-time continuity for the mature person who submits to this halting instruction." [14]

The 1928 meeting of the Department of Adult Education of the NEA heard a series of speakers assess the areas in which the universities, libraries, and public schools each had a unique role. Its Commission on Coordination then urged that "organizations and agencies serving within this field endeavor to find, not only their own peculiar task, but also to discover in what ways their service may be facilitated and improved through coordination and articulation of their service with that of other organizations and agencies," to the end that "waste, confusion, and duplication" may be prevented within communities. [15]

Lyman Bryson pointed to the societal need for the coordination of adult education, on the rationale that adult education is one of the ways "by which all the resources of a social group may be put to work for the betterment of life," the stake in this undertaking being that "our success in managing our difficult civilization may hang upon the use we make of the learning power which is ours as long as we are alive." [16]

To Floyd Reeves the most pressing need was "to prevent wasteful or undesirable duplication, to fill existing gaps, and to make education facilities available to all adults who desire them and who would benefit by them." [17]

Cyril Houle advocated preserving the values of "diversity of operation and control" of the many adult educational agencies, but felt that through better contact with one another "each agency might then improve its own services from a greater knowledge of and experience with the objectives, practices, and personnel of the other agencies." He could also see that "the total range of service to the adult population might be improved with the elimination by individual agencies of gaps and duplication and the promotion of joint activities directed toward a more extended and complete program." [18]

In the view of Robert Blakely the sharpest need is for a *philosophy,* so that no matter what problems adult educators are facing they share a common cause and are abidingly aware of that sharing; and a *goal,* so that no matter on what sectors they are working, all are paying attention to the common front— their eyes on the same checkpoint: a lofty and distant peak of achievement.[19]

Other leaders of the field have pointed to the need for joint planning by all organizations on behalf of the total community,[20] for giving the adult educational movement a sense of direction,[21] and, in fact, an almost infinite list of additional needs.[22]

Clearly, there has been widespread recognition in the field of the need for coordination at the local, state, and national levels. But as the preceding statements illustrate, little agreement has existed regarding the priority order of the needs and therefore regarding the focus of coordinative efforts. In consequence, when a coordinative organization has attempted to focus on a particular set of needs, as the AAAE focused on the collection and dissemination of information, it has lost the support of those who felt other needs were more important. On the other hand, when a coordinative organization has attempted to meet a variety of needs, as did the AEA in its first eight years, it has lost the support of those who felt that it was not giving the field a unifying sense of direction.

CONCEPTS OF COORDINATION

If there has been little agreement regarding the focal need for coordination of the adult educational field, there has been probably even less agreement on the best or most appropriate or most feasible means of satisfying this need. The AAAE chose the primary method of knowledge acquisition and dissemination, in the faith that a better informed field would voluntarily become a better coordinated field, and secondarily used the method of bilateral relationships with selected organizations. The AEA, on the other hand, chose the method of providing a positive instrument of joint planning for one dimension of the field, but left the coordination of other dimensions to natural processes and permissive consultation.

The preponderant sentiment has consistently favored coordination at the local, state, and national levels through a voluntary organization of some sort established expressly for this purpose. But, as pointed out previously, there has been some difference among local and state groups as to whether the preferable form of organization is an association of individual members or a council of organizational representatives, or a combination of these forms. Similar alternative forms have been proposed for coordinative organizations at the national level. The AAAE, for example, was wholly an individual membership organization that operated essentially as a service agency. The NEA Department of Adult Education was an individual membership organization that operated essentially as a professional society. The AEA was a combination of an association of individual members and a council of agency representatives.

Other leaders have proposed that coordination of the field should be achieved by a "holding company" of national organizations modeled somewhat after the National Education Association;[23] by the public schools at the local level[24] and the state department of education at the state level;[25] or by the federal government.[26] One of the early students of the problem of coordination suggested that it should be achieved not organizationally so much as programmatically by "advancing individual welfare and social progress through the development of seven great arts." [27]

When tested against the comprehensive view of the adult educational field presented at the beginning of this chapter, these concepts of coordination appear partial and incomplete. They do not encompass all dimensions of the field as conceptualized in this analysis, and they tend to be political in the sense that they accommodate themselves to the present reality only and have no sense of direction toward a fully matured field.

FORCES AFFECTING COORDINATION

Certainly any long-run plan for guiding the development of the adult educational field toward greater maturity must take into account the forces affecting its coordination. In the course of tracing the development of the field—and especially of its co-ordinative organizations—in the preceding chapters, it has become clear that a number of forces have been at work both for and against the further development of intercommunication and joint planning among the various elements of the field. The strongest of these forces can be summarized as follows:

Forces Favoring Further Coordination

1. The overlapping of the "markets" of the various adult educational activities results in pressure from the "consumers" for better integrated services. Although this force is seldom applied directly in the form of mass demands for coordinated planning, it is felt by the adult educators as a consequence of the choices made by their constituents. For example, when labor union members choose to participate in university programs rather than in union-sponsored programs, a pressure is exerted on both institutions to work together.

2. The marginality of the adult educational role in most institutional settings induces adult educators to seek mutual support, status, and problem-solving help across institutional lines.

3. The fact that advances in knowledge and method occurring in one element of the field have implications for other elements causes adult educators to seek beyond their own particular segments for personal growth.

4. As adult education has become increasingly recognized as a discrete activity, adult educators in each segment have come increasingly to look upon the adult educators in other segments as their natural allies in the struggle for recognition, power, and financial support.

5. There has been an increasing recognition on the part of adult educators of a growing commonality of interests cutting across segmental lines. For example, in a study of a sample of adult educational leaders in the public schools, proprietary schools, personnel training, and the American Association of University Women conducted by Thurman White in 1950, they were shown to have high common interest in the following nine areas:

1. To gain a better understanding of the basic needs which cause adults to participate in educational programs.
2. To gain a clearer insight into the changing interests of adults in vocations, religion, family, leisure time activities health, and other areas of life.
3. To increase one's ability to apply psychological principles to the selection of objectives.
4. To acquire techniques for relating our program more closely to the needs and interests of adults.
5. To acquire techniques for relating our program more closely to the general needs of the community.
6. To become more skillful in recognizing the community needs and resources that are important to adult education programs.
7. To develop a better understanding of the kinds of educational materials more suitable for mature people.
8. To become more skillful in recognizing the community needs and resources that are important to adult education programs.
9. To become more familiar with the procedures for "keeping up" with new developments and materials for adult education programs.[28]

Forces Opposing Further Coordination

1. The lack of agreement on the ultimate goals of adult education tends to set up a resistance in some adult educators toward working together on common problems on which they do agree. The fact is that different models of the desirable ends of education exist. For example, adult educators in liberal education institutions view the end product of education as an individual who can think responsibly for himself, whereas adult educators associated with some doctrinaire institutions—especially in the economic, political, and religious areas—view the desirable end product to be the individual who believes in their

doctrine. These differences sometimes produce emotional blocks to cooperation at any level.

2. In the hierarchy of multiple memberships held by most adult educators, the primary group membership—usually the institution that is paying the salary—tends to make demands on time, energy, interest, resources, and loyalty that inhibit substantial attention to memberships lower down the scale of commitment, such as in the general education field.

3. The competition of the various institutions and program areas for response from the same or overlapping target-populations tends to induce feelings of rivalry that inhibit full exchange of information and experience and whole-hearted cooperation.

4. Perceptions of difference in status among various segmental groupings within the field tend to induce feelings of inferiority, fear of domination, and other emotions that obstruct cooperation. Brunner found, for instance, that perceptions of dominance in the AEA of "the university people," "the professors," "the public school people," or, more generally, "those interested in formal education," on the one hand, and of "the group dynamics people" on the other, operated as a serious deterrent to cooperative efforts within the organization.[29]

5. The fact that the adult education workers in the various segmental groupings entered into their adult educational roles from different backgrounds of training and experience has produced differences in vocabularies, differences in theoretical and philosophical positions, and differences in methodological approaches which interfere with communications and present barriers to cooperation.[30]

6. The confusion that often exists in the minds of participants in coordinative organizations as between their roles as individual adult educators, in which they speak for themselves, and their roles as representatives of organizations, in which they speak for their organizations, complicates the operation of coordinative organizations.

7. The effectiveness of a coordinative organization is highly dependent upon the volunteer energies of its members for committee work and other organizational responsibilities, and these energies are made difficult to obtain by such common conditions

as lack of money for face-to-face meetings, difficulty of communication, and the competition of other interests.

8. Without a clear and comprehensive map of the field to be coordinated, it is difficult to construct a coordinative organizational structure in which the component parts of the field feel represented and in which a functional division of labor is possible. The lack of such a comprehensive picture of the field has, in fact, probably been one of the strongest forces opposing coordination up to 1960.

The difficulties experienced between 1924 and 1960 in developing successful coordinative organizations on every level would seem to indicate that these forces for and against coordination are nearly enough in balance to prevent substantial progress—with the favorable forces being perhaps more persistent, if not much stronger. A careful analysis of the historical record gives some evidence, however, of a basic tendency in the field that seems to have the effect of gradually weakening the opposing forces and strengthening the favorable forces.[31]

CHAPTER VIII

❦

THE FUTURE

OF ADULT EDUCATION

The ground on which the historian stands becomes progressively less firm as he moves from describing the past through interpreting the present to predicting the future. But trends which become discernible from a study of the past do not just dissolve in the present. While they may not determine the future course of events, trends at least suggest some probabilities that may be subtly influencing the minds of men who help to shape the future. It is in the spirit of projecting certain of the more visible trends of the past into probabilities regarding the future development of adult education that the first part of this chapter is written. Then the spirit will change sharply to one of examining some probabilities that emerge from a radically new set of assumptions.

SOME PREDICTIONS BASED ON PRESENT TRENDS AND ASSUMPTIONS

Given the continuation of the present direction of movement of our society, and especially of our educational system for youth, the following predictions regarding the future development of education for adults can be made with considerable security:

1. The size of the "student body" of adult education will continue to expand. This prediction is based on two assumptions: (1) the absolute number of adults in our population is increasing, and (2) the pace of social and technological change that induces adults to engage in self-improvement is accelerating. Adults

269

provide a potential student body about twice the size of that provided by children and youth, and presumably should constitute the largest segment of our national educational enterprise. But this potential cannot be achieved under the present assumptions that basic learning is primarily a function of youth and that adult education is primarily a short-term, spasmodic, need-meeting and gap-filling activity. Therefore, while the total number of adults who participate in organized learning activities in a given year may exceed the total number of youth students, they will still constitute a highly ephemeral and intellectually immobile student body. And the total volume of attendance-hours by adults will remain substantially under the volume accumulated by youth, with the result that while the absolute size of the adult student body may exceed that of youth, its volume of work will remain smaller.

2. The educational level of the student body of adult education will continue to rise. One consequence of this trend might be to place an increasing pressure toward excellence in curriculum and instruction on adult educators; but the danger is that under present assumptions "excellence" will be defined in rather sterile academic terms. Another possible consequence of this trend is that adults might turn increasingly toward self-education, especially if they find that organized adult educational programs are not geared to their real needs.

3. The resources and facilities for the education of adults will gradually expand. Public support for the education of youth became increasingly generous as society came to recognize its stake in the development of an educated citizenry, and this recognition of a societal stake is now being extended to the education of adults. The expansion of resources for adult education will probably be most visible in public institutions of education, but an increasing number of private institutions, including industry, will be perceived as having an educational responsibility toward their employees and clients, and will construct facilities and employ specialists for the fulfillment of this responsibility.

4. The curriculum and methodology of adult education will become increasingly differentiated from those designed for children and youth. Adult learning experiences will more and more

be organized around the problems and processes of real life rather than according to academic subjects. Old educational forms will be modified: courses for credit will be converted into non-credit courses for learning; traditional academic degrees will give way to special degrees for adults. New forms will be invented: some that are now in the embryonic stage of development include residential centers for continuing education, training laboratories, closed circuit television, and community colleges; others now on the horizon include teaching machines, electronic data processing and feedback devices, game-theory case problems, subliminal stimuli, and the use of mass media for two-way communication and interactive learning. Attempts will continue to be made to find a "core curriculum" for adults, but these are doomed to only partial success at best so long as education is perceived as primarily a function of youth.

5. There will be a rapid expansion in the body of knowledge about the education of adults. Research resources will be increasingly focused on the developmental processes of the adult years, the nature of adult learning, environmental factors affecting adult learning, characteristics of adults as learners, and institutional arrangements for the education of adults. It is highly probable that an enormous untapped potential for human growth and achievement will soon be discovered.

6. The role of the adult educator will become increasingly differentiated from other roles and training for this role will become increasingly specialized. A growing number of people will enter full-time careers in adult education, and an even larger number will seek to acquire the competencies required to perform the part-time adult educational component of such roles as business executive, youth leader, social worker, minister, and civil servant. Programs of graduate education in adult education in universities and in-service training in operating agencies will expand proportionately.

At the very least, if the conditions under which adult education continues to develop remain essentially as they are now, adult education is soon bound to match elementary, secondary, and higher education in size and significance. It will continue to be a dynamic field to observe and an exciting field to be in. But it will be tied to a set of assumptions about the nature of learning that have not changed substantially since they were formulated in the Middle Ages.

SOME PROBABILITIES BASED ON NEW ASSUMPTIONS

The new frontiers of adult education predicted above, even though based on current trends and assumptions, may seem visionary. But the odds are high that they are already archaic; they may, indeed, be more relevant to the world of the past than to the world of the future.

For a new force has been introduced into the dynamics of civilization that requires an entirely new set of assumptions about the purpose and nature of education. This force is so new and so subtle that it is only beginning to be discerned by a few of the more sensitive analysts of culture. This force is, very simply, the fact that the time-span of cultural revolution has for the first time in history become compressed into less than the lifetime of an individual.

Alfred North Whitehead heralded the appearance of this phenomenon in 1931 with these words:

Our sociological theories, our political philosophy, our practical maxims of business, our political economy, and our doctrines of education, are derived from an unbroken tradition of great thinkers or of practical examples, from the age of Plato in the fifth century before Christ, to the end of the last century. The whole of this tradition is warped by the vicious assumption that each generation will live substantially amid the conditions governing the lives of its fathers and will transmit those conditions to mould with equal force the lives of its children.

We are living in the first period of human history for which this assumption is false. . . . The note of recurrence dominates the wisdom of the past, and still persists in many forms even where explicitly the fallacy of its modern application is admitted. The point is that in the past the time-span of important change was considerably longer than that of a single human life. Thus mankind was trained to adapt itself to fixed conditions. But today this time-span is considerably shorter than that of human life, and accordingly our training must prepare individuals to face a novelty of conditions.[1]

The present generation of adults is the first generation in the history of civilization that is having to live in a world that is different in its essential character from the world into which they were born. The consequences of this fact for education have come to dominate much of Margaret Mead's thinking, as reflected in this passage:

Within the lifetime of ten-year-olds the world has entered a new age, and already, before they enter the sixth grade, the atomic age has been followed by the age of the hydrogen bomb. . . . Teachers who never heard a radio until they were grown have to cope with children who have never known a world without television. Teachers who struggled in their childhood with a buttonhook find it difficult to describe a buttonhook to a child brought up among zippers. . . . From the most all-embracing world image to the smallest detail of daily life the world has changed at a rate which makes the five-year-old generations further apart than world generations or even scores of generations were in our recent past, than people separated by several centuries were in the remote past. The children whom we bear and rear and teach are not only unknown to us and unlike any children there have been in the world before, but also their degree of unlikeness itself alters from year to year.[2]

No wonder Dr. Mead was forced to conclude that the purpose of teaching has now changed from teaching what we know to teaching what we don't know!

Some Required New Assumptions about Education for Children and Youth

The introduction of this new force into our culture—the compressing of the time-span of major social change into less than a single lifetime—requires a whole new set of assumptions about the education of both youth and adults. It is necessary to examine those regarding children and youth first, since they largely determine the requirements for the education of adults.

1. *The purpose of education for the young must shift from focusing primarily on the transmission of knowledge to the development of the capacity to learn.* Traditionally, the central purpose of education has been to transmit culture from one gen-

eration to the next. And always before this purpose has served society well, since our ancestors were born into a world that they could rely on to be essentially the same when they died. What they learned from their fathers about how to think, what to think, how to make a living, and how to relate to other people proved to be adequate throughout their own lifetimes and they had to add very little to these learnings to equip their sons and daughters to live adequately throughout their lifetimes.

But in the modern era much of what we learned in our youth becomes at best inadequate and at worst obsolete and even untrue by the time we have to apply it in adult life. This phenomenon is highly visible in regard to science education; it is widely accepted now that a scientific education is good for about seven years. The phenomenon is also highly visible in regard to vocational education; automation and technological advances render thousands of workers obsolete almost daily. The phenomenon is less visible, and perhaps therefore more insidious, in regard to other human competencies. Ways of thinking about art, music, literature, and drama that we of the current generation of adults learned in our youth ill equipped us to keep up with the sequence of intellectual revolutions that have occurred in the last quarter century. Attitudes that we learned at a time when world power was controlled by Caucasian peoples are no longer functional in a world in which world power is shifting to colored peoples. In fact, the very bases of understanding ourselves as human beings shift like ocean sands as the researchers of psychology, sociology, anthropology, medicine, and other human sciences uncover new facts and insights about us.

If it is true that the time-span of cultural revolution is now less than the lifetime of a human being, the needs of society and the needs of individuals can no longer be served by education that merely transmits knowledge. The new world then requires a new purpose for education: *the development of the capacity in each individual to learn, to change, to create a new culture* throughout the span of his life. Certainly knowledge must continue to be transmitted, but no longer as an end in itself—only as a means to the end of mastering the ability to learn. The central mission of elementary, secondary, and higher education must become, then, not teaching youth what they need to know, but teaching them how to learn what is not yet known. The substance of youth education therefore becomes process—the process of learning; and accordingly the substance of adult education becomes content—the content of man's continually expanding knowledge.

2. *The curriculum of education for the young must shift from subject-mastery basis of organization to a learning-skill basis of organization.* If youth are to be taught *how* to learn over *what* to learn, then learning activities will have to be organized as ever broadening and deepening sequences of inquiries in which the students find the answers to their own questions. The curriculum will be organized around problem areas or questions rather than around fragmented subject areas. Fortunately, excellent starts have already been made in organizing certain sequences in this way, especially in mathematics and some sciences. [3] But a school curriculum that has changed only in degree and not in kind from the medieval trivium and quadrivium still has a major revolution ahead of it before it can meet the requirements of the modern world.

3. *The role of the teacher must be redefined from "one who primarily transmits knowledge" to "one who primarily helps students to inquire."* This shift will, in turn, require a new kind of training for teachers, in which relatively less emphasis is placed on the acquisition of huge volumes of subject content to greater emphasis on understanding the processes of learning and on gaining skill in guiding (and serving as a resource to) students in conducting self-inquiries.

4. *A new set of criteria must be applied to determine the readiness of youth to leave full-time schooling.* If knowledge is doomed to obsolescence every few years, then it is no longer valid to test the readiness of a student to graduate by testing how much information he has acquired. Rather, it would seem that three radically different criteria are required.

First, has the student mastered the tools of learning? To measure a student against this criterion will require instruments that will provide data that would answer such questions as these: Can he read up to his capacity? (It is estimated that the average high school and college graduates today can read only at half their trainable capacities—yet reading is the primary tool of continuing learning.) Can he think symbolically? Can he ask

questions that get at the heart of the matter and that can be an-
swered through inquiry? Does he know how to collect and analyze various kinds of data? Does he understand the basic concepts
and can he use the basic methods of the various intellectual
disciplines? Can he communicate effectively with populations
that are relevant to his welfare? Is he familiar with and able to
use the important sources of knowledge?

Second, has the student developed an insatiable appetite for
learning? If he is leaving formal schooling feeling that he has
finished a full meal at the table of knowledge, then he is not
ready to graduate; he needs more education. But if he is leaving
with an overwhelming sense of dissatisfaction with his inadequa-
cies and a burning desire to overcome them, he is prepared for
the adult world.

Third, does he have a definite, but flexible, plan for continuing
his learning? Certainly before his final year is completed every
student should have skilled guidance in (1) diagnosing his individual needs for continuing learning, (2) identifying the resources available to him in the community for satisfying these
needs, and (3) building a personal program of further learning
that will possess continuity, sequence, and integration. It would
help to symbolize the concept of learning as a lifelong process if
every institution for the education of youth would convert its
graduation ritual into an exchange between the student, who
would hand the president a scroll detailing his plans for continuing learning, and the head of the institution, who would hand the
student a certificate stating that the institution has taught the
student all it now knows about how to learn but will continue to
make its resources available to him for further inquiry.

New Perspectives for Adult Education

Should it come to pass that education is redefined as a lifelong
process rather than as a function of youthful years, then with the
emergence into adulthood of the first generation of youth who
have been taught how to learn rather than what to think, the role
of adult education in society would begin to be transformed.

1. Certainly adult education would then become the largest
and most significant dimension of our national educational enter-

prise. Almost all adults would perceive "going to school" as being as normal a part of the daily pattern of living as "going to work" has been in the past, for this is what they would have been brought up to expect. In fact, going to school and going to work (even going to work as a housewife) may come to be seen as interrelated aspects of the same process as employers and communities come to treat continuing learning and work, and continuing learning and citizenship, as two sides of the same coin. The problem of what to do about increasing leisure as the work week becomes shorter would become meaningless, because the work week would be redefined as the work-study week. Under these circumstances, the size of the adult student body would grow to be at least twice the size of the youth student body in numbers and probably of about equal size in volume of attendance hours.

2. The number of institutions providing opportunities for continuing learning would greatly increase, and existing educational institutions would greatly expand their programs for adults. Every industrial firm, government agency, health and welfare agency, and voluntary association would have to provide for the continuing learning of its employees, clients, and members as a condition of survival. Adult education would become as fixed a part of their budgets, buildings, and organizational structures as production, marketing, public relations, and administration now are. Schools and colleges would have an enrollment of part-time adult students twice the size of full-time youth students, and would have specially designed facilities and specially trained faculties to serve them.

3. A special curriculum would be constructed to provide adults with a continuous, sequential, and integrated program of lifelong learning. With youths entering into adulthood knowing how to learn, the curriculum of adult education would gradually turn from consisting of a hodgepodge of remedial activities to a positive program of sequential development. Certainly the curriculum would provide for adults to keep up to date on major developments of new knowledge and methods in both those areas of life that concern every citizen (the generalist dimension) and those areas in which each individual makes his vocation (the specialist dimension).[4] Thus there would probably be two parallel curriculums for adults, roughly corresponding to what we

now think of as general education and vocational education, but each would be keyed to the actual life problems confronted by the adult learners, and in this sense would not be traditional "core curriculums" but rather flexible programs that help people move in the general direction of greater maturity (such as broadening concepts, increasing independence of thought, sharpening skills, and deepening interests). Certainly the curriculum would also take into account the changing developmental tasks of adults as they move through the life span. The choices available to the young man and woman who are starting a career, raising a family, and trying to find new social relationships would be quite different from the choices available to middle aged or older adults whose developmental tasks are vastly different. The curriculum would be designed both to help adults to prepare for entering the next phase of development and for achieving fulfillment in their present phase of development.

4. An integrated adult education movement would emerge that would help to bring a sense of unity and articulation into the field of adult education equivalent to that now existing in the field of youth education. The general characteristics of such a movement would probably be somewhat along the lines described in the preceding chapter, but its mission would be quite different under the new assumptions we are now dreaming about than it could be under the existing assumptions. Its new mission would be primarily to engage the representatives of the various institutions concerned with the education of adults in the construction of a master plan for human growth during the adult years that would enable each institution to make those contributions to an individual's development that it is uniquely qualified to make, and to make these contributions in such a way that they would build cumulatively on the contributions of all other institutions. Its primary responsibility would be to shape up the uniquely adult curriculum described above and to bring the multiplicity of resources for adult learning into harmonious effort to carry out this curriculum.

5. We would start to create "educative communities." The social scientists are amassing evidence that the most significant and lasting changes in human behavior are achieved not by the direct instruction of individuals but by producing changes in their en-

vironment. For example, an individual is more likely to develop attitudes and skills of civic participation by living in a community in which opportunities for civic participation are rich and are rewarding than by attending a series of lectures on the subject. Accordingly, the adult education of the future would be perceived as serving a clientele not only of individuals but of organizations and total communities. This phase of the mission of adult education would be concerned with "teaching" organizations and communities to plan ways of work that will not only get things done but also will further the growth of persons. Howard Y. McClusky of the University of Michigan visualizes that when this millennium is reached doctors will not only treat illness but will "explain the way to abundant health," firemen will not only put out fires but spend a larger share of their time and energy training us to prevent fires, policemen will be more interested in helping to develop careful drivers than in giving tickets, and sales clerks will be more concerned with helping customers make wise choices than in selling whatever they can persuade a sucker to buy.[5] In a totally educative community everybody would be always partly a teacher and partly a learner; the highest social approval would be reserved for those activities and those persons concerned with improving the quality of human competence; and every decision by every organization and government agency would be evaluated in part according to its effect on the development of citizens toward increasing self-direction and enlightenment.

WHICH WAY WILL
ADULT EDUCATION GO?

If the line of reasoning to this point is even roughly correct, it seems clear that the fate of adult education rests on what happens in youth education.

If youth education continues to define education as primarily the process of transmitting the culture from one generation to the next, then adult education is doomed to advance only in the technology of meeting ephemeral needs and remedying gaps in the existing equipment of adults. For the student body of adult education will continue to be populated by people who perceive their education as essentially completed and who view additional education as merely an occasional vitamin, not as part of a balanced diet throughout life. The educational vacuum will continue to be filled for the most part by vocational and avocational palliatives, sectarian propagandizing, and frustrated attempts to provide a program of positive human development. Adult education would still be useful and necessary under these conditions, but it would be peripheral to a society that is on the verge of exploring the moon.

But if youth education should start flooding the adult student body with graduates who perceive learning as a lifelong process and who have learned how to learn, then adult education can become an instrument for helping individuals and society to realize to an increasing degree the enormous untapped power of human potentiality. The development of a race of human beings who are capable of approaching their full potentiality would then be possible, and the consequences in terms of the political, social, and cultural implications for our civilization would be incalculable. In fact, the concept of lifelong learning may well be our last secret weapon against the destruction of civilization. It is clearly our only insurance against the obsolescence of man.

The obstacles to the reorganization of our national educational system according to the concept of lifelong learning are great. Adults cling to the notion that the education that was good for them is good for their children. Unless they themselves become bored or dissatisfied they resist engaging in serious learning for themselves. Intellectual mobility is not yet a top priority value in our society. The breakthrough to the new day of lifelong learning will not occur, therefore, unless the current generation of adults is dramatically confronted with the fact of the threat of obsolescence. This, then, is the central challenge of the modern adult education movement. It must educate adults about the new meaning of education, and especially it must help the educators of youth to re-examine the effects of what they do in the schools on the quality of the learning their children engage in when they become adults. The highest priority subject matter for adult education in the immediate future is education about education. If that succeeds, then all education would become unified into a "lifelong education movement."

PART FOUR

SEQUEL

CHAPTER IX

※

SOME OBSERVATIONS ON

THE FOLLOWING FIFTEEN YEARS

(1961-1976)

As a historian moves in his reporting and analysis closer to his own time, his perspective—and therefore his role—changes. He no longer has the benefit of intervening decades to help him judge which events were passing meteors and which were permanent additions to the firmament. He cannot be secure about his ability to distinguish between fads and trends. His role becomes more that of a chronicler than that of a historian. He has to start talking more in terms of "as I see it" than in terms of "as it was." Hence the change in the title of this chapter to "Some Observations." Of necessity, a greater proportion of the material presented in this chapter is based on personal experience and observation and a lesser proportion on documentation than has been true of previous chapters. The reader becomes, therefore, an equally responsible participant-observer.

THE SOCIAL SETTING

The fifteen years from 1961 through 1976 were troubled, disorderly, and confusing—not only in America but worldwide. Perhaps, as some social analysts believe, these were the beginning years of an era of transition from a world of merely rapid change to a world of explosive change.[1] Another explanation, falling back on the Hegelian dialectic, could be that these were years in which antitheses to old theses were generated, so that soon we shall be entering into an era of new syntheses. Whatever the meaning of its events turns out to be, this era was one of turmoil for those who lived through it.

The characteristics of the population of the United States continued to change in important ways. In size it increased from over 180 million (including armed forces abroad) in 1960 to over 210 million in 1973, with a projected total by the year 2000 of up to 251 million.[2] As the population has grown larger, it has also resumed the trend toward becoming older. Throughout our history the median age of the American population has been rising from the tender age of 16 revealed in the second biennial census in 1800 to 30.2 in 1950. Then it dipped with the post-war baby boom to 28.0 in 1970 and started rising again in 1972 It is projected that it will be somewhere between 29.1 and 32.7 in the year 2000.[3] Clearly, America was in the early stages in the 1970's of having to shift from being a youth-oriented to an adult-oriented culture.

The half-century trend of population movement from the country to the cities continued during the sixties. Rural population decreased 0.3 percent while the populations of Standard Metropolitan Statistical Areas (cities of 50,000 or more and the surrounding counties economically integrated with the city) increased 16.6 percent and urban areas increased 19.2 percent.[4] However, as one demographer has pointed out, while it is apparent that the larger communities have a disproportionate amount of the population, "Nevertheless, only 36 percent of the total population lives in cities of 50,000 or more. In other words, almost half of the urban population still lives in fairly small cities."[5] Furthermore, "More than four-fifths of the national growth took place in the SMSA's, and in these areas more than four-fifths of the total growth took place outside the cities designated as central cities. The areas within the SMSA's but outside the central cities, often called suburbs, now for the first time in our history include more population than the central cities themselves, or more than is found in the nonmetropolitan portion of the United States."[6]

The central cities appeared to be in the process of becoming populated predominantly by Blacks and other minorities of low socioeconomic status. But this tended to be characteristic mostly of the metropolitan areas in the Northeast; in other parts of the country, especially in the South and West, "the pattern runs the other way—high socioeconomic status in the cities and lower status in the suburbs."[7] These shifts were part of the more general phenomenon of the continuously increasing mobility of Americans—31.8 percent changed their residence in 1973, over half of them to different cities,[8] thus putting into question the validity of such sacred cows in the American tradition as neighborhood roots, sense of community, and local control.

The American population also continued to become better educated, with the median number of years of school completed by persons 25 and over rising from 10.5 in 1960 to 12.2 in 1970.[9] But this central tendency statistic conceals pockets of serious deficiencies in the educational attainment of our population. For example, in a national survey made in 1971 it was estimated that 21.2 million adults (about 10 percent of our population but just about one of every five adults) "lacked reading skills at the 'survival' level, such as the ability to read the telephone book or fill out a simple job application."[10] And in 1970 the National Advisory Council on Adult Education reported that approximately 28 percent of all persons 16 years of age and older and 48 percent of those 25 years and older had less than a high school education.[11] The National Association for Public Continuing and Adult Education estimated that in 1975 there were 23,015,688 persons age 16 and over with less than an elementary school education.[12] The representation of Blacks and other minorities was higher in these statistics than their proportion of the total population.

On the social scene this fifteen-year period was characterized by intense and widespread protest, violence, attack on established institutions, and social disorganization. The period opened with clarion calls for the better life by President Kennedy in his proclamation of "The New Frontier" and by President Johnson in his proclamation of "The Great

Society." Aspirations were raised for the elimination of poverty, of inequality in education and work and civil rights, and of urban decay; reduction of crime, unemployment, and illiteracy; and improvement in health care, race relations, international relations, the status of women, economic opportunity, care of the aging, governmental services, and the quality of the environment.

But that cheerful dream was soon displaced by the nightmare of the Vietnam war. What had begun as a training mission to advise our South Vietnam allies in 1961 had escalated to full American involvement in open hostilities with an attack by North Vietnamese PT boats on a United States destroyer in the Gulf of Tonkin on August 2, 1964. On July 28, 1965, President Johnson announced that the United States armed forces in Vietnam would be increased from 75,000 to 125,000 and the draft would be doubled to support the war in the Far East. The following October there began a crescendo of anti-war demonstrations in the universities and cities of the country that reached its peak following the invasion of Cambodia in 1970 and did not subside until the treaty ending United States involvement in Vietnam was signed on January 28, 1973. In addition to its direct costs in terms of lives, materials, and money, the Vietnamese war incurred perhaps even greater indirect costs, including disillusionment with American leadership, a decade of violence and police brutality, the dislocation of our economy and the deep recession of the early seventies, the invasion of domestic privacy by our intelligence agencies, the growth of a military-industrial complex, and no doubt other costs still to be realized.

The social scene was further disturbed by a staccato barrage of other crises and violence:

- —1961: failure of the invasion of Cuba at the Bay of Pigs; a flurry of airplane hijackings; the erection of the Berlin wall.
- —1962: the Cuban missile crisis.
- —1963: the assassination of President Kennedy; race riots in Montgomery, Alabama and Cambridge, Maryland.
- —1964: the "Long Hot Summer" of race riots.
- —1965: the Civil Rights March on Selma, Alabama; the Watts riot in Los Angeles; anti-war rallies.

−1966: founding of the Black Panthers; more race riots and anti-war demonstrations.

−1967: more anti-war demonstrations; race riots in 127 cities; Haight-Asbury "Summer of Love" in San Francisco; spread of "Hippies" and "flower-children" around the country.

−1968: assassinations of Robert Kennedy and Martin Luther King; the My Lai Massacre in South Vietnam; seizure of university buildings in Columbia, Duke, Oregon, and San Francisco State universities; race riots in 125 cities; street fighting at the Democratic National Convention in Chicago; more anti-war demonstrations.

−1969: hijacking of sixty-five airplanes; ejection of students by police from the administration building at Harvard; more anti-war demonstrations; shooting of Chicago Black Panther leader by police while he lay asleep in bed.

−1970: killing of four students at Kent State University by national guardsmen during a campus demonstration against the Cambodian invasion; a nationwide student protest strike.

−1971: arrest of 12,000 anti-war demonstrators in Washington; publication in the *New York Times* of the "Pentagon Papers" revealing that the American public had been lied to.

−1972: President Nixon's visit to China; assassination attempt on Governor George Wallace, forcing him to withdraw from the presidential race; burglary of the Democratic National Committee headquarters in the Watergate building in Washington.

−1973: occupation of the trading post and church at Wounded Knee, South Dakota, by activists of the American Indian Movement; televised Senate hearings into Watergate break-in; war in Middle East between Israel and Syria and Egypt; Spiro Agnew's plea of *nolo contendere* to a charge of evading income tax and his resignation of the vice presidency; an oil embargo by Arab nations producing an energy crisis around the world.

−1974: formal hearings by the House Judiciary Committee on the impeachment of Richard Nixon; Nixon's resignation; a full pardon of Nixon by President Ford for all crimes Nixon may have committed.

−1975: sentencing of four Nixon Administration officials found guilty of the Watergate cover-up; evacuation of the last Americans from Vietnam; college campuses quiet.

—1976: widespread violations of the law and the rights of citizens by intelligence agencies revealed by a Senate Committee; decision by the Supreme Court upholding the rights of States to establish laws permitting abortion; Congress rocked by sex scandals.

It seems all the more remarkable, in light of these turbulent events, that considerable progress was made in achieving the goals of "The Great Society" on several fronts. In foreign affairs our aid to developing countries through the Peace Corps, the Agency for International Development, the World Bank, and other programs, demonstrated the innate idealism and generosity of the American people; and our relations with the U.S.S.R. and China became less tense. In race relations the passage of the Civil Rights Act of 1964, along with a number of Supreme Court decisions, produced substantial gains in the integration of public accommodations (including public schools in the South, although busing remained an issue in many parts of the North), increasing influence of Blacks in elections, and reduction of job discrimination. New federal agencies were established to deal with such social problems as protection of the environment, protection of consumer rights, the reduction of crime, the improvement of health care, the improvement of the quality of education, the improvement of the status of women (although adoption of the Equal Rights Amendment awaited action by several States), the development of new sources of energy, and the improvement of services to the elderly. But these remained issues, along with the reduction of poverty, the elimination of illiteracy, the control of multinational corporations, the restoration of confidence in government, and the achievement of world peace and prosperity, on the agenda for the era ahead.

On the economic scene the major concerns during this period were inflation and unemployment. As summarized by the *Congressional Quarterly*:

Inflation became a chronic and corrosive condition of American life during the decade 1965-1975. Through war and peace, plenty and shortages, expansions and contractions, prices rose persistently and the dollar's value dwindled.

By the end of that decade, prices were skyrocketing at rates of 10 percent or more a year, making a "double-digit inflation" an increasingly troubling threat to economic stability, as well as to the well-being of individual Americans.[10]

Unemployment ranged between 5 percent and over 9 percent, although for some segments of the population, such as Black young adult males, it ranged to over 30 percent.[14]

But at a deeper level, social analysts were beginning to worry that perhaps the very structure of the world economy was changing in such a way that former assumptions, concepts, models, and strategies for understanding and to some extent controlling it were no longer applicable. Alvin Tofler, for example, observed that the growth of domestic conglomerate firms and transnational corporations, the shift of wealth from the have-nations to the have-not nations (especially the oil-producing countries), and other structural changes create a totally new set of conditions that may result in an economic explosion—"Ecospasm."[15]

In science and technology, developments in this period were so fast and so varied that many scientists and laymen alike were worried lest they be getting out of hand. The conquest of space, the development of transistors and miniaturization of electronic circuits, the expansive use of com puters in hundreds of new fields of application, the extension of the use of laser beams, the prospect of being able to manipulate genetic structures, the discovery and distribution of myriad new drugs, the launching of scores of communication satellites that make instant transmissions around the world commonplace, and the transplanting of human organs provide just a taste of technological developments during this period. The setting of boundaries, goals, ethical standards, and methods of control for science and technology loomed as high priorities on the agenda for the next era.

Developments in the arts were equally confusing. An era that witnessed the construction of two of the finest centers for the performing arts ever conceived—the Lincoln Center in New York and the Kennedy Center in Washington—also witnessed the unleashing of waves of pornographic literature, motion pictures, and plays. Rock and Roll and country music dominated the air waves and record shops. In 1961 Newton N. Minow, Chairman of the Federal Communications Commission dubbed television "a vast wasteland" and said, "It is not enough to cater to the nation's whims—you must also serve the nation's needs." But criticism of the medium's saturation with soap operas, games of greed, and programs of violence appeared to have little effect. Literary critics of the period used such labels as "the literature of reduction," "the literature of exhaustion," "compositions and decompositions in the languages of contemporary life," and "culture of disparagement" to convey their assessment of the quality of literary production during this span of time.[16] In the fine arts what appeared to be "a decade of irresponsibility" to some was perceived by others as a really new kind of art, "Conceptual Art," described by one supporter as:

> . . .one that has shown less and less dependence on the art object and eventually has eliminated it altogether. In its place it substitutes process, real or imagined or both, as the essence of a new aesthetic experience. . . The new art embraces nonart materials and other ordinary things. For that reason it achieves a structural relationship with the environment of here and now or, in other words, the new art is a more public art.[17]

Finally, the educational scene was as turbulent, confused, and fermentative as the other scenes. In addition to the demonstrations, rallies, strikes, boycotts, and sit-ins associated with school desegregation and anti-war protest, there were direct attacks on the quality of education[18] and even on the legitimacy of organized education at all.[19] There were a variety of responses at the local level with the establishment of experimental schools of a variety of sorts—ungraded schools, open classrooms, alternative schools, community schools, and the like, and with new curriculums such as the "new math," "new social studies," competency-based education, and the like.[21] Countering these experimental solutions were numerous pressures to return the school to "teaching the basics."

The federal government also responded to the "crisis in the classroom" with the greatest infusion of legislation, funds, and direction into the national educational enterprise in history. Until the 1960's federal aid to education had been limited to land grants (such as the Ordinances of 1785 and 1787; the Morrill Act of 1862 for land-grant colleges) or for the funding of special programs (such as the Smith-Lever Act of 1914 for the Agricultural Extension Service; the Smith-Hughes Act of 1917 for vocational education; the anti-depression agencies—C.C.C., N.Y.A., P.W.A., and W.P.A.—in the thirties; the Service Man's Readjustment Act—the "G.I. Bill"—in 1941; the Impact Laws reimbursing local schools near military installations in the 1940s and 50s; and the National Defense Education Act of 1958 to stimulate education in science, foreign language, and mathematics). Congress was not ready for a shift to general aid to education when President Kennedy proposed it in the School Assistance Act of 1961 and the National Education Improvement Act of 1963, and both acts were defeated. But under the leadership of President Johnson, with the help of what he called "The Education Congress of 1963," the dam broke and out poured the following flood of general support for education:

- The Higher Education Facilities Act of 1963
- The Economic Opportunity Act of 1964
- The Civil Rights Act of 1964
- Dozens of acts for funding manpower development programs, library services, health professions educational assistance, mental retardation programs, and the like
- The giant of them all, the Elementary and Secondary Education Act of 1965 "to strengthen and improve education quality and educational opportunity in the Nation's elementary and secondary schools."

As a result of these and other acts, federal funds for education and related activities grew from $3.8 billion in 1960 to $16.5 billion in 1970.[22] Although this flow had been cut back to $14.9 billion in 1973 by the Nixon Administration, the principle of general aid to education by both direct grants and grants to States by the federal government had been established. A new role for the federal government in education had been defined, and the role of the United States Office of Education was elevated to that of a superagency, with authorization to give active leadership to the national educational enterprise.

This was the social setting for the most explosive growth of adult education in our national history.

INSTITUTIONAL DEVELOPMENTS IN ADULT EDUCATION

Business and Industry

The forces that caused an upsurge in education in industry following World War II—the greatly increased level of skill required as a result of automation and mechanization, the shortage of broadly educated and flexible executive talent, and the increasing acceleration of technological change—continued to be an influence in this era. But new forces were added. One set of forces emanated from the equal employment opportunity and civil rights legislation of the federal government, which required employers to take affirmative action in the integration and advancement of women and minorities in their companies. Another set came from the labor unions, which increasingly included educational benefits as demands in their contract negotiations. But perhaps even more fundamentally, a strong set of forces was produced by changes that took place during this period in management theory and philosophy. As reflected in the literature and in the programs of schools of business administration, there was a clear shift in emphasis away from the definition of the role of the executive as essentially a manager of logistics toward larger responsibility as a developer of human resources.[23]

A clear picture of industrial adult education was difficult to obtain, as Nader points out:

> Statistics on adult education in business and industry are almost impossible to find and the validity of those available is high questionable. One difficulty is in the definition of terms, as not all those engaged in training activites even agree they are functioning in the field of adult education . . . Another difficulty arises from the fact that some activities, such as on-the-job training, do not readily lend themselves to data gathering.[24]

Nevertheless, there were convincing clues that the adult educational services provided by business and industry to employees and their families, customers, and the general public, continued to expand in volume, variety, and quality. The membership of the American Society for Training and Development, which represents only the tip of the training personnel iceberg, grew from around 4000 in 1960 to around 10,000 in 1976. The American Management Associaton's seminars and institutes for supervisors and executives, which could be described in a small brochure in the early sixties, required a large catalog in 1976. Whereas only a handful of consulting firms specializing in training and development existed in 1960, the Consultant Directory published in the *Training and Development Journal* in November, 1972, contained 190 listings. A study of training, education, and personnel development in a cross-sectional sample of 62 corporations carried out by Stanley Peterfreund Associates in 1975 produced these findings:

> Training, education, and personnel development activity [T/E/D] and cost is massive and rising. In only five of the 62 companies is there a complete absence of formal training, inhouse. Only three of the 62 pay for no outside educational activity.
>
> Four out of five have responsibility for all formal training for all personnel under a single designated executive or manager.
>
> The large majority of these 62 companies report more activity, in greater variety, in '75 than in '70. Even in the midst of a recession, only a small minority expect to do less in '75 than in '74. (Revisits to 10 of these organizations in 1976 revealed that nine of the ten had spent more in 1975). And looking ahead, two-thirds anticipate they'll be doing more in 1980 than they are now. The level of T/E/D activities is on the uptrend!
>
> Of the 37 organizations from which we were able to get some documented costs the range was from $0 to over $20,000,000 per company. On a per-employee basis, the 37 companies spent an average of $161 per employee.
>
> One out of four companies has one or more separate, dedicated facilities—separate buildings or locations whose only use is for T/E/D. These companies usually also have space dedicated to T/E/D within other company facilities. Thirty percent more have dedicated T/E/D space, but none in buildings specifically built or maintained for that purpose.

More frequently than ever before, corporate education and training people and their functional department heads are full-time "professionals." The T/E/D functional office is in many ways becoming more importantly recognized, thus providing an additional career path in its own right. The trend, in fact, is to upgrade the function organizationally (in some cases splitting it out from Personnel, or even making Personnel the subordinate function).

The trend is away from a programmatic approach, with stand-alone courses and episodic activity, toward T/E/D as a process, as a rationalized system. Continuing education, in turn, becomes more closely integrated with other corporate objectives and planning. In this process, the individual becomes the focus. Less is approached on a universal basis; far more emphasis is given to customizing, individual options, self-motivation. This alters the role of the functional T/E/D staff, which traditionally has done the training and now (much more often) becomes the orchestrator of T/E/D—a resource, consultant, adviser—while the T/E/D activity itself becomes decentralized.

We see a growing tendency to view one's employees as a resource, and money spent in training, education, and personnel development as an "investment" rather than an "expense."[25]

It is clear that the trends which began in the preceding era have continued and accelerated during this period. Business and industry have indeed become major adult educational institutions.

Colleges and Universities

The trends which were identified in the previous era (page 84-90) continued and many of them accelerated during this period. Enrollments in extension, according to the Bureau of the Census, increased from 843,923 in 1952 to 3,367,000 in 1972.[26] The scope of services—notably in the expansion of continuing professional development activites for physicians, nurses, engineers, teachers, and others; the establishment of regional learning resource centers; the creation of statewide networks of computer-assisted instruction; and many others—continued to broaden. The curriculum steadily became increasingly organized around the real life tasks and problems of adults, with content being geared to competency development rather than rote learning. Administrative responsibility for extension activities tended to become more centralized and elevated in the university hierarchy, with many universities raising the office of dean of extension to that of vice president or vice chancellor. Extension staffs continued to grow in size, stature, and differentiation of role; and an increasing number of position announcements specified the possession of a doctorate in adult education as a prerequisite. The budgetary allocations for continuing education continued to increase, both absolutely and in relation to the budgets of other units of the universities; and, incidentally, the income from extension activities became an increasingly important factor in the economic health of many institutions of higher education. More and more continuing education centers designed expressly for the education of adults appeared on campuses around the country. Orientation and inservice education programs to provide teachers of adults with the new concepts and methodologies of adult learning became an integral part of the operations of most extension programs.

Houle characterized this era in these words in 1967:

> We are now well launched on the greatest forward surge of growth which higher adult education has ever known, more broadly based, more maturely conceived, and more universally accepted than at any other time in our history. The social determinist would find no root cause to explain this growth, in the same sense that the end of a long war created the last major thrust. We have, instead, only the maturing of many trends, which, interacting together, have created wide-spread support for advanced forms of adult learning. The ideas of 15 years ago have come into their own. We were prophets. . .we have worked hard and successfully to create programs, and now we reap the reward. We sense that we are still nearer the beginning than the end of a spurt of growth whose culmination we cannot yet see.[27]

Houle sensed correctly; the spurt of growth in the next ten years dwarfed that of the preceding decade. These were some of the new developments:

There was a massive infusion of funds into the higher adult education system by the federal government. There was a role for extension in almost every piece of social legislation enacted during this period—the Higher Education Act, the Elementary and Secondary Education Act, the Higher Education Facilities Act, the Manpower Development and Training Act, the Public Health Service Act, the Housing and Urban Development Act, the Foreign Assistance Act, and the Civil Rights Act.[28] The National Advisory Council on Extension and Continuing Education identified 184 discrete federal programs in extension, continuing education, and community service funded at $6.714 billion in 1972, with about $2.35 billions going directly to institutions of higher education.[29] As a result of these new programs tremendous demands were put on universities for providing training—the Vista volunteers, Peace Corps recruits, job corpsmen, community action leaders, Head Start teachers, paraprofessional workers in rural and innercity projects, employees of government agencies—community problem-solving service, consultation, and other services. Although many benefits accrued to higher adult education from this infusion of funds, leaders of the field expressed concerns about several possible negative consequences: (1) With most federal funds designated for special projects rather than for support of basic continuing programs, there is a tendency toward program fragmentation and diversion from central goals. (2) Since many federal projects are of a crash nature with short lead time for planning and unrealistic deadlines, they produce a diversion of energy from long-run objectives and a constant climate of crisis. (3) Status within and among institutions is strongly influenced by a dean's success in obtaining federal grants or contracts, producing a new spirit of competitiveness among colleagues and a tendency to value "grantsmanship" over broader professional competencies.[30] Perhaps as significant as the entry of the federal government into supporting higher adult education in the mid-sixties was the fact that attempts by the Nixon and Ford Administrations in the early seventies to cut back these appropriations were largely resisted by Congress. And as this period drew to a close, Senator Walter Mondale introduced a bill, the "Lifetime Learning Act," to support research and development, teacher training, curriculum development, conversion of facilities to serve adult participants, development of techniques for guidance and counseling of adults, development and dissemination of media materials appropriate for adults, and assessment of the role of gerontology and related fields to identify educational needs and goals of elderly Americans.

There was an extraordinary proliferation of community colleges across the country. In fact, this institutional form had become such a significant and discrete part of the higher education enterprise that its development during this period will be treated in a separate section.

Growing pressures from a variety of sources to make higher education more accessible to more people—especially part-time working adult students—produced a rash of nontraditional and external degree programs. Small experiments in making undergraduate degrees available to adults at their convenience, such as the Goddard College program started in the thirties and the special degrees for adults in such places as Brooklyn College and the University of Oklahoma (Bachelor of Liberal Studies) in the fifties, suddenly mushroomed into an epidemic of new external degree programs and other nontraditional study forms in the early seventies. And by the mid-seventies this epidemic was spreading throughout the body of the higher education establishment and starting to bring about transformations in its mission, structure, program, educational strategies, clientele, policies, and relationships with the larger society. Higher education responded to the pressure with minimal resistance—and in many cases without outright enthusiasm—because as the pool of youth available for college enrollment declined, finding a new clientele became a matter of survival.

A Commission on Non-Traditional Study was formed in 1971 under the auspices of the College Entrance Examination Board and the Educational Testing Service and funded by the Carnegie Corporation of New York and the Educational Foundation of America to study the phenomenon. The three publications produced during its two-year lifetime documented the need and demand, rationale, revolutionary implications, and widespread diffusion of nontraditional alternatives for higher education.[31] Samuel Gould, the Chairman of the Commission, has a very appealing definition of nontraditional study in his "Preface" to *Diversity By Design*. He is describing the process the Commission went through in trying to agree on what they were supposed to be investigating:

> Despite our lack of a completely suitable definition, we always seemed to sense the areas of education around which our interests centered. This community of concern was a mysterious light in the darkness, yet not at all mysterious in retrospect. Most of us agreed that non-traditional study is more an attitude than a system and thus can never be defined except tangentially. This attitude puts the student first and the institution second, concentrates more on the former's need than the latter's convenience, encourages diversity of individual opportunity rather than uniform prescription, and de-emphasizes time, space, and even course requirements in favor of competence, and, where applicable, performance. It has concern for the learner of any age and circumstance, for the degree aspirant as well as the person who finds sufficient reward in enriching life through constant, periodic, or occasional study.[32]

These new programs tended to possess one or more of the following characteristics: (1) open admissions; (2) granting of credit for learning outside of academia through a variety of assessment procedures (including the College-Level Examination Program, the College Proficiency Examination Program, and interviews by panels or individual mentors); (3) awarding of degrees solely by examination; (4) utilization of part-time non-faculty teachers and mentors; (5) development of individualized learning programs by students with or without the assistance of mentors; (6) fulfillment of learning objectives through contracts; (7) utilization of unconventional methods of learning and teaching (television, audiotapes, videotapes, films, programmed instruction, learning modules, work-study programs, computerized instruction, undirected experience, independent study projects); and (8) inclusion of noneducational institutions (business and industry, community organizations, government agencies) in an educational consortium. A survey conducted for the Commission in 1972 identified 351 nontraditional programs already in existence; but new programs were launched so frequently thereafter that the College Entrance Examination Board was forced to establish a special Office of New Degree Programs to keep its information up to date.[33]

A method for quantifying the value of noncredit continuing education activities, the Continuing Education Unit (CEU) was introduced and widely adopted. Originally developed by a group of thirty-three national educational, professional, business and labor associations, and government agencies, through a Task Force to Study the Feasibility and Implementation of a Uniform Unit for the Measurement of Noncredit Continuing Education Programs, the CEU was approved in 1971 by the Southern Association of Colleges and Schools and spread rapidly across the country. It was used especially widely for advancement and relicensing in the professions. But institutions also found it to be a simple matter to translate CEUs into full-time student equivalencies which can, in turn, be translated into state and federal institutional support formulas.[34]

The special problems of urban society caused urban universities to become more deeply involved in research and educational programs directly concerned with city living and city planning. Many universities created special administrative units and academic programs (e.g., urban affairs centers) to conduct research, offer instruction, or provide services related to urban problems. Others incorporated these activities into existing operations. Some state universities, notably Wisconsin, established urban extension agents who serve urban areas in much the same way that agricultural extension agents have served rural areas for over half a century, and bills have been introduced repeatedly into Congress for a national urban extension program.[35]

The proportion of older part-time students in credit programs continued to increase steadily. A new high of 38.4 percent part-time students was reached in 1975 opening fall enrollments in all postsecondary institutions (56.1 percent of credit students in community colleges were part-time). In 1974, 3.2 million, or one-third of the 9.8 million credit students were 25 and over; and of these 1,025,000 were over 35—an increase of 30.2 percent over the previous year. Of these, 80 percent were attending on a part-time basis.[36] In fact, the report of the Committee on the Financing of Higher Education for Adult Students of the American Council on Education in 1974 proposed that it was no longer meaningful to distinguish between "adult" and "regular" students ("It is the central premise of this report that *all* students in postsecondary institutions are adults with adult responsibilities").[37] It seemed clear that as nontraditional and external degree programs continued to make higher education accessible to older working students, adults would continue to constitute an increasing proportion of the clientele of higher education.

New delivery systems for reaching large numbers of people spread over extensive geographic areas were being developed. The Union of Experimenting Colleges and Universities (University Without Walls), headquartered at Antioch College, allowed students to work toward undergraduate and graduate degrees without requiring residence on any of the campuses of the thirty-plus members of its consortium. The University of Maryland offered full degree programs on scores of overseas bases of the Department of Defense for military personnel and their dependents. Brigham Young University reached more than a quarter of a million students through a nationwide and worldwide network of centers. Nova University, of Fort Lauderdale, Florida, offered several master's and doctoral degree programs anywhere in the United States where thirty or more students are able to be enrolled in a cluster for regular periodic sessions. Pennsylvania State University, the University of Nebraska, the University of Wisconsin, the California State University and College System, and many other state systems, deliver both credit and noncredit programs through networks of university centers, multimedia systems, and consortial arrangements with other institutions in the state.

New ways of financing higher continuing education were being explored and developed. A major breakthrough occurred in federal support for continuing education when provision was made for the first time for basic opportunity grants to be made available to part-time, students in the 1975 appropriation for Title IV of the Higher Education Act Amendments of 1972. A number of special task forces and commissions were exploring alternatives for state support for continuing higher education—notably in New York, New Jersey, Massachusetts, California, and Iowa.[38] The alternatives being considered included: (1) state financing of leadership positions, (2) state financing of information and counseling services, (3) state aid to institutions for adult students, (4) institutional incentive grants, (5) extensions of state aid to part-time and noncredit students, (6) an educational entitlement approach in which individuals are provided with vouchers entitling them to obtain educational services from institutions of their choice, and (7) tax incentives either to individuals or to employers. At the close of this period recommendations were ready to be presented to several state legislatures regarding one or more of these alternatives.

There was a tendency for institutions of higher education to join together into consortia to share resources and operate programs—and often to offer external degrees. These consortia frequently included noneducational organizations, such as corporations, government agencies, and community organizations, as full members. Some consortia were local or metropolitan in scope (e.g., the Bridgeport, Connecticut, Higher Education Consortium), while other were statewide (e.g., State University of New York, California State University and College System), regional (e.g., East Central College Consortium, Colleges of Mid-America), or national (e.g., Union of Experimenting Colleges and Universities). The concept of "learning systems" was being superimposed on the older concept of "educational institutions."

Graduate programs for training professional adult education workers expanded. In 1960 thirteen universities offered master's and doctor's degrees in adult education and produced a few score of graduates; in 1976 some sixty-five universities were graduating hundreds of professional workers. Indeed, adult education was by that time one of the few educational specialties in which the demand for trained workers was greater than the supply.

Community Colleges and Technical Institutes

Until the beginning of this era, the two-year college was such a peripheral part of the total higher education picture that it was simply incorporated into the statistics of colleges and universities (as in previous sections of this book) or of secondary education (as in the case of some earlier works). In 1953 only 265,799 students were enrolled in 518 two-year institutions, and these figures had grown to only 852,373 students in 633 institutions by 1963. Between 1963 and 1973 enrollment had skyrocketed to 2,919,650 and the number of institutions to 999.[39] The bibliography of a comprehensive survey of the literature of the field in 1962 listed only 19 books on junior and community colleges published between 1927 and 1960.[40] A similar bibliography in 1974 listed 65 books published since 1960.[41]

No doubt the forces which produced this phenomenal growth in a little over a decade included all of those that produced the ferment in higher education in general. But several forces seemed to have special potency for the community colleges: (1) an increasing shift from the manufacturing to the service industries produced a larger demand for skilled technicians and paraprofessionals—especially in the allied health fields; (2) faith in the power of education to open doors to social and economic opportunity caused the "new entrants" into higher education to be more career-oriented in their educational goals; (3) the egalitarian spirit of "The Great Society" stimulated federal legislation and aid directed toward the community college as a key institution in bringing about societal reform and opportunity for minorities; (4) the shorter commuting distances to most community colleges and their lower tuitions made it possible for working people to engage in higher education through part-time study; (5) the "open door" admission policy of most community colleges rendered past academic difficulties less a barrier to entry; and (6) increased competitiveness for admission to four-year colleges during the sixties caused many students to turn to the community colleges for the first two years of their baccalaureate programs.

Originally junior colleges provided general academic programs similar to the freshman and sophomore years of four-year colleges, since most of them served as "finishing schools" for young women or "prep schools" for young men and women. As community colleges evolved, they retained this component, typically labelled "the transfer program." A second component, "the terminal program," was added to provide career training. A third component, continuing education, grew in the image of university extension but with a more diversified program of noncredit adult educational activities. A fourth component, which was still in the early stages of development at the close of this period was the community service program. Harlacher cites this component as the one that makes the community college a uniquely American institution. He points out that "A junior college is an institution that primarily duplicates organizationally and fulfills philosophically the first two years of the four-year senior college. On the other hand, a true community college connotes an institution that has developed beyond an isolated entity into an institution seeking full partnership with its community. In the process, the community college becomes for its district community a cultural center, a focal point of intellectual life, a source of solidarity and a fount of local pride."[42]

Harlacher further observed that:

The soundly conceived community service program recognizes the college's obligation to accept the following responsibilities:

1. Become a center of community life by encouraging the use of college facilities and services by community groups when such use doesn't interfere with the college's regularly scheduled day and evening programs.

2. Provide educational services for all age groups which utilize the special skills and knowledge of the college staff and other experts to meet the needs of community groups and the college district community at large.

3. Provide the community with the leadership and coordination capabilities of the college, assist the community in long-range planning, and join with individuals and groups in attacking unsolved problems.

4. Contribute to and promote the cultural, intellectual and social life of the college district community and the development of skills for the profitable use of leisure time.[43]

Because the community colleges are the only higher education institution with the mission of providing exclusively educational services—they have no obligation to provide knowledge-production services, as do the senior institutions—they have been free to focus on the improvement of learning and teaching. As a result, they have spawned many innovations, the most promising of which could well be the learning laboratory or learning resources center. The "Learning Lab," as it came to be called, is a facility—usually associated with a library and a media center—to which an individual can come off the street at almost any time of day or night and develop a program of individualized learning with the help of an educational counselor. Learning programs consisted of various combinations of tutorial, peer-helping, independent reading, watching videotapes or listening to audio-tape cassettes, undertaking field projects, interviews with resource people, small group projects, multimedia modules, and laboratory experiments. Learning Labs proved to be especially effective with students who deviate from the academic mode—both slow- and fast-learners, since they can learn at their own pace, in their own style, and without fear of competitive failure.[44]

As de Tocqueville might have reported, had community colleges been in existence in 1831, I have observed educational institutions of all sorts and in no other have I found the optimism, exuberance, seriousness of purpose, and pleasure in learning that characterized every community college I have visited.

Cooperative Extension Service

As was pointed out in Chapter IV, the *Statement of Scope and Responsibility* (The "Scope Report") of 1958, which had outlined the purpose and priorities of Cooperative Extension for the next decade, outlined nine areas from which local states and counties could decide on emphases.

Six of these areas were continuations of the traditional focus on agricultural efficiency, marketing and distribution, conservation and use of natural resources, management on the farm and in the home, family living, and youth development. But three were new directions: leadership development, community improvement and resource development, and public affairs education. From the perspective of almost two decades later Paul Miller interpreted the meaning of this report as follows:

> The implication of the report was clear: Activity at local levels may not be transformed but, without breaking with the past, they were urged to turn more toward technological humanism and away from the more familiar vocationalism. Cooperative Extension seemed to be electing the option of becoming more broadly educational rather than narrowing its emphasis to technical agriculture. In keeping with its new mission, reforms in personnel training were reflected in the founding of the National Center for Extension Administration at the University of Wisconsin by the W. K. Kellogg Foundation. The report fostered widespread discussions about the competence of Cooperative Extension. The epochal crises surrounding the cities and economic and social class issues of poverty caught the Cooperative Extension Service in the rocky Washington terrain.[45]

A new policy statement, *A People and a Spirit*, was released in November, 1968, after two years of effort by a Joint Study Committee of the Department of Agriculture and the National Association of State Universities and Land-Grant Colleges.[46] The nine areas of the "Scope Report" were absorbed into three: "agricultural and related industries," "social and economic development," and "quality of living." A fourth and new area, "international extension," was added.

Miller's interpretation of the meaning of this policy statement was as follows:

> . . .the truly profound aspect of the more recent report is that it interprets what Cooperative Extension wants to do within the needs of the United States *as a whole*. Fully a third of the report is devoted to explaining the way informal catalytic education, carried on by a development organization, could help achieve goals for all America and help solve priority issues. Indeed, the urban crisis and rural deprivation are treated as aspects of the same issue.

The report sees the main urban problems flowing from conditions in rural communities making most of its residents so poor and unhappy that they would rather go any other place than to remain. The gains of agricultural productivity seem to have gone to processors and consumer rather than to small and medium-sized farmers; by some quirk of economic cause and effect, the modernization of American agriculture has left one in every four rural Americans poor.[47]

The specific program recommendations of the Extension Study Committee were as follows:

1. Agriculture and Related Industries
   —Increase program emphasis in marketing and farm business management.
   —Reduce the relative percentage of effort in husbandry and production programs.
   —Take advantage of the capability of commercial agricultural firms to provide a part of the technological information.
2. Social and Economic Development
   —Expand efforts in educational programs of social and economic development.
   —Make significantly greater efforts to assist low-income farmers in decisions other than agricultural production, including selection of alternative vocations.
   —Expand program activity dealing with natural resources and the environment.
3. Quality of Living
   —Expand Extension programs of youth and family education.
   —Expand sharply the educational programs to help the disadvantaged and the alienated.
   —Emphasize the disciplines of social and behavioral sciences as well as those of home economics in filling positions to support future programs related to the family.
   —Assign personnel to work in Extension youth programs who are qualified in disciplines relevant to the education and motivation of youth.
   —Adapt and expand 4-H as well as provide additional youth activities where 4-H is not a suitable mechanism for meeting specific problems.
   —Undertake continuing national as well as state dialog with leaders of cooperating organizations, to seek ways by which each organization can assist in meeting the emerging broad human development problems.

      —Conduct programs in the quality of living category in urban as well as rural areas.

4. International Extension
      —Evolve long-range program strategy from the U.S. overseas agricultural development programs. The strategy should provide for a formally planned and specifically financed Extension component and define the nature of relationships under which such long-term programs will function.
      —Make effort to adapt existing U.S. institutions, including Cooperative Extension Service, to long-range overseas programs of agricultural development.
      —Direct major initial emphasis in Extension programs abroad toward increased agricultural production and marketing.
      —Develop Cooperative Extension field support for approved agricultural development activities sponsored by private industry in other nations.
      —Establish International Extension Training Centers at one or more land-grant universities.[48]

Some clues as to how these recommendations affected actual program operation of the Extension Service can be gathered from an overview, *Cooperative Extension Service Programs*, published in June, 1976. Because the report is not organized according to the categories used by the Extension Study Committee, many of the following quotations relate to two or more of the categories:

    — Extension agents and specialists conducting adult Extension programs in agriculture and natural resources devote approximately 70% of their time to work with commercial farmers, 25% with small and low-income farmers (gross income of $20,000 or less), and about 5% to work with home gardeners . . . . Much of the continuing work with small, part-time, and low-income farmers is carried on as a part of the regular program where recommendations on production practices do not vary greatly from one clientele group to another. About 55% of the total staff resources devoted to agriculture and natural resources programs is expended on programs designed specifically to meet special needs of low-income farmers.

    — Extension has a highly competent, well trained and highly skilled staff of about 3,000 Extension agricultural agents and more than 3,000 specialists and specialized multi-county area staff members whose primary responsibility, dedication and interest is to better serve the American farmer and rancher. While these individuals have as a primary responsibility to serve the commercial farmer in the United States, they will continue with the assistance of paraprofessionals to provide leadership and program support for programs designed to help the small or low-income farmer.

— During 1975 Extension, through its community development work in rural America, provided assistance to 50,832 community projects, made over 9,000 surveys and feasibility studies, conducted almost 55,000 workshops and conferences reaching some two million people, and prepared thousands of publications and other pieces of educational materials.

— Congress first earmarked funds specifically for community resource development work in the mid-1950's as a pilot effort. In recent years Congress has been earmarking $1 million under the Smith-Lever Act 3(d) and $1.5 million under Title V of the Rural Development Act of 1972, which is administered in close cooperation with the Cooperative State Research Service (CSRS) as a joint research-extension effort in rural development. Approximately 200 counties are now being served on a concentrated effort under Title V programs.

— In 1975, 36.7% of the total farm youth population participated in 4-H. The numbers of youth participating in organized 4-H Clubs and 4-H special interest groups reached an all-time high in 1975, with 80.1% of these youth coming from farms, open country and towns and cities under 50,000 population, and 19.9% lived in suburbs and in central cities of 50,000 and over. Most of the 4-H participants in large metropolitan areas resulted from programs designated by Congressional appropriations specially earmarked for urban 4-H and 4-H-type nutrition programs in inner cities. Currently, approximately 25% of the youth participating in 4-H-youth programs are from minority ethnic and racial groups.

— In addition to youth participating in 4-H Clubs and 4-H special interest groups, 819,369 youth were enrolled in 4-H Expanded Food and Nutrition Education Programs primarily for low-income city youth, and 724,679 were enrolled in instructional 4-H TV Program Series. A total of 431,289 youth attended Extension 4-H Youth conducted camps in 1975.

— Approximately 4,000 professional Extension home economists and 7,000 paraprofessionals assisted by 700,000 volunteer leaders extend home and family living education to 10 million families annually. Many of these leaders are among the approximately 600,000 Extension homemakers in 35,000 different organized clubs in 41 states and Puerto Rico. Virtually all of these homemakers are rural.

— Extension's Expanded Food and Nutrition Education Program has reached more than a million "hard-to-reach" families and two million low-income youth since its inception in 1969. According to Congressional intent, this program must be directed to units or communities of low income. Seventy percent of the EFNEP families live outside of cities with population of 50,000 or over.[49]

As one rereads the recommendations in *A People and A Spirit* one gets the impression that the Joint Committee had in mind a greater shift from agricultural technology toward social and economic development and quality of living, from service to education, than this overview of Extension programs reflects. (And no mention was made in the report of activities under the Joint Committee's heading of "International Extension").

Miller has observed that all three major policy statements of 1948, 1958, and 1968, confronted Cooperative Extension with "a crossroad of decision," which he defined in these words:

One choice led down the road to a more open casting of Cooperative Extension as adult education, toward a unique pattern for extending the knowledge and the talent of the university to the people, and expanding from rural to urban problems. The other choice would have Cooperative Extension continue to view itself as a development organization for solving problems, to maintain its loyalty to commercial agriculture, to stress achievement of high levels of farm production efficiency, to strengthen the ties to specialized commodity associations. This choice would define Cooperative Extension as a specialized technical service.[50]

Miller then goes on to project the consequences of each choice and the forces opposing the first one:

Following the adult education model would bring Cooperative extension squarely into the scene which includes General Extension and many other forms of continuing education. This direction would likely weaken the ties to farm organizations and legislative centers, for these groups would interpret (as they often have) the move as a decline of interest in rural people. Broadening the program in the adult education mold would require interest and support of the parent university beyond the interests of the colleges of agriculture. General faculties new to the scene often view agrarian traditions as parochial, limiting, and attuned to the past rather than to the challenges of the new society. Agricultural faculties are not altogether close to other faculties on their own campuses, and have remained somewhat distinct from the national community of science and technology. Moreover, at issue is Cooperative Extension's ability to broaden its base at the knowledge center so that it has the resources to aid new clients.

The other alternative would sharpen and strengthen the Cooperative Extension system as an elite technical service for commercial agriculture. While it would remain loyal to old covenants with legislatures, farm organizations, and government agencies, this approach would come in conflict with present reality: the availability of many private technical services to farmers, the strong consumer interest at odds with self-interest of farmers.[51]

Although the policy statements of 1948, 1958, and 1968 appeared to be urging the Extension Service to move toward the first choice, the policy decisions that set actual programs and services appeared to retain prime loyalty to the second choice and give token acknowledgement to the first. The bulk of Extension's services continued to go to commercial agriculture, but gradually increasing attention was being paid to the adult educational needs of low-income farmers and the urban poor. Considering Cooperative Extension's enormous success in building a strong base of support among the farmers and their organizations and legislative representatives, it is understandable that its policy-makers would want to do nothing that would jeopardize such a dependable source of lifeblood.

The Cooperative Extension Service continued to grow in size during this period, although more gradually than its more glamorous siblings in the educational family—the community colleges and university nontraditional study programs—described in preceding sections of this chapter. Its "faculty" of federal and state staffs and county agents had grown from the 14,812 level (of full-time equivalents) reported in 1958 to 16,732 in 1975. Its total budget grew from $150,098,000 in 1961 to $501,036,000 in 1976—of which 39 percent was from federal funds, 41 percent from state appropriations, 18 percent from county funds, and 2 percent from non-tax sources. It is not possible to compare the total "student body" with that in 1960 as reported in Chapter IV, since the basis and method of collecting and reporting statistics was changed in 1968 to a computerized National Extension Management System (EMIS) that was coordinated with a network of State Extension Management Systems (SEMIS). But some indication of the growth in volume of services can be obtained from a comparison of 94,313,395 contacts (the number of times the Extension Service is contacted for information and educational services) in 1972 with 111,644,600 contacts in 1975.[52]

One state-level development during this period that may turn out to be worthy of note was the experimentation by land-grant colleges in several states with various patterns for integrating their general extension and agricultural extension structures and services. No general trend had emerged, however, by the end of the period.

Foundations

With the termination of the Fund for Adult Education of the Ford Foundation in 1961, the level of foundation contributions to the field was greatly reduced. But the major foundations continued to support special projects, especially innovative approaches to reaching the educationally disadvantaged. Indeed, one observer credits the foundations with pioneering many of the programs that were incorporated into federal government's Great Society movement:

> Principles and practices of community development were encouraged and nurtured by the Carnegie Corporation and a wide range of such rural and urban programs that are now supported by federal funds. Theories, methods and practices of community development have infused the poverty program, the extensive rural development activities of the Cooperative Extension Service, the eight pilot urban-studies centers funded by the Ford Foundation and much of the work now being done under Title I of the Higher Education Act. Educational (and now public) television owes its existence to foundation initiative which has been continued through federal funds. International affairs education for adults would certainly not have achieved its present state, precarious though it is, without foundation support... Also the foundations have had the courage and wisdom to venture into study of issues that were emerging but not yet clearly established as key or critical areas for public concern. In the mid-sixties support by foundations for citizen education in world affairs tapered off but new areas were encouraged—relating to poverty, civil rights, and equality of educational opportunity.[53]

The Carnegie Corporation was without question the single most potent force in bringing policy leadership to the ferment in higher education through its support of the Carnegie Commission on Higher Education, the Commission on Non-Traditional Study, and numerous programs of the College Entrance Examination Board and Educational Testing Service. The Mott Foundation was the moving force in the rapid spread of the community school movement. The Ford Foundation gave massive support to innovative attacks on urban, poverty, and civil rights problems. The Kellogg Foundation subsidized the establishment of five additional centers for continuing education (bringing the total to ten) —at Notre Dame, New Hampshire (the New England Center for Continuing Education), Columbia, Oxford, and California Polytechnic State College; but the movement it had promoted had resulted in the construction of over eighty university continuing education centers under independent financing.[54]

Government Agencies

As has been documented repeatedly in preceding sections, the federal government took a historic turn in the early sixties in providing legislation, financial support, and policy leadership to education in general. In regard to adult education, the initial federal thrust was on providing training to unemployed heads of households who had previous employment experience. The Area Redevelopment Act (1961) and the Manpower Development and Training Act (1962) sought to aid those persons whose unemployment was caused by geographic shifts in the demand for labor and changes in skill requirements resulting from technological advances.

By 1964, although the general employment picture was improving, disproportionately high concentrations of unemployment remained for Blacks, for non-English-speaking adults, and for the undereducated. With the passage of the Economic Opportunity Act of 1964, the Adult Basic Education Program was established. This program sought to remedy the inequities of educational disadvantage by offering persons 18 years of age and older the opportunity to develop reading, writing, language, and mathematical skills to enable them to obtain employment. The Office of Economic Opportunity provided funds to the U.S. Office of Education to administer the program until the Adult Education Act of 1966 (Title III of the 1966 Amendments to the Elementary and Secondary Education Act—P.L. 89-750) placed the program entirely within the U.S. Office of Education.

Under this landmark Act, adult basic and secondary level educational programs were established in each of the states and territories. Funds were available to state and local education agencies to meet the costs of instruction, to employ and train qualified adult educators, and to develop specialized curriculums and techniques appropriate for adult learners. Enrollments in programs under the Adult Education Act increased from 37,991 in fiscal year 1965 to almost one million in fiscal year 1974.[55]

The original Adult Education Act in 1966 established an eight-member Advisory Committee on Adult Basic Education which in the 1970 Amendments was enlarged to a fifteen-member National Advisory Council on Adult Education with the following responsibilities: (1) advising the Commissioner of Education in preparation of general regulations; (2) advising the Commissioner with respect to policies and procedures governing state plans and policies to eliminate duplication; (3) advising the Commissioner with respect to coordination of programs offering adult education activities and services; (4) reviewing the administration and effectiveness of programs; and (5) making annual reports to the President of findings and recommendations relating to adult education activities and services. For the first time in history the federal government had established a national body with express authority to influence national policy regarding adult education. During the next five years the National Advisory Council conducted studies, convened consultations, and published findings and recommendations which in fact did affect legislation and programs.[56]

The 1970 Amendments to the Adult Education Act (P.L. 91-230) authorized the establishment of state advisory councils on adult education with the obvious hope of providing the same kind of policy leadership for state governments that the National Council had demonstrated at the national level. In 1975 the National Council made a survey of state councils and found:

... that twenty-six state advisory councils for adult education are now in existence, although two are not operational. Twenty-three states and territories indicated no council and no plans to establish one. Six states indicated that their councils are combined in some way with vocational, technical, or community education.

The prevailing sentiment appeared to be one of resistance to councils whose membership was mandated by the federal government.[57]

Research, statistical, publications, and advisory services to the field of adult education by the federal government were greatly strengthened and expanded during this period with the establishment of several new agencies. A National Center for Educational Statistics was created within the U.S. Office of Education in 1965 with a congressional mandate to collect "such statistics and facts as shall show the condition and progress of education in the several States and Territories . . ."[58] Its regular publications in adult education included *Adult Basic Education Program Statistics* (annual), a comprehensive picture of participants and programs from the Bureau of Census Current Population Survey, *Participation In Adult Education* (triennial starting in 1969); *Adult Education in Public Education Systems* (triennial); *Adult and Continuing Education in Institutions of Higher Education* (biennial); and *Adult Education in Community Organizations* (triennial). There appeared to be some hope that the statistical jungle of adult education could become civilized. The Educational Resources Information Center (ERIC) was established in the Office of Education at about the same time and in 1973 was moved to the newly-created National Institute of Education. As a part of the reorganization, the Clearinghouse in Adult Education, originally located at Syracuse University, was moved to Northern Illinois University and amalgamated with the Clearinghouse in Career Education. One of a network of sixteen Clearinghouses, the

Clearinghouse in Career Education stores in a computer data from journal articles, significant project reports, research reports, curriculum guides, bibliographies, survey results, speeches, conference proceedings, and other sources. These data can then be retrieved and made available to users in print or microfiche.

Inservice education for governmental employees continued to expand in keeping with the policy guidelines of the Government Employees Training Act of 1958 and leadership from the Civil Service Commission. By 1976 almost 750,000 civilian employees were reached through 83 agency-operated centers, the National Independent Study Center opened by the Civil Service Commission in 1976, and 120 off-campus study centers in cooperation with colleges and universities. Another third of a million military personnel participated in a variety of training programs conducted by the Department of Defense.[59]

Numerous federal agencies, such as the Public Health Service, the National Park Service, the National Edowment for the Humanities, The National Science Foundation, the Office of Consumer Affairs, and the Bureau of Indian Affairs, to cite a small sample, continued to provide educational programs and services to selected segments of the public.

Health and Welfare Agencies

The trends that characterized the preceding era (1921-1961) in the development of voluntary health, welfare, and recreational institutions were largely reinforced, but to some extent modified by new forces in the 1961-1976 period. The expanding role of government in dealing with problems of poverty, illness (e.g., Medicare and Medicaid), social rehabilitation, drug addiction, crime, poor nutrition, inadequate housing, urban decay, and the like, both made new funds available to voluntary organizations and complicated their roles. As Hoffer points out, "Relationships between various government entities and private social welfare agencies in the 1960's are widely disparate and highly fluid. . . On one point, however, there is virtually unanimous agreement: that only the resources of government are sufficient for health services, public assistance and other income-maintenance programs. Private agency support for this principle, sometimes begrudgingly accorded, is granted on the grounds that only the taxing power of government is adequate to the task.[60] Although there were many examples of cooperation between the private and the public sectors of the field during this period, clarification of their appropriate roles for the future remained on the agenda for the next era.

Independent Centers

A major new institutional form in this category became established during this period—the educational brokerage agency.

The concept of educational brokering has roots that go back to the early years of the adult education movement. Many libraries began to maintain card files of community resources to which clients could be referred. Since 1923 the Educational Exchange of Greater Boston (formerly the Prospect Union Educational Exchange) had been providing adult educational information and counseling. Several local adult education councils, notably in Cleveland, Denver, and New York, provided similar services. But as we entered the decade of the seventies it appeared that educational brokering was an idea whose time had come.

Brokerage agencies began popping up all over the country under a variety of names—Center for Adult Learning in Boulder, Colorado; Career Counseling Service in Providence, Rhode Island; Educational Opportunity Center Program in Boston; Regional Learning Service of Central New York in Syracuse; Center for Open Learning in Demopolis, Alabama; Community-Based Counseling for Adults in Madison, Wisconsin; Rockland County Guidance Center for Women, Nyack, New York; and the Learning Exchange in Evanston, Illinois. There appeared to be four patterns of organization among the new centers: (1) Free-standing agencies, which are attached to no other institution and are supported by combinations of client fees, state and federal funds, and contracts with corporations. (2) New units in existing systems (such as the Hudson Community College Commission in Jersey City), in which governance structures are linked to the broader system and funding comes mainly from the system. (3) Consortium centers, in which a headquarters staff coordinates a network of counselor-advocates located in the individual colleges of the consortium who advise clients of learning opportunities throughout the network. And (4) new units within established institutions (such as the School for New Learning at DePaul University) which are funded and administered by a single institution, yet refer clients to a variety of institutions.

Educational brokering has been described as:

... an intermediary function, a mechanism by which adults may take advantage of the broad array of learning opportunities in their communities. Brokers aid individuals through advisement, assessment and advocacy as they move into the often strange territory of postsecondary education. Brokers help people to make personal and career decisions, select appropriate educational resources and embark on learning programs. The distinctiveness of brokering arises from (1) the ways clients are reached and served in their own communities, usually utilizing existing resources, and (2) perhaps most important, the new educational role of client advocate. The interests of individuals, not institutions, are the focus of brokers' advocacy efforts.[61]

Many of the brokering agencies gained their initial support from the Fund for the Improvement of Postsecondary Education and the National Institute for Education. But between 1974 and 1976 support for local and state brokering agencies was built into legislation in California, Massachusetts, New Jersey, and Pennsylvania. On January 1, 1976, the National Center for Educational Brokering was established "to promote educational brokering through technical assistance, publications, and public policy studies and recommendations." It published a monthly *Bulletin* describing new developments.

Another institutional form which evolved and flourished during this period was the Human Growth Center. The National Training Laboratories had been established in the late forties under the auspices of the National Education Association and a group of universities to conduct research and engage in training in human relations and group dynamics. It popularized the "T-group," "sensitivity training," and "the laboratory method" as vehicles for helping people gain increased self-understanding and improve their interpersonal skills at its summer sessions at Bethel, Maine. Its basic method of learning through the analysis of unstructured group experience was widely adopted in industry, educational institutions, and voluntary organizations during the fifties and sixties. But early in the sixties a group of the "graduates" of Bethel began shifting the emphasis from group and interpersonal processes to personal growth, with heavy emphasis on self-awareness, expanded states of consciousness, meditation, emotional and physiological release, self-actualization, and other activities bordering on the psychotherapeutic or mystical. The prototype center, Esalen Institute, at Big Sur, California, spawned over one hundred independent "growth centers" across the country by the mid-seventies. They were linked into a loose association that came to be known as "The Human Potential Movement" and their professional workers banded together in the American Humanistic Psychology Association.

Labor Unions

No national comprehensive system of labor education had evolved in the United States by the close of this period, as was the case in many European countries. Programs continued to be planned and operated by local union councils, university centers, or individual national unions. Emphasis continued to be on increasing the competence of members and staff to function in the union in such areas as collective bargaining, union administration, communications, trade union history and structure, and legislative issues, although some programs dealt with broad social problems such as civil rights, poverty, urban affairs, and international relations.

A survey conducted in 1965 and 1966 found that about 40 of more than 180 national unions sponsor some consistent educational activity. Conferences lasting one to three days were the most common activity of national unions, with 34 unions holding them. Twenty-two unions conducted 253 one-week resident schools for local union leaders with an enrollment of 19,085. State and local central bodies conducted a variety of educational activities, the most common being one-week residential schools; 26 of these enrolling 2444 in 1966. A variety of imaginative programs by local unions were identified, but figures were not available for the total number held or the number of participants. Twenty-three university centers conducted 1066 short courses for local unionists with an enrollment of 27,433 during the two-year period, and in addition sponsored a variety of conferences and residential schools.[62]

One of the leaders of the field summarized the status of labor education in this country during this period as follows:

Labor educators have demonstrated the ability to involve unionists, mostly blue-collar workers, in non-vocational, voluntary adult education. Unionists do respond to educational opportunity when they are approached through their unions; when the education is conducted under auspices in which they have confidence, in a style that involves them in the learning process; and when the subject matter is relevant to their concerns. Once they are drawn into education activity and have a successful experience, many worker-students are motivated toward education that is broader in scope, has long-range goals, or deals with controversial issues.

Very few unions that initiate educational activity give it up. Rapidly growing unions and unions facing new problems turn to education to help them. The number of university centers continues to increase. . .

Yet labor education remains peripheral to the adult education movement in the United States. Very few unions take it seriously enough to invest sufficient funds for a meaningful program. . .

Unless there is a major breakthrough in scale, based on a massive infusion of union or public funds, or both, the present situation will continue. In some unions, and for some unionists, labor education will be meaningful. But for the total union movement and for the nation, labor education will represent an indication of what might be done rather than a major accomplishment.[63]

Libraries

Few major new institutional developments occurred in library adult education during this period. Monroe observed that the use of community studies begun in the fifties spread in the sixties and "led to the rejection of the concept of 'the general reader' and to the development of services for more clearly identified groups: students, teachers; the aging; labor; the handicapped; the disadvantaged. Close study brought to light large numbers of potential library users of whose interests and needs the library has been unaware."[64] Accordingly, there was increased emphasis on the development of new approaches to serving disadvantaged adults.[65] These outreach programs were supported by federal funds from the Economic Opportunity Act, the Manpower Development and Training Act, and the Library Services and Construction Act during the 1960's and early 1970's.

A significant new development did occur, however, with the founding in 1975 of the Continuing Library Education Network and Exchange (CLENE). A study commissioned by the National Commission on Libraries and Information Science and completed in 1974 had identified the continuing education of library personnel as a top priority need of the field.[66] Initially financed by ten state library agencies and a grant from Title II-B of the Higher Education Act, CLENE expected to be supported eventually through membership dues. It started publishing a newsletter in September, 1975, and held its first national assembly in January, 1976.

Mass Media

This was an era of expansive productivity, creativity, and controversy in educational technology—the use of media in learning and teaching. It was characterized by extravagant fads, unfulfilled hopes, and some significant new institutional developments.

Printed materials continued to roll off the presses in rising volume. Without question more books on adult education, higher education, community education, the future of education, and related subjects were published between

1961 and 1976 than in the preceding forty years. New curricular materials based on engaging learners in discovery were developed for the elementary and secondary grades in mathematics, physics, the social sciences, and other subjects, and many of them were adapted for adult learners, especially in remedial programs. With the impetus emanating from the "Great Society" emphasis on education of the undereducated, new publishers discovered the need for adult-level texts and workbooks for adult basic education and started filling the void. Improvements in the technology and economics of photocopying resulted in the production of a growing volume of teacher-made materials, reprints, reports, student products, and other materials, giving rise to questions about the violation of the copyright laws.[67]

The volume of periodical literature showed a parallel increase. The journals of related disciplines (anthropology, counseling psychology, developmental psychology, educational psychology, social psychology, sociology, administration, and the like) began presenting a growing number of articles on adult education. Several new periodicals specifically on continuing education came into being, including *Continuing Education in Nursing, Convergence* (published by the International Council for Adult Education), *Continuing Education for Adults* (published by the Library for Continuing Education at Syracuse University), the *Journal of Extension, Continuing Education Reports* (published by the University of Chicago), *Community College Review*, (published by North Carolina State University) *Community Education Journal, New Directions for Community Colleges*, and *New Directions for Higher Education*. The accelerating rapidity of developments in this era brought forth several new newsletters, including *AEA Dateline* (by the Adult Education Association of the U.S.A.), *Adult and Continuing Education Today* (by Today Publications and News Service), *NUEA Newsletter* (by the National University Extension Association), and *Education Recaps* (by the Educational Testing Service's Office of New Degree Programs). All except the last one featured current developments in Congress and the federal agencies.

The information explosion became so overwhelming to

users that a new institutional form—the information clearing-house—was created to collect documents, evaluate them, abstract them, classify them, store their data in computers, and devise systems for retrieving the data for users. In addition to the ERIC Clearinghouses previously mentioned, information centers were established at Montclair State College in New Jersey for adult basic education materials; in the National Education Association in Washington for public school adult education materials; at the Library of Continuing Education at Syracuse University for archival materials; and in various professional organizations for their specialized materials.[68] Obviously the technology of data storage and retrieval—"information science"—was developing rapidly in this period and no doubt would flower in the next decade.

The use of teaching machines and programmed instruction experienced a dramatic growth during the sixties, much of it spurred on by commercial exploitation. A number of corporations invested heavily in producing and marketing the hardware and software for this burgeoning new technology, and for a while educators worried lest the machine replace the teacher. But by the early seventies the teaching machine had taken its place as just one of a number of resources available to help learners and many of the commercial ventures went bankrupt. Programmed instruction proved to be a most valuable resource for some of the more basic kinds of learning —especially when used in conjunction with human interaction —and became one of the foundational elements of many learning laboratories and remedial programs.

The computer also came into prominence in this period as a medium for a variety of educational purposes. It was used extensively for improving administrative efficiency—monitoring admissions, class scheduling, room assignment, grade recording, inventorying materials and equipment, and providing other data for decision making. It became an almost mandatory instrument for collecting and analyzing data in research. But it was also used increasingly as a facilitator of learning, through computer-assisted instruction, simulation exercises, data retrieval, and problem-solving in mathematics, engineering, and the sciences. The most striking technological development in this field was miniaturization, which made possible the manufacture of pocket calculators and mini-computers that were of a size and within a price range that made them widely available.

Substantial advances and refinements were made in the use of audio-visual aids. Scores of established publishing companies and more scores of specialized producers turned out films, film strips, audiocassettes, multimedia packages, exhibits, displays and recordings on practically every subject imaginable. The *Catalog of United States Government Produced Audiovisual Materials* for 1974-75 contained 4.500 items, described in 356 pages, available from the National Audiovisual Center of the General Services Administration. As a consequence of the miniaturization of electronic equipment, portable videotaping recorders and projectors became available and were widely used to produce home-made audio-visual aids and to provide learners with immediate feedback on their performance. A major trend developed during this period away from the isolated use of individual audio-visual aids toward their incorporation into complex learning systems (or modules or packages). For example, the ROCOM Division of the Hoffman-La Roche Drug company produced a multimedia system for use in the inservice education of nurses in intensive coronary care that consisted of a dozen films, thirty film strips, a dozen audiotapes, a text, a coordinator's manual (specifying, among other things, various group activities), a learner's workbook, and a package of diagnostic and progress-assessment instruments.

An elaborate version of the concept of learning systems was the dial-access network. One of the most complex networks was established by the Lister Hill National Center for Biomedical Communications, which used a communication satellite to connect isolated communities in Alaska with medical specialists, set up cable television networks in the ghettos of Denver and New York City, and made available a variety of diagnostic systems and computer-aided instruction to medical students, physicians, and allied health professionals via telephone lines, teletype, TWX, and other devices.[69] Other more or less complex systems were established by other institutions, notably university extension.[70]

An institutional form that experienced widespread growth during this period in educational institutions of every type was the media center. Often closely associated physically and in personnel with libraries and learning laboratories, media centers combined the functions of helping teachers prepare audio-visual materials, collecting and disseminating commercially-produced materials, producing their own materials, and designing learning systems, including dial-access networks. The role of media specialist became a new specialty for which graduate training programs were established in several universities.

But the medium that produced the greatest hope, disappointment, and controversy, was television. The functions of the Educational Television and Radio Center, which had been financed largely by foundation grants and contributions from local stations, were taken over in 1967 by the Corportion for Public Broadcasting, created by the Public Broadcasting Act of 1967 and financed by federal appropriations. There was a raging argument over what the scope of this new government-sponsored agency should be. The Carnegie Commission on Educational Television recommended that television programming directed at the general community (cultural-informational television) was an appropriate function for national public television, but that instructional television, designed for use in the classroom or other formal educational settings, was another domain that was not appropriately the domain of public television.[71] However, the Commission recommendations were altered by Congress when it included radio in "public broadcasting" and changed again when the Corporation for Public Broadcasting decided to include "educational broadcasting" in its domain.

In 1969 the Corporation commissioned the National Instructional Television Center to make a study of the contemporary scene and recommend future directions for continuing public education broadcasting. Blakely sum-

marizes the study's findings regarding the contemporary
scene in 1968 as follows:

... continuing education programming accounted for two of fifty-six
total broadcast hours (3.4 percent) of the week's schedule for a typical
public television station. Most of the series or comprehensive programs
were produced by public broadcasting stations for their own use only;
one-third of them were used by other stations; only 5 percent were
produced initially for national use, and most of these were in specialized
areas of professional education.

Usually programs were initiated "to fill a need" which the station
identified intuitively or some group in the community pressed for.

Most of the programs, radio and television both, were essentially lectures or illustrated lectures. Few provided opportunities for involvement.

The median audience for each continuing education program in
radio was reported as 1,000 and in television as 10,000. Most programs
were consistently directed to middle- and upper-class audiences.

There was little evidence that activities to accompany continuing
education broadcasts were planned.

There was little evidence that the programs were developed with the
aid of audience research.[72]

The study's general recommendation was that the Corporation give leadership in a national project to make a systematic
approach to continuing public education broadcasting, which
the Corporation implemented by establishing an Adult
Learning Programs Service (ALPS). In 1972 ALPS proposed
its first program, ALPS ONE, which would make available
to adults who had not completed high school general educational instruction of the same quality at the adult level as
"Sesame Street" was at the child level. Within weeks of the
submission of the proposal President Nixon vetoed the bill
to provide two-year support to the Corporation, the chair-
manship of the Board of the Corporation changed hands,
and the proposal was tabled. There were indications in press
reports in 1976 that the Corporation may be considering
renewing the process of upgrading continuing education
public broadcasting.[73]

Meantime, instructional television continued to be used
extensively, both by local educational stations and by local
educational institutions through closed-circuit programming.

Several statewide networks were producing series for local use. For example, the Maryland State Department of Education developed a series of thirty "telelessons" with an accompanying manual in 1972-74 under the title "Basic Education: Teaching the Adult," for the purpose of helping to train teachers of adult basic education. Several state universities (e.g. Maryland, Nebraska, Wisconsin, Michigan State) were planning or operating degree programs modeled after the British Open University, in which television was employed along with correspondence study, short-term residential session, and other media.[74]

Museums and Art Institutes

The trends of the preceding era, as described in Chapter IV, continued without substantial change. Advances in electronic technology made it possible for museums to engage viewers in participative interaction in new ways. Several new "indigenous museums" came into being, including an Indian village in Plymouth Colony, Massachusetts, and several reconstructed ghost towns in the Far West. The putting of art into action in an "audience-activating environment" was a major focus of the Chicago Museum of Contemporary Art, opened in 1967.[75]

A survey of museum use made in 1965 found that museums were conducting formally organized classes serving 4,500,000 adults, and that about 14 percent of all museums had programs for adults.[76]

Proprietary Schools

Although the statistics on enrollment in proprietary schools are difficult to obtain, there are clues that these schools experienced considerable growth during the sixties, with special stimulation from the G.I. Bill and the expansion of the service industries. The National Center for Educational Statistics estimated an enrollment of 1,393,000 students in private trade, vocational, and business schools in 1972.[77] Clark and Sloan, in their 1966 study, *Classrooms on Main*

Street, found that there were more than 35,000 of what they called "specialty schools"—which they classified as follows: business schools; training in selected industries (e.g., construction, transportation, retailing); skilled trade preparation (e.g., truck drivers, repairmen); semi-professional occupations (e.g., airplane pilots and attendants, radio announcers, commercial artists); personal—and protective —service occupations (e.g., barbers, private policemen, detectives); and leisure-time occupations (golf professionals, arts and crafts leaders).[78]

Charges of unethical practices and other abuses, especially charges by the Veterans Administration, continued to plague this segment of the field. Just as the National Home Study Council had been organized in the preceding era to solve this problem for the correspondence schools, the Continuing Education Council came into being in 1974 to establish and monitor standards for proprietary institutions not covered by existing accrediting agencies. The first institutions approved by its Accrediting Commission in 1975 included Dale Carnegie Institutes, the Professional Training Division of the Boy Scouts of America, the Continuing Education Program of the National Association of Accountants, and the Educational Services Department of the Portland Cement Association.[79]

Public Schools

Statistical procedures and methods had not become satisfactorily standardized during this period, but they were good enough to support the conclusion that it was a period of substantial growth in public school adult education. The estimate of a total enrollment of 4,373,054 participants in 1956-57 cited in Chapter IV had grown to 7,070,867 in 1969-70, according to the same government agency.[80] The National Association for Public Continuing and Adult Education estimated that in 1974-75 there were 8,624,100 enrollments in public school adult educational programs, based on figures submitted by State Departments of Education. Of these, 1,087,344 were in adult basic education programs, 1,109,212 were in high school diploma programs, 413,006

were in high school equivalency programs, 108,708 were in
Americanization and citizenship programs, 666,600 were
in business and commercial programs, and 5,239,230 were in
general education programs.[81] This same source estimated
that in 1973-74 there were 18,346 full-time and 151,797
part-time administrative and instructional staff members.[82]

A large part of this growth was no doubt a result of the
infusion of funds into the public school system from the
"Great Society" programs of the federal government. For
example, four federally-sponsored programs (Adult Basic
Education, Adult Vocational Education, Civil Defense
Adult Education, and Manpower Development and Training)
accounted for 39 percent of the enrollments for 1968-69.[83]
But obviously more leadership was being supplied by state
departments of education: in 1959 only twenty-five states
employed state directors of adult education, some of whom
also had other assignments, while in 1970 there were full-
time directors in all fifty states and Puerto Rico.[84]

This was an era of experimentation and innovation in
curriculum construction and instructional strategies, triggered
by the infusion of new knowledge and insights about adult
learning processes. Reference has already been made in the
section on mass media to changes in curricular materials and
the use of the new media. But something more fundamental
than the improvement and enrichment of old curriculum
approaches was happening—a totally new way of thinking
about how the curriculum should be organized was evolving.
The traditional organizing principle, subject-matter transmission, which had permeated education since the trivium
and quadrivium of the Middle Ages, was giving way to the
organizing principle of competency development.

The notion that education should be concerned with the
development of competencies as well as or instead of the
acquisition of academic subject matter has been explored
in the literature of education since ancient times. But during
the late forties and fifties practical techniques were developed
for specifying observable behaviors that education should
result in, translating these behaviors into concrete educational
objectives, arranging conditions and strategies that would

assure the achievement of these behaviors (e.g., programmed instruction), and then measuring the actual level of performance of these behaviors achieved. During the sixties discontent with the mechanistic character of this approach began to develop, and toward the end of that decade the notion of defining educational outcomes in terms of the more functional concept of competencies began to gain currency. The first models of desired competencies were developed for the education of teachers, and during the early seventies a considerable number of competency-based teacher education (CBTE) programs appeared on the scene, stimulated by grants from the Bureau of Research in the U.S. Office of Education to support the development of "Educational Specifications for a Comprehensive Undergraduate and Inservice Teacher Education Model." Soon competency models also began being developed for elementary and secondary levels of youth education.[85]

Teachers of adults had long known that many adults, particularly those who had not achieved in school, responded negatively to the traditional academic curriculum, and the literature of the field from the 1920's on contained accounts of individual attempts to organize specific learning experiences (but not total curriculums) around practical life situations. One of the first attempts to construct a comprehensive curriculum on the basis of competencies needed in coping with life was that of Winthrop R. Adkins at Teachers College, Columbia University. Starting in 1965 he and his associates developed Life Skills Education models, and "structured inquiry" learning experiences for such "curriculum tracks" as Managing a Career, Developing One's Self and Relating to Others, Managing Home and Family Responsibilities, Managing Leisure Time, and Exercising Community Rights, Opportunities, and Responsibilities.[86]

The greatest swell of competency-based education for adults occurred, however, following the report of the findings of the Adult Performance Level (APL) Study in October, 1975.[87] Funded with $1 million from the Office of Education's Adult Education Division, the first phase of the Study —an assessment of the functional competency of American adults—took just over four years to complete. Its general finding that one out of five (19.8 percent) adults lacked the skills and knowledge needed to function effectively, another 33.9 percent were marginally competent, and only about 46.3 percent were functioning with any degree of real competence, jolted the educational world.[88]

The Study identified five general knowledge areas as necessary to adult competence: occupational knowledge, consumer economics, government and law, health, and community resources. After the general knowledge areas were identified, data were reanalyzed to determine the skills involved in adult competency. Four primary skills seemed to account for the vast majority of requirements placed on adults: (1) communications skills (reading, writing, speaking, and listening), (2) computation skills, (3) problem-solving skills, and (4) interpersonal relations skills. The findings allowed for the construction of a general theory of adult functional competency, as follows:

1. Functional competency is a construct which is meaningful only in a specific societal context. A corollary of this thesis is that, just as functional competency is culture-bound, it is perhaps even more closely bound to the technological state of a particular society. The person who is functionally competent in one society may be incompetent in another. Furthermore, as technology changes, the requirements for competency change.

2. Functional competency does not consist just of a single skill or even a set of skills. Relevant to the skills and general knowledge areas identified by APL research, functional competency is two-dimensional; it is best described as the application of a set of skills to a set of general knowledge areas which result from the requirements imposed upon members of a society. . . .

3. Adult competency is a function of both individual capabilities and societal requirements. To restate the thesis: A person is functionally competent only to the extent that he or she can meet the requirements which are extant at a given point in time. If the requirements change and the individual does not adapt by either acquiring more or different knowledges and skills, then that person becomes less competent. Functional competence is a dynamic process, rather than a static state.

4. Functional competency is directly related in a mathematical sense to success in adult life. . . . However we define functional competency, we expect more competent adults to be more successful.[89]

The Study then undertook to develop a framework for curriculums based on APL objectives. By matching the battery of general skills with the general knowledge areas the Study team under the direction of Norvell Northcutt arrived at 65 objectives that can determine a person's ability to cope with everyday living. This new curricular approach can be illustrated by one of the modules in the Occupational Knowledge set:

Goal: To develop a level of occupational knowledge which will enable adults to secure employment in accordance with their individual needs and interests, in relation to the economic contingencies of life.

Objective 1: To build a working vocabulary related to the materials and situations of the occupational experience.

Task 1: Using words commonly found in employment situations (applications, on the job, etc.), to verbally associate the word with its meaning.

Task 2: To be able to read the words in sentence and phrase context used in T-1, or in work orders, signs, etc.

Task 3: To be able to correctly spell the words used in T-1.

Task 4: To be able to follow directions in a given work order. [90]

Even before the Study was completed many state departments of education and local school systems had started developing APL competency-based programs and materials and conducting workshops to help teachers become competent in using the new approach. [91] As this period was drawing to a close it appeared that competency-based education was spreading from adult basic education to other content areas of public school adult education.

Another major development in public school adult education during this period was the vigorous growth of the "Community School" or "Community Education" movement. Although such educational pioneers as Comenius, Rousseau, Pestalozzi, Spencer, and Dewey had proclaimed the notion that schools had a social responsibility to improve the community as well as educate the child, [92] it was not until Frank J. Manley initiated the Community School Program (later known as the Mott Program of the Flint Board of Education) in Flint, Michigan in 1936 that an operational model existed. The movement spread gradually during the forties and fifties, largely through the osmotic effects of the Mott Foundation's clinical preparation program for Educational Leadership begun in 1943. The tempo of expansion accelerated during the sixties and early seventies with increasing support from the Mott Foundation and the federal government.

By June, 1975, there were 4,344 community schools (2,647 in elementary schools and 1,697 in secondary schools) in 850 different school districts across the country. There were 1,300 full-time and 1,400 part-time community school directors operating programs that served 4,566,269 adults enrolled in formal credit and noncredit courses and an additional 2,245,055 persons participating weekly in nonformal or nonenrolled activities. A total of 75 Centers for Community Education Development (15 of which were regional centers) had been established to provide training and consultative services.[93] To serve the professional needs of this growing movement a National Community School Education Association was founded in 1965.

Community Education has been defined as: "A process that concerns itself with everything that affects the well-being of all citizens within a given community. This definition extends the role of Community Education from one of the traditional concept of teaching children to one of identifying the needs, problems, and wants of the community and then assisting in the developing of facilities, programs, staff, and leadership toward the end of improving the entire community."[94] Or, more simply, community education is "the process that achieves a balance and a use of all the institutional forces in the education of the people—all of the people—of the community."[95] A typical statement of the objectives of a community school was that of the Wilmington, Delaware, Community School Program, which undertook to serve:

1. As an educational center—as a place where children, youth, and adults have opportunities for study and learning.
2. As a neighborhood center—as a place where citizens of all ages may take part in such things as sports, physical fitness programs, in-

formal recreation, instrumental music, arts and crafts, golden-agers clubs, choral groups, and other similar leisure-time activities.

3. As a center for community services—as the place where individuals and families may obtain counseling services, health services, youth employment services, and the like.

4. As a center of neighborhood or community life—the idea being that the school serves as the institution that assists citizens in the study and solution of significant neighborhood or community problems. Informal discussion groups are an important aspect of the program and better communication between school and community is a welcome result.[96]

The community school movement was providing a richer model for public school adult education than the traditional "evening school" model, and it seemed to be sweeping the country.

The National Education Association's structure for serving public school adult education underwent several changes during this period. As was pointed out in Chapter VI, the National Association for Public School Adult Education was a department of the National Education Association and the staff of the Division of Adult Education of the NEA served as its secretariat. In effect, the mass membership of the NEA, which consisted overwhelmingly of classroom teachers, was subsidizing NAPSAE, along with many other NEA Departments which did not require NEA membership. In 1968 the NEA Representative Assembly voted to establish several different bases of affiliation for its nonmember associated organizations. NAPSAE chose to become a "National Affiliate" in 1969, which enabled it to continue its headquarters in the NEA building under a rental agreement but otherwise to operate as an autonomous organization. At that time it also changed its name to the National Association for Public Continuing and Adult Education, so as to broaden its base beyond public school adult educators to community college and government agency personnel. It continued the membership services described in Chapter VI, but became increasingly active in influencing federal legislation and policies. The Division of Adult Education was continued, with its focus primarily on developing understanding and support for adult education on the part of the NEA membership.[97]

Religious Institutions

This was an era of ferment in religious institutions, as in most other institutions and in society at large. As summarized by Stokes:

The 1960's were a period of far-reaching reexamination of the role of religion in a changing society. The tremendous membership growth in religious institutions which followed World War II leveled off. Social patterns underwent major change with the development of Sunday shopping habits, the proliferation of opportunities for weekend outings and the increasing affluence to make them possible, and a high mobility that loosened institutional ties. All of these factors contributed to a growing feeling on the part of many persons, particularly young adults, that the church was not keeping pace with the changing culture. As a result, two things happened: there was a lessening of active participation in the nation's religious communities, together with a growing awareness on the part of astute churchmen of the drastic need for many changes in the program and image of the religious institution.[98]

In his review of the literature of religious adult education between 1965 and 1973, Long found certain trends that were common among the Protestant, Catholic, and Jewish religious institutions:

—Literature concerning religious adult education appeared to be increasing in quantity.
—Adult education in churches and synagogues was generally experiencing differentiation and integration.
—Adult education sponsored by religious institutions seemed to be in a fluid and dynamic state, with increasing activity in Protestant, Catholic, and Jewish institutions.
—Within the dynamic, fluid framework of developing programs, pluralism is the watchword. There was no one accepted philosophy or concept. There appeared to be some kind of broad agreement on general objectives.
—Conceptual bases of adult education programs ranged from strict religious concepts to secular concepts. Protestant, Catholic, and Jewish institutions could be found dispersed along the continuum from secular emphasis to religious emphasis.
—Programming reflected the individual desires of the local congregations.
—The literature contained interesting references to innovative efforts

to involve adults in inquiry, direct experience, direct ministry efforts, and improved dialogue.

—There is sufficient evidence in the literature to indicate a trend toward "more and better" adult education programs sponsored by religious institutions. The need also seemed so great that progress, while meaningful and important, may not be as significant as it might appear.[99]

But certain unique developments occurred in each of the three major religious communities.

Many Protestant denominations enlarged their denominational adult religious education staffs to produce new curricular series, conduct leadership training workshops, and provide other services to their local churches. A central theme in most of the new programs was the relevancy of religion to problems and issues of life. For example, following guidelines proposed by the Curriculum Committee of the General Board of Education of the Methodist Church in 1965, a new adult curriculum organized around several basic questions (e.g., How can I find meaning in life? What has the Bible to say about the basic issues of life?) was developed.[100] For each subject area denominational headquarters supplied a study book, a book of readings, and a discussion guide. The United Presbyterian Church, U.S.A., developed a new series of paperback adult study materials, Decade Books, for "the person who finds that his childhood church school education isn't sufficient for today's questions of faith." The United Church of Christ combined its program for men's and women's groups into a new form, "Lay Life and Work," dealing with the concerns of lay people in day-to-day living. Almost all programs emphasized small group techniques, and some denominations engaged extensively in some form of sensitivity training.

The National Council of Churches focused its energy increasingly on providing stimulation and resources in support of denominational programming. The report of its Cooperative Curriculum Project in 1965 became the keystone for many of the new curricular thrusts.[101] It also sponsored a number of Interdenominational Strategy Conferences on such topics as "Christian Parenthood," "Young Adults," "The Aging,"

"Education and Vocation," and "Controversy and Conflict."

The major momentum for change in the Catholic Church came from the Second Vatican Council in 1962-65, which, among many other things, legitimated a shift from almost exclusive focus on the education of children toward increasing concern for the education of adults. The section of "Christus Dominus" on Catechetical training illustrates this shift, as well as the opening of the doors of the Church to the social sciences:

> Catechetical training is intended to make men's faith become living, conscious, and active, through the light of instruction. Bishops should see to it that such training be painstakingly given to children, adolescents, young adults, and even grownups. In this instruction a proper sequence should be observed as well as a method appropriate to the matter that is being treated and to the natural disposition, ability, age, and circumstances of life of the listener. Finally, they should see to it that this instruction is based on sacred Scripture, tradition, the liturgy, the teaching authority, and life of the Church.
>
> Moreover, they should take care that catechists be properly trained for their task, so that they will be thoroughly acquainted with the doctrine of the Church and will have both a theoretical and a practical knowledge of the laws of psychology and of pedagogical methods.[102]

In 1968 a Division of Adult Education was established in the National Church headquarters in Washington, D.C., creating a focal point for adult education on a par with divisions for elementary, secondary, and higher education. In 1972 responsibility for giving leadership in adult education programming was transferred to the National Center for Religious Education, a move which Ryan interpreted as reflecting a new emphasis and a real conviction about adult education on the part of the Bishops.[103] Two pronouncements released by the American Bishops in 1972, *The General Catechetical Director* and *To Teach as Jesus Did*, placed adult education first in the category of educational priorities —the first declaring: "Today more than ever before it is important to recognize that learning is a lifelong experience— consequently the continuing education of adults is activated not at the periphery of the Church's educational mission, but at its center."[104]

A contributing (or, at least, supporting) factor in the expansion of adult education in the Catholic Church was the
steady decline in enrollment of children and youth in the
parochial schools, thus making both physical facilities and
personnel available to serve adults. A new institutional form
came into being, the Catholic Adult Education Center,
often located in abandoned parochial schools and staffed
by priests, nuns, and lay teachers formerly on the faculties
of those schools. By the mid-seventies over a dozen such
centers had been established in the Archdiocese of Chicago,
with a coordinative Center for Adult Learning providing
leadership training and program-planning consultation to
local parishes. Similar centers existed in Detroit, Baltimore,
Los Angeles, and San Francisco.

Although the Administrative Board and the General Assembly of U.S. Bishops had urged the American Church to
place its emphasis on religious education, many dioceses
and local parishes chose to include in their programs such
life-centered areas as marriage education, parent education,
lay leadership training. and personal enrichment and self-
actualization. Thus, the Church needed leaders who were
competent in both theology and adult educational theory
and methodology, with the result that increasing numbers
of nuns and priests were enrolling in graduate programs
in adult education and a growing number of professionally-
trained lay adult educators were being employed. Ryan
reported that in 1976 there were over 1,500 professional
Directors of Religious Education or Religious Education
Coordinators in local parishes.[105]

A survey of adult Jewish education made by the American
Association for Jewish Education in 1964 found that although
there was still a strong emphasis on Jewish tradition, increasingly this emphasis was put in the context of Jewish consciousness within the culture of the times. The study also
indicated that no central themes appeared to be emerging
to give a sense of a coherent movement to the widely diversified activities of the temples and synagogues.[106]

Toward the end of this period there seemed to be a re-
surgence of interest in religion, as evidenced by rising church

attendance, prayer breakfasts by government leaders, open injection of religious faith into the 1976 presidential election, and other signs. The consequences of this trend for adult education in religious institutions remained to be seen in the era ahead.

Voluntary Organizations

One of the most striking developments of this era was the rising awareness in the country of volunteerism as a major national resource. In 1965 the Office of Manpower Research, Manpower Administration, of the U.S. Department of Labor, with the assistance of the Bureau of the Census, undertook a survey "to assess the economic and social contribution of volunteers."[107] The survey found that during the year ending November, 1965, 21,656,000, or about 16 percent, of the persons over age 14 "contributed their labor to some health, education, or welfare services for the general good."[108] Using the Department of Labor survey as the benchmark for estimates of "organized" volunteer manhours and adding estimates of "unorganized" volunteer work from a study by the University of Michigan Institute of Social Research at about the same time,[109] plus data he obtained from a study of a small sample of national voluntary organizations of his own, Wolozin estimated that volunteers contributed a total of 4.158 billion hours of labor in 1964 with an estimated value of over $25 billion.[110]

Although there was strong evidence that the corps of volunteer workers continued to grow in the traditional voluntary organizations in the fields of social service, health care, youth agencies, religious stewardship, and community service,[111] the greatest new growth in "organized" volunteer work was in government. Many of the "New Society" programs—The Peace Corps, the Jobs Corps, the Vista (later ACTION) program, Head Start, Upward Bound, the Community Action Projects, and the like—made extensive use of volunteers, many of them drawn from outside the middle class population traditionally associated with volunteering. But the explosive growth in volunteerism came in the "unorganized" (meaning nonestablishment type) endeavors of citizens to cope with social problems or influence social policy.

Kitzmiller and Ottinger characterize this development as follows:

Over the past two decades organized, independent citizen action has become an extremely potent force in our society. With increasing frequency—and success—citizens with common grievances or objectives have been stepping outside the existing political and social structures to organize *ad hoc* groups and press their causes by exerting new types of pressures on those structures. These *ad hoc* groups differ from the more traditional citizens' organizations in that they seek to *change* institutions instead of working through them and they feel free to employ methods that would be considered shrill, extreme and even dangerous or anarchical by such organizations.[112]

Some of the new citizen-action movements tended to focus on a single issue, such as civil rights (Southern Christian Leadership Conference), environmental protection (Sierra Club, Wilderness Society, CONCERN), the Vietnam War (the Vietnam Moratorium), women's liberation (NOW), abortion (Right to Life), and the like. Others, such as Ralph Nader's Public Citizen and John Gardner's Common Cause, served as vehicles for attacking the multitude of problems confronting the citizenry, such as housing, consumer protection, waste disposal, transportation, taxes, crime, pollution, governmental efficiency, and the like. Some of these operated only at the national level, essentially as lobbyists, while others involved citizens in attacking local and state problems as well as national problems through local and state chapters.

New organizations were also created during this period to coordinate the programs of individual action groups and systematize their efforts. Examples in the field of "organized" volunteerism included the Association for Administration of Volunteer Services, Association of Volunteer Bureaus, Corporate Volunteer Coordinators Council, and the National Society of Directors of Volunteer Services. Examples of organizations serving the "unorganized" voluntary movements were the National Center for a Voluntary Society,

the National Center for Voluntary Action, and the Alliance
for Volunteerism. A vehicle for stimulating, assembling, and
disseminating scholarly research on volunteerism was created
with the founding in 1971 of the Association of Voluntary
Action Scholars and the beginning of the publication of its
quarterly *Journal of Voluntary Action Research.*

Although the emphasis in the new volunteerism was on
action for social change, there was a heavy educational
component in the work of most of the new organizations
—education regarding both the substance of public issues
and the skills of citizen participation and organizational
leadership. There was growing evidence that volunteer work
could be experiential learning at its best.[113]

NATIONAL ORGANIZATION AND COORDINATION

The urge to bring a greater degree of unity and coherence
to the field of adult education that was documented in
Chapters VI and VII gained its most visible expression with
the convening in December, 1969, of a Galaxy Conference
of Adult Education Organizations in Washington, D.C. The
notion of having a number of the national organizations in
the field hold their annual meetings simultaneously in the
same city, so that they could come together for some joint
sessions, evolved from a meeting of the leaders of seventeen
organizations convened at Syracuse University in 1964 to
discuss the creation of its Library of Continuing Education.
As a result of these discussions an Ad Hoc Committee of
Adult Education Organizations was formed in 1966 to plan
the Galaxy Conference in 1969. (In 1967 the "Ad Hoc"
was dropped from the title.)

A total of 2,508 representatives of twenty organizations,
eight of which held their annual meetings there, attended
the Galaxy Conference. They took two actions subject to
later ratification by their respective organizations: (1) the
adoption of a statement of goals for the adult education
movement, "Imperatives for Action," and (2) the adoption
of a constitution for a new organization, the Coalition of
Adult Education Organizations.[114]

The constitution of the CAEO stated that "The overall purpose of the Coalition is to provide a basis for cooperation and action among the several organizations and associations in promoting adult and continuing education." It then specified that in carrying out the overall purpose, the Coalition shall endeavor:

1. To identify and focus on major issues in adult education.

2. To facilitate exchange of information about resources, action and plans of the organizations which are the members of the Coalition.

3. To facilitate the exchange of information about various aspects of adult education including: programs, financial support, legislation, administration, professional development, publications research, selection of faculty and staff.

4. To facilitate joint planning on projects to serve the field of adult education.

5. To be a resource for information and consultative services concerning adult education.

6. To promote the support of government, foundations and agencies to achieve educational opportunity for *all* persons.

7. To cooperate with other groups, agencies, and organizations in the achievement of these goals.[115]

By the mid-1970's the CAEO had grown to include nineteen member organizations and one associate member, representing diverse elements of the field, as follows:

Adult Education Association of the U.S.A.
Adult Student Personnel Association
American Library Association
American Association of Community and Junior Colleges
American Society for Training and Development
Association for Continuing Higher Education
Association for Continuing Professional Education
Institute of Lifetime Learning
Library of Continuing Education, Syracuse University
National Association of Black Adult Educators
National Association for Public Continuing and Adult
     Education
National Community Education Association
National Council of Churches
National Council of Community Services and Continuing
     Education

National Education Association
National Home Study Council
National University Extension Association
United States Association of Evening Students
University and College Labor Education Association
National Multimedia Center for Adult Education/National
    Adult Education Clearing house (Associate Member)

An assessment of the accomplishments of the Coalition in its first six years was provided in an editorial in its June, 1976, newsletter:

The Coalition of Adult Education Organizations represents the efforts of a number of national organizations with a common interest in adult and continuing education to come together at regular intervals to share in the process of interassociational communication and action. The Coalition plays not only a protective role with regard to existing adult educational programming and funding but also an advocacy role in an effort to develop, maintain and improve a balanced system of adult and continuing education throughout the United States. . . .

Over the past several years the process of coalition has led to a number of successful efforts in the areas of legislative action, cooperative programming, interassociational goal setting, education accounting systems assessment, data collection and policy planning, international programming, professional development, and adult education program research funding. The Coalition has developed increasing visibility in both the congressional and the executive offices in Washington, particularly among certain strategic sections of the U.S. Office of Education and pertinent National Advisory Councils. We have also maintained communication with appropriate private sector groups and other associations which share our interest in lifelong learning. A quick glance through the agenda of our CAEO meetings over the past several years yields convincing evidence of the responsible role we have played.

The Coalition and its members have been criticized for failing to produce statements and reports which capture the imagination of adult educators and for failing to inspire such professionals to work together in their setting or collectively on a state or national basis. We are the first to admit that the Coalition has not had a strong or indeed much grass roots visibility at all. In fact, some of our more agonizing discussions over the years have been related to whether such visibility is appropriate. . . .[116]

Obviously the CAEO was in the process of overcoming

some of the obstacles in the way of achieving a national coordinating organization in this complex field discussed in Chapter VI. The soundness of its choosing a symbiotic model rather than a coercive model for achieving its purposes remained to be demonstrated in the era ahead.

CHARACTERISTICS OF THE FIELD

The generalizations made about the characteristics of the field made in Chapter VII apply remarkably well to the field as it continued to evolve during the subsequent fifteen years.

The field proved itself to be indeed highly flexible and expansive. As has been documented earlier in this chapter, it adapted to a host of new social needs and served elements of the population previously unreached; it spread to an ever wider spectrum of institutions; it developed new techniques and media; and it recruited and trained large numbers of new personnel to deliver its services. Enrollment figures in almost every institutional setting showed dramatic increase. Although there are no reliable statistics regarding participation in the total field, since the trend was upward in all those segments of the field for which reliable statistics were available, the trend for the field as a whole could be assumed to be upward. A survey by the Response Analysis Corporation of Princeton, New Jersey in 1972 showed that better than one out of every three, or 32.1 million adults engaged in adult education that year.[117] Considering that this survey did not include the massive participation in "unorganized" voluntary activity described in the "Voluntary Organization" section of this chapter, it would seem to be reasonable to double that figure for comparison with the estimated participation of 49.5 million in 1955 that appears in Table 7.

The field continued to be a multidimensional social system, although it appeared that the institutional dimension was growing more strongly than the subject-matter, geographical, or personnel dimension—as evidenced particularly by the establishment of the Coalition of Adult Educational Organizations as the principal symbol of a potentially unified field.

The field continued to be highly interactive, as evidenced

by the Galaxy Conference of 1969 and a multitude of inter-association conferences at the local, regional, and national levels.[118]

Perhaps most importantly, great progress was made during this period in the development of a distinctive theory, curriculum, and methodology of adult education. Successful teachers of adults had long known that they couldn't teach adults as children have traditionally been taught. But there was little research-based knowledge about the unique characteristics of adult learners, and no comprehensive theory of adult learning to provide guidelines for program designers and teachers. During the fifties attempts began to be made to extract principles from the reports of successful teachers regarding their deviations from traditional practices, and a theoretical framework began to evolve empirically.[119] Then during the sixties new knowledge about the developmental stages and learning processes of adulthood started being produced by developmental psychologists, clinical psychologists, sociologists, anthropologists, and adult educators, and a comprehensive theory started taking shape. In the mid-sixties the label "andragogy" was imported from Europe (where it had been coined as early as 1833) to differentiate the new body of theory from "pedagogy," which was the label traditionally applied to the education of children. The new theory required a different approach to curriculum construction (task- or problem-centered rather than subject-centered units of learning), a different role for the teacher (facilitator and resource person rather than transmitter), a different role for the learner (active inquirer rather than passive recipient), and a different methodology (experiential rather than transmittal).[120] As these concepts became increasingly widely understood, the programs and practices of adult education came to look more and more different from those of traditional schooling. But toward the end of this period teachers of children and youth were discovering that the new theoretical framework had some implications for their practice, and andragogy was beginning to take on the meaning of "the art and science of helping human beings learn" rather than its original definition as "the art and science of teaching adults."

Finally, and partly as a result of the emergence of a comprehensive theory of adult learning, adult education continued to become increasingly differentiated as a field of study and practice—although, as the previous sentence suggests, the sharp distinction between youth and adult education appeared to be starting to blur. However, as previously noted in this chapter, specialized graduate programs for the training of professional adult educators continued to proliferate, the volume of inservice education programs rose, and the production of literature on adult education increased to flood proportions.

THE FUTURE OF ADULT EDUCATION

In Chapter VIII a number of predictions, required new assumptions, and new perspectives are listed which were made from the perspective of the author in 1962. The fact that the trends between 1961 and 1976 followed the predictions as well as they did suggests that the trends between 1921 and 1961 on which they were based were stable trends, not anomalies.

The first prediction was that the size of the "student body" of adult education would continue to expand. It has been documented above that indeed it has continued to expand, and probably at a more rapid rate than ever before in history. The fact that the previously-cited survey of the Response Analysis Corporation of Princeton, New Jersey, found that there were 79.8 million "would-be learners" who reported an interest in more education, of whom only 38 percent were currently engaged in education, suggests that this trend will continue well into the future.[121] In fact, there are strong indications that many formerly predominantly youth-serving institutions—especially high schools, colleges, community colleges, and universities—may become predominantly adult-serving institutions within the foreseeable future.

The second prediction is that the educational level of the student body of adult education would continue to rise. As was pointed out in the opening section of this chapter, the median number of years of school completed by persons

25 and over rose from 10.5 in 1960 to 12.2 in 1970 and was projected to rise to around 15 in the year 2000.

The third prediction was that the resources and facilities for the education of adults will gradually expand. The only part of that prediction that went wrong was the "gradually." In earlier sections of this chapter evidence has been presented of enormous and rapid expansion, especially in business and industry, colleges and universities, community colleges, government agencies, and the public schools. With the predicted continuing increase in the need and market for adult education, there is no reason to believe that its resources will not continue to expand.

The fourth prediction was that the curriculum and methodology of adult education will become increasingly differentiated, and this has been documented in the preceding section. With predictable increasing research on the aging process and adult learning, this trend will not only continue but will accelerate.

The fifth prediction, that there will be a rapid expansion in the body of knowledge about the education of adults has also been documented above. Looking into the future, it is predictable that among the new frontiers of discovery will be life-span developmental processes, environmental influences on learning, biological and chemical factors in learning, and extrasensory phenomena in learning.

The sixth prediction, that the role of the adult educator will become increasingly differentiated, along with training for that role, has been documented in the preceding section; and there are no signs that this trend will slacken in the next several decades. Indeed, schools of education in universities across the country, seeing the handwriting on the wall, are shifting their emphasis from the preparation of administrators and teachers for elementary, secondary, and higher education to the preparation of adult educators.

Also in Chapter VIII some implications were drawn concerning the education of children and youth that in 1962 seemed rather farfetched. The timing I had in mind for them was well into the twenty-first century. The basic thrust of the implications was that the central mission of formal schooling would be to produce self-directed lifelong learners. Well, lo and behold, in 1972 the International Commission on the Development of Education established by UNESCO, in its report, *Learning To Be: The World of Education Today and Tomorrow*, issued a resounding declaration that all of education must be reorganized with all feasible speed around the concept of learning as a lifelong process.[122] Almost immediately the Unesco Institute for Education adopted "the implications of the concept of lifelong education for the school curriculum" as the focus of its research and development work around the world. It produced three monographs analyzing the concept of lifelong education and presenting a variety of possible models for reorganizing the schools in congruence with it.[123] Other institutions around the world and in this country (notably the U.S. Office of Education and Phi Delta Kappa) picked up the theme. It seemed clear in 1976 that this would become the central organizing concept for all of education within perhaps not more than a decade or two.

If so, the chances are that a new institutional form—perhaps a lifelong learning center—will come into being to serve all ages. A number of partial prototypes of such a new institutional form are already in existence—learning labs, regional learning centers, educational brokerage agencies, library reader advisers, educational consortiums, and the like. There seemed to be agreement among the educational futurists of the seventies that the new institutional form would tap into all the resources of every community, creating "educative communities" and ending the monopoly of formal educational institutions.[124]

Perhaps the basic guidelines for shaping this new institutional form are those proposed by the International Commission on the Development of Education:

The concept of education limited in time (to 'school age') and confined in space (to school buildings) must be superseded. School education must be regarded not as the end but as the fundamental component of total educational activity, which includes both institutionalized and out-of-school education. A proportion of educational activity should be de-formalized and replaced by flexible, diversified models. Excessive prolongation of compulsory schooling, which is beyond certain countries' capacities, must be avoided. The extension of continual training will more than compensate for the shorter average duration of initial studies. Briefly, education must be conceived of as an existential continuum as long as life.

"Closed" educational systems should be made 'open.' We must gradually eliminate rigid distinctions between primary, secondary and post-secondary education. Short-cuts and branch-articulations should be introduced into educational channels.

Special attention should be paid to fostering education for pre-school-age children by selecting and cultivating the most positive forms of family and community associations in this work. All available means, conventional and unconventional, should be applied to developing basic education.

General education and technical training should be reconciled. Character and intelligence training should be harmonized. Education and work should be closely associated. Technology should be ever-present in the educational process, both as content and as guiding method. Technical education, which is unnecessarily expensive, should be supplemented and in many cases replaced by out-of-school professional training. Training should be so organized as to facilitate reconversion during employment, to lead to optimum professional mobility and to produce the greatest possible yield from the points of view both of the national economy and the trainees themselves. Narrow, premature specialization should be done away with.

There should be more diversified higher-education institutions. Universities should be turned into multi-purpose establishments open to adults and young people, and designed as much for continual training and periodic upgrading as for specialization and scientific research.

Education should be individualized and personalized to the utmost and constitute a preparation for self-learning. The processes of instruction and learning should be accelerated wherever this is in the learner's and the community's joint interest. New techniques for reproducing and communicating educational material, which are eminently suited to most envisaged innovations, should be introduced at a quicker pace, while technology in general should be regarded as a source of new pedagogic methods (where the cost of equipment is not excessive) and as means of making educational activity more democratic.

Educational management should be democratized, and the general public should play a large part in all decisions affecting education.[125]

It should be noted in passing that the above statement is not the ranting of a group of irresponsible education radicals, but the careful thinking of respectable representatives of "the establishment"—the former Prime Minister and Minister of Education of France, the former President of the Inter-American Development Bank, a Professor of Nuclear Physics at the University of Damascus, the Minister of Foreign Affairs and former Minister of Education of the People's Republic of the Congo, a member of the Academy of Pedagogical Sciences of the U.S.S.R., the former Minister of Higher Education and Sciences of Iran, and the Adviser on International Education of the Ford Foundation.

Clearly, "lifelong education," which until the early seventies had been used as a synomym for continuing or adult education, was taking on a new meaning. It was coming to mean the organization of the total educational enterprise as one continual process from birth to death. Obviously, a new institutional form was in the process of development to accommodate this new conception. And when this new institutional form has finally taken shape, adult education, as we have known it, will have disappeared. There will no longer be early childhood educators, youth educators, and adult educators. There will only be facilitators and resource persons of self-directing lifelong learners.

NOTES

CHAPTER I

1. See Louis B. Wright, *The Cultural Life of the American Colonies*, p. 126. New York: Harper and Brothers, 1957.
2. C. Hartley Grattan, *In Quest of Knowledge*, p. 139. New York: Association Press, 1955.
3. Wright, *op. cit.*, p. 25.
4. Robert F. Seybolt, *Source Studies in American Colonial Education: The Private School*, p. 35. Bureau of Educational Research Bulletin No. 28. University of Illinois Bulletin, XXIII, No. 4. Urbana, Ill.: University of Illinois Press, 1925. By permission.
5. Ellwood P. Cubberley, *The History of Education*, p. 365. Boston: Houghton Mifflin Company, 1920.
6. Eleanor T. Glueck, *The Community Use of Schools*, pp. 1ff. Baltimore: The Williams and Wilkins Company, 1927.
7. Seybolt, *Source Studies in American Colonial Education, op. cit.*, p. 101.
8. Wright, *op. cit.*, p. 129.
9. *Ibid.*
10. Oliver Garceau, *The Public Library in the Political Process*, pp. 6–7. New York: Columbia University Press, 1949.
11. *Ibid.*, p. 16.
12. Grattan, *op. cit.*, pp. 138–39.
13. R. Freeman Butts and Lawrence A. Cremin, *A History of Education in American Culture*, p. 76. New York: Holt, Rinehart and Winston, Inc., 1953.
14. Alfred C. True, *A History of Agricultural Extension Work in the United States, 1785–1923*, p. 8. U.S. Department of Agriculture Miscellaneous Publication No. 15. Washington, D.C.: Government Printing Office, 1928.
15. *Ibid.*, p. 19.
16. James Truslow Adams, *Frontiers of American Culture*, pp. 157–158. New York: Charles Scribner's Sons, 1944.
17. *Handbook of Adult Education in the United States, 1948*, Mary L. Ely, ed., p. 316. New York: Institute of Adult Education, 1948.
18. Grattan, *op. cit.*, p. 140.
19. Wright, *op. cit.*, pp. 242ff.

CHAPTER II

1. Charles A. Beard and Mary R. Beard, *A Basic History of the United States,* p. 79. New York: Doubleday Company, Inc., 1944.
2. *Ibid.,* p. 153, citing Isaiah Thomas, *History of Printing,* 1810.
3. Herbert B. Adams, "Educational Extension in the United States," *Report of the U.S. Commissioner of Education for 1899–1900,* p. 300. Washington, D.C.: Government Printing Office, 1910.
4. Henry Barnard, ed., *American Journal of Education,* XIV (1864), 535.
5. Henry Barnard, ed., *Connecticut Common School Journal,* I (1838), 40.
6. Cecil B. Hayes, *The American Lyceum,* p. 34. U.S. Office of Education Bulletin No. 12. Washington, D.C.: Government Printing Office, 1932.
7. Carl Bode, *The American Lyceum: Town Meeting of the Mind,* p. 250. New York: Oxford University Press, 1956.
8. From an address by John J. Pettibone, director of extension of Indiana University, National University Extension Association, *Proceedings of the First National University Extension Conference at Madison, Wisconsin, March 10–12, 1915,* p. 227.
9. Charles A. Beard and Mary R. Beard, *The Rise of American Civilization,* p. 764. New York: The Macmillan Company, 1930.
10. T.R. Adam, *The Museum and Popular Culture,* p. 8. New York: American Association for Adult Education, 1939.
11. Alexis de Tocqueville, *Democracy in America,* Vol. II, Phillips Bradley, ed., p. 114. New York: Alfred A. Knopf, Inc., 1954. By permission.
12. *Ibid.,* p. 115.
13. *Ibid.,* p. 118.
14. C. Hartley Grattan, *In Quest of Knowledge,* p. 147. New York: Association Press, 1955.
15. Bernard E. Meland, *The Church and Adult Education,* p. 13. New York: American Association for Adult Education, 1939.
16. Malcolm MacLellan, *The Catholic Church and Adult Education,* Vol. VIII, No. 5, p. 20. Washington, D.C.: Catholic Education Press, 1935. By permission of the Catholic University of America Press.
17. *Ibid.,* p. 21.
18. Alfred C. True, *A History of Agricultural Extension Work in the United States, 1785–1923,* p. 24. U.S. Department of Agriculture

Miscellaneous Publication No. 15. Washington, D.C.: Government Printing Office, 1928.

19. Ellwood P. Cubberley, *The History of Education,* p. 672. Boston: Houghton Mifflin Company, 1920.

20. *Ibid.,* p. 699.

21. Ellwood P. Cubberley, *Public Education in the United States,* rev. ed., p. 587. Boston: Houghton Mifflin Company, 1947.

22. Grace M. Glynn, "Public School Adult Education in Rhode Island," p. 1. Providence: State Department of Education, May, 1957. (Mimeographed).

23. Lawrence F. Greenberger, "Adult Education through Evening High Schools," pp. 43–45. Unpublished doctoral dissertation, University of Pittsburgh, 1936.

24. Excerpts from the *Annual Reports of the Cincinnati Board of Education* for 1841, 1842, and 1857.

25. *Fifteenth Annual Report of the Board of Managers for the Year Ending March 15, 1851,* p. 12. Cleveland: Board of Education, 1851.

26. Chicago Board of Education, "A Historical Review of the Chicago Public Evening Schools," pp. 1-3. Chicago: Board of Education, 1937. (Mimeographed).

27. *Eleventh Annual Report of the Baltimore Board of School Commissioners, 1839,* p. 6.

28. *Twenty-eighth Annual Report of the Baltimore Board of School Commissioners, 1856,* p. 38.

29. Buffalo Educational Council, *Adult Education in a Community,* pp. 5-6. New York: American Association for Adult Education, 1927.

30. *Annual Report of the St. Louis Board of Education for 1859–1960.*

31. Quoted in Adams, "Educational Extension in the United States," *op, cit.,* p. 302.

CHAPTER III

1. Rebecca Richmond, *Chautauqua: An American Place,* p. 75. New York: Duell, Sloan and Pearce Inc., 1943.

2. John S. Noffsinger, *Correspondence Schools, Lyceums, Chautauquas,* pp. 4–7. New York: The Macmillan Company, 1926. By permission.

3. L.H. Bailey, *Farmers' Institutes, History and Status in the United States and Canada,* pp. 24ff. U.S. Department of Agriculture, Office of Experiment Stations Bulletin 79. Washington, D.C.: Government Printing Office, 1900.

4. Alfred C. True, *A History of Agricultural Extension Work in the*

United States, 1785–1923, p. 129. U.S. Department of Agriculture Miscellaneous Publication No. 15. Washington, D.C.: Government Printing Office, 1928.

5. O.H. Kelley, *Origin and Progress of the Order of Patrons of Husbandry in the United States,* cited in *ibid.,* p. 123.

6. Marius Hansome, "The Development of Workers' Education," Theodore Brameld, ed., *Workers' Education in the United States,* pp. 52ff. New York: Harper and Brothers, 1941.

7. See *Apprenticeship Past and Present,* 3d ed., U.S. Department of Labor, Bureau of Apprenticeship. Washington, D.C.: Government Printing Office, 1955.

8. See A.B. Beatty, *Corporation Schools.* Bloomington, Ill.: Public School Publishing Co., 1918.

9. Nathaniel Peffer, *New Schools for Older Students,* p. 174. New York: The Macmillan Company, 1926. By permission.

10. John R. Morton, *University Extension in the United States,* p. 12. Birmingham, Ala.: University of Alabama Press, 1953.

11. American Society for the Extension of University Teaching, *Proceedings of the First Annual Meeting of the National Conference on University Extension.* Philadelphia: J. B. Lippincott Company, 1892.

12. Baldwin M. Woods and Helen V. Hammarberg, "University Extension in the United States of America," *Universities in Adult Education,* p. 131. Paris: UNESCO, 1952. By permission.

13. F.M. Rosentreter, *The Boundaries of the Campus,* p. 48. Madison, Wis.: University of Wisconsin Press, 1957. By permission of the copywright owners, the Regents of the University of Wisconsin.

14. National University Extension Association, *Proceedings of the Conference at Madison, Wisconsin,* March 10–12, 1915, pp. 211, 235.

15. American Society for the Extension of University Teaching, *Proceedings of the First Annual Meeting, op. cit.,* pp. 56–57.

16. National University Extension Association, *Proceedings of the NUEA at Chicago,* April 12–14, 1916, p. 8.

17. Rosentreter, *op. cit.,* pp. 53–54.

18. Morton, *op. cit.,* pp. 10–11.

19. Alvin Johnson, *The Public Library: A People's University,* pp. 24–25. New York: American Association for Adult Education, 1938.

20. Superintendent's Reports, Cleveland Public Schools, for the years indicated.

21. Chicago Board of Education, "A Historical Review of the Chicago Public Evening Schools," pp. 1–3. Chicago: Board of Education, 1937. (Mimeographed.)

22. Burton R. Clark, *Adult Education in Transition*, p. 48. Berkeley, Calif.: University of California Press, 1956.

23. J. Ernest Kuehner, assistant to the superintendent, St. Louis Board of Education, in a letter to the author September 3, 1957.

24. *Sixty-third Annual Report of the Cleveland Board of Education, 1898–1899*, p. 47.

25. Homer Kempfer, *Adult Education*, p. 155. New York: McGraw-Hill Book Company, Inc., 1955.

26. Clark, *op. cit.*, pp. 48–49.

27. Chicago Board of Education, *op. cit.*, pp. 14–15.

28. *Ohio State Laws*, 1922, Chapter 19, Sec. 767.

29. *Laws of Pennsylvania*, 1842, Act. No. 38, Sec. 5.

30. *Massachusetts Acts and Resolves*, 1847, Chapter 137.

31. *Annual Report of the Evening and Junior High Schools, 1919–1920*, Cleveland Public Schools.

32. Chicago Board of Education, *op. cit.*, p. 9.

33. *Report of the Superintendent, Cleveland Public Schools, 1887–1888*, p. 107.

34. *Ibid.*, p. 22.

35. Walter C. Eells, ed., *American Junior Colleges*, p. 11. Washington, D.C.: American Council on Education, 1940.

36. *Ibid.*, p. 18.

37. Mary L. Ely and Eve Chappel, *Women in Two Worlds*, p. 121. New York: American Association for Adult Education, 1938.

38. Alan E. Hugg, "Informal Adult Education in the Y.M.C.A.," p. 85. Unpublished doctoral dissertation, Faculty of Philosophy, Columbia University, 1950.

39. Frank E. Hill, *Educating for Health*, p. 19. New York: American Association for Adult Education, 1939.

40. Frank E. Hill, *Man-Made Culture*, pp. 146–147. New York: American Association for Adult Education, 1938.

41. Malcolm MacLellan, *The Catholic Church and Adult Education*, Vol. VIII, No. 5, p. 21. Washington, D.C.: Catholic Education Press, 1935. By permission of the Catholic University of America Press.

42. *Ibid.*, p. 23.

43. Theodore L. Low, "The Place of the Museum in Adult Education," *Handbook of Adult Education in the United States*, 1948, Mary L Ely, ed., p. 236. New York: Institute of Adult Education, 1948.

44. Thomas Gehring and Roberta Venable, "The Education of the Freedmen," Rehabilitative School Authority, Commonwealth of Virginia, Richmond 1976. (Mimeographed.)

CHAPTER IV

1. U.S. Bureau of the Census, *Statistical Abstract of the United States: 1961*, pp. 23, 26. Washington, D.C.: Government Printing Office, 1961.
2. U.S. Bureau of the Census, *Statistical Abstract of the United States: 1956*, p. 33. Washington, D. C.: Government Printing Office, 1956.
3. William J. Carr, "Education," J. Frederic Dewhurst, ed., *America's Needs and Resources*, pp. 379–380. New York: Twentieth Century Fund, 1955.
4. For a detailed analysis of these changes, see Dewhurst, *America's Needs and Resources, op. cit.,* pp. 130–431.
5. Henry S. Commager, *The American Mind*, p. 43. New Haven, Conn.: Yale University Press, 1950.
6. Charles R. Mann, "Education for More than the Job," *Journal of Adult Education,* I (February, 1929), 56.
7. See Chester I. Barnard, *Organization and Management*, pp. 3–9. Cambridge, Mass: Harvard University Press, 1948.
8. Harold Clark and Harold Sloan, *Classrooms in the Factories*, p. 14. Rutherford, N.J.: Fairleigh Dickinson University, 1958. By permission.
9. Leon Brody, "Educational Activities of Corporations," *Handbook of Adult Education in the United States*, 1948, Mary L. Ely, ed., p. 13. New York: Institute of Adult Education, 1948.
10. Clark and Sloan, *op. cit.,* pp. 15–16, 25.
11. A consolidated index listing the titles of 446 separate courses offered by six corporations, in *ibid.,* pp. 84–97. See also O.M. Serbein, *Educational Activities of Business.* Washington, D.C.: American Council on Education, 1961.
12. Peter E. Siegle, *New Directions in Liberal Education for Executives,* pp. 1–2. Chicago: Center for the Study of Liberal Education for Adults, 1958. By permission.
13. Clark and Sloan, *op. cit.,* pp. 134–135.
14. U.S. Office of Education, *Biennial Survey of Education in the United States, 1950–1952:* Chapter 1, "Statistical Summary of Education, 1951–1952," p. 45. Washington, D.C.: Government Printing Office, 1955.
15. John R. Morton, *University Extension in the United States,* pp. 133–134. Birmingham: University of Alabama Press. 1953.
16. Cyril O. Houle and Charles A. Nelson, *The University, the Citizen, and World Affairs,* pp. 61–73. Washington, D.C.: American Council on Education, 1956.

17. Morton, *op. cit.*, pp. 105–18.

18. See Bernard H. Stern, *How Much Does Experience Count* and *Adults Grow in Brooklyn*. Reports of the Brooklyn College Experimental Degree Project for Adults. Chicago: Center for the Study of Liberal Education for Adults, 1955. Also see Center for the Study of Liberal Education for Adults, *College Without Classes*. Chicago: the Center, 1961.

19. See Stuart Demerest, Galway Kinnell, and Alvin Johnson, *New Directions in University Adult Education: A Symposium*. Notes and Essays No. 11. Chicago: Center for the Study of Liberal Education for Adults, 1955.

20. See James B. Whipple, *Especially for Adults*. Notes and Essays No. 19. Chicago: Center for the Study of Liberal Education for Adults, 1957.

21. Morton, *op. cit.*, pp. 10–11. See also John P. Dyer, *Ivory Towers in the Market Place*, p. 38. Indianapolis: The Bobbs-Merrill Company, Inc., 1956.

22. Morton, *op. cit.*, pp. 73–78. See also James T. Carey, *The Development of the University Evening College*, pp. 29–43. Chicago: Center for the Study of Liberal Education for Adults, 1961.

23. For some of the more imaginative examples of this trend, see *A Review of 1957*, pp. 53–67. Chicago: Center for the Study of Liberal Education for Adults, 1958.

24. Morton, *op. cit.*, p. 96.

25. Dyer, *Ivory Towers in the Market Place, op. cit.*, pp. 42–43.

26. Morton, *op. cit.*, p. 97.

27. *Ibid.*, p. 65.

28. *Ibid.*, p. 66.

29. See Center for the Study of Liberal Education for Adults, "Conference Report: Evaluation of Liberal Adult Education." Chicago: the Center, 1959. (Mimeographed).

30. James E. Crimi, *Adult Education in the Liberal Arts Colleges*, p. 3. Chicago: Center for the Study of Liberal Education for Adults, 1957.

31. U.S. Department of Agriculture, *The Cooperative Extension Service Today: A Statement of Scope and Responsibility*, p. 3. Washington, D.C.: Federal Extension Service, April, 1958.

32. U.S. Bureau of the Census, *op. cit.*, p. 195.

33. Edmund deS. Brunner, "The Cooperative Extension Service of the United States Department of Agriculture," *Handbook of Adult Education*, 1948, *op. cit.*, p. 99.

34. *Ibid.*, p. 98.

35. See Joseph L. Matthews, "The Cooperative Extension Service of

the United States," Charles P. Loomis, *et al., Rural Social Systems and Adult Education,* p. 64. East Lansing, Mich.: Michigan State College Press, 1953.

36. Amelia S. Gordy, *Extension Activities and Accomplishments 1960,* p. 13. U.S. Department of Agriculture Extension Service Circular No. 533. Washington, D.C.: Government Printing Office, 1961.

37. U.S. Department of Agriculture, *op. cit.,* pp. 5–12.

38. Gordy, *op. cit.,* pp. 1, 9.

39. Joseph L. Matthews, "The Cooperative Extension Service," *Handbook of Adult Education in the United States,* 1960, p. 222, Malcolm S. Knowles, ed. Chicago: Adult Education Association, 1960.

40. Gordy, *op. cit.,* p. 7.

41. *Ibid.,* p. 34.

42. Letter of June 10, 1959, to the author from Florence Anderson, Secretary of the Carnegie Corporation of New York.

43. W.K. Kellogg Foundation, *The First Twenty-five Years,* p. 11. Battle Creek, Mich.: The Foundation, 1955.

44. W.K. Kellogg Foundation, *Annual Reports,* from 1945 to 1959. Battle Creek, Mich.: The Foundation, 1945-1959.

45. Fund for Adult Education, *Annual Report,* 1951, p. 12. White Plains, N.Y.: Fund for Adult Education, 1951.

46. Fund for Adult Education, *Continuing Liberal Education,* p. 11. Report for 1957–1959. White Plains, N.Y.: Fund for Adult Education, 1959.

47. *U.S. 85th Congress,* S. 385, Public Law 85–507, July 7, 1958. Government Employees Training Act.

48. Cyril O. Houle, Elbert W. Burr, Thomas H. Hamilton, and John R. Yale, *The Armed Services and Adult Education.* Washington, D.C.: American Council on Education, 1947.

49. Albert R. Munse and Edna D. Booher, *Federal Funds for Education—1956–1957 and 1957–1958,* pp. 116–117. U.S. Office of Education Bulletin 1959, No. 2. Washington, D.C.: Government Printing Office, 1959.

50. Marie D. Wann and Marthine V. Woodward, *Participation in Adult Education,* U.S. Office of Education Circular No. 539. Washington, D.C.: Government Printing Office, 1959.

51. G.L. Maxwell, "In Appreciation of a Great Leader," *Adult Education Bulletin,* VII (December, 1942), 39–40.

52. Ambrose Caliver, "Adult Education Activities of Government Agencies," *Handbook of Adult Education,* 1960, *op. cit.,* p. 243.

53. Munse and Booher, *op. cit.,* p. 18.

54. *A Design for Democracy.* An abridgment of a report of the Adult

Education Committee of the British Ministry of Reconstruction, 1919. New York: Association Press, 1956.

55. *Culture in Canada*. A Study of the Findings of the Royal Commission on National Development in the Arts, Letters, and Sciences, 1949-1951, Albert A. Shea, ed. Toronto: Canadian Association for Adult Education, 1952.

56. President's Commission on Higher Education, *Higher Education for American Democracy*, Vol. I, "Establishing the Goals," pp. 96-98. New York: Harper and Brothers, 1947.

57. President's Committee on Education Beyond the High School, *Second Report to the President*, p. 67. Washington, D.C.: Government Printing Office, 1957.

58. *Ibid.*, pp. 72–73.

59. Joe R. Hoffer, "Adult Education in Voluntary Social Welfare Organizations," *Handbook of Adult Education*, 1960, *op. cit.*, pp. 367-370.

60. Levitte Mendel, "Adult Education through Voluntary Health Organizations," *ibid.*, p. 258.

61. Frank J. Bruno, *Trends in Social Work*, p. 367. New York: Columbia University Press, 1957.

62. See especially *Handbook of Adult Education*, 1960, *op. cit.*, pp. 568, 575, 583, 596, and 602–603.

63. Adult Education Council of Greater Chicago, "A First Manual," p. 19. Chicago: The Council, 1956. (Mimeographed).

64. A comprehensive study of the history, variety, status, and future of residential adult education is provided in Robert H. Schacht, "Residential Adult Education: An Analysis and Interpretation." Unpublished doctoral dissertation, University of Wisconsin, 1957. See also: Royce S. Pitkin, *The Residential School in American Adult Education*. Notes and Essays No. 14. Chicago: Center for the Study of Liberal Education for Adults, 1956.

65. Robert H. Schacht and Henry Klein, "Adult Education in Independent and Residential Schools," *Handbook of Adult Education*, 1960, *op. cit.*, p. 273.

66. Lawrence Rogin, "Survey of Workers Education," *Journal of the American Labor Education Service*, 30th Anniversary Issue, 1958, p. 5. By permission.

67. Joseph Mire, *Labor Education*, pp. 23–31. Madison, Wis.: Inter-University Labor Education Committee, 1956.

68. John D. Connors, "Labor Education Today and Tomorrow," reprint from *The American Federationist*, October, 1956.

69. Mire, *op. cit.*, pp. 125–136.

70. Connors, *op. cit.*

71. Mire, *op. cit.,* pp. 70–71.

72. William S. Learned, *The American Public Library and the Diffusion of Knowledge*. New York: Harcourt, Brace & World, Inc., 1924.

73. "Libraries and Adult Education," *Handbook of Adult Education in the United States,* 1936, Dorothy Rowden, ed., p. 77. New York: American Association for Adult Education, 1936.

74. American Library Association, *Libraries and Adult Education*, p. 7. New York: The Macmillan Company, 1926. By permission.

75. *Ibid.,* p. 9.

76. Helen Lyman Smith, *Adult Education Activities in Public Libraries,* p. 56. Chicago: American Library Association, 1954.

77. American Library Association, *op. cit.,* pp. 54–57.

78. Smith, *op. cit.,* pp. 1–2.

79. Grace T. Stevenson, "The ALA Adult Education Board," *ALA Bulletin,* XLVIII (April, 1954), 229

80. See Lester Asheim, *Training Needs of Librarians Doing Adult Education Work*. Chicago: American Library Association, 1955.

81. Charles H. Hewitt, "Grant Evaluation Study," p. 178. Chicago: American Library Association, 1958. (Mimeographed).

82. Cyril O. Houle, "The Use of Print in Adult Educational Agencies," *Adult Reading,* 55th Yearbook of the National Society for the Study of Education, Part II, pp. 166–169. Chicago: University of Chicago Press, 1956.

83. For example: W.S. Gray and Ruth Munroe, *Reading Interests and Habits of Adults*. New York: The Macmillan Company, 1929; Douglas Waples and Ralph W. Tyler, *What People Want to Read About*. Chicago: University of Chicago Press, 1931; Guy T. Buswell, *How Adults Read*. Chicago: University of Chicago Press, 1937; Douglas Waples, *et al., What Reading Does to People*. Chicago: University of Chicago Press, 1940; W.S. Gray and Bernice Rogers, *Maturity in Reading*. Chicago: University of Chicago Press, 1956.

84. Houle, *op. cit.,* p. 170.

85. Frank E. Hill, *Listen and Learn: Fifteen Years of Adult Education on the Air,* p. 17. New York: American Association for Adult Education.

86. *Ibid.,* p. 33.

87. American Council on Education, Association for Education by Radio-Television, Association of Land-grant Colleges and Universities, National Association of Educational Broadcasters, National Association of State Universities, National Council of Chief State School Officers, and National Education Association.

88. "Telecourses for Credit," Vol. V, Forward. East Lansing, Mich.:

Michigan State University Continuing Education Service, 1958. (Mimeographed).

89. Fund for Adult Education, *Continuing Liberal Education, op. cit.,* pp. 31–32.

90. See Ronald Shilen, *Able People Well Prepared,* pp. 15–16. White Plains, N.Y.: The Fund for Adult Education, 1961.

91. Noffsinger, *Correspondence Schools, Lyceums, Chautauquas,* pp.15-16. New York: The Macmillan Company, 1926. By permission.

92. *Ibid.,* pp. 88–89.

93. Homer H. Kempfer, "State Programs of General Adult Education," *Adult Education Journal,* VI (April, 1948), 76.

94. See especially the following: Lawrence F. Greenberger, "Adult Education through Evening Schools," pp. 43–45. Unpublished doctoral dissertation, University of Pittsburgh, 1936; Homer Kempfer, *Adult Education Activities of the Public Schools,* Report of a Survey, 1947-1948. U.S. Office of Education Pamphlets No. 107. Washington, D.C.: Government Printing Office, 1949; National Association of Public School Adult Educators, *A Study of Urban Public School Adult Education Programs.* Washington, D.C.: NEA Division of Adult Education Service, 1952; Edward Olds, *Financing Adult Education in America's Public Schools and Community Councils.* Report of the National Commission on Adult Education Finance. Chicago: Adult Education Association, 1954.

95. Watson Dickerman, *Outposts of the Public School,* p. 13. New York: American Association for Adult Education, 1938.

96. Morse A. Cartwright, *Ten Years of Adult Education,* p. 60. New York: The Macmillan Company, 1935.

97. Carnegie Corporation of New York, Office Memorandum, Series II: Adult Education, No. 15, *op. cit.,* p. 20.

98. National Education Association, *Proceedings of the Department of Adult Education,* June 19, 1925, p. 8.

99. Cf. Cartwright, *op. cit.,* p. 60, and *Handbook of Adult Education,* 1936, *op. cit.,* p. 167; cf. Kempfer, *Adult Education Activities, op. cit.,* p. 21, and Paul Essert, *Creative Leadership of Adult Education,* p. 35. Englewood Cliffs, N.J.: Prentice-Hall, Inc., 1951. See also National Association of Public School Adult Educators, *A Study of Urban Public School Adult Education Programs, op. cit.,* p. 4.

100. John Holden, *Adult Education Services of State Departments of Education.* U.S. Office of Education Miscellaneous Bulletin No. 31. Washington, D.C.: Government Printing Office, 1959.

101. *Ibid.,* p. 24

102. Eduard C. Lindeman, *The Meaning of Adult Education,* pp. 8–9. New York: New Republic, Inc., 1926. By permission.

103. C. Hartley Grattan, *In Quest of Knowledge,* p. 229. New York: Associated Press, 1955.

104. State of California, *Partial Report of the Senate Interim Committee on Adult Education,* pp. 237–238. Senate Resolution 185. Sacramento, Calif.: California State Printing Office, 1953.

105. *Ibid.,* p. 241.

106. Robert A. Luke, "The Emergency in Education Extends into Adult Education," *The Public School Adult Educator,* I (May, 1958), 51.

107. The University of the State of New York Advisory Council on Adult Education, "A Platform for Continuing Education for Adults and the State of New York," pp. 12–13. Preliminary edition. Albany: State Department of Education, 1959. (Mimeographed).

108. Leon F. Miller, "Statutory Provisions for Public School Adult Education and their Implementation." Unpublished doctoral dissertation, Department of Education, University of Chicago, 1950.

109. Holden, *op. cit.,* p. 28.

110. Kempfer, *op. cit.,* p. 15.

111. Adult Education Association of the U.S.A., *Creating a Climate for Adult Learning,* p. 12. Chicago: The Association, 1959.

112. Donald Deffner, "The Church's Role in Adult Education," pp. 103–104. Unpublished doctoral dissertation, Graduate Division, University of California, Berkeley, 1956.

113. *Ibid.,* p. 205.

114. W. Randolph Thornton, "More Power to You," *International Journal of Religious Education,* XXXIII (May, 1957), 2.

115. For a description of the project, see Paul Bergevin and John McKinley, *Design for Adult Education in the Church.* Greenwich, Conn.: The Seabury Press, 1958.

116. See Lawrence C. Little, ed., *Charting the Future Course of Christian Adult Education in America.* Pittsburgh: Department of Religious Education, University of Pittsburgh, 1958.

117. See Sister Jerome Keeler, "Catholic Approaches and Problems," *Adult Leadership,* VII (February, 1959), 236.

118. Leon Feldman, "Trends in Adult Jewish Education." A reprint from *Congress Weekly,* Vol. XXI, No. 7 (February, 1954). New York: The Jewish Education Committee of New York.

119. *Ibid.*

120. Lily Edelman, "Jewish Approaches and Problems,' *Adult Leadership,* VII (February, 1959), 238.

121. Leon Feldman, *op. cit.*

122. For a study of this phenomenon in depth, see Richard H. Shryock, *National Tuberculosis Association, 1904–1954: A Study of the*

Voluntary Health Movement in the United States. New York: National Tuberculosis Association, 1957.

123. Max Birnbaum, "Adult Education in General Voluntary Organizations," *Handbook of Adult Education,* 1960, *op. cit.,* p. 384.

124. William C. Rogers, "Minnesota Voluntary Associations," Minneapolis: University of Minnesota Extension Division, n.d. (Mimeographed).

CHAPTER V

1. American Society for the Extension of University Teaching, *Proceedings of the First Annual Meeting, of the National Conference on University Extension,* pp. 15–16. Philadelphia: J. B. Lippincott Company, 1892.

2. National University Extension Association, *Proceedings of the NUEA at Chicago, April 12–14, 1916,* pp. 194–196.

3. For a detailed description of the center's activities, see Center for the Study of Liberal Education for Adults, *A Review of 1958: Future Directions of the Center, and a Report of Current Activities.* Chicago: The Center, 1959.

4. Another factor was the traditional hostility of the AFL toward the National Education Association, which it perceived to be a "company union" in competition with its own American Federation of Teachers, and which it felt wielded disproportionate power in the new Adult Education Association.

5. For a detailed description of its activities, see Joseph Mire, *Labor Education.* Madison, Wis.: Inter-University Labor Education Committee, 1956.

6. *Adult Education Journal,* V (April, 1946), 78, 94; VI (April, 1947), 85.

7. *Ibid.,* V (April, 1946), 94.

8. American Association for Adult Education, *Annual Report of the Director, 1948–1949,* p. 8.

9. *Adult Education Journal,* VII (July, 1948), 140.

10. A concise history of the NEA is given in the *NEA Handbook,* Centennial Edition, 1956–1957, pp. 49–80.

11. *Journal of Adult Education,* II (January, 1930), 85–86.

12. Morse Cartwright, *Ten Years of Adult Education,* p. 72. New York: The Macmillan Company, 1935.

13. See Dorothy Rowden, "Community and State Organizations of Adult Education Agencies," *Handbook of Adult Education in the*

United States, 1934, Dorothy Rowden, ed., p. 44. New York: American Association for Adult Education, 1934. Also see Ralph A. Beals, "Regional Organizations of Adult Education Agencies," *Handbook of Adult Education in the United States,* 1936, Dorothy Rowden, ed., p. 197. New York: American Association for Adult Education, 1934.

14. See C.S. Marsh, *Adult Education in a Community: A Survey of the the Facilities Existing in the City of Buffalo, New York.* New York: American Association for Adult Education, 1926.
15. See Frank Lorimer, *The Making of Adult Minds in a Metropolitan Area.* New York: The Macmillan Company, 1931.
16. *Handbook of Adult Education,* 1934, *op. cit.,* pp. 48–50.
17. American Association for Adult Education, *Annual Report of the Director, 1939–1940,* p. 27.
18. *Journal of Adult Education,* VIII (April, 1949), 98–100.
19. C. Scott Fletcher, "The Program of the Fund for Adult Education," *Adult Education,* II (December, 1951), 64.
20. See "Workshops" on "Building Better Communities," *Adult Leadership,* IV (May, 1955), 9–27; "Improving Communication among Local Organizations," *ibid.* (November, 1955); "Working Together for Adult Education," *ibid.* (December, 1955), 13–25; and "Representative Councils in Action," *ibid.,* V (May, 1956), 11–23.
21. Edward Olds, *Financing Adult Education in America's Public Schools and Community Councils,* pp. 70–77. Report of the National Commission on Adult Education Finance. Chicago: Adult Education Association of the U.S.A., 1954.
23. Ruth Kotinsky, *Adult Education Councils,* p. 153. New York: American Association for Adult Education, 1940.
24. Lyman Bryson, *A State Plan for Adult Education,* pp. 8–9. New York: American Association for Adult Education, 1934.
25. *Ibid.,* p. 8.
26. *Ibid.,* pp. 61–62.
27. For a composite picture of state organizations as they had developed by 1953, see Andrew Hendrickson, "A Typical State Association," *Adult Education,* III (May, 1953), 142.
28. *Handbook of Adult Education,* 1936, *op. cit.,* p. 204.
29. American Association for Adult Education, *Annual Report of the Director, 1937–1938,* p. 22.
30. See Warren H. Schmidt, "The AEA Area Organization and Conferences Project: A summary Report," *Adult Education,* VI (Autumn, 1955), 42–55.

CHAPTER VI

1. See: American Society for the Extension of University Teaching, *Proceedings of the First Annual Meeting of the National Conference on University Extension*, p. 7. Philadelphia: J.B. Lippincott Company, 1892; and Ellen C. Lombard, *Cooperation in Adult Education*, p. 3. U.S. Bureau of Education Home Education Circular No. 6. Washington, D.C.: Government Printing Office, 1924.
2. Carnegie Corporation, Office Memorandum, Series II, Adult Education No. 15, *op. cit.*, p. 5.
3. Carnegie Corporation, Office Memorandum, Series II: Adult Education, No. 1: Letter of June 6, 1924, from F.P. Keppel to Members of the Advisory Committee. (Mimeographed).
4. Carnegie Corporation, Office Memorandum, Series II: Adult Education, No. 3: Statement by E.C. Lindeman; No. 4: Statement by J.C. Dana; No. 5: Statement by E.D. Martin; No. 8: Amplified Statements by J.E. Russell, Charles A. Beard, A.E. Cohn, and E.D. Martin.
5. Carnegie Corporation, Office Memorandum, Series II: Adult Education, No. 10: Tentative Program, December 8, 1924.
6. A national Adult Education Association had been incorporated in 1923 "to promote adult education in peoples' colleges." Carnegie Corporation, Office Memorandum, Series II: Adult Education, No. 20: Digest of Proceedings of National Conference on Adult Education and First Meeting of the American Association for Adult Education, March 26, 1926.
7. Carnegie Corporation, Office Memorandum, Series II: Adult Education, No. 15, *op. cit.*
8. Carnegie Corporation, Office Memorandum, Series II: Adult Education, No. 20, *op. cit.*, p. 5.
9. Carnegie Corporation, Office Memorandum, Series II: Adult Education, No. 18: Digest of Proceedings of Regional Conference on Adult Education, New York, December 15, 1925, pp. 27–28.
10. *Loc. cit.*
11. Carnegie Corporation, Office Memorandum, Series II: Adult Education, No. 20, *op. cit.*, p. 23.
12. Carnegie Corporation, Office Memorandum, Series II: Adult Education, No. 18, *op. cit.*, p. 31.
13. Carnegie Corporation, Office Memorandum, Series II: Adult Education, No. 20, *op. cit.*, pp. 17–18.
14. *Ibid.*, p. 40.
15. The information and quotations on purposes, goals, and policies

have been taken, unless otherwise indicated, from a comprehensive review of the first twenty years of the AAAE's operation in American Association for Adult Education, *Annual Report of the Director, 1944–1945*, pp. 9–32.

16. American Association for Adult Education, *Annual Report of the Director, 1928–1929*, p. 2.

17. American Association for Adult Education, *Proceedings of the Third Annual Meeting, May 14–16, 1928*, p. 122.

18. American Association for Adult Education, *Annual Report of the Director, 1926–1927*, pp. 13–15. See also the annual report for 1929–1930, p. 19.

19. American Association for Adult Education, *Annual Report of the Director, 1943–1944*, p. 16.

20. American Association for Adult Education, *Annual Report of the Director, 1929–1930*, p. 2.

21. *Journal of Adult Education*, I (June, 1929), 321.

22. American Association for Adult Education, *Annual Report of the Director, 1946–1947*, p. 19.

23. American Association for Adult Education, *Annual Report of the Director, 1939–1940*, p. 51.

24. *Ibid.*, p. 49.

25. American Association for Adult Education, *Annual Report of the Director, 1941-1942*, p. 11.

26. *Journal of Adult Education*, III (April, 1931), 230–231.

27. For a rationale of this policy, see American Association for Adult Education, *Annual Report of the Director, 1926–1927*, p. 7.

28. American Association for Adult Education, *Annual Report of the Director, 1943–1944*, pp. 12-13.

29. American Association for Adult Education, *Annual Report of the Director, 1934–1935*, p. 24.

30. For a detailed description of plans for the new institute, see *Journal of Adult Education*, XIII (June, 1941), 308–309.

31. American Association for Adult Education, *Annual Report of the Director, 1935–1936*, pp. 6-7.

32. *Journal of Adult Education*, XIII (June, 1941), 306.

33. National Education Association, *Proceedings of the Sixty-fifth Annual Meeting*, LXV (1927), 328.

34. *Ibid.*, pp. 331–332.

35. National Education Association, *Proceedings of the Sixty-sixth Annual Meeting*, LXVI (1928), 303.

36. *Adult Education Bulletin*, III (October, 1938), 25.

37. *Loc. cit.*

38. *Adult Education Bulletin*, IV (January, 1940), 42.

39. Adult Education Association of the U.S.A., *First Annual Report, 1952*, p. 11.

40. Paul H. Sheats, "A Final Report on Negotiations with the AAAE," *Adult Education Bulletin*, VIII (April, 1944), 112.

41. American Association for Adult Education, *Annual Report of the Director, 1944–1945*, pp. 10–11.

42. For a list of "Some of the Problems in Adult Education," see *Adult Education Bulletin*, XI (February, 1947), 87–88.

43. American Association for Adult Education, *Minutes of the Executive Board, October 26, 1949*, p. 5.

44. *Adult Education Bulletin*, XIII (August, 1949), 162.

45. *Progress Report of the Joint Committee of the American Association for Adult Education and the NEA Department of Adult Education, May, 1950*, p. 3. (Mimeographed).

46. *Ibid.*, p. 2.

47. For a summary report of this workshop, see *Adult Education*, I (October, 1950), 5–12.

48. American Association for Adult Education, *Minutes of the Meeting of the Executive Board, September 3, 1950*, p. 3.

49. *Adult Education*, I (October, 1950), 7.

50. See especially the following: *Annual Reports* of the AEA for 1951-1959; Adult Education Association, "Working Paper for a Long-run Plan of Development," p. 2. Chicago: The Association, 1953. Mimeographed); Adult Education Association, "Developmental Needs of the Adult Education Movement." Chicago: The Association, November 1, 1954. (Duplicated); Adult Education Association, *Minutes of the 1956 Delegate Assembly*, pp. 14–15; Adult Education Association, "A proposed Plan of Development for the Five Years, 1957–1962," pp. 3–5. Chicago: The Association, 1956. (Mimeographed).

51. For summaries of the various studies, see: Malcolm S. Knowles, "Direction-Finding Processes in the AEA," *Adult Education*, VIII (Autumn, 1957), 41–42; Committee on Social Philosophy, "Issues Confronting the AEA," *Adult Education*, VII (Winter, 1957), 99-103; Robertson Sillars, ed., *Seeking Common Ground in Adult Education*, Adult Education Monograph No. 4. Chicago: Adult Education Association, 1958.

52. Edmund deS. Brunner, *et al.*, "The Role of a National Organization in Adult Education," p. 351. New York: Bureau of Applied Social Research, Columbia University, 1959. (Mimeographed).

53. See Grace T. Stevenson, "The Executive Committee Studies the Brunner Report," *Adult Leadersip*, VIII (March, 1960), 284–285 and IX (June, 1960), 53–74; and Glenn S. Jensen, "Our Organization

Meets Its Challenges," *Adult Leadership,* IX (April, 1961), 306–311.

54. Coolie Verner and Wilbur C. Hallenbeck, "A Challenge to the Adult Education Association," *Adult Education,* II (April, 1952), 136–137.

55. "What Are We Trying to Do," *Adult Leadership,* I (May, 1952), 1–2.

56. For detailed accounts of these controversies, see Robertson Sillars, "Some Problems of Publications Policy in the Adult Education Association of the U.S.A." Unpublished doctoral dissertation, Teachers College, Columbia University, 1954. Also, Brunner, *et al.,* "The Role of a National Organization in Adult Education," *op. cit.,* pp. 52–63.

57. For another evaluation of the AAAE's contribution, see: C. Hartley Grattan, *In Quest of Knowledge,* p. 123. New York: Association Press, 1955.

CHAPTER VII

1. Morse A. Cartwright, *Ten Years of Adult Education,* p. 60. New York: The Macmillan Company, 1935.

2. Paul L. Essert, *Creative Leadership of Adult Education,* p. 37. Englewood Cliffs, N.J. Prentice-Hall, Inc., 1951.

3. Malcolm S. Knowles, "Adult Education in the United States," *Adult Education,* V (Winter, 1955), 76.

4. Marie D. Wann and Marthine V. Woodward, *Participation in Adult Education,* pp. 3–4. U.S. Department of Health, Education, and Welfare, Office of Education Circular No. 539. Washington, D.C.: Government Printing Office, 1959.

5. Cyril O. Houle, "Professional Education for Educators of Adults," *Adult Education,* VI (Spring, 1956), 132–133.

6. See Brunner's review of research on adult educational participation in *An Overview of Adult Education Research,* pp. 89–118. Chicago: Adult Education Association, 1959.

7. See J.R. Kidd, *How Adults Learn,* pp. 33–57. New York: Association Press, 1959.

8. Coolie Verner, "The Literature of Adult Education," *Handbook of Adult Education in the United States, 1960,* Malcolm S. Knowles, ed., p. 171. Chicago: Adult Education Association, 1960.

9. Brunner, *et al., op. cit.,* pp. 1–7.

10. Cyril O. Houle, "The Doctorate in Adult Education," *Adult Education,* XI (Spring, 1961), 131–140. Boston University was the fif-

teenth university to inaugurate a graduate degree program, in the spring of 1960.

11. Based on Cyril O. Houle, "The Field of Adult Education," p. 13. Chicago: Department of Education, University of Chicago, n.d. (Mimeographed).
12. Burton R. Clark, *Adult Education in Transition: A study of Institutional Insecurity*, pp. 148–149. University of California Publications in Sociology and Social Institutions, Vol. I, No. 2, Berkeley, Calif.: University of California Press, 1956.
13. Frederick P. Keppel, *Education for Adults and Other Essays*, p. 38. New York: Columbia University Press, 1926.
14. W.S. Bittner, "Cooperation for Adult Education," *School and Society*, XX (September 6, 1924), 297–300.
15. National Education Association, *Proceedings of the Sixty-sixth Annual Meeting, 1928*, LXVI, p. 278.
16. Lyman Bryson, *Adult Education*, pp. 198–199. New York: American Book Company, 1936.
17. Floyd W. Reeves, "Adult Education: What Is It and Where Is It Going?" *Adult Education Bulletin*, II (October, 1937), 3.
18. Cyril O. Houle, "The Co-ordination of Public Adult Education at the State Level," pp. 1–2. Unpublished doctoral dissertation, Department of Education, University of Chicago, 1940.
19. Robert J. Blakely, *Adult Education in a Free Society*, J.R. Kidd, ed., p. 14. Toronto: Guardian Bird Publications, 1958.
20. Howard Y. McClusky, "Mobilizing the Community for Adult Education," Paul Sheats, *et al.*, *Adult Education: The Community Approach*, p. 295. New York: Holt, Rinehart and Winston, Inc., 1953.
21. C. Hartley Grattan, *In Quest of Knowledge*, p. 276–277. New York: Association Press, 1955.
22. For additional references to statements on the need for co-ordination, see Houle, "The Co-ordination of Public Adult Education at the State Level," pp. 2–4. Unpublished doctoral dissertation, Department of Education, University of Chicago, 1940.
23. Robert A. Luke, "The AEA and the Field of Adult Education," *Adult Education*, IV (March, 1954), 135–136.
24. American Vocational Association, *Adult Education*, p. 69. Minneapolis: William Wood Dunwoody Industrial Institute Press, 1928. Also see *Education for American Life*, pp. 62–63. New York State University Regents' Inquiry into the Character and Cost of Public Education in the State of New York. New York: McGraw-Hill Book Company, Inc., 1938.
25. Baldwin M. Woods and Helen V. Hammarberg, "University Ex-

tension in the United States of America," *Universities in Adult Education*, pp. 139–140. Paris: UNESCO, 1952. By permission.

26. Advisory Committee on Education, *Report of the Committee*, pp. 135–137. Washington: Government Printing Office, 1938.

27. William H. Stacy, *Integration of Adult Education*, pp. 8–9. Contributions to Education No. 646. New York: Teachers College, Columbia University, 1935.

28. Thurman White, "Some Common Interests of Adult Education Leaders," *Adult Education*, VI (Spring, 1956), 160.

29. Edmund deS. Brunner, *et al.*, "The Role of a National Organization in Adult Education," pp. 222–230. New York: Bureau of Applied Social Research, Columbia University, 1959. (Mimeographed).

30. See Kenneth D. Benne, "Some Philosophic Issues in Adult Education," *Adult Education*, VII (Winter, 1957), 67–82; and Malcolm S. Knowles, "Philosophical Issues that Confront Adult Educators," *Adult Education*, VII (Summer, 1957), 234–240.

31. For proposed strategies for the further development of a coordinated field see Malcolm S. Knowles, "The Development of a Co-ordinated Adult Educational Movement in the United States," pp. 456–461. Unpublished doctoral dissertation, Department of Education, University of Chicago, 1960.

CHAPTER VIII

1. Alfred N. Whitehead, "Introduction," Wallace B. Donham, *Business Adrift*, pp. viii–xix. New York: McGraw-Hill Book Company, 1931. By permission.

2. Margaret Mead, *The School in American Culture*, pp. 33–34. Cambridge, Mass.: Harvard University Press, 1959. By permission.

3. For examples, see the following pamphlets in the series on "New Dimensions in Higher Education" by the U.S. Office of Education: No. 1: "Independent Study"; No. 2: "Effectiveness in Teaching"; and No. 7: "Quest for Quality." Washington, D.C.: Government Printing Office, 1960.

4. For an elaboration of this concept, see Stuart Chase, *Some Things Worth Knowing*. New York: Harper & Brothers, 1958.

5. Howard Y. McClusky, "Adult Education—Our Secret Weapon," *Adult Leadership*, I (October, 1952), 26.

CHAPTER IX

1. See David Bell, ed., "Toward the Year 2000: Work in Progress," *Daedalus* (Summer, 1967); Buckminster Fuller, *Operating Manual for Spaceship Earth*. Carbondale, Illinois: Southern Illinois University Press, 1969; and Alvin Toffler, *Future Shock*. New York: Random House, 1970.

2. U.S. Bureau of the Census, *Statistical Abstract of the United States: 1974*, pp. 5-7. Washington, D.C.: Government Printing Office, 1974.

3. *Ibid.*, pp. 6, 31.

4. *Ibid.*, p. 19.

5. Ronald Weber, ed., *America in Change*, p. 28. Notre Dame, Ind.: University of Notre Dame Press, 1972.

6. *Ibid*, pp. 30-31.

7. *Ibid.*, p. 30.

8. *Statistical Abstract, 1974, op. cit.*, p. 37.

9. *Ibid.*, p. 116

10. *Perspectives of Adult Education in the U.S. and a Projection for the Future*, p. 3. U.S. Office of Education, Publication No. (OE) 72-181. Washington, D.C.: Government Printing Office, 1972.

11. *Adult Education: State Demographic Data*, p. xi. Washington, D.C.: National Advisory Committee on Adult Education, 1973.

12. *Public Continuing and Adult Education 1975 Almanac*, p. 39. Washington, D.C.: National Association for Public Continuing and Adult Education, 1975.

13. "Inflation and Unemployment," *Congressional Quarterly*, 1975.

14. *Statistical Abstract, 1974, op. cit.*, p. 342.

15. Alvin Toffler, *The Eco-Spasm Report*. New York: Bantam, 1975.

16. *America in Change, op. cit.*, pp. 220-238.

17. *Ibid.*, p. 205.

18. For examples, see the writing of Kenneth Clark, Robert Coles, Edgar Z. Friedenberg, Paul Goodman, John Holt, Herbert Kohl, George B. Leonard, Neil Postman, Carl Rogers, Charles E. Silberman, and Charles Weingartner.

19. Ivan Illich, *Deschooling Society*. New York: Harper and Row, 1970.

20. See George B. Leonard, *Education and Ecstasy*. New York: Dell Publishing Co., 1968; Charles E. Silberman, *Crisis in the Classroom*. New York: Random House, 1970; Melvin Silberman, *et al*, *The Psychology of Open Teaching and Learning*. Boston: Little,

Brown, 1972; and Alvin Toffler, *Learning for Tomorrow*. New York: Random House, 1974.

21. In addition to the above, see Patricia Cross, *Accent on Learning*. San Francisco: Jossey-Bass, 1976; John I. Goodlad, *et al*, *The Changing School Curriculum*. New York: The Fund for the Advancement of Education, 1966; and Jerrold R. Acharias and Stephen White, "The Requirements for Major Curriculum Revision," in Robert W. Health, ed., *New Curricula*. New York: Harper and Row, 1964.

22. *Statistical Abstract, 1974, op. cit.*, p. 143.

23. See the writings of Chris Argyris, Robert Blake, Rensis Likert, Douglas McGregor, Alfred Marrow, and Leonard Nadler.

24. Leonard Nadler, "Business and Industry," *Handbook of Adult Education in the U.S., 1970*, R.M. Smith, G.F. Aker, and J.R. Kidd, eds., p. 316. New York: Macmillan, 1970.

25. Stanley Peterfreund, "Education in Industry—Today and in the Future," Training and Development Journal, XXX (May, 1976), 30-40. For selected case descriptions of continuing education in corporations, see Sally J. Olean, *Changing Patterns in Continuing Education for Business*. Boston: Center for the Study of Liberal Education for Adults, 1967.

26. National Center for Educational Statistics, *Digest of Educational Statistics 1975*, p. 136. Washington, D.C.: Government Printing Office, 1975. However, the 1974-75 joint report of the Association of Continuing Higher Education and the National University Extension Association, *Programs and Registrations*, pp. 40-41, showed a total registration in the 244 out of possible 355 member institutions that reported of 6,420,671 (3,064,173 credit and 3,356,498 noncredit) students. Discrepancies of this sort are not uncommon in the statistics of adult education, owing to differences in definitions and in data-collection methods.

27. Cyril O. Houle, "From Craft Toward Profession," *The Continuing Task*. Boston: Center for the Study of Liberal Education for Adults, 1967.

28. *Federal Support for Adult Education*. Washington, D.C.: Adult Education Association of the U.S.A., 1968.

29. *A Question of Stewardship: A Study of the Federal Role in Higher Continuing Education*. Washington, D.C.: National Advisory Council on Extension and Continuing Education, 1972.

30. Malcolm S. Knowles, *Higher Adult Education in the United States*, p. 38. Washington, D.C.: American Council on Education, 1969.

31. Samuel Gould and K. Patricia Cross, *Explorations in Non-Tradi-*

tional Study. San Francisco: Jossey-Bass, 1972; Samuel Gould, Chairman, Commission on Non-Traditional Study, *Diversity By Design.* San Francisco: Jossey-Bass, 1973; Cyril O. Houle, *The External Degree.* San Francisco: Jossey-Bass, 1973; See also: K. Patricia Cross, *Accent on Learning.* San Francisco: Jossey-Bass, 1976; Theodore Hesburg, Paul A. Miller, and Clifton R. Wharton, Jr., *Patterns for Lifelong Learning.* San Francisco: Jossey-Bass, 1973; Ohmer Milton, *Alternatives to the Traditional.* San Francisco: Jossey-Bass, 1972; and Dyckman W. Vermilye, *Lifelong Learners: A New Clientele for Higher Education.* San Francisco: Jossey-Bass, 1974.

32. *Diversity By Design, op. cit.,* p. xv.
33. Cyril O. Houle, *The External Degree, op. cit.,* p. 13 and p. 174.
34. *NUEA Newsletter,* V (November 10, 1972), 3.
35. Thomas Cummings, *Political Backgrounds of Adult Education.* Boston: Center for the Study of Liberal Education for Adults, 1967.
36. *The PER Report,* I (August 2, 1976), 2 (Postsecondary Education Resources, Inc., Fairfax, Virginia).
37. *Ibid.,* p. 5.
38. For example, see: "Financing Lifelong Learning: Rationale and Alternatives," a working paper for the Study of Adult Education in New York State, State Department of Education, Albany, New York, April 8, 1975 (mimeographed); "The Third Century: Postsecondary Planning for the Nontraditional Learner," a report prepared for the Higher Education Facilities Commission of the State of Iowa by the Office of New Degree Programs of the Educational Testing Service, May, 1976; and "Postsecondary Alternatives to Meet the Educational Needs of California's Adults," prepared for the California Legislature, Sacramento, California, September, 1975.
39. National Center for Educational Statistics, *The Condition of Education, 1975,* p. 190. Washington, D.C.: Government Printing Office, 1975.
40. Ralph R. Fields, *The Community College Movement.* New York: McGraw-Hill, 1962.
41. "Master Bibliography," Department of Adult and Community College Education, North Carolina State University, 1974 (mimeographed).
42. Ervin L. Harlacher, "Community Colleges," *Handbook of Adult Education, 1970, op. cit.,* pp. 213-214.
43. Ervin L. Harlacher, *The Community Dimension of the Community*

College, p. ii. Washington, D.C.: American Association of Junior Colleges, 1967.

44. John C. Van Druff, "Learning Labs in Adult Education," *Adult Leadership*, XXIII (September, 1974), 72-73.

45. Paul A. Miller, *The Cooperative Extension Service: Paradoxical Servant—The Rural Precedent in Continuing Education*, p. 20. Syracuse: Publications in Continuing Education, Syracuse University, 1973.

46. Joint USDA-NASULGC Extension Study Committee, *A People and A Spirit*. Washington, D.C.: Extension Service, U.S. Department of Agriculture, 1968.

47. Paul A. Miller, *op. cit.*, p. 21.

48. *A People and A Spirit*, *op. cit.*, pp. 91-93.

49. *Cooperative Extension Service Programs: A Unique Partnership Between Public and Private Interests*, pp. 14-19. Washington, D.C.: Extension Service, U.S. Department of Agriculture, 1976.

50. Paul A. Miller, *op. cit.*, p. 17.

51. *Ibid.*, pp. 17-18.

52. All statistics in this paragraph were obtained from EMIS and supplied to the author by the office of Edwin L. Kirby, Administrator, Extension Service, United States Department of Agriculture, August, 11, 1976.

53. Hilton Power, "Education for Social and Public Responsibility, *Handbook of Adult Education, 1970, op. cit.*, pp. 461-462.

54. See Joseph Dermer (ed.), *Where Large Foundations Make Their Grants*. New York: Public Service Materials Center, 1974; and Harold J. Alford, *Continuing Education in Action: Residential Centers for Lifelong Learning*. New York: Wiley, 1968.

55. For a detailed description of these Acts and programs, see National Advisory Council on Adult Education, *An Historical Perspective: The Adult Education Act, 1964-1974*. Washington, D.C.: National Advisory Council on Adult Education, 1974. The material in this section was drawn from this source.

56. See *Interim Report*, 1971, and *Annual Reports* for subsequent years. Washington, D.C.: National Advisory Council on Adult Education.

57. *1976 Annual Report*, p. 12. Washington, D.C.: National Advisory Council on Adult Education, 1976.

58. National Center for Educational Statistics, *Projects, Products, and Services of the National Center for Educational Statistics*, p. 1. Washington, D.C.: Government Printing Office, 1973.

59. See U.S. Civil Service Commission, *Employee Training in the*

Federal Service, Washington, D.C.: Government Printing Office. Published annually since 1967.

60. Joe R. Hoffer, "Health and Welfare Agencies," *Handbook of Adult Education, 1970, op, cit.*, p. 340.

61. *Bulletin of the National Center for Education Brokering*, I (March, 1976), 1. Published by the Center, 405 Oak Street, Syracuse, N.Y. 13203.

62. Lawrence Rogan, "Labor Unions," *Handbook of Adult Education, 1970, op. cit.*, pp. 304-307.

63. *Ibid,.* p. 312.

64. Margaret Monroe, "Public Libraries and Museums," *Handbook of Adult Education, 1970, op. cit.*, p. 246.

65. See, for example, Priscilla Gotsick, "Adult Basic Education and Public Libraries: Services to the Disadvantaged," *Adult Leadership*, XXXI (April, 1973), 329-346.

66. Elizabeth W. Stone, Ruth K. Patrick, and Barbara Conroy, *Continuing Library and Information Science Education.* Washington, D.C.: Government Printing Office, 1974.

67. For a comprehensive review of the continuing education publication scene, see A.N. Charters and W.M. Rivera, *International Seminar on Publications in Continuing Education.* Syracuse: Publications in Continuing Education, Syracuse University, 1972.

68. For a detailed description of the adult education clearinghouses, see Roger De Crow, "Information Resources and Services," *Handbook of Adult Education, 1970, op. cit.*, pp. 75-90.

69. See National Library of Medicine, *The Lister Hill National Center for Biomedical Communications Report to the Congress*, April, 1972. DHEW Publication No. (NIH) 72-268. Washington, D.C.: Government Printing Office, 1972.

70. For example, see Charles A. Wedemeyer and Robert E. Najem, *AIM: From Concept to Reality: The Articulated Instructional Media Program at Wisconsin.* Syracuse: Publications in Continuing Education, Syracuse University, 1969.

71. Carnegie Commission on Educational Television, *Public Television.* New York: Harper and Row, 1967.

72. Robert J. Blakely, *The Use of Instructional Television in Adult Education: A Review of Some Recent Developments*, p. 9. Syracuse: Publications in Continuing Education, Syracuse University, 1974.

73. For controversial analyses of educational broadcasting during this period, see Robert A. Carlson, *Educational Television In Its Cultural and Public Affairs Dimension: A Selected Literature*

Review of Public Television As An Issue in Adult Education.
Syracuse: Publications in Continuing Education, Syracuse University, 1973; and John Ohliger, *Listening Groups: Mass Media in Adult Education.* Boston: Center for the Study of Liberal Education for Adults, 1967.

74. For a comprehensive analysis of the impact of the new media on society, see Peter H. Rossi and Bruce J. Biddle (eds.), *The New Media and Education.* Chicago: Aldine, 1966.

75. Margaret Monroe, "Public Libraries and Museums," *op. cit.*, pp. 254-255.

76. American Association of Museums, *A Statistical Survey of Museums in the United States and Canada.* Washington, D.C.: American Association of Museums, 1965.

77. National Center for Educational Statistics, *Participation in Adult Education, 1972* in *Digest of Education Statistics, 1975, op. cit.*, p. 136.

78. Harold F. Clark and Harold S. Sloan, *Classrooms on Main Street.* New York: Teachers College, Columbia University, 1966.

79. "List of Continuing Education Agencies Accredited by the Continuing Education Council, Fall, 1975," Continuing Education Council, 6 North 6th Street, Richmond, Virginia, 23219. (mimeographed).

80. The U.S. Office of Education—National Center for Educational Statistics, *Adult Education in Public School Systems, 1968-69 and 1969-70*, p. 23. Washington, D.C.: Government Printing Office, 1970. Note that community college enrollment of 1,275,961 must be subtracted from the total enrollment of 8,346,828 in "the public education system" figure.

81. *Public Continuing and Adult Education 1976 Almanac*, p. 43. Washington, D.C.: National Association for Public Continuing and Adult Education, 1976.

82. *Ibid.*, pp. 47, 49.

83. *Adult Education in Public Schools Systems, 1968-69 and 1969-70, op. cit.*, p. 17.

84. Robert E. Finch, "Public Schools," *Handbook of Adult Education 1970, op. cit.*, p. 236.

85. For a comprehensive overview of these developments, see W. Robert Houston, *Exploring Competency-Based Education.* Berkeley: McCutcheon, 1974.

86. See Winthrop R. Adkins, "Life Skills Education for Adult Learners," *Adult Leadership*, XXII (June, 1973), 55-84.

87. See "The Adult Performance Level Study," APL Project, Uni-

versity of Texas, Austin, Texas, 1973 (mimeographed); and Norvell Northcutt, *et al*, "Adult Functional Competency: A Summary," APL Project, University of Texas, Austin, Texas, 1975 (mimeographed).

88. Edith Roth, "APL: A Ferment in Education," *American Education*, XII (May, 1976).

89. "Adult Functional Competency: A Summary," *op. cit.*, pp. 2-3.

90. "A Curriculum for ABE: Goals, Objectives, Tasks," APL Project, University of Texas, Austin, Texas, 1976.

91. For examples, see "The Texas APL Competency-Based High School Diploma Program," The APL Project, University of Texas, Austin, Texas. "Adult Competency Instructional Guides" by Harry Frank, Vocational and Adult Education Department, Auburn University, Auburn, Alabama; Mary Mulvey, "Project ERA/COPE, " Providence, Rhode Island Public Schools Adult Education Program; "Just around the Corner," Mississippi Authority for Educational Television, Jackson, Mississippi; and "Partnership in Learning," World Education, New York.

92. See E.G. Olsen, "Standing on the Shoulders of Pioneers," *Community Education Journal*, V (November-December, 1975), 8-12.

93. "Community School Statistics for the School Year 1974-1975," *Community Education Journal, ibid*, p. 56.

94. J.D. Minzey and C.R. Olsen, *The Role of the School in Community Education*, pp. 31-32. Midland, Mich.: Pendell, 1969.

95. Maurice F. Seay, *et al, Community Education: A Developing Concept*, p. 11. Midland, Mich.: Pendell, 1974.

96. J.B. Elzy, "From the Ashes of the Riots—The Wilmington, Delaware, Community School Program Is Born," *Community Education Journal*, III (January, 1973), 20.

97. For a detailed account of these events, see Robert A. Luke, "The NEA and Adult Education," *Adult Leadership*, XX (June, 1971), 42-78.

98. Kenneth Stokes, "Religious Institutions," *Handbook of Adult Education, 1970, op. cit.*, p. 354.

99. Huey B. Long, *Adult Education in Church and Synagogue: A Review of Selected Recent Literature*, pp. 41-42. Syracuse: Publications in Continuing Education, Syracuse University, 1973.

100. *Design for Methodist Curriculum*. Nashville: General Board of Education, The Methodist Church, 1965.

101. Kenneth D. Barringer, "Religious Education for Adults," *Adult Leadership*, XVII (May, 1968), 10-34.

102. Quoted in James R. Schaefer, *Program Planning for Adult Christian Education*, p. 96. New York: Newman Press, 1972.
103. Leo V. Ryan, "New Focus in the Roman Catholic Adult Education Movement," *Adult Leadership*, XXIV (May, 1976), 314.
104. *Ibid.*, p. 315.
105. *Ibid.*, p. 314.
106. *Proceedings, National Conference on Adult Jewish Education, February 20, 1965, New York City: A Summary Report.* New York: American Association for Jewish Education, 1965. See also, Marvin M. Beckerman, "Adult Jewish Education: Present and Future Directions," *Religious Educator*, LXVIII (January-February, 1973), 84-95.
107. Manpower Administration, U.S. Department of Labor, *Americans Volunteer*, p. ii. Manpower/Automation Research Monograph No. 10. Washington, D.C.: Government Printing Office, 1969.
108. *Ibid.*, pp. 3-4.
109. J.N. Morgan, I.A. Sirageldin, and N. Baerwaldt, *Productive Americans*. Ann Arbor, Mich.: Institute for Social Research, University of Michigan, 1966.
110. Harold Wolozin, "The Economic Role and Value of Volunteer Work in the United States: An Exploratory Study," *Journal of Voluntary Action Research*, IV (January-April, 1975), 38-40.
111. See "AHA Survey Report," *Hospitals, the Journal of the American Hospital Association*, XLII (March 16, 1968); Guion G. Johnson, *Volunteers in Community Service*. Chapel Hill, N.C.: University of North Carolina Press, 1967; David Horton Smith, "Voluntary Action and Voluntary Groups," in Alex Inkeles, ed., *Annual Review of Sociology*. Palo Alto, Calif.: Annual Review Publications, 1975.
112. W.M. Kitzmiller and Richard Ottinger, *Citizen Action: Vital Force for Change*, p. 1. Washington, D.C.: Center for a Voluntary Society, 1971.
113. See Richard A. Graham, "Voluntary Action and Experimental Education," *Journal of Voluntary Action Research*, II (October, 1973), 186-193.
114. For a detailed account of the Galaxy Conference and its antecedents, see A.N. Charters, *Report on the 1969 Galaxy Conference of Adult Education Organizations*. Syracuse: Publications in Continuing Education, Syracuse University, 1971.
115. *Ibid.*, p. 33.
116. Robert A. Allen, Jr. "What Is CAEO: An Editorial," *CAEO News*, II (June, 1976), 1.

117. *Diversity By Design, op. cit.*, p. 17.

118. My first book, *Informal Adult Education* (New York: Association Press, 1950), was such an attempt.

119. See R.J. Kidd, *How Adults Learn.* New York: Association Press, 1973; M.S. Knowles, *The Modern Practice of Adult Education: Andragogy versus Pedagogy.* New York: Association Press, 1970; M.S. Knowles, *The Adult Learner: A Neglected Species.* Houston: Gulf Publishing Co., 1973; M.S. Knowles, *Self-Directed Learning: A Guide for Learners and Teachers.* New York: Association Press, 1975; and Allen Tough, *The Adult's Learning Projects.* Toronto: Ontario Institute for Studies in Education, 1971.

120. *Diversity By Design, op. cit.*, pp. 15-17.

121. Edgar Faure, Chairman, International Commission on the Development of Education, *Learning To Be: The World of Education Today and Tomorrow.* Paris: Unesco, 1972.

122. R.H. Dave (ed.), *Lifelong Education and School Curriculum.* Monograph No. 1. Hamburg: Unesco Institute for Education, 1973.; R.H. Dave and N. Stiemerling, *Lifelong Education and the School: Abstracts and Bibliography.* Monograph No. 2. Hamburg: Unesco Institute for Education, 1973.; R.H. Dave (ed.), *Reflections on Lifelong Education and the School.* Monograph No. 3. Hamburg: Unesco Institute for Education, 1975.

123. For example, see Stephen R. Graubard, "University Cities in the Year 2000." *Toward the Year 2000, Daedalus*, 96 (Summer, 1967), 817-822; Louis Rubin (ed.)., *The Future of Education: Perspectives on Tomorrow's Schooling.* Boston: Allyn and Bacon, 1975; Alvin Toffler (ed.)., *Learning for Tomorrow: The Role of the Future in Education.* New York: Random House, 1974; and the abovecited Unesco Institute for Education monographs.

124. *Learning To Be, op. cit.*, pp. 233-234.

BIBLIOGRAPHY

OF GENERAL SOURCES

ADAM, THOMAS R., *The Civic Value of Museums.* New York: American Association for Adult Education, 1937.
———, *Education for International Understanding.* New York: Institute of Adult Education, Columbia University, 1948.
———, *Motion Pictures in Adult Education.* New York: American Association for Adult Education, 1940.
———, *The Museum and Popular Culture.* New York: American Association for Adult Education, 1939.
———, *The Workers' Road to Learning.* New York: American Association for Adult Education, 1940.
ADAMS, HERBERT B., "Educational Extension in the United States." *Report of the U.S. Commissioner of Education for 1899–1900.* Washington, D.C.: Government Printing Office, 1901.
ADAMS, JAMES TRUSLOW, *Frontiers of American Culture: A Study of Adult Education in a Democracy.* New York: Charles Scribner's Sons, 1944.
ADULT EDUCATION ASSOCIATION OF THE U.S.A., *Creating a Climate for Adult Education.* Report of a National Conference on Architecture for Adult Education. Chicago: The Association, 1959.
ADVISORY COMMITTEE ON EDUCATION, *Report of the Committee.* Washington, D.C.: Government Printing Office, 1938.
AMERICAN ASSOCIATION FOR ADULT EDUCATION, *Adult Education and Democracy.* New York: The Association, 1936.
AMERICAN FEDERATION OF LABOR-CONGRESS OF INDUSTRIAL ORGANIZATIONS, *Labor and Education in 1955.* Reports of the Executive Council of the AFL, the President of the CIO, and the First Constitutional Convention of the AFL and CIO on Education in 1955. AFL-CIO Publication No. 34. Washington, D.C.: AFL-CIO, 1956.
AMERICAN LIBRARY ASSOCIATION, *Experimental Projects in Adult Educa-*

tion. A Report of the ALA Adult Education Subgrant Project. Chicago: The Association, 1956.

————, *Libraries and Adult Education*. New York: The Macmillan Company, 1926.

AMERICAN VOCATIONAL ASSOCIATION, *Adult Education*. Minneapolis: William Wood Dunwoody Industrial Institute Press, 1927.

ASHEIM, LESTER, *Training Needs of Librarians Doing Adult Education Work*. Report of the Allerton Park Conference, November 14–16, 1954. Chicago: American Library Association, 1955.

BAILEY, L.H., *Farmers' Institutes, History and Status in the United States and Canada*. U.S. Department of Agriculture, Office of Experiment Stations, Bulletin No. 79, 1900. Washington, D.C.: Government Printing Office, 1900.

BARBASH, JACK, *Universities and Unions in Workers Education*. New York: Harper Brothers, 1955.

BEALS, RALPH A., *Aspects of Post-collegiate Education*. New York: American Association for Adult Education, 1935.

————, AND LEON BRODY, *The Literature of Adult Education*. New York: American Association for Adult Education, 1941.

BEARD, CHARLES A., AND MARY R. BEARD, *A Basic History of the United States*. New York: Doubleday & Company, Inc., 1944.

————, AND ————, *The Rise of American Civilization*. New York: The Macmillan Company, 1930.

BEATTY, A.J., *Corporation Schools*, Bloomington, Ill.: Public School Publishing Co., 1918.

BELTH, MARC, AND HEBERT SCHUELER, *Liberal Education for Adults Re-examined: The Queens College Program*. Notes and Essays No. 25. Chicago: Center for the Study of Liberal Education for Adults, 1959.

BENSON, CLARENCE H., *History of Christian Education*. Chicago: Moody Press, 1943.

BERELSON, BERNARD, *The Library's Public*. Report of the Public Library Inquiry. New York: Columbia University Press, 1949.

BERGEVIN, PAUL, AND JOHN MCKINLEY, *Design for Adult Education in the Church*. Greenwich, Conn.: The Seabury Press, 1958.

BIDDLE, WILLIAM, *The Cultivation of Community Leaders*. New York: Harper and Brothers, 1953.

BITTNER, WALTON S., AND HERVEY F. MALLORY, *University Teaching by Mail*. New York: The Macmillan Company, 1933.

BLAKELY, ROBERT J., *Adult Education in a Free Society*, J.R. Kidd, ed., Toronto: Guardian Bird Publications, 1958.

BODE, CARL, *The American Lyceum: Town Meeting of the Mind*. New York: Oxford University Press, 1956.

BOGUE, JESSE P., *The Community College*. New York: McGraw-Hill Book Company, 1950.

BRAMELD, THEODORE, ed., *Workers' Education in the United States*. Fifth Yearbook of the John Dewey Society. New York: Harper & Brothers, 1941.

BRUNNER, EDMUND DE S., *Community Organization and Adult Education*. Chapel Hill, N. C.: University of North Carolina Press, 1942.

————, *An Overview of Adult Education Research*. Chicago: Adult Education Association, 1959.

————, AND IRVING LORGE, *Rural Trends in Depression Years*. New York: Columbia University Press, 1937.

————, WILLIAM L. NICHOLS, II, AND SAM D. SIEBER, "The Role of a National Organization in Adult Education." A Report to the Executive Committee of the Adult Education Association. Chicago: Adult Education Association, 1959. (Duplicated).

————, AND E. HSIN-PAO YANG, *Rural America and the Extension Service*. New York: Teachers College, Columbia University, 1949.

BRUNO, FRANK J., *Trends in Social Work, 1874-1956*. New York: Columbia University Press, 1957.

BRYSON, LYMAN, *Adult Education*. New York: American Book Company, 1936.

————, *The Next America*. New York: Harper & Brothers, 1952.

————, *A State Plan for Adult Education*. New York: American Association for Adult Education, 1934.

BURCH, GLEN, *Challenge to the University: An Inquiry into the University's Responsibility for Adult Education*. Notes and Essays No. 35. Chicago: Center for the Study of Liberal Education for Adults, 1961.

BUTTS, R. FREEMAN, AND LAWRENCE A. CREMIN, *A History of Education in American Culture*. New York: Holt, Rinehart and Winston, Inc., 1953.

CAREY, JAMES T., *The Development of the University Evening College*. A Research Report. Chicago: Center for the Study of Liberal Education for Adults, 1961.

————, *Forms and Forces in University Adult Education*. A Research Report. Chicago: Center for the Study of Liberal Education for Adults, 1961.

CARSKADON, THOMAS R., AND GEORGE SOULE, *U.S.A. in New Dimensions: The Measure and Promise of America's Resources*. New York: The Macmillan Company, 1957.

CARTER, JEAN, *Parents in Perplexity*. New York: American Association for Adult Education, 1938.

——, AND JESS OGDEN, *Everyman's Drama: A Study of the Non-commercial Theater in the United States.* New York: American Association for Adult Education, 1938.

——, AND ——, *Small Communities in Action.* New York: Harper & Brothers, 1946.

CARTWRIGHT, MORSE A., *Ten Years of Adult Education.* New York: The Macmillan Company, 1935.

——, ed., *Unemployment and Adult Education.* New York: American Association for Adult Education, 1931,

——, AND GLEN BURCH, *Adult Adjustment.* New York: Teachers College, Columbia University, 1945.

CENTER FOR THE STUDY OF LIBERAL EDUCATION FOR ADULTS, *College Without Classes: Credit through Examinations in University Adult Education.* Chicago: The Center, 1961.

——, "Evaluation of Liberal Education." Second Conference Report. Chicago: The Center, 1959. (Mimeographed).

——, *A Review of 1957: Center Activities and Projects.* Chicago: The Center, 1958.

——, *A Review of 1958: Future Directions of the Center, and a Report of Current Activities.* Chicago: The Center, 1959.

CHICAGO BOARD OF EDUCATION, "A Historical Review of the Chicago Public Evening Schools." Chicago: Board of Education, 1937. (Mimeographed).

CLARK, BURTON R., *Adult Education in Transition: A Study of Institutional Insecurity.* University of California Publications in Sociology and Social Institutions, Vol. I, No. 2. Berkeley, Calif.: University of California Press, 1956.

——, *The Marginality of Adult Education.* Notes and Essays No. 20. Chicago: Center for the Study of Liberal Education for Adults, 1958.

CLARK, HAROLD, AND HAROLD SLOAN, *Classrooms in the Factories.* Rutherford, N.J.: Fairleigh Dickinson University, 1958.

——, *et al., The Pursuit of Solvency for Higher Education in the U.S.A.* New York: McGraw-Hill Book Company, 1959.

COMMAGER, HENRY STEELE, *The American Mind.* New Haven: Yale University Press, 1950.

——, ed., *Living Ideas in America.* New York: Harper & Brothers, 1951.

COOK, ALICE, AND DOUTY, AGNES, *Labor Education Outside the Union.* Ithaca: Cornell University Press, 1959.

CREESE, JAMES, *The Extension of University Teaching.* New York: American Association for Adult Education, 1941.

CRIMI, JAMES E., *Adult Education in the Liberal Arts Colleges.* Notes and Essays No. 17. Chicago: Center for the Study of Liberal Education for Adults, 1957.

CUBBERLEY, ELLWOOD P., *The History of Education.* Boston: Houghton Mifflin Company, 1920.

———, *Public Education in the United States,* rev. ed., Boston: Houghton Mifflin Company, 1947.

Culture in Canada. A Study of the Findings of the Royal Commission on National Development in the Arts, Letters, and Sciences (1949-1951). Albert A. Shea, ed., Toronto: Canadian Association for Adult Education, 1952.

DAIGNEAULT, GEORGE H., ed., *The Changing University.* A Report on the Seventh Annual Leadership Conference. Chicago: Center for the 'Study of Liberal Education for Adults, 1959.

DEFFNER, DONALD L., "The Church's Role in Adult Education." Unpublished doctoral dissertation, Graduate Division, University of California, 1956.

DEMAREST, G. STUART, AND GALWAY KINNEL, *New Directions for University Adult Education: Institution-Centered.* Notes and Essays, No. 11. Chicago: Center for the Study of Liberal Education for Adults, 1955.

A Design for Democracy. An Abridgment of a Report of the Adult Education Committee of the British Ministry of Reconstruction commonly called "The 1919 Report." New York: Association Press, 1956.

DEWHURST, J. FREDERIC AND ASSOCIATES, *America's Needs and Resources: A New Survey.* New York: Twentieth Century Fund, 1955.

DICKERMAN, WATSON, *Outposts of the Public School.* New York: American Association for Adult Education, 1938.

DONAHUE, WILMA, *Education for Later Maturity.* New York: William Morrow & Company, Inc., 1955.

DYER, JOHN P., *Ivory Towers in the Market Place: The Evening College in American Education.* Indianapolis: Bobbs-Merrill Co., 1956.

EDWARDS, NEWTON, AND HERMAN G. RICHEY, *The School in the American Social Order.* Boston: Houghton Mifflin Company, 1947.

EELS, WALTER C., ed., *American Junior Colleges.* Washington, D.C.: American Council on Education, 1940.

ELY, MARY L., *Adult Education in Action.* New York: American Association for Adult Education, 1936.

———, *Why Forums?* New York: American Association for Adult Education, 1937.

———, and Eve Chappell, *Women in Two Worlds.* New York: American Association for Adult Education, 1938.

ENGLEHARDT, NICKOLAUS L., AND NICHOLAUS L. ENGLEHARDT, JR., *Planning the Community School.* New York: American Book Company, 1940.

ESSERT, PAUL L., *Creative Leadership of Adult Education.* Englewood Cliffs, N.J.: Prentice-Hall, Inc., 1951

EVANS, OWEN D., *Educational Opportunities for Young Workers*. New York: The Macmillan Company, 1926.

FISHER, DOROTHY CANFIELD, *Why Stop Learning?* New York: Harcourt, Brace & World, Inc., 1927.

FISHER, GALEN M., *Public Affairs and the Y.M.C.A., 1844–1944*. New York: Association Press, 1948.

FLEXNER, JENNIE M., *Readers' Advisory Service*. New York: American Association for Adult Education, 1934.

———, AND B.C. HOPKINS, *Readers' Advisors at Work*. New York: American Association for Adult Education, 1941.

FUND FOR ADULT EDUCATION, *Continuing Liberal Education*. Report for 1955–1957. White Plains, N.Y.: The Fund, 1957.

GARCEAU, OLIVER, ed., *The Public Library in the Political Process: A Report of the Public Library Inquiry*. New York: Columbia University Press, 1949.

GLUECK, ELEANOR T., *The Community Use of Schools*. Baltimore: Williams and Wilkins, 1927.

GLYNN, GRACE M., "Public School Adult Education in Rhode Island." A Summary of a Survey Submitted to the Principals of Adult Education Programs. Providence: State Department of Education of Rhode Island, May, 1957. (Mimeographed).

GORDY, AMELIA S., *Extension Activities and Accomplishments, 1960*. U.S. Department of Agriculture Extension Service Circular No. 533. Washington, D.C.: Government Printing Office, 1961.

GRATTAN, C. HARTLEY, *American Ideas About Adult Education*. New York: Bureau of Publications, Teachers College, Columbia University, 1959.

———, *In Quest of Knowledge*. New York: Association Press, 1955.

GRAY, WILLIAM S., AND BERNICE E. LEARY, *What Makes a Book Readable?* Chicago: University of Chicago Press, 1935.

———, AND RUTH MUNROE, *Reading Interests and Habits of Adults*. New York: The Macmillan Company, 1929.

———, AND BERNICE ROGERS, *Maturity in Reading: Its Nature and Appraisal*. Chicago: University of Chicago Press, 1956.

GREENBERGER, LAWRENCE F., "Adult Education through Evening High Schools." Unpublished doctoral dissertation, University of Pittsburgh, 1936.

GREENE, JAMES H., *Organized Training in Business*. Harper & Brothers, 1937.

GRUENBERG, BENJAMIN C. *Science and the Public Mind*. New York: McGraw-Hill Company, 1935.

GRUMMAN, RUSSEL M., ed., *University Extension in Action*. Chapel Hill, N.C.: University of North Carolina Press, 1946.

HACKER, LOUIS M., *The Shaping of the American Tradition*. New York: Columbia University Press, 1947.

HALL-QUEST, ALFRED L., *The University Afield*. New York: The Macmillan Company, 1926.

Handbook of Adult Education in the United States, Dorothy Rowden, ed. New York: American Association for Adult Education, 1934.

Handbook of Adult Education in the United States, Dorothy Rowden, ed. New York: American Association for Adult Education, 1936.

Handbook of Adult Education in the United States, Mary L. Ely, ed. New York: Institute of Adult Education, Columbia University, 1948.

Handbook of Adult Education in the United States. Malcolm S. Knowles, ed. Chicago: Adult Education Association, 1960.

HAWKINS, GAYNELL, *Educational Experiments in Social Settlements*. New York: American Association for Adult Education, 1937.

———, *Education for Social Understanding: Programs of Case Work and Group Work Agencies*. New York: American Association for Adult Education, 1940.

HAYES, CECIL B., *The American Lyceum*. U.S. Office of Education Bulletin No. 12, 1932. Washington, D.C.: Government Printing Office, 1932.

HENRY, NELSON B., ed., *Adult Reading*. 55th Yearbook of the National Society for the Study of Education, Part II. Chicago: University of Chicago Press, 1956.

HERRING, JOHN W., *Social Planning and Adult Education*. New York: The Macmillan Company, 1933.

HEWITT, DOROTHY, AND KIRTLEY F. MATHER, *Adult Education: A Dynamic for Democracy*. New York: Appleton-Century-Crofts, Inc., 1937.

HILL, FRANK E., *Educating for Health*. New York: American Association for Adult Education, 1939.

———, *Listen and Learn: Fifteen Years of Adult Education on the Air*. New York: American Association for Adult Education, 1937.

———, *Man-Made Culture: The Educational Activities of Men's Clubs*. New York: American Association for Adult Education, 1938.

———, *School in the Camps*. New York: American Association for Adult Education, 1935.

———, *Training For the Job*. New York: American Association for Adult Education, 1940.

HILL, RICHARD W., AND MARION TURNER, *Fifty Years of Banking Education*. New York: American Institute of Banking, 1950.

HODGEN, MARGARET T., *Workers' Education in England and the United States*. New York: E.P. Dutton & Co., Inc., 1925.

HOLDEN, JOHN B., *Adult Education Services of State Departments of*

Education. U.S. Office of Education Miscellaneous Bulletin No. 31. Washington, D.C.: Government Printing Office, 1959.

HOULE, CYRIL O., "The Co-ordination of Public Adult Education at the State Level." Unpublished doctoral dissertation, Department of Education, University of Chicago, 1940.

————, *Libraries in Adult and Fundamental Education.* The Report of the Malmo Seminar. Paris: UNESCO, 1951.

————, *Major Trends in Higher Adult Education.* Notes and Essays No. 24. Chicago: Center for the Study of Liberal Education for Adults, 1959.

————, ELBERT W. BURR, THOMAS H. HAMILTON, AND JOHN R. YALE, *The Armed Services and Adult Education.* Washington, D.C.: American Council on Education, 1947.

————, AND CHARLES A. NELSON, *The University, the Citizen, and World Affairs.* Washington, D.C.: American Council on Education, 1956.

HUDSON, ROBERT B., *Radburn, A Plan of Living.* New York: American Association for Adult Education, 1934.

HUGG, ALAN E., "Informal Adult Education in the Y.M.C.A.: A Historical Study." Unpublished doctoral dissertation, Faculty of Philosophy, Columbia University, 1950.

HUMBLE, MARION, *Rural America Reads: A Study of Rural Library Service.* New York: American Association for Adult Education, 1938.

HURLBUT, J.L., *The Story of Chautauqua.* New York: G.P. Putnam's Sons, 1921.

JOHNSON, ALVIN, *The Clock of History.* New York: W.W. Norton & Company, Inc., 1946.

————, *Deliver us from Dogma.* New York: American Association for Adult Education, 1934.

————, *The Public Library—A People's University.* New York: American Association for Adult Education, 1938.

KAPLAN, ABBOTT, *Study and Discussion in the Liberal Arts.* White Plains, N.Y.: The Fund for Adult Education, 1960.

KAPLAN, MAX, *Leisure in America: A Social Inquiry.* New York: John Wiley & Sons, Inc., 1960.

KEELER, SISTER JEROME, ed., *Handbook of Catholic Adult Education.* Milwaukee: The Bruce Publishing Company, 1959.

W. K. KELLOGG FOUNDATION, *Continuing Education, An Evolving Form of Adult Education.* Battle Creek, Mich.: The Foundation, 1960.

————, *The First Twenty-five Years.* Battle Creek, Mich.: The Foundation, 1955.

KEMPFER, HOMER H., *Adult Education.* New York: McGraw-Hill Book Company, 1955.

———, *Adult Education Activities of the Public Schools.* U.S. Office of Education Pamphlet No. 107. Washington, D.C.: Government Printing Office, 1949.

———, AND GRACE S. WRIGHT, *One Hundred Evening Schools.* U.S. Office of Education Bulletin 1949 No. 4. Washington, D.C.: Government Printing Office, 1949.

KEPPEL, FREDERICK P., *Education For Adults and Other Essays.* New York: Columbia University Press, 1926.

KERRISON, IRVINE L.H., *Workers' Education at the University Level.* New Brunswick, N.J.: Rutgers University Press, 1951.

KIDD, J.R., *How Adults Learn.* New York: Association Press, 1959.

KING, C. WENDELL, *Social Movements in the United States.* New York: Random House, Inc., 1956.

KNOWLES, MALCOLM S., "The Development of a Co-ordinated Adult Educational Movement in the United States." Unpublished doctoral dissertation, Department of Education, University of Chicago, 1960.

KOTINSKY, RUTH., *Adult Education and the Social Scene.* New York: Appleton-Century-Crofts, Inc., 1933.

———, *Adult Education Councils.* New York: American Association for Adult Education, 1940.

———, *Elementary Education of Adults.* New York: American Association for Adult Education, 1941.

LANDIS, BENSON Y., AND J.D. WILLARD, *Rural Adult Education.* New York: The Macmillan Company, 1933.

LEARNED, WILLIAM S., *The American Public Library and the Diffusion of Knowledge.* New York: Harcourt, Brace & World, Inc., 1924.

LINDEMAN, EDUARD C., *The Meaning of Adult Education.* New York: New Republic, Inc., 1926.

LITTLE, LAWRENCE C., ed., *Charting the Future Course of Christian Adult Education in America.* Pittsburgh: Department of Religious Education, University of Pittsburgh, 1958.

LOMBARD, ELLEN C., *Cooperation in Adult Education.* U.S. Bureau of Education Home Education Circular No. 6. Washington, D.C.: Government Printing Office, 1924.

———, *Home Education by Means of Reading Courses and the Co-operation of State and National Agencies.* U.S. Bureau of Education Home Education Circular No. 2. Washington, D.C.: Government Printing Office, 1922.

LOOMIS, CHARLES P., et al., *Rural Social Systems and Adult Education.* East Lansing, Mich.: Michigan State College Press, 1953.

LORD, RUSSEL R., *The Agrarian Revival: A Study of Agricultural Extension.* New York: American Association for Adult Education, 1939.

LORIMER, FRANK, *The Making of Adult Minds in a Metropolitan Area.* New York: The Macmillan Company, 1931.

LUNDBERG, GEORGE A., et al., *Leisure: A Suburban Study.* New York: Columbia University Press, 1934.

MACCORMICK, AUSTIN H., *Education of Adult Prisoners.* New York: National Society of Penal Information, 1931.

MACLELLAN, MALCOLM, *The Catholic Church and Adult Education.* Washington, D.C.: Catholic Education Press, 1935.

MAGOWAN, KENNETH, *Footlights Across America.* New York: Harcourt, Brace & World, Inc., 1929.

MARSH, C.S., *Adult Education in a Community: A Survey of the Facilities Existing in the City of Buffalo, New York.* New York: American Association for Adult Education, 1926.

MATHER, L. K., *The New American School for Adults.* Washington, D.C.: National Education Association Division of Adult Education Service, 1955.

MELAND, BERNARD E., *The Church and Adult Education.* New York: American Association for Adult Education, 1939.

MERRIFIELD, CHARLES, *Leadership in the Voluntary Enterprise.* New York: Oceana Publications, 1961.

MEZIROW, J.D., AND DOROTHEA BERRY, *The Literature of Liberal Adult Education.* New York: Scarecrow Press, 1960.

MILLER, LEON F., "Statutory Provisions for Public School Adult Education and their Implementation." Unpublished doctoral dissertation, Department of Education, University of Chicago, 1950.

MIRE, JOSEPH, *Labor Education.* Madison, Wis.: Inter-University Labor Education Committee, 1956.

MORTON, JOHN R., *University Extension in the United States.* Birmingham, Ala.: University of Alabama Press, 1953.

MUNSE, ALBERT R., AND EDNA D. BOOHER, *Federal Funds for Education, 1956–1957 and 1957–1958.* Bulletin 1959, No. 2, U.S. Office of Education. Washington, D.C.: Government Printing Office, 1959.

NATIONAL ASSOCIATION OF PUBLIC SCHOOL ADULT EDUCATORS, *Public School Adult Education: A Guide for Administrators and Teachers.* Washington, D.C.: National Education Association, 1956.

NATIONAL EDUCATION ASSOCIATION, *NEA Handbook, 1956–1957.* Centennial Edition. Washington, D.C.: The Association, 1956.

———, *A Study of Urban Public School Adult Education Programs.* Washington, D.C.: NEA Division of Adult Education Service, 1952.

NEUFFER, FRANK R., *Administrative Policies and Practices of Evening Colleges, 1953.* A Report. Chicago: Center for the Study of Liberal Education for Adults, 1953.

NEW YORK ADULT EDUCATION COUNCIL, *A Picture of Adult Education*

in the New York Metropolitan Area. New York: The Council, 1934.
NEW YORK STATE UNIVERSITY, *Education for American Life.* The Regents' Inquiry into the Character and Cost of Public Education in the State of New York. New York: McGraw-Hill Book Company, 1938.
NOFFSINGER, JOHN S., *Correspondence Schools, Lyceums, Chautauquas.* New York: The Macmillan Company, 1926.
OLDS, EDWARD, *Financing Adult Education in America's Public Schools and Community Councils.* Report of the National Commission on Adult Education Finance. Chicago: Adult Education Association of the U.S.A., 1954.
OVERSTREET, HARRY A., AND BONARO W. OVERSTREET, *Leaders for Adult Education.* New York: American Association for Adult Education, 1941.
————, *Where Children Come First.* A Study of the P.T.A. Idea. Chicago: National Congress of Parents and Teachers, 1949.
OZANNE, JACQUES, *Regional Surveys of Adult Education.* New York: American Association for Adult Education, 1934.
PACEY, LORENE M., *Readings in the Development of Settlement Work.* New York: Association Press, 1950.
PEFFER, NATHANIEL, *Educational Experiments in Industry.* New York: The Macmillan Company, 1932.
————, *New Schools for Older Students.* New York: The Macmillan Company, 1926.
PETERSON, RENEE AND WILLIAM PETERSON, *University Adult Education.* New York: Harper & Brothers, 1960.
PHINNEY, ELEANOR, *Library Adult Education in Action: Five Case Studies.* Chicago: American Library Association, 1956.
PITKIN, ROYCE S., *The Residential School in American Adult Education.* Notes and Essays No. 14. Chicago: Center for the Study of Liberal Education for Adults, 1956.
POSTON, RICHARD, *Democracy Is You: A Guide to Citizens Action.* New York: Harper & Brothers, 1953.
————, *Small Town Renaissance.* New York: Harper & Brothers, 1950.
POWELL, JOHN W., *Education for Maturity.* New York: Hermitage House, Inc., 1949.
————, *Learning Comes of Age.* New York: Association Press, 1956.
————, *School for Americans: An Essay in Adult Education.* New York: American Association for Adult Education, 1941.
PRESIDENT'S COMMISSION ON HIGHER EDUCATION, *Higher Education for American Democracy.* Vol. I, "Establishing the Goals." New York: Harper & Brothers, 1947.
PRESIDENT'S COMMITTEE ON EDUCATION BEYOND THE HIGH SCHOOL. *Sec-*

ond Report to the President. Washington, D.C.: Government Printing Office, 1957.

REEVES, FLOYD W., THOMAS FANSLER, AND CYRIL O. HOULE, *Adult Education.* New York: McGraw-Hill Book Company, 1938.

RICHMOND, REBECCA, *Chautauqua, An American Place.* New York: Duell, Sloan, & Pearce, Inc., 1943.

RITCHIE, HARRY E., "Adult Education in the Cleveland Public Schools." Unpublished doctoral dissertation, Graduate School, Western Reserve University, 1940.

ROBINSON, EDWARD S., *The Behavior of the Museum Visitor.* New York: American Association of Museums, 1928.

ROSENTRETER, FREDERICK M., *The Boundaries of the Campus: A History of the University of Wisconsin Extension Division 1885–1945.* Madison, Wis.: The University of Wisconsin Press, 1957.

Rotary—Fifty Years of Service. Evanston, Ill.: Rotary International, 1954.

ROWDEN, DOROTHY, *Enlightened Self-Interest: A Study of Educational Programs of Trade Associations.* New York: American Association for Adult Education, 1937.

SCHACHT, ROBERT H., "Residential Adult Education—An Analysis and Interpretation." Unpublished doctoral dissertation, University of Wisconsin, 1957.

SCHNEIDER, FLORENCE H., *Patterns of Workers' Education.* Washington, D.C.: American Council on Public Affairs, 1941.

SCHRAMM, WILBUR, *The Impact of Educational Television.* Urbana, Ill.: University of Illinois Press, 1961.

SCHWERTMAN, JOHN B., *I Want Many Lodestars.* Notes and Essays No. 21. Chicago: Center for the Study of Liberal Education for Adults, 1958.

SERBEIN, OSCAR N., *Educational Activities of Business.* Washington, D.C.: American Council on Education, 1961.

SEYBOLT, ROBERT F., *Source Studies in American Colonial Education: The Private School.* Bureau of Educational Research Bulletin No. 28. University of Illinois Bulletin, XXIII, No. 4. Urbana, Ill.: University of Illinois Press, 1925.

SHAW, WILFRED B., *Alumni and Adult Education.* New York: American Association of Adult Education, 1929.

SHEATS, PAUL H., CLARENCE D. JAYNE, AND RALPH B. SPENCE, *Adult Education: The Community Approach.* New York: Holt, Rinehart and Winston, Inc., 1953.

SHILEN, RONALD, *Able People Well Prepared: The Adult Education and the Mass Media Fellowship Programs, 1952–1961, of the Fund for*

Adult Education. White Plains, N.Y.: The Fund for Adult Education, 1961.

SHRYOCK, RICHARD H., *National Tuberculosis Association, 1904–1954: A Study of the Voluntary Health Movement in the United States.* New York: National Tuberculosis Association, 1957.

SIEGLE, PETER E., *New Directions in Liberal Education for Executives.* Chicago: Center for the Study of Liberal Education for Adults, 1958.

————, and James B. Whipple, *New Directions in Programming for University Adult Education.* Chicago: Center for the Study of Liberal Education for Adults, 1957.

SILLARS, ROBERTSON, ed., *Seeking Common Ground in Adult Education.* Adult Education Monograph No. 4. Chicago: Adult Education Association, 1958.

————, "Some Problems of Publications Policy in the Adult Education Association of the U.S.A." Unpublished doctoral thesis, Teachers College, Columbia University, 1954.

SMITH, HELEN LYMAN, *Adult Education Activities in Public Libraries.* A Report of the ALA Survey of Adult Education Activities in Public Libraries and State Library Extension Agencies of the United States. Chicago: American Library Association, 1954.

SMITH, HILDA W., *Women Workers at the Bryn Mawr Summer School.* New York: Affiliated Schools and American Association for Adult Education, 1929.

SMITH, PAYSON, et al., *Education in the Forty-eight States.* Advisory Committee on Education Staff Study No. 1. Washington: Government Printing Office, 1939.

SORENSON, HERBERT, *Adult Abilities.* Minneapolis: University of Minnesota Press, 1938.

SPENCE, RALPH B., AND BENJAMIN SHANGOLD, *Public School Adult Education in New York State 1944–1947.* University of New York Bulletin No. 1391. Albany: University of the State of New York, May 1, 1950.

STACY, WILLIAM H., *Integration of Adult Education.* Teachers College, Columbia University Contributions to Education, No. 646. New York: Bureau of Publications, Teachers College, Columbia University, 1935.

STATE OF CALIFORNIA, *Partial Report of the Senate Interim Committee on Adult Education.* (Senate Resolution 185). Sacramento, Calif.: California State Printing Office, 1953.

STERN, BERNARD H., *Adults Grow in Brooklyn.* Report No. 2, The Brooklyn College Experimental Degree Project for Adults. Chicago: Center for the Study of Liberal Education for Adults, 1955.

————, *How Much Does Adult Experience Count?* A Report of the

Brooklyn College Experimental Degree Project. Chicago: Center for the Study of Liberal Education for Adults, 1955.

————, and Ellsworth Missal, *Adult Experience and College Degrees.* A Report of the Experimental Degree Project at Brooklyn College, 1954–1958. Cleveland: The Press of Western Reserve University, 1960.

STONE, FERDINAND F., AND JESSIE A. CHARTERS, *Alumni Interest in Continuing Education.* Columbus: Ohio State University Press, 1932.

STUDEBAKER, JOHN W., *The American Way.* New York: McGraw-Hill Book Company, 1935.

SWEENEY, CHARLES P., *Adult Working-Class Education in Great Britain and the United States.* U.S. Department of Labor, Bureau of Labor Statistics Bulletin No. 271, Miscellaneous Series. Washington, D.C.: Government Printing Office, 1920.

SWIFT, FLETCHER H., AND JOHN W. STUDEBAKER, *What Is This Opportunity School?* New York: American Association for Adult Education, 1932.

TAYLOR, JED H., *Library Service for the C.C.C.* New York: American Association for Adult Education, 1937.

————, *Organization of C.C.C. Camp Library-Reading Rooms.* New York: American Association for Adult Education, 1938.

THOMPSON, CLEM O., *University Extension in Adult Education.* Bloomington, Ind.: National University Extension Association, 1943.

THOMSEN, CARL, SIDNEY, EDWARD, AND MIRIAM D. TOMPKINS, *Adult Education Activities for Public Libarries.* Paris: UNESCO, 1950.

THORNDIKE, EDWARD L., *Adult Interests.* New York: The Macmillan Company, 1935.

————,*et al., Adult Learning.* New York: The Macmillan Company, 1928.

TIBBITTS, CLARK, AND WILMA DONAHUE, *Aging in Today's Society.* Englewoods Cliffs, N.J.: Prentice-Hall, Inc., 1960.

TOCQUEVILLE, ALEXIS DE, *Democracy in America,* Vol. II. Phillips Bradley, ed., New York: Alfred A. Knopf, Inc., 1954.

TRUE, ALFRED C., *A History of Agricultural Extension Work in the United States, 1785–1923.* U.S. Department of Agriculture, Miscellaneous Publication No. 15, October, 1928. Washington, D.C.: Government Printing Office, 1928.

TYSON, LEVERING, *Education Tunes In: A Study of Radio Broadcasting in Adult Education.* New York: American Association for Adult Education, 1930.

UNESCO, *Adult Education, Current Trends and Practices.* New York: Columbia University Press, 1949.

————, *International Directory of Adult Education*. New York: Columbia University Press, 1954.

————, *Universities in Adult Education*. Paris: UNESCO, 1952.

U.S. BUREAU OF THE CENSUS, *Historical Statistics of the United States, Colonial Times to 1957*. Washington, D.C.: Government Printing Office, 1960.

————, *Statistical Abstract of the United States: 1956*. Washington, D.C.: Government Printing Office, 1956.

————, *Statistical Abstract of the United States: 1961*. Washington, D.C.: Government Printing Office, 1961.

UNITED STATES BUREAU OF LABOR STATISTICS, *Directory of International and National Labor Unions in 1955*. Bulletin No. 1185. Washington, D.C.: Government Printing Office, 1956.

UNITED STATES DEPARTMENT OF AGRICULTURE, Federal Extension service, *The Cooperative Extension Service Today*. A Statement of Scope and Responsibility. Washington, D.C.: Federal Extension Service, 1958.

UNITED STATES DEPARTMENT OF LABOR, Bureau of Apprenticeship, *Apprenticeship Past and Present*. Third Edition. Washington, D.C.: Government Printing Office, 1955.

UNITED STATES DEPARTMENT OF LABOR, *Our Manpower Future, 1955-1965*. Population Trends, Their Manpower Implications. Washington, D.C.: Government Printing Office, 1957.

United States 85th Congress, S. 385, Public Law 85-507, July 7, 1958. Government Employees Training Act.

UNITED STATES OFFICE OF EDUCATION, *Biennial Survey of Education in the United States, 1946–1948*. Chapter 2: "Statistics of State School Systems, 1947–1948." Washington, D.C.: Government Printing Office, 1950.

————, *Biennial Survey of Education in the United States, 1950–1952*. Chapter 1: "Statistical Summary of Education, 1951–1952." Washington, D.C.: Government Printing Office, 1955.

————, *Biennial Survey of Education in the United States, 1948–1950*. Chapter 2: "Statistics of State School Systems, 1949–1950." Washington, D.C.: Government Printing Office, 1952.

————, *Biennial Survey of Education in the United States, 1950–1952*. Chapter 2: "Statistics of State School Systems: Organization, Staff, Pupils, and Finances, 1951–1952." Washington, D.C.: Government Printing Office, 1955.

UNITED STATES COMMITTEE ON LABOR AND PUBLIC WELFARE, *Fact Book on Aging*. Studies of the Aged and Aging. Selected Documents, Vol. XI. Washington, D.C.: Government Printing Office, 1957.

VAN DE WALL, WILLEM, *The Music of the People.* New York: American Association for Adult Education, 1939.

WANN, MARIE D., AND MARTHINE V. WOODWARD, *Participation in Adult Education.* U.S. Department of Health, Education, and Welfare, Office of Education Circular No. 539. Washington, D.C.: Government Printing Office, 1959.

WAPLES, DOUGLAS, BERNARD BERELSON, AND FRANKLYN BRADSHAW, *What Reading Does to People.* Chicago: University of Chicago Press, 1940.

————, AND RALPH TYLER, *What People Want to Read About.* Chicago: University of Chicago Press, 1931.

WARE, CAROLINE F., *Labor Education in Universities.* New York: American Labor Education Service, 1946.

WARNCKE, RUTH, "The Library-Community Project of the American Library Association." Report, 1955–1960. Chicago: The Association, 1960. (Mimeographed).

WESTPHAL, EDWARD P., *The Church's Opportunity in Adult Education.* Philadelphia: The Westminster Press, 1941.

WHIPPLE, JAMES B., *Especially for Adults.* Notes and Essays No. 19. Chicago: Center for the Study of Liberal Education for Adults, 1957.

WICKENDON, W.E., AND R.H. SPAHR, *A Study of Technical Institutes.* New York: Society for the Promotion of Engineering Education, 1931.

WILLIAMS, WILLIAM E., AND A.E. HEATH, *Learn and Live.* Boston: Marshall Jones, 1937.

WILSON, LOUIS R., ed., *The Role of the Library in Adult Education.* Chicago: University of Chicago Press, 1937.

WINCHESTER, B.S., *The Church and Adult Education.* New York: Richard R. Smith, 1930.

WOODYARD, ELLA, *Culture at a Price: A Study of Private Correspondence Schools Offerings.* New York: American Association for Adult Education, 1940.

WORKERS EDUCATION BUREAU OF AMERICA, *Labor and Education.* Washington, D.C.: American Federation of Labor, 1939.

WORLD ASSOCIATION FOR ADULT EDUCATION, *International Handbook of Adult Education.* London: The Association, 1929.

WRIGHT, LOUIS B., *The Cultural Life of the American Colonies.* New York: Harper & Brothers, 1957.

SUPPLEMENTAL BIBLIOGRAPHY

FOR PART IV

Adult Education: State Demographic Data. Washington, D.C.: National Advisory Committee on Adult Education, 1973.

Alford, Harold J. *Continuing Education in Action: Residential Centers for Lifelong Learning.* New York: Wiley, 1968.

Alter, Henry C. *Of Messages and Media: Teaching and Learning by Public Television.* Boston: Center for the Study of Liberal Education for Adults, 1968.

American Association of Museums. *A Statistical Survey of Museums in The United States and Canada.* Washington, D.C.: American Association of Museums, 1965.

Anderson, D.W., ed. *Competency Based Teacher Education.* Berkeley: McCutchan, 1974.

Association of Continuing Higher Education and National University Extension Association. *Programs and Registrations, 1974-1975.* Washington, D.C.: National University Extension Association, 1975.

Bell, David, ed., "Toward the Year 2000: Work in Progress," *Daedalus* (Summer, 1967).

Benne, K.D., L.P. Bradford, J.R. Gibb, and R. Lippitt. *The Laboratory Method of Changing and Learning.* Palo Alto, Cal., Science and Behavior Books, 1975.

Birenbaum, William B., ed. *From Class to Mass Learning.* "New Directions for Community Colleges," No. 7. San Francisco: Jossey-Bass, 1974.

Blakely, Robert J. *The Use of Instructional Television in Adult Education: A Review of Some Recent Developments.* Syracuse: Publications in Continuing Education, Syracuse University, 1974.

Bradford, L.P. *National Training Laboratories: Its History 1947-1970.* Bethel, Me.: L.P. Bradford, 1974.

Carlson, Robert A. *Educational Television In Its Cultural and Public Affairs Dimension: A Selected Literature Review of Public Television As An Issue in Adult Education.* Syracuse: Publications in Continuing Education, Syracuse University, 1973.

Carnegie Commission on Educational Television. *Public Television*. New York: Harper and Row, 1967.

Carnegie Commission on Higher Education. *The Capitol and the Campus: State Responsibility for Post-Secondary Education*. New York: McGraw-Hill, 1971.

———, *A Chance to Learn*. New York: McGraw-Hill, 1971.

———. *Continuity and Discontinuity*. New York: McGraw-Hill, 1973.

———, *Less Time More Options: Education Beyond High School*. New York: McGraw-Hill, 1971.

———, *The Open Door Colleges: Policies for the Community College*. New York: McGraw-Hill, 1970.

Carnegie Council on Policy Studies. *The Federal Role in Post-Secondary Education*. San Francisco: Jossey-Bass, 1975.

Carnegie Foundation for the Advancement of Teaching. *More Than Survival: Prospects for Higher Education in a Period of Uncertainty*. San Francisco: Jossey-Bass, 1975.

———, *The States and Higher Education*. San Francisco: Jossey-Bass, 1976.

Charters, A.N. *Report on the 1969 Galaxy Conference of Adult Education Organizations*. Syracuse: Publications in Continuing Education, Syracuse University, 1971.

———, and W.M. Rivera. *International Seminar on Publications in Continuing Education*. Syracuse: Publications in Continuing Education, Syracuse University, 1972.

Clark, Harold F., and Harold S. Sloan. *Classrooms on Main Street*. New York: Teachers College, Columbia University, 1966.

———, *Classrooms in the Military*. New York: Teachers College, Columbia University, 1964.

Clifford, Geraldine J. *The Shape of American Education*. Englewood Cliffs, N.J.: Prentice-Hall, 1975.

Cohen, Arthur M., *et al. College Responses to Community Demands: The Community College in Challenging Times*. San Francisco: Jossey-Bass, 1975.

———, *New Perspectives on the Community College*. San Francisco: Jossey-Bass, 1971.

Commission on Non-Traditional Study. *Diversity By Design*. San Francisco: Jossey-Bass, 1973.

Cooperative Extension Service Programs: A Unique Partnership Between Public and Private Interests. Washington, D.C.: Extension Service, U.S. Department of Agriculture, 1976.

Cross, K. Patricia. *Accent on Learning*. San Francisco: Jossey-Bass, 1976.

———, *Beyond the Open Door: New Students to Higher Education*. San Francisco: Jossey-Bass, 1971.

Cummings, Thomas. *Political Backgrounds of Adult Education*. Boston: Center for the Study of Liberal Education for Adults, 1967.

Dave, R.H., ed. *Lifelong Education and School Curriculum*. Monograph No. 1. Hamburg: Unesco Institute for Education, 1973.

———, *Reflections on Lifelong Education and the School*. Monograph No. 3. Hamburg: Unesco Institute for Education, 1975.

Dave, R.H., and N. Stiemerling. *Lifelong Education and the School: Abstracts and Bibliography*. Monograph No. 2. Hamburg: Unesco Institute for Education, 1973.

De Crow, Roger, and Stanley Grabowski, eds. *Research and Investigation in Adult Education: 1968 Register*. Washington, D.C.: Adult Education Association of the U.S.A., 1968. (Subsequent Registers, prepared by the ERIC Clearinghouse on Adult Education, available for 1969, 1970, 1971, 1972).

Dermer, Joseph, ed. *Where Large Foundations Make Their Grants*. New York: Public Service Materials Center, 1974.

Design for Methodist Curriculum. Nashville: General Board of Education, The Methodist Church, 1965.

Eble, Kenneth E. *A Perfect Education*. New York: Macmillan, 1968.

Faure, Edgar, Chairman, International Commission on the Development of Education. *Learning to Be: The World of Education Today and Tomorrow*. Paris: Unesco, 1972.

Federal Support for Adult Education Washington, D.C.: Adult Education Association of the U.S.A., 1968.

Fields, Ralph R. *The Community College Movement*. New York: McGraw-Hill, 1962.

Franklin, Richard. *Patterns of Community Development*. New York: Public Affairs Press, 1966.

Freire, Paulo. *Pedagogy of the Oppressed*. New York: Herder and Herder, 1970.

Fuller, Buckminster. *Operating Manual for Spaceship Earth*. Carbondale, Ill.: Southern Illinois University Press, 1969.

Goodlad, John I., et al. *The Changing School Curriculum*. New York: The Fund for the Advancement of Education, 1966.

Gould, Samuel, and K. Patricia Cross. *Explorations in Non-Traditional Study*. San Francisco: Jossey-Bass, 1972.

Goulet, L.R., and P.B. Baltes. *Life-Span Developmental Psychology*. New York: Academic Press, 1970.

Griffith, William S., and Ann P. Hayes, eds. *Adult Basic Education: The State of the Art*. Washington, D.C.: U.S. Government Printing Office, 1970.

Harlacher, Ervin L. *The Community Dimension of the Community College*. Washington, D.C.: American Association of Junior Colleges, 1967.

Heath, Robert W., ed. *New Curricula*. New York: Harper and Row, 1964.

Henderson, A.D., and J.G. Henderson. *Higher Education in America: Problems, Priorities, and Prospects*. San Francisco: Jossey-Bass, 1974.

Henry, David D. *Challenges Past, Challenges Present: An Analysis of American Higher Education Since 1930*. San Francisco: Jossey-Bass, 1975.

Hesburg, Theodore, Paul A. Miller, and Clifton R. Wharton, Jr. *Patterns for Lifelong Learning*. San Francisco: Jossey-Bass, 1973.

Houle, Cyril O., *et al. The Continuing Task: Reflections on Purpose in Higher Continuing Education*. Boston: Center for the Study of Liberal Education for Adults, 1967.

Houle, Cyril O. *The External Degree*. San Francisco: Jossey-Bass, 1973.
————, *The Inquiring Mind*. Madison: University of Wisconsin Press, 1961.

Houston, Robert. *Exploring Competency-Based Education*. Berkeley: McCutchan, 1974.

Huber, J. *Changing Women in a Changing Society*. Chicago: University of Chicago Press, 1973.

Illich, Ivan. *Deschooling Society*. New York: Harper and Row, 1970.

Ingalls, John D. *Human Energy*. Reading, Mass.: Addison-Wesley, 1976.

Inkeles, Alex, ed. *Annual Review of Sociology*. Palo Alto, Cal.: Annual Review Publications, 1975.

Jensen, Gale, A.A. Liveright, and Wilbur Hallenbeck. *Adult Education: Outlines of an Emerging Field of University Study*. Washington, D.C.: Adult Education Association of the U.S.A., 1964.

Johnson, B. Lamar. *Changes in the Two-Year College*. New York: Macmillan, 1969.

Johnson, Guion G. *Volunteers in Community Service*. Chapel Hill, N.C.: University of North Carolina Press, 1967.

Johnstone, W.C., and R.J. Rivera. *Volunteers for Learning*. Chicago: Aldine, 1965.

Joint USDA-NASULGC Extension Study Committee, *A People and A Spirit*. Washington, D.C.: Extension Service, U.S. Department of Agriculture, 1968.

Kidd, J.R. *How Adults Learn*. New York: Association Press, 1973.

Kitsmiller, W.M., and Richard Ottinger. *Citizen Action: Vital Force for Change*. Washington, D.C.: Center for a Voluntary Society, 1971.

Knowles, Malcolm S. *The Adult Learner: A Neglected Species*. Houston: Gulf Publishing Co., 1973.

―――, *Higher Adult Education in the United States*. Washington, D.C.: American Council on Education, 1969.

―――, *The Modern Practice of Adult Education: Andragogy versus Pedagogy*. New York: Association Press, 1970.

―――, *Self-Directed Learning: a Guide for Learners and Teachers*. New York: Association Press, 1975.

―――, and Hulda F. Knowles. *Introduction to Group Dynamics*. New York: Association Press, 1973.

Lee, Robert E. *Continuing Education for Adults Through the American Public Library, 1833-1964*. Chicago: American Library Association, 1966.

Leonard G.B. *Education and Ecstasy*. New York: Delacarte Press, 1968.

Little, Lawrence C. *Wider Horizons in Christian Adult Education*. Pittsburgh: University of Pittsburgh Press, 1962.

Liveright, A.A. *A Study of Adult Education in the United States*. Boston: Center for the Study of Liberal Education for Adults, 1968.

Long, Huey B. *Adult Education in Church and Synagogue: A Review of Selected Recent Literature*. Syracuse: Publications in Continuing Education, Syracuse University, 1973.

Loeser, Herta. *Women, Work, and Volunteering*. Boston: Beacon Press, 1974.

Manpower Administration, U.S. Department of Labor. *Americans Volunteer*. Washington, D.C.: Government Printing Office, 1969.

Marquis Academic Media. *Yearbook of Adult and Continuing Education*. Chicago: Marquis Who's Who, 1975.

McKenzie, Leon. *Adult Religious Education*. West Mystic, Conn.: Twenty-Third Publications, 1975.

Miller, Paul A. *The Cooperative Extension Service: Paradoxical Servant― The Rural Precedent in Continuing Education*. Syracuse: Publications in Continuing Education, Syracuse University, 1973.

Milton, Ohmer. *Alternatives to the Traditional*. San Francisco: Jossey-Bass, 1972.

Minzey, J.D., and C.R. Olsen. *The Role of the School in Community Education*. Midland, Mich.: Pendell, 1974.

Monroe, Margaret E. *Library Adult Education*. New York: Scarecrow Press, 1963.

Morgan, J.N., I.A. Sirageldin, and N. Baerwaldt. *Productive Americans*. Ann Arbor, Mich.: Institute for Social Research, University of Michigan, 1966.

National Advisory Council on Adult Education. *Annual Reports*, 1972-1976. Washington, D.C.: National Advisory Council on Adult Education, 1972-1976.

——, *An Historical Perspective: The Adult Education Act, 1964-1974*. Washington, D.C.: National Advisory Council on Adult Education, 1974.

——, *Interim Report*. Washington, D.C.: National Advisory Council on Adult Education, 1971.

National Center for Educational Statistics. *Adult Education in Community Organizations, 1972*. Washington, D.C.: Government Printing Office, 1974.

——, *The Condition of Education, 1975*. Washington, D.C.: Government Printing Office, 1975.

——, *Digest of Educational Statistics, 1975*. Washington, D.C.: Government Printing Office, 1975.

——, *Projects, Products, and Services of the National Center for Educational Statistics*. Washington, D.C.: Government Printing Office, 1973.

National Library of Medicine. *The Lister Hill National Center for Biomedical Communications Report to the Congress, April, 1972*. DHEW Publication No. (NIH)72-268. Washington, D.C.: Government Printing Office, 1972.

Newman, F. *Report on Higher Education*. Washington, D.C.: Government Printing Office, 1971.

Niemi, John A., ed. *Mass Media and Adult Education*. Englewood Cliffs, N.J.: Educational Technology Publications, 1971.

Ohliger, John. *Listening Groups: Mass Media in Adult Education*. Boston: Center for the Study of Liberal Education for Adults, 1967.

Olean, Sally J. *Changing Patterns in Continuing Education for Business*. Boston: Center for the Study of Liberal Education for Adults, 1967.

Patterson, Franklin. *Colleges in Consortium*. San Francisco: Jossey-Bass, 1974.

Perspectives of Adult Education in the U.S. and a Projection for the Future. U.S. Office of Education Publication No. (OE) 72-181. Washington, D.C.: Government Printing Office, 1972.

Popiel Elda S., ed. *Nursing and the Process of Continuing Education*. St. Louis: C.V. Mosby, 1973.

Postman, Neil, and C. Weingartner. *Teaching as A Subversive Activity*. New York: Delacorte Press, 1969.

Proceedings, National Conference on Adult Jewish Education, Feb-

ruary 20, 1965, New York City: A Summary Report. New York: American Association for Jewish Education, 1965.

Public Continuing and Adult Education 1976 Almanac. Washington, D.C.: National Association for Public Continuing and Adult Education, 1976.

A Question of Stewardship: A Study of the Federal Role in Higher Continuing Education. Washington, D.C.: National Advisory Council On Extension and Continuing Education, 1972.

Rauch, David B. *Priorities in Adult Education.* New York: Macmillan, 1972.

Robertson, D.B., ed. *Voluntary Associations: A Study of Groups in Free Societies.* Washington, D.C.: Center for a Voluntary Society, 1973.

Rossi, Peter H., and Bruce J. Biddle, eds. *The New Media and Education.* Chicago, Aldine, 1966.

Rouche, John E. *Salvage, Redirection, or Custody? Redirection in the Community Junior College.* Washington, D.C.: American Association of Junior and Community Colleges, 1968.

Rubin, Louis, ed. *The Future of Education: Perspectives on Tomorrow's Schooling.* Boston: Allyn and Bacon, 1975.

Sanders, H.C. ed. *The Cooperative Extension Service.* Englewood Cliffs, N.J.: Prentice-Hall, 1966.

Schaefer, James R. *Program Planning for Adult Christian Education.* New York: Newman Press, 1972.

Schindler-Rainman, Eva, and Ronald Lippitt. *The Volunteer Community.* Washington, D.C.: The Center for a Voluntary Society, 1971.

Seay, Maurice F., et al. *Community Education: A Developing Concept.* Midland, Mich.: Pendell, 1974.

Shannon, T.J., and C.A. Schoenfeld. *University Extension.* New York: Center for Applied Research in Education, 1965.

Silberman, Charles E. *Crisis in the Classroom.* New York: Random House, 1970.

Silberman, Melvin, et al. *The Psychology of Open Teaching and Learning.* Boston: Little, Brown, 1972.

Smith, R.M., G.F. Aker, and J.R. Kidd, eds. *Handbook of Adult Education in the United States, 1970.* New York: Macmillan, 1970.

Stone, Elizabeth W., Ruth K. Patrick, and Barbara Conroy. *Continuing Library and Information Service Education.* Washington, D.C.: Government Printing Office, 1974.

Toffler, Alvin. *The Eco-Spasm Report.* New York: Bantam, 1975.

_____, *Future Shock.* New York: Random House, 1970.

_____, *Learning for Tomorrow: The Role of the Future in Education*. New York: Random House, 1974.

Tough, Allen. *The Adult's Learning Projects*. Toronto: Ontario Institute for Studies in Education, 1971.

U.S. Bureau of the Census. *Statistical Abstract of the United States: 1974*. Washington, D.C.: Government Printing Office, 1974.

U.S. Civil Service Commission. *Employee Training in the Federal Service*. Washington, D.C.: Government Printing Office. Published annually since 1967.

U.S. Office of Education-National Center for Educational Statistics. *Adult Education in Public Schools Systems, 1968-69 and 1969-70*. Washington, D.C.: Government Printing Office, 1970.

Vermilye, Dyckman W., ed. *Learner-Centered Reform: Current Issues in Higher Education 1975*. San Francisco: Jossey-Bass, 1975.

Vermilye, Dyckman W. *Lifelong Learners: A New Clentele for Higher Education*. San Francisco: Jossey-Bass, 1974.

Verner, Coolie, and Alan Booth. *Adult Education*. Washington, D.C.: The Center for Applied Research in Education, 1964.

Weber, Ronald, ed. *America in Change*. Notre Dame, Ind.: University of Notre Dame Press, 1972.

Wedemeyer, Charles A., and Robert E. Najem. *AIM: From Concept to Reality: The Articulated Instructional Media Program at Wisconsin*. Syracuse: Publications in Continuing Education, Syracuse University, 1969.

BIBLIOGRAPHY

FOR THE 1994 REISSUE

Abruzzese, Roberta S. *Nursing Staff Development: Strategies for Success*. St. Louis: Mosby-Year Books, 1992.

American Association of Community and Junior Colleges. *Building Communities: A Vision for A New Century* Washington, DC: American Association of Community and Junior Colleges, 1988.

American Council on Education. *Principles of Good Practice for Alternative and External Degree Programs for Adults*. Washington, DC: American Council on Education, 1990.

American Society for Training and Development. *Facts About Retraining America's Workforce*. Alexandria, VA: American Society for Training and Development, 1987.

Apps, Jerold W. *The Adult Learner on Campus*. Chicago: Follett, 1981.

———. *Improving Practice in Continuing Education*. San Francisco: Jossey-Bass, 1985.

———. *Mastering the Teaching of Adults*. Malabar, FL: Krieger, 1991.

———. *Problems in Continuing Education*. New York: McGraw-Hill, 1979.

Aslanian, C.B., and H.M. Brickel. *Americans in Transition: Life Changes As Reasons for Adult Learning*. Princeton, NJ: College Entrance Examination Board, 1980.

Association of Independent Colleges and Schools. *Private Career Education: A National Resource in an Ever-Changing Society*. Washington, DC: Association of Independent Colleges and Schools, 1986.

Basseches, M. *Dialectical Thinking and Adult Development*. Norwood, NJ: Abex Publishing, 1984.

Beatty, Paulette R., and Mary Alice Wolf. *Connecting With Older Adults*. Malabar, FL: Krieger, 1994.

Beder, Hal. *Adult Literacy: Issues for Policy and Practice*. Malabar, FL: Krieger, 1991.

Belenky, M.F., et al. *Women's Ways of Knowing: The Development of Self, Voice, and Mind*. New York: Basic Books, 1986.

Binstock, R.W., et al., eds. *Handbook of Aging and the Social Sciences*. New York: Von Nostrand Reinhold, 1985.

Birren, J.E., and Schaie, K.W. *Handbook of the Psychology of Aging*. New York: Von Nostrand Reinhold, 1985.

Bittel, Bill. *Adult Learners' Survival Skills*. Malabar, FL: Krieger, 1990.

Boo, M.R., and L.E. Decker. *The Learning Community*. Alexandria, VA.: National Community Education Association, 1985.

Boone, Edgar J. *Developing Programs in Adult Education*. Englewood Cliffs, NJ: Prentice-Hall, 1985.

Boone, Edgar J., Ronald W. Shearon, Estelle White, and Associates. *Serving Personal and Community Needs Through Adult Education*. San Francisco: Jossey-Bass, 1980.

Botkin, James W., Mahdi Elmandjra, and Mircea Malitza. *No Limits to Learning: Bridging the Human Gap*. A Report to the Club of Rome. New York: Pergamon Press, 1979.

Boud, David, and Virginia Griffith, eds. *Appreciating Adults Learning: From the Learners' Perspective*. London: Kogan Page, 1987.

Boyd, Robert D., Jerold W. Apps, and Associates. *Redefining the Discipline of Adult Education*. San Francisco: Jossey-Bass, 1980.

Boyle, P.G. *Planning Better Programs*. New York: McGraw-Hill, 1981.

Brocket, R., ed. *Continuing Education in the Year 2000*. San Francisco: Jossey-Bass, 1987.

———, ed. *Ethical Issues in Adult Education*. New York: Teachers College Press, 1988.

Brookfield, Stephen D. *Adult Learners, Adult Education, and the Community*. New York: Teachers College Press, 1984.

———. *Developing Critical Thinkers: Challenging Adults to Explore Alternative Ways of Thinking and Acting*. San Francisco: Jossey-Bass, 1987.

———. *Learning Democracy: Eduard Lindeman on Education and Social Change*. Dover, NH: Croom-Helm, 1987.

———. *Understanding and Facilitating Adult Learning*. San Francisco: Jossey-Bass, 1986.

Brown, H.D. *Principles of Language Learning and Teaching*. Englewood Cliffs, NJ: Prentice-Hall, 1980.

Brundage, B. *Adult Learning Principles and Their Application to Program Planning*. Toronto: Ministry of Education, 1980.

Burnham, Byron R. *Evaluating Human Resources and the Organization*. Malabar, FL: Krieger, 1994.

Caffarella, Rosemary S. *Program Development and Evaluation Resource Book for Trainers*. New York: Wiley, 1988.

Campbell, D.C. *The New Majority: Adult Learners in the University*. Edmonton: University of Alberta Press, 1984.

Candy, Philip C. *Self-Direction for Lifelong Learning: A Comprehensive Guide to Theory and Practice*. San Francisco: Jossey-Bass, 1991.

Cantor, Jeffry A. *Delivering Instruction to Adult Learners* Middletown, OH: Sall and Emerson, 1992.

Carlson, Robert A. *The Americanization Syndrome: A Quest for Conformity*. Dover, NH: Croom-Helm, 1987.

Carnevale, Anthony P., Leila J. Gainer, and Janice Villet. *Training In America: The Organization and Strategic Role of Training*. San Francisco: Jossey-Bass, 1990.

Cassara, Beverly B., ed. *World Survey of Adult Education*. Malabar, FL: Krieger, 1994.

Castrovilli, M., ed. *Army Continuing Education*. New York: School Guide Publications, 1988.

Cell, E. *Learning to Learn from Experience*. Albany, N.Y.: State University of New York Press, 1984.

Cervero, R.M. *Effective Practice in Continuing Professional Education*. San Francisco: Jossey-Bass, 1988.

Chacon, M., et al. *Chicanas in Postsecondary Education: Executive Summary*. Stanford, CA: Center for Research on Women, 1982.

Charters, Alexander N., and Associates. *Comparing Adult Education Worldwide*. San Francisco: Jossey-Bass, 1981.

Chickering, A.S., et al. *The Modern American College*. San Francisco: Jossey-Bass, 1981.

Ciofalo, Andrew, ed. *Internships: Perspectives on Experiential Learning*. Malabar, FL: Krieger, 1992.

Cohen, A.M., and F.B. Brawer. *The American Community College*. San Francisco: Jossey-Bass, 1982.

Cohen, Norman H. *Mentoring Adult Learners: A Guide for Educators and Trainers*. Malabar, FL: Krieger, 1994.

Collins, M. *Competence in Adult Education: A New Perspective*. Lanham, MD: University Press of America, 1987.

Collins, Z.W., ed. *Museums, Adults and the Humanities: A Guide to Educational Programming*. Washington, DC: American Association of Museums, 1981.

Commission on Higher Education and the Adult Learner. *Adult Learners: Key to the Nation's Future*. Columbia, MD: The Commission on Higher Education and the Adult Learner, 1984.

Commission of Professors of Adult Education. *Graduate Programs in Adult Education: United States and Canada*. Washington, DC: American Association of Adult and Continuing Education, 1986.

Commons, M.L., F.A. Richards, and C. Armon, eds. *Beyond Formal Operations: Late Adolescent and Adult Cognitive Development*. New York: Praeger, 1984.

Commons, M.L., J. Synnott, F.A. Richards, and C. Armon, eds. *Adult Devel-*

opment: Camparisons and Applications of Developmental Models. New York: Praeger, 1989.

Confessore, Cary J., and Sharon J. Confessore. *Guideposts to Self-Directed Learning.* King of Prussia, PA: Organization Design and Development, 1992.

Conrad, J.P., and J. Cavros. *Adult Offender Education Programs.* Sacramento, CA: American Justice Institute, 1981.

Cookson, Peter, ed. *Program Planning for the Training and Education of Adults: North American Perspectives.* Malabar, FL: Krieger, 1994.

Council of Chief State School Officers, *Community Education and State Agencies: Initiative, Activities, and Leadership.* Washington, DC: Council of Chief State School Officers, 1986.

Craig, Robert L. *Training and Development Handbook,* 3rd ed. New York: McGraw-Hill, 1987.

Cranton, Patricia. *Planning Instruction for Adult Learners.* Middletown, OH: Wall and Emerson, 1989.

————. *Working with Adult Learners.* Middletown, OH: Wall and Emerson, 1992.

Cronbach, Lee J., and Associates. *Toward Reform of Program Evaluation.* San Francisco: Jossey-Bass, 1980.

Cropley, A.J. *Towards a System of Lifelong Education.* Elmsford, NY: Pergamon Press, 1980.

Cross, K. Patricia. *Adults as Learners.* San Francisco: Jossey-Bass, 1981.

Crux, Sandra C. *Learning Strategies for Adults.* Middletown, OH: Wall and Emerson, 1991.

Daloz, Laurent A. *Effective Teaching and Mentoring.* San Francisco: Jossey-Bass, 1986.

Darkenwald, Gordon C., and Sharan B. Merriam. *Adult Education: Foundations of Practice.* New York: Harper and Row, 1982.

Dean, Gary J. *Designing Instruction for Adult Learners.* Malabar, FL: Krieger, 1994.

Decker, L.E. *Foundations of Community Education.* Charlottesville, VA: Community Collaborators, 1980.

Deschler, D., ed. *Evaluation for Program Improvement.* San Francisco: Jossey-Bass, 1984.

Draves, Bill. *The Free University: A Model for Lifelong Learning.* Chicago: Follett, 1980.

Dwyer, R. *Labor Education in the U.S.* Metuchen, NJ: Scarecrow Press, 1977.

Edelson, Paul J. *The Struggle for Control of Adult Education in America.* Malabar, FL: Krieger, 1994.

Eisner, F.W., and S.M. Dobbs. *The Uncertain Profession: Observations on the State of Museum Education in Twenty American Art Museums.* Los Angeles: J. Paul Getty Center for Education in the Arts, 1986.

Elias, John L. *The Foundations and Practice of Adult Religious Education*. Malabar, FL: Krieger, 1993.

———. *Paulo Freire: Pedagogue of Liberation*. Malabar, FL: Krieger, 1993.

———. *Studies in Theology and Education*. Malabar, FL: Krieger, 1986.

Erikson, E.H. *The Life Cycle Repeated: A Review*. New York: Norton, 1982.

Eurich, Nell P. *Corporate Classrooms: The Learning Business*. Princeton, NJ: Carnegie Foundation for the Advancement of Teaching, 1985.

———. *The Learning Industry: Education for Adult Workers*. Princeton, NJ: The Carnegie Foundation for the Advancement of Teaching, 1990.

Fingeret, Arlene. *Adult Literacy Education: Current and Future Directions*. Columbus, OH: ERIC Clearinghouse on Adult, Career, and Vocational Education, 1984.

Foltz, N.T., ed. *Handbook of Adult Religious Education*. Birmingham, AL: Religious Education Press, 1986.

Fowler, J. *Stages of Faith: The Psychology of Human Development and the Quest for Meaning*. New York: Harper & Row, 1981.

Freedman, L. *Quality in Continuing Education*. San Francisco: Jossey-Bass, 1987.

Galbraith, Michael W., ed. *Adult Learning Methods*. Malabar, FL: Krieger, 1990.

———, ed. *Education in the Rural American Community: A Lifelong Process*. Malabar, FL: Krieger, 1992.

———, ed. *Facilitating Adult Learning*. Malabar, FL: Krieger, 1991.

Gangel, Kenneth O., and James C. Wilhoit. *The Christian Educator's Handbook of Adult Education*. Wheaton, IL: Victor Books, 1993.

Garrison, D. Randy, ed. *Research Perspective in Adult Education*. Malabar, FL: Krieger, 1994.

Garrison, D. Randy, and Doug Shale, eds. *Education At A Distance: From Issues to Practice*. Malabar, FL: Krieger, 1990.

Gibb, Jack R. *Trust: A New View of Personal and Organizational Development*. Los Angeles: Guild of Tutors Press, 1978.

Gilligan, C. *In a Different Voice: Psychological Theory and Women's Development*. Cambridge, MA: Harvard University Press, 1982.

Glaser, E.M., H.H. Abelson, and K.N. Garrison. *Putting Knowledge to Use*. San Francisco: Jossey-Bass, 1983.

Gould, R. *Transformation: Growth and Change in Adult Life*. New York: Simon and Schuster, 1978.

Grabowski, Stanley M., et al. *Preparing Educators of Adults*. San Francisco: Jossey-Bass, 1981.

Green, J.S., S.J. Grosswald, E. Suter, and D.B. Walthall, eds. *Continuing Education for the Health Professions*. San Francisco: Jossey-Bass, 1984.

Green, L.W., and Others. *Health Education Planning: A Diagnostic Approach*. Palo Alto, CA: Mayfield, 1980.

Groome, T. *Christian Religious Education: Sharing Our Story and Vision*. New York: Harper & Row, 1980.

Gross, Ronald, ed. *Invitation to Lifelong Learning*. Chicago: Follett, 1982.

———. *The Lifelong Learner*. New York: Simon and Schuster, 1977.

Guba, Egon G., and Yvonna S. Lincoln. *Effective Evaluation: Improving the Usefulness of Evaluation Results Through Responsive and Naturalistic Approaches*. San Francisco: Jossey-Bass, 1981.

Gueulette, D., ed. *Microcomputers for Adult Learning: Potentials and Perils*. Chicago: Follett, 1982.

Harman, D. *Illiteracy: A National Dilemma*. New York: Cambridge Book Co., 1987.

Harri-Augstein, Sheila, and Laurie Thomas. *Learning Conversations: The Self-Orhanized Way to Personal and Organizational Growth*. New York: Routledge, 1991.

Hayes, Charles D. *Self-University*. Wasilla, AK: Autodidactic Press, 1989.

Heermann, B. *Teaching and Learning With Computers*. San Francisco: Jossey-Bass, 1988.

Holmberg, B. *Status and Trends of Distance Education*. Dover, NH: Croom-Helm, 1986.

Hone, K.A. *Serving the Rural Adult: Inventory of Model Programs in Rural Adult Postsecondary Education*. Manhattan, KS: Kansas State University, 1984.

Houle, Cyril O. *Continuing Learning in the Professions*. San Francisco: Jossey-Bass, 1980.

———. *The Literature of Adult Education: A Bibliographic Essay*. San Francisco: Jossey-Bass, 1992.

———. *Patterns of Learning: New Perspectives on Life-Span Education*. San Francisco: Jossey-Bass, 1984.

Hudson, Frederic M. *The Adult Years: Mastering the Art of Self-Renewal*. San Francisco: Jossey-Bass, 1991.

Hughes, J.W., ed. *Ministering To Adult Learners: A Skills Workbook for Christian Educational Leaders*. Washington, DC: United States Catholic Conference, 1981.

Isley, P.J., and J. Niemi. *Recruiting and Training Volunteers*. New York: McGraw-Hill, 1981.

Jarvis, Peter. *Adult Learning in the Social Context*. Dover, NH: Croom-Helm, 1987.

Jarvis, Peter, ed. *Perspectives On Adult Education and Training in Europe*. Malabar, FL: Krieger, 1992.

Jarvis, Peter. *The Sociology of Adult and Continuing Education*. Dover, NH: Croom-Helm, 1985.

Jarvis, Peter, ed. *Twentieth Century Thinkers in Adult Education: International Perspectives on Adult and Continuing Education*. New York: Routledge, 1987.

Jarvis, Peter, and Nicholas Walters. *Adult Education and Theological Interpretations*. Malabar, FL: Krieger, 1993.

Keegan, D. *The Foundations of Distance Education*. Dover, NH: Croom-Helm, 1986.

Kegan, R. *The Evolving Self: Problem and Process in Human Development*. Cambridge, MA: Harvard University Press, 1982.

Klevins, Chester, ed. *Materials and Methods in Adult and Continuing Education: International—Illiteracy*. Los Angeles: Klevins Publications, 1987.

Knowles, Malcolm S. *Andragogy in Action: Applying Modern Principles of Adult Learning*. San Francisco: Jossey-Bass, 1984.

———. *The Making of an Adult Educator: An Autobiographical Journey*. San Francisco: Jossey-Bass, 1989.

———. *Using Learning Contracts*. San Francisco: Jossey-Bass, 1986.

Knox, Alan B. *Adult Development and Learning*. San Francisco: Jossey-Bass, 1977.

———, et al. *Developing, Administering, and Evaluating Adult Education*. San Francisco: Jossey-Bass, 1980.

Knox, Alan B. *Helping Adults Learn*. San Francisco: Jossey-Bass, 1986.

Kolb, D.A. *Experiential Learning Experience As the Source of Learning and Development*. Englewood, NJ: Prentice-Hall, 1984.

Kreitlow, Burton W., and Associates. *Examining Controversies in Adult Education*. San Francisco: Jossey-Bass, 1981.

Laird, D. *Approaches to Training and Development*. Reading, MA: Addison-Wesley, 1985.

Langenbach, Michael. *Curriculum Models in Adult Education*. Malabar, FL: Krieger, 1993.

Langerman, P.D., and D.H. Smith, eds. *Managing Adult and Continuing Education Programs and Staff*. Washington, DC: American Association for Adult and Continuing Education, 1979.

Larson, G.A. *Adult Education for the Handicapped*. Columbus, OH: ERIC Clearinghouse on Adult, Career, and Vocational Education, 1982.

Lenz, E. *The Art of Teaching Adults* New York: Holt, Rinehart & Winston, 1982.

Levinson, D.J., et al. *Seasons of A Man's Life*. New York: Knopf, 1978.

Lillard, L., and H. Tab. *Private Sector Training: Who Can Get It and What Are Its Effects?* Santa Monica, CA: Rand Corporation, 1986.

Lincoln, Yvonna S., and Egon G. Guba. *Naturalistic Inquiry*. Beverly Hills, CA: Sage, 1983.

Long, Huey B. *New Perspectives on the Education of Adults in the United States*. New York: Nichols, 1987.

Long, Huey B. et al. *Self-Directed Learning: Application and Theory*. Athens, GA: Adult Education Department of the University of Georgia, 1988.

Long, Huey, B. *Self-Directed Learning: Emerging Theory and Practice*. Norman, OK: Oklahoma Research Center for Continuing Professional and Higher Education of the University of Oklahoma, 1989.

Long, Huey, B. Roger Hiemstra, et al. *Changing Approaches to Studying Adult Education*. San Francisco: Jossey-Bass, 1980.

Lumsden, D.B., ed. *The Older Adult as Learner: Aspects of Educational Gerontology*. Washington, DC: Hemisphere, 1985.

Lutheran Church of America. *Guides for Adult Education*. Philadelphia: Lutheran Church in America, 1986.

McCrae, R.R., and P.T. Costa. *Emerging Lives, Enduring Dispositions: Personality in Adulthood*. Boston: Little, Brown, 1984.

McFee, L., and H. Neufeldt. *Education of the Black Adult in the U.S.: An Annotated Bibliography*. Westport, CT: Greenwood Press, 1985.

McKenzie, Leon. *Adult Education and the Burden of the Future*. Washington, DC: University Press of America, 1978.

———. *Adult Education and Worldview Construction*. Malabar, FL: Krieger, 1991.

———. *The Religious Education of Adults*. Birmingham, AL: Religious Education Press, 1982.

McLagan, Patricia. *Models for Excellence: The Conclusions and Recommendationa of the ASTD Training and Development Competency Study*. Alexandria, VA: American Society for Training and Development, 1983.

McNett, I. *Demographic Imperatives: Implications for Educational Policy*. Washington, DC: American Council on Education, 1983.

Madaus, C.F., M. Scriven, and D.L. Stufflebeam. *Evaluation Models: Viewpoints on Educational and Human Services Evaluation*. Boston: Kluwer-Nijhoff, 1983.

Malatesta, C.Z., and C.E. Izard. *Emotion in Adult Development*. Beverly Hills, CA: Sage, 1984.

Margolis, R.J. *Rural Postsecondary Education*. Manhattan, KS: Kansas State University, 1981.

Marsick, Virginia, ed. *Learning in the Workplace*. Dover, NH: Croom-Helm, 1987.

Matkin, G.W. *Effective Budgeting in Continuing Education*. San Francisco: Jossey-Bass, 1985.

Merriam, Sharan B. *Case Study Research in Education: A Qualitative Approach*. San Francisco: Jossey-Bass, 1988.

———. *Selected Writings on Philosophy and Adult Education*. Malabar, FL: Krieger, 1984.

———. *Themes of Adulthood Through Literature*. New York: Teachers College Press, 1983.

Merriam, Sharon B., and Rosemary Caffarella. *Learning in Adulthood: A Comprehensive Guide*. San Francisco: Jossey-Bass, 1991.

Merriam, Sharon B., and Carolyn Clark. *Lifelines: Patterns of Work, Love, and Learning in Adulthood*. San Francisco: Jossey-Bass, 1991.

Merriam, Sharon B., and Phyllis M. Cunningham, eds. *Handbook of Adult and Continuing Education*. San Francisco: Jossey-Bass, 1989.

Merriam, Sharon B., and Edwin L. Simpson. *A Guide to Research for Educators and Trainers of Adults*. Malabar, FL: Krieger, 1989.

Meyers, C. *Teaching Students to Think Critically*. San Francisco: Jossey-Bass, 1986.

Mezirow, Jack, and Associates. *Fostering Critical Reflection in Adulthood: A Guide to Transformative and Emancipatory Learning*. San Francisco: Jossey-Bass, 1990.

Moore, Allen B., and James A. Feldt. *Racilitating Community and Decision-making Groups*. Malabar, FL: Krieger, 1991.

Morrison, I., and K. Rubenson. *Recurrent Education in an Information Economy*. Toronto: Canadian Association of Adult Education, 1987.

Murray, Margo, with Marna A. Owen. *Beyond the Myths and Magic of Mentoring*. San Francisco: Jossey-Bass, 1991.

Nadler, Leonard. *Corporate Human Resources Development: A Management Tool*. New York: Van Nostrand Reinhold, 1980.

————. *Designing Training Programs: The Critical Events Model*. Reading, MA: Addison-Wesley, 1982.

Nadler, Leonard, ed. *The Handbook of Human Resources Development*. New York: John Wiley and Son, 1984.

Norris, Joye A., and Paddy Kennington. *Developing Literacy Programs for Homeless Adults*. Malabar, FL: Krieger, 1992.

Norris, Neal A., ed. *Community College Futures: From Rhetoric to Reality*. Stillwater, OK: New Forums Press, 1989.

Norton, L., and B. Sims. *The Status of Correctional Education in the U.S.*. Columbus, OH: National Center for Research in Vocational Education, 1988.

Nowlen, P.M. *A New Approach to Continuing Education for Business and the Professions: The Performance Model*. New York: Macmillan, 1988.

Ohliger, John. *Basic Choices in Adult Education*. Madison, WI: Basic Choices, 1983.

————. *The Fictional Adult Educator*. Madison, WI: Basic Choices, 1988.

————. *Millenia: The Past, The Present Issues, and the Future of Adult Education: A Quotational Bibliography*. Madison, WI: Basic Choices, 1988.

Olgren, C.H., and L.A. Parker. *Teleconferencing Technology and Applications*. Dedham, MA: Artech House, 1983.

Oliver, L.P. *Study Circles: Coming Together for Personal Growth and Social Change*. Washington, D.C.: Seven Locks Press, 1987.

Parent, Neal, ed. *Adult Learning and the Parish*. Dubuque, IA: William C. Brown, 1985.

Patterson, R.W.K. *Values, Education, and the Adult*. Boston: Routledge, 1979.

Patton, Michael Q. *Creative Evaluation*. Beverly Hills, CA: Sage, 1981.

————. *Practical Evaluation*. Beverly Hills, CA: Sage, 1982.

————. *Qualitative Evaluation Methods*. Beverly Hills, CA: Sage, 1980.

————. *Utilization-Focused Evaluation*. Beverly Hills, CA: Sage, 1978.

Paulston, R.G., ed. *Other Dreams, Other Schools: Folk Colleges in Social and Ethnic Movements*. Pittsburgh: University of Pittsburgh Press, 1979.

Perelman, L. *The Learning Enterprise: Adult Learning, Human Capital, and Economic Development*. Washington, DC: Council of State Planning Agencies, 1984.

Peters, John M., et al. *Building An Effective Adult Education Enterprise*. San Francisco: Jossey-Bass, 1980.

Peters, John M., Peter Jarvis, et al. *Adult Education: Evolution and Achievements in a Developing Field of Study*. San Francisco: Jossey-Bass, 1991.

Peterson, D.Z. *Facilitating Education for Older Learners*. San Francisco: Jossey-Bass, 1983.

Peterson, G.A., ed. *The Christian Education of Adults*. Chicago: Moody Press, 1984.

Peterson, R.E., et al. *Adult Education and Training in Industrialized Countries*. New York: Praeger, 1982.

————, et al. *Lifelong Learning In America*. San Francisco: Jossey-Bass, 1979.

Piskurich, George M. *Self-Directed Learning: A Practical Guide to Design, Development, and Implementation*. San Francisco: Jossey-Bass, 1993.

Philips, K., and D. Ballorado. *Affective Aspects of Adult Literacy Programs*. San Francisco: National Adult Literacy Project, 1985.

Prawl, S., R. Medlin, and J. Gross. *Adult and Continuing Education Through the Cooperative Extension Service*. Columbia, MO: Extension Division, University of Missouri, 1984.

Renner, M.J., and M.R. Rosenzweig. *Enriched and Impoverished Environments: Effects on Brain and Behavior*. New York: Springer-Verlag, 1987.

Ricard, Virginia B. *Developing Intercultural Communication Skills*. Malabar, FL: Krieger, 1993.

Roberts, H. *Alternative Adult Education*. New York: Methuen, 1988.

Romaniuk, J. *The Older Adult Learner in Higher Education: An Anylsis of State Public Policy*. Washington, DC: National Council on the Aging, 1982.

————. *Tuition-Waiver Policies for Older Adults: Impact on States and Institutions of Higher Education*. Washington, DC: National Council on the Aging, 1982.

Rouche, J.E., and G.A. Baker. *Access and Excellence: The Open Door College*. Washington, DC: Community College Press, 1987.

Rybash, J.M., W.J. Hoyer, and P.A. Roodin. *Adult Cognition and Aging: Developmental Changes in Processing, Knowing, and Thinking*. Elmsford, NY: Pergamon, 1986.

Schaie, K.W., and L.L. Willis. *Adult Development and Aging*. Boston: Little Brown, 1986.

Schindler-Rainman, Eva, and Ronald Lippitt. *The Volunteer Community: Creative Use of Human Resources*. Fairfax, VA: NTL Learning Resources, 1985.

Schlossberg, Nancy K., Ann Q. Lynch, and Arthur W. Chickering. *Improving Higher Education Environments for Adults*. San Francisco: Jossey-Bass, 1989.

Schon, Donald A. *Educating the Reflective Practitioner*. San Francisco: Jossey-Bass, 1987.

Scott, N.A. *Returning Women Students: A Review of Research and Descriptive Studies*. Washington, DC: National Association of Women Deans, Administrators, and Counselors, 1980.

Shore, I., and P.A. Freire. *A Pedagogy for Liberation*. South Hadley, MA: Bergin and Gargey, 1987.

Simerly, R.G., ed. *Strategic Planning and Leadership in Continuing Education*. San Francisco: Jossey-Bass, 1987.

Smelser, N.J., and E.H. Erikson. *Themes of Work and Love in Adulthood*. Cambridge, MA: Harvard University Press, 1980.

Smith, N.L. *New Techniques for Evaluation*. Beverly Hills, CA: Sage, 1981.

Smith, Robert M. *Learning How To Learn: Applied Theory for Adults*. Englewood Cliffs, NJ: Prentice Hall, 1982.

Smith, Robert M., ed. *Theory Building for Learning How To Learn*. Chicago: Educational Studies Press, 1987.

Smith, Robert M., *Learning To Learn Across the Life Span*. San Francisco: Jossey-Bass, 1990.

Solow, K., and G. Walker. *The Job Training Partnership Act: Service to Women*. New York: Grinker Associates, 1986.

Stanage, Sherman M. *Adult Education and Phenomenological Research: New Directions for Theory, Practice, and Research*. Malabar, FL: Krieger, 1987.

Stern, M.S., ed. *Power and Conflict in Continuing Professional Education*. Belmont, CA: Wadsworth, 1983.

Stevens-Long, Judith. *Adult Life: Developmental Processes*. Palo Alto, CA: Mayfield, 1979.

Stewart, David W. *Adult Learning in America: Eduard Lindeman and His Agenda for Lifelong Education*. Malabar, FL: Krieger, 1987.

Stokes, Kenneth, ed. *Faith Development in the Adult Life Cycle*. New York: Sadlier, 1983.

Strother, G.B., and J.P. Klus. *Administration of Continuing Education*. Belmont, CA: Wadsworth, 1982.

Stubblefield, Harold W. *Towards a History of Adult Education in America: The Search for a Unifying Principle*. Dover, NH: Croom-Helm, 1988.

Sullivan, Eugene. *Guide to External Degree Programs in the U.S.* 2nd ed. New York: Macmillan, 1983.

Taylor, R., K. Rockhill, and R. Fieldhouse. *University Adult Education in England and the U.S.A.* Dover, NH: Croom-Helm, 1985.

Thomas, Laurie F., and Sheila Harri-Augstein. *Self-Organized Learning: Foundations of a Conversational Science for Psychology*. New York: Routledge, 1985.

Tittle, C.K., and E.R. Denker. *Returning Women Students in Higher Education: Defining Policy Issues*. New York: Praeger, 1980.

Toffler, Alvin. *The Third Wave.* New York: William Morrow, 1980.

Tough, Allen M. *Intentional Changes: A Fresh Approach to Helping People Change.* New York: Cambridge University Press, 1982.

Treadway, D.M. *Higher Education in Rural America: Serving the Adult Learner.* New York: College Entrance Examination Board, 1984.

Troll, P.B. *Continuations: Adult Development and Aging.* Monterey, CA: Brooks/Cole, 1982.

Tuijnman, Albert, and Max van der Kamp. *Learning Across the Lifespan: Theories, Research, Policies.* New York: Pergamon, 1992.

Union of American Hebrew Congregations. *To See the World Through Jewish Eyes: Guidelines for Adult Jewish Studies.* New York: Union of American Hebrew Congregations, 1988.

U.S. Department of Defense. *Voluntary Education Programs for Military Personnel.* Directive N. 1322.8. Washington, DC: U.S. Department of Defense, 1987.

Valore, L., and G.E. Diehl. *Effectiveness and Acceptance of Home Study.* Washington, DC: National Home Study Council, 1987.

Vaughn, G.B. *The Community College in America.* Washington, DC: Community College Press, 1985.

Ventura, C. *Education for Older Adults: A Catalog of Program Profiles.* Washington, DC: National Council on the Aging, 1982.

Verduin, John R., Jr., and Thomas A. Clark. *Distance Education: The Foundations of Effective Practice.* San Francisco: Jossey-Bass, 1991.

Vigilanti, John A. *Academic Freedom and the Adult Student in Catholic Higher Education.* Malabar, FL: Krieger, 1992.

Vogel, L.J. *The Religious Education of Older Adults.* Birmingham, AL: Religious Education Press, 1984.

Vogel, Linda J. *Teaching and Learning in Communities of Faith: Empowering Adults Through Religious Education.* San Francisco: Jossey-Bass, 1991.

Warner, P.D., and J.A. Christenson. *The Cooperative Extension Service: A National Assessment.* Boulder, CO: Westview Press, 1984.

Wedemeyer, C.A. *Learning at the Back Door: Reflections on Non-traditional Learning in the Lifespan.* Madison, WI: University of Wisconsin Press, 1981.

Weinstock, R. *The Greying of the Campus.* New York: Educational Facilities Laboratories, 1978.

Williams, D., ed. *Naturalistic Evaluation.* San Francisco: Jossey-Bass, 1986.

Witkin, B.R. *Assessing Needs in Educational and Social Programs.* San Francisco: Jossey-Bass, 1984.

Wlodkowski, Raymond J. *Enhancing Adult Motivation to Learn.* San Francisco: Jossey-Bass, 1985.

INDEX

Academies, *see* Private schools
Accreditation, 133, 327
Adam, Thomas, 20
Adams, Herbert, 47
Adams, James T., 10, 14
Adams, John, 10
Adams, Sam, 13
Addams, Jane, 65
Adkins, Winthrop R., 329
Administration of adult education
in business and industry, 80, 293
in colleges and universities, 85-86, 88, 102, 301
in Cooperative Extension, 92-93, 309-310
in government agencies, 98-103, 313-314
in health and welfare agencies, 105
in labor unions, 110, 318-319
in libraries, 113, 116
in mass media, 324
in public schools, 58-59, 141-142, 328, 333
in religious institutions, 145, 148-149, 150-151, 335-337
in voluntary associations, 152-153, 339-340
Adult basic education, 285, 304, 312-314, 321, 322, 326
See also Fundamental education, Literacy education
Adult education
articulation with youth education, 278, 346-349
See also Field of adult education
Adult Education, 204, 217, 236-237
Adult Education Act, 313
Adult Education Association
and adult education councils, 178-179
assessment of, 244-246
commissions and committees of, 233
conferences of, 238-240

Adult Education Association
(*continued*)
and coordination of adult education, 263-264, 340-343
and Council of National Organizations, 227-230
delegate assembly of, 225-226
direction-finding activities of, 222
effect of Fund for Adult Education on, 221-222
executive committee of, 227
field services of, 239-240
financing of, 241-243
founding of, 217
grants from Fund for Adult Education, 223, 242
and liberal education, 221-222
membership of, 223-224
officers of, 224-225
organizational structure of, 224-235
preparations for, 218-219
publications of, 236-238, 256
purposes, goals, and policies of, 219-222
and regional organizations, 187-188
relationship with the Fund for Adult Education, 241-242
relationship of segmental organizations with, 158-175
research by, 240
sections of, 233-234
staff of, 234-235
and state associations, 186
study of by Bureau of Applied Social Research, 222, 224, 226
Adult Education Bulletin, 136, 204, 213, 236, 293-294
Adult education councils, *see* Councils
Adult Education Journal, 204, 236
Adult education movement, *see* Field of adult education
Adult educational functions and roles, delineation of
in business and industry, 80

417

Trends in adult education (*continued*)
in voluntary associations, 152, 338-340
in workers' education, 109-111
True, Alfred, 23, 40-41
Tuition, 82, 87, 144
Turner, Frederick, 47
Tyler, Ralph, 114

Uniform lessons, 73, 146
Union of Experimenting Colleges and Universities, 300, 301
Union Leadership Academy, 111
United Christian Adult Movement, 145-146
United Church of Christ, 335
United Hebrew Charities, 66
United Presbyterian Church, 335
UNESCO
participation in by the Adult Education Association, 240
participation in by the American Association for Adult Education, 207
study of lifelong education, 347-349
U.S. National Commission for, 99
United States Agricultural Society, 22, 23
United States Armed Forces Institute, 99
United States Bureau of the Census, 100, 250
United States Department of Agriculture, *see* Cooperative Extension Service
United States Department of Education, 53
United States Government, *see* Government agencies
United States Military Academy, 32
United States Office of Education
Adult Education Section, 100-101, 164, 240
Federal Radio Project, 124
precursors to, 53
public forum project, 136-137
statistics of, 100, 134-135, 143
University Broadcasting Council, 124
University extension
administration of, 85-86, 294-295
Channing on, 32-33

University extension (*continued*)
cooperation with other institutions, 161, 301
curriculum development in, 50, 84-85, 294
decline of, 48-49
developments in, 46-50, 83-90, 294-301
differentiation of function in, 86, 295
enrollment in, 84, 294
facilities of, 87-89, 295
financing of, 295-296, 300-301
and libraries, 47
methods in, 89-90, 295
number of, 50, 84
origins in English universities, 47
precursors of, 14-15, 18, 32-33
See also Colleges and universities
University Settlement, 65
University Without Walls, 300
Urban extension, 299

Van Druff, John C., 374
Van Hise, Charles R., 49
Vatican Council II, 336
Vermilye, Dyckman, 373
Verner, Coolie, 226, 256
Veterans' education, 85, 101, 133, 137
Veterans' organizations, 68
Vietnam War, 286
Vincent, John, 36
Vocational education
in correspondence schools, 132
developments in during Colonial period, 6-7; 1780-1865, 15; 1866-1920, 45-46, 56, 59-60; 1921-1961, 80-81, 135-137, 142, 144
in labor unions, 109
legislation for, 59-60, 312-313
policy of AAAE on, 195-196
professional society for, 176
in public schools, 55, 59-60
See also Agricultural education, Business and industry, Workers' education
Voluntary associations
coordinative organizations for, 175
developments in, 21-22, 60-72, 151-154, 338-340